INDIGENOUS THEORIES
OF CONTAGIOUS DISEASE

This book is dedicated to the memory of
my father, Marshall Green

INDIGENOUS THEORIES OF CONTAGIOUS DISEASE

EDWARD C. GREEN

ALTAMIRA
PRESS

A Division of
ROWMAN & LITTLEFIELD PUBLISHERS, INC.
Lanham • New York • Toronto • Oxford

ALTAMIRA PRESS
A division of Rowman & Littlefield Publishers, Inc.
A wholly owned subsidiary of The Rowman & Littlefield Publishing Group, Inc.
4501 Forbes Boulevard, Suite 200
Lanham, MD 20706
www.altamirapress.com

PO Box 317
Oxford
OX2 9RU, UK

British Library Cataloguing in Publication Information Available

Library of Congress Cataloguing-in-Publication Data

Green, Edward C.
  Indigenous theories of contagious disease. Edward C. Green.
    p. cm.
  Includes bibliographical references and index.
  ISBN 0-7619-9199-9 (cloth); ISBN 0-7619-8941-2 (paperback)
  1. Medical anthropology—Africa, Southern. 2. Communicable diseases—Africa,
Southern. 3. Public health—Africa, Southern. 4. Traditional medicine—Africa, Southern.
5. Africa, Southern—Social life and customs. I. Title.
GN296.5.A35 G74

Printed in the United States of America

℗™ The paper used in this publication meets the minimum requirements of American
National Standard for Information Sciences—Permanence of Paper for Printed Library
Materials, ANSI/NISO Z39.48–1992.

TABLE OF CONTENTS

Foreword, by W. Penn Handwerker   7

Acknowledgments   9

Introduction   11

Chapter One: African Health Beliefs   21

Chapter Two: Pollution and Other Contagion Beliefs   55
               among Bantu Speakers

Chapter Three: Resistance to Illness and the   89
               Internal Snake Concept

Chapter Four: Childhood Diarrhea   107

Chapter Five: Sexually Transmitted Diseases and AIDS   135

Chapter Six: Malaria, Tuberculosis, and Other   179
               Infectious Diseases

Chapter Seven: Indigenous Contagion Theory in   217
               Broader Perspective

Chapter Eight: Theoretical Implications   245

References   271

Author Index   293

Subject Index   299

About the Author   311

FOREWORD

Edward Green's *Indigenous Theories of Contagious Disease* opens the way for the development of effective working relationships between biomedical health service providers and indigenous healers and for more effective health promotion and disease prevention across the world.

Indigenous healers provide roughly 80% of the medical services used worldwide. Before seeking expert advice, people everywhere apply their personal medical knowledge. Biomedically trained policymakers and service providers routinely confuse what they know with material reality. In doing this, by ignoring or dismissing indigenous and personal medical theories, they miss potentially key insights into improved characterizations of illness. They also rule out the possibility of understanding why so few people actively and effectively take their advice and recommendations, or of improving on their initial advice and recommendations.

Green develops this argument while he exhaustively and with painstaking detail documents indigenous contagion theory (ICT). He thus reveals a line of medical theorizing and practice that addresses critical global health promotion/disease prevention issues: childhood diarrhea, HIV/AIDS and other sexually transmitted infections, malaria, and tuberculosis, to name only a few. Green analyzes specific ICTs and biomedical equivalents as different sets of knowledge that address the same health promotion/disease prevention issues, although they may call the same thing by different names and although ICTs often frame issues in terms (e.g., pollution) alien to biomedical health providers. He thus shows how we can open effective lines of communication and coordination between the biomedically trained people who direct global health promotion/ disease prevention efforts, the indigenous healers who provide the vast majority of medical services, and the client populations both aim to serve. Green focuses on African theories and practices, but he reviews evidence that ICTs occur globally.

While *Indigenous Theories of Contagious Disease* makes an important contribution to applied medical anthropology, Green also contributes to more general theoretical concerns in the field. His argument suggests a way to reframe issues so as to draw together what have been divergent lines of inquiry: biological and ecological studies that focus on disease, environment, and population, and cultural and ethnomedical studies that focus on socially constructed definitions of and responses to illness.

Green's analysis also draws our attention to a still more general issue. In 1871, Edward Tylor defined culture as everything we learn and thus share with other people because we live our lives as social creatures. Margaret Mead made the anthropological concept of culture a core element of popular culture. But today, in the face of increasing face-to-face cultural diversity, most people don't recognize that they have a culture, and most people who talk about cultural diversity don't understand what this means. Irrespective of age, gender, class, and ethnicity, culture remains largely something that "other" people have. What we know consists of immutable elements of experience—Truth with a capital T. What others know too often reflects ignorance, myth, or "cultural blinders."

The barriers to understanding and effective working relationships that Green addresses thus extend far beyond global health promotion/disease prevention. Green makes clear that different menus can describe equivalent meals and that understanding this is an essential first step toward the development of mutually beneficial social interaction in culturally diverse settings.

W. Penn Handwerker
University of Connecticut

8

ACKNOWLEDGMENTS

The author's research was funded by the Swiss Development Cooperation and the European Community (Mozambique) and the U.S. Agency for International Development (Swaziland, South Africa, Zambia, and Mozambique). The author thanks Josefa Marrato, Emanuelle Wilsonne, Annemarie Jurg and other colleagues in the Mozambique Ministry of Health, along with Nokhutula Mofamere for help with research, as well as M. Masauso Nzima, Karen Romano, Hubert Allen, and Deborah Hollitzer-Allen for sharing valuable research data. Mitch Allen, John Janzen, D. Michael Warren, Mary Douglas, Ann McElroy, Marvin Harris, Maurice Eisenbruch, Alma Gottlieb, Robert Hahn, Constance McCorkle, Daniel Halperin, Charlie Cheney, Gery Ryan, and three anomymous reviewers made valuable suggestions on sections of the manuscript and/or ideas pursued in this book. H. Russell Bernard deserves special mention for the quality and quantity of his highly useful suggestions and for his moral support. My wife, Suzie McLaughlin, listened patiently and commented wisely throughout the development of this book. Of course, only the author should be held accountable for conclusions reached and opinions expressed here.

INTRODUCTION

The popular stereotype of African indigenous medicine is of magic, witchcraft, sorcery, and spirit possession, set against a background of throbbing drums. Unfortunately, this does not come from Hollywood and comic books alone. A number of health researchers and anthropologists have lent it scientific credibility. One problem with this stereotype is that it has made it easy for Western-trained officials of public health programs to dismiss African medicine as "meaningless pseudo-psychological mumbo-jumbo, which is positively harmful" (Motlana, in Freeman and Motsei 1992:1186). Asuni (1979:33) has written that infection and germs are "alien concepts" that may be incompatible with the knowledge of Nigerian traditional healers.

There is a widespread belief among health professionals that influences the annual allocation of millions of dollars of development assistance. This belief is that African medicine is a "system that is irreconcilable with our own" (Foulkes 1992:122). Health professionals can cite classic and recent anthropological studies to support this view. Secure in their minds that they have done the right thing by rejecting African medicine, health officials promote Western allopathic medicine as if there were no medical system already in place, as if Africa were a tabula rasa. When Africans do not quickly embrace whatever is offered them from the alien system, they are criticized for being stubborn or backward.

How accurate is the stereotype? I have conducted ethnomedical research in a half dozen African countries and have found that when it comes to the diseases that account for greatest morbidity and mortality (i.e., those biomedically classified as infectious and contagious), the indigenous and biomedical etiologic models are, in fact, not very different in fundamental and important ways.[1]

Why are etiologic models important? Anthropologists generally hold that the cause attributed to illness is the key to understanding indigenous theories of illness, as well as the practices associated with the theory, notably treatment and prevention. (Recently, anthropologists have tended to use the word "illness" to denote an indigenous or folk construct, and "disease" to denote a biomedical construct [see Hahn 1984, following Feinstein 1967]. The distinction in terms came to be used widely in anthropology after work by Eisenberg and Kleinman in the late 1970s and early 1980s). A number of influential anthropologists and health professionals, generalizing about how tribal and peasant peoples interpret the causes of illness, have concluded that most Africans interpret most illnesses in some supernatural or "personalistic" manner that invokes witchcraft, sorcery, or spirits of some sort (see, e.g., Murdock 1980; Foster 1983).

Anthropological opinion has changed considerably since the 1970s and especially since the 1980s, at least in part because of the involvement of anthropologists in applied research in infectious disease areas such as childhood diarrhea and sexually transmitted diseases (Inhorn and Brown 1990, 1998). Yet, even today, some anthropologists argue that *all* illnesses are understood personalistically in Africa, that in the end, "everything boils down to witchcraft" (Pool 1994a:12). Others acknowledge that some illnesses are conceived naturalistically, but that these tend to be minor, nonserious, and—by implication—scarcely worth our consideration (e.g., Opala and Boillot 1996:6).

Yet I have found that Africa's most serious diseases tend to be interpreted within a framework that is essentially naturalistic and impersonal. Diseases like malaria, tuberculosis, schistosomiasis, cholera, amoebic dysentery, AIDS and other sexually transmitted diseases, typhoid, and acute respiratory infections including pneumonia, yellow fever, leprosy, and dengue are usually understood within a framework or a body of health knowledge that I call indigenous contagion theory (ICT). ICT is most unsupernatural in character: One becomes ill because of impersonal exposure. One comes into contact with something that anyone could come into contact with—not because an avenging spirit or an ill-intended person singles one out for misfortune in the form of sickness.

Contagion theory in sub-Saharan Africa comprises at least three interrelated types of etiologic belief: (1) "naturalistic infection," or what has been called folk germ theory; (2) "mystical contagion," more often called pollution; and (3) environmental dangers. A fourth type might be included: illness resulting from taboo violation, at least when the immediate cause of illness is physical contact. For now, let us look at the three main types more closely.

Naturalistic infection has been defined as an "invasion of the victim's body by noxious microorganisms, with particular but not exclusive reference to the germ theory of disease" (Murdock 1980:9). In most societies that hold to this theory, the agents of infection are described as worms or tiny insects rather than germs.[2]

Pollution, or what Murdock (1980) has called mystical contagion, is actually not so mystical when examined closely. In the anthropological sense, pollution denotes a belief that people will become ill as a result of contact with, or contamination by, a substance or essence considered dangerous because it is unclean or impure. Africans considered to be in an unclean or polluted state are often kept apart from other people, since they are considered contagious until ritually purified. In central Mozambique, as well as Bangladesh and elsewhere, several kinds of children's diarrhea and/or dehydration are believed to be caused by contact with polluting essences (they are also often believed to be caused by eating bad or spoiled food). One source of pollution that may appear mystical is unfaithful behavior on the part of a parent: If a mother or father commits adultery, he or she acquires a contaminating essence that makes the child sick. The immediate cause is physical contact with the child, or drinking "hot," "spoiled," or "contaminated" breast milk. This belief tends to reinforce the importance of fidelity in marriage. To the extent that this is successful, what happens when Western medicine makes

13

Africans feel that their traditional health beliefs are harmful superstitions that should be abandoned?

A third component of contagion theory, environmental dangers, is based on the belief that elements in the physical environment can cause or spread illness. One expression of this is the idea that contagious illness can be carried in the air or wind. For example, the Bemba of Zambia believe that tuberculosis is an "illness in the air," spread by inhalation of unclean dust carried by the wind. The Bambara of Mali seem to classify smallpox, measles, and other contagious illness as "wind illness," because only wind has sufficiently widespread contact with the body to cause outbreaks (Imperato 1974:15). Drawing on my fieldwork, *tifo temoya* (illness in the air) is a general Swazi term denoting illnesses that are contracted through inhalation. Colds, influenza, tuberculosis, severe (malarial?) headaches, and some types of contagious childhood diarrhea are examples of illnesses carried through the air and inhaled. Recognition of this sort of contagious disease, along with sound preventive practices, is also found in African veterinary practices, as described in Chapter One.

These three components of contagion theory relate to perceived rules or laws, observed cause-and-effect relationships, the natural environment, and/or the involvement of material things, thereby meeting the definitional criteria of "naturally caused," according to Janzen and Prins (1981:429–431). They are not supernatural or personalistic in character. I agree with Murdock (1980), who classifies infection theories of sickness as naturalistic. However, he classifies contagion or pollution theories as mystical, and I suggest that pollution beliefs, as well as those relating to environmental dangers, are naturalistic or quasi-naturalistic. They involve an impersonal process of illness through contact or exposure. Polluted individuals are not singled out for illness or misfortune by a human or superhuman force; they typically become polluted from mere contact, from being in the wrong place at the wrong time.

Perhaps African contagion theory can be interpreted as an expression of what an earlier generation of anthropologists called "native genius" in observing the contagiousness of certain illnesses, in discerning the empirical cause-and-effect relationship between certain kinds of contact with an illness and the spread of the same illness. Perhaps the isolation, avoidance, or social marginalization of people in polluted states serves to quarantine those who, in fact, could be a health threat to others because of their contagiousness.

Certainly, not all African health beliefs and practices are naturalistic, rational, or health promotive. Some are not by objective, scientific standards, and these are discussed in detail in Chapter Eight. A full analysis of African contagion beliefs would also show that magical spells and ill will are thought to be sent through the air and be able to infect people. Certainly a full description of every type of physical and mental illness in a range of African societies would reveal ample evidence of personalistic theories of illness causation, and witchcraft, sorcery, and spirit beliefs are part of the same cultural construction of knowledge as naturalistic, impersonal etiology. But my argument is that those involved in promoting public health in Africa should take the trouble to learn about the existing medical systems before trying to supplant them with what sounds to most Africans like Western scientific mumbo-jumbo.

In short, I propose that there is a domain of ethnomedical thought that can be called indigenous contagion theory and that it comprises three interrelated subdomains. The subdomain of pollution beliefs receives the most attention in this book because: (1) It seems to be a major explanatory metaphor for contagious illness; (2) It may be the most complex and symbol-laden component of indigenous contagion theory; (3) It may be a source of confusion about the degree to which personalistic or supernatural thinking dominates African health beliefs; and (4) In spite of its importance in African ethnomedicine, it has been largely overlooked by anthropologists and health researchers.

Let me comment on terminology. While pollution beliefs in southern Africa have features in common with similar ideas in India and elsewhere, use of the word "pollution" may obscure the somewhat distinctive nature of contagion theory in Africa. And it is a loaded, pejorative term. On the other hand, I feel I must use the term because it is important in this analysis to distinguish pollution from naturalistic infection and environmental dangers. Moreover, the word is well established among anthropologists and others who write about the Indian subcontinent and elsewhere. It becomes useful in Chapter Seven when I show that parallels exist between Africa and other parts of the world regarding pollution and other indigenous contagion beliefs.

This book has an applied intent as well as a scholarly one. Many millions of dollars are spent annually for public health programs that are designed to modify behavior and otherwise intervene in ways intended to prevent contagious diseases. These diseases are currently making a strong

15

comeback after several decades in which antibiotics, immunizations, environmental sanitation, and other interventions seemed to be making substantial health gains.

If there are to be effective interventions, it is more important than ever to understand how Africans (and others) understand contagious diseases. If the evidence shows that diseases that are biomedically classified as infectious and contagious tend not to be interpreted supernaturally, but rather belong to an interpretive system that is essentially rational, empirically based, promotive of good health, and not very different from Western biomedicine in important ways (once we learn to decode the symbolic language), then those who control international funds must deal with ethnomedical research findings—and with indigenous systems themselves. I hope to show that this is what we must do in order to develop culturally meaningful health programs that Africans and others will accept.

Illnesses that are thought to be caused by pollution and other means of contagion are unlike other illnesses in several ways that have important public health implications. Tradition-bound Africans are often characterized as being fatalistic; it is thought that they believe that illness cannot be prevented. Yet, as Ngubane (1977) has observed, the "mystical force" of pollution is not normally considered open to any manipulation or supplication. It is impersonal. The breach of proper behavior is automatically punishable by illness or by the social marginalization of those seen as polluted. It is unlike ancestor-sent illness, witchcraft, or sorcery illness, where supplication to God or lesser spirits or manipulation of medicines or rituals can lead to reprieve. This is not to say that pollution illness is so naturalistic that mundane treatments (e.g., Western medicine) will suffice. In fact, pollution illness usually requires some sort of ritual purification that only indigenous specialists can perform. Such rituals may appear mystical, yet, as Durkheim recognized early on, they may also exhibit practical hygienic measures that do protect against the spread of disease.

Consider illness prevention, the goal of public health. Pollution and other illnesses that are believed contagious, unlike those of supernatural origin, are often considered preventable because they relate to conditions that may be avoidable or modifiable. According to my findings in southern Africa, many naturally caused illnesses (those that "just happen," "illness of God") are thought to be unpreventable because they "have no

16

cause." Illnesses believed due to witchcraft, sorcery, or spirits likewise cannot be prevented because superhuman will or magic cannot be thwarted by mere human effort.

Yet, contagious illnesses stand out among naturally caused illnesses because they may be prevented by blocking or avoiding contact with agents of naturalistic infection or pollution, or by avoiding exposure to elements in certain environments. They may also be prevented by medicines intended to provide protection against future opportunities for contact with such agents or elements. Or prevention may depend on certain types of behavior; often this means following social norms and avoiding taboos and other social transgressions.

For applied medical anthropology and public health, this suggests that prevention strategies for contagious disease can build on an existing etiologic belief system. African and biomedical beliefs about causation and prevention appear compatible in the domain of contagious disease, in ways they are not in other areas of disease. Contagious illnesses are also often thought to be treatable as well as possibly preventable by foreign or Western-biomedical means, unlike illnesses of presumed supernatural origin. An exception may be certain pollution illnesses that require ritual purification.

Pollution and other indigenous contagion beliefs therefore are an area of potential interface between African and Western medicine. But this potential has not been realized. There has not been much research about pollution beliefs and related elements of ICT. I think many health researchers have missed and continue to miss the significance of a crucial area of African ethnomedicine due to an expectation or mind-set that finds supernatural thinking everywhere. There has been a trend toward recognition of naturalism in African ethnomedicine beginning in the mid-1970s (e.g., Warren 1974; Fortes 1976; Janzen and Prins 1981; Yoder 1982; de Zoysa et al. 1984). But there has already been some reaction to this and there has been an attempt to reassert the old magic-witchcraft paradigm of African medicine. For example, Robert Pool recently argued that "in the final instance, everything boils down to witchcraft" (1994a: 12) in African ethnomedicine. Pool's ideas are discussed in Chapter Two.

With even some anthropologists still contributing to the witchcraft-sorcery stereotype, it is not surprising that African health officials often dismiss the idea of accommodating local health beliefs. The prevailing view is that indigenous health beliefs are worse than superstitious nonsense—they are dangerous. The view of most health officials is something like, "We can't build on traditional health beliefs because they are based mainly on witchcraft superstitions, which are dangerous and socially divisive, so let's simply start with a clean slate and teach what we know from modern medicine." This attitude also constrains the development of accommodating public health programs in developing countries outside of Africa, a topic taken up in the last chapter.

In my view, indigenous contagion beliefs express essentially the same process of infection as modern germ theory attempts to, but in an idiom to which we are unaccustomed. A pioneer of African ethnomedicine, E. E. Evans-Pritchard—the scholar most closely associated with African witchcraft theories—asked: "Is Zande thought so different from ours that we can only describe their speech and actions without comprehending them, or is it essentially like our own though expressed in an idiom to which we are unaccustomed?" (1937:4).

We do no injustice to science and medicine, and certainly not to public health, if we build on—rather than ignore or confront—indigenous contagion beliefs in our attempts to mitigate the ravages of infectious diseases. The details of exactly how to develop effective programs based on African contagion beliefs need to be developed, and they will differ between countries and perhaps societies within countries. Some suggestions are offered in this book about sexually transmitted and diarrheal diseases. At the very least, preventive health education campaigns could adopt the language, metaphors, and symbolism of ICT to become more meaningful and acceptable to the intended audience and therefore to better motivate adoption of certain behaviors or "technologies" (e.g., condoms, oral rehydration salts).

This book focuses on southern Africa because that is where my applied research has taken me. However, I cite enough evidence from other parts of Africa to suggest that the rationality and naturalism of health beliefs of the south can be found elsewhere in the continent and beyond. It is easier to find evidence of impersonal illness causation in the well-documented ethnomedical systems of China, India, the Middle East, and Latin America than it is in sub-Saharan Africa. Chinese, Ayurveda, Unani, and humoral pathology are acknowledged to be based on essentially naturalistic causality. Thus, it may be sufficient to explode myths of excessive supernaturalism in Africa, where health beliefs are widely regarded as the most magical in the world, a view supported by some respected anthropologists (e.g., Foster 1983:20). If we conclude that there has been excessive supernaturalism attributed to Africans, this has doubtless happened elsewhere.

In Chapter Seven, I take up the issue of the global relevance of the proposed analytic construct of indigenous contagion theory. I show that contagious diseases like syphilis, pneumonia, and tuberculosis tend to be thought of in ways similar to African ICT. Researchers, however, often do not know how to interpret and classify odd-seeming findings that not only do not conform to the biomedical model, but also may differ from the prevailing emic models of the region (e.g., humoral pathology in Latin America). I argue that ICT is needed as an analytic construct by anthropologists and health practitioners in many parts of the world. I also discuss the broader issues of the use and nonuse of relevant ethno-medical findings in designing and implementing public health programs in all developing countries. The point is, the same etic mind-set that is quick to dismiss indigenous medicine in Africa also constrains the development of more effective health programs in many other parts of the world.

In Chapter Eight, I explain why ICT is found in association with contagious illnesses in diverse, widely separated regions of the world, as well as in the recorded history of medicine from different periods and places. This leads to a discussion of the utility of what has been called the adaptation paradigm. Consideration of adaptation in association with contagion theory calls for examination of paradigms in contemporary medical anthropology, such as the biocultural-ecological and so-called critical medical anthropology.

NOTES

1. "Biomedicine" refers to Western-style, cosmopolitan medicine, including its branch of public health, and it is distinguished from African "traditional" (although dynamic, adaptive, and changing) systems of "indigenous medicine." "Contagious" disease usually refers to disease transmission that is direct, by contact, while with "infectious" disease, transmission is indirect, through the medium of water, air, or contaminated articles (Pelling 1993:309).

2. I have found many such germ concepts in my research (e.g., *kadoyo* among the Bemba [Zambia]; *iciwane* among the Zulu [South Africa]; *liciwane* among the Swazi [Swaziland]; *atchi-koko* among the Macua of northern Mozambique; *khoma* among the Shona of central Mozambique; and—to take an example from others' research in west Africa—*kokoro* among the Yoruba of Nigeria [Foster et al. 1996]). Sexually transmitted diseases are often thought to involve such infection agents—not witchcraft.

CHAPTER ONE

AFRICAN HEALTH BELIEFS

This chapter deals with the types of explanations that predominate in understandings of illness in southern Africa. I present evidence from ethnography that suggests that although pollution and other contagion beliefs and related practices have been recognized by some since at least the turn of the century, their significance has been largely overlooked. Anthropologists and others have given much greater emphasis to more exotic-seeming areas of ethnomedicine, namely witchcraft, sorcery, magic, and spirit beliefs.

ETHNOGRAPHIC OVERVIEW

Findings presented in this book evolve from a number of ethnolinguistic groups in east-central and south-central Africa. To understand how these groups relate to each other, and to provide some basis for understanding the relative homogeneity of ethnomedical beliefs and practices found in central and southern Africa, I present an ethnographic overview of the region derived from G. P. Murdock's seminal work, *Africa: Its People and Their Cultural History* (1959). My own research findings come from three general groups in Murdock's classification: the Central Bantu, the Shona/Thonga clusters, and the Nguni.

Central Bantu

This group occupies the savanna, dry forest, and upland grasses, stretching from the Atlantic to the Indian oceans, that lie just to the south of the equatorial rain forest. Despite a high degree of social organizational and other uniformity, there are sufficient ethnolinguistic differences to justify recognition of eight subgroupings or clusters: the Kongo, Kimbundu, Kwango, Kasai, Lunda, Bemba, Maravi, and Yao. Of the groups discussed in detail in this book, the Nyanja belong to the Maravi cluster, the Bemba belong to the Bemba cluster, and the Macua (Makua) belong to the Yao cluster (Murdock:1959:290–306). Keep in mind that Murdock's profiles describe a way of life now nearly 40 years in the past.

The economy of the central Bantu has been based traditionally on swidden horticulture rather than the cattle pastoralism that is typical of the groups to the south. Maize, millet, sorghum, and eleusine are primary crops of the eastern division of the broader group; groundnuts and sweet potatoes are also cultivated. Traditional settlement pattern of the Central Bantu is compact (and formerly stockaded) villages arranged around a central plaza, although groups of the Kwango and eastern Yao cluster live in dispersed homesteads or small hamlets, typical of groups to the south. Each settlement has a hereditary headman and an advisory council of elders. Age-grades and secret societies are rare. There is a fair degree of social stratification, with most groups distinguishing privileged nobility or royalty from commoners.

With few exceptions, matrilineal descent prevails among the Central Bantu, and the resulting descent groups are exogamous, meaning they must marry outside the group. Bride-price and polygyny (plural wives as distinct from plural husbands) tend to be the rule, and residence is traditionally avunculocal—boys leave their father's home at some age to live with their maternal uncles.

There is an interesting difference between the western and eastern branches of the Central Bantu: The eastern groups traditionally lacked livestock, "native money, or other movable property in substantial amounts," so they tended to be poor (Gluckman 1945; Murdock 1959: 300) and often substituted bride-service for bride-price.[1] And groups in the west tended to be integrated within complex states (such as the kingdom of Kongo) whereas eastern groups tended not to be—the Makonde (immediate neighbors of the Macua in Mozambique), for example, recognized no authority higher than the hamlet/village headman.

Of interest to AIDS epidemiology nowadays, most groups of the five western clusters practice male circumcision, while most eastern groups do not (although the Macua for the most part do, probably due to Islamic influence). Among populations in which AIDS is a heterosexually transmitted disease, male circumcision has been found to protect against STD and HIV infection (Bongaarts et al. 1989; Moses et al. 1994; Seed et al. 1995; Caldwell and Caldwell 1996).

Shona/Thonga

This subgroup consists of two clusters of many tribes, including the Shona and Thonga, and it occupies a geographical position between the Central Bantu to the north and west, and the Nguni to the south (Murdock 1959:374–380). The groups included here are mainly agricultural. Maize is the primary crop, followed in importance by millet, eleusine, rice, beans, earth peas, manioc, groundnuts, pumpkins, and sweet potatoes. Animal husbandry is important to the Thonga, but subsidiary among the Shona. Both groups live in dispersed hamlets or homesteads (kraals). Descent is primarily patrilineal, unlike their matrilineal Central Bantu neighbors. Murdock (p. 377) believes the Shona once shared the kinship system of its neighbors to the north but after the introduction of cattle, shifted to patrilineal descent, patrilocal residence, and bride-price payments, the pattern found among the Thonga. Both Shona and Thonga have been organized in states of relatively modest size. A king resides in a royal court in a capital village/town, maintains a court of advisers, and receives tribute from outlying chieftaincies (Murdock 1959:378).

Nguni

This subgroup represents the southern extension of Bantu speakers, and it includes the three clusters: the Nguni proper (including the Zulu,

Swazi, and Xhosa discussed in this book), the Ndebele, and the Ngoni (Murdock 1959:380–385). The "Ndebele proper" are those of today's Zimbabwe (some 20% of that country's population). The Ngoni are descended from Nguni speakers who fled the wars and raids of King Shaka Zulu around 1820, migrating with their cattle as far north as Lake Victoria. Today, most are found in Zambia, Malawi, and Tanzania where they have mixed among Central Bantu groups.

Animal husbandry (especially cattle keeping) and agriculture are both important for the Nguni. Cattle are important for prestige, bridewealth payments, and milk; goats sheep and dogs are also kept, as are—since their introduction by Europeans—horses, donkeys, pigs, and chickens. Maize has succeeded sorghum as the staple crop; subsidiary crops include bananas, beans, gourds, watermelons, eleusine, millet, earth peas, groundnuts, pumpkins, and sweet potatoes. The settlement pattern is one of dispersed homesteads, or kraals. Polygyny is common except among the Xhosa; each wife has her own hut within the kraal. All groups are strongly patrilineal; residence is patrilocal and patriarchal. All groups are organized into complex states.

As with the Thonga, kings (demoted to paramount chiefs by colonial authorities) enjoyed near absolute power, resided in a royal court in a capital village or town, maintained a court of advisers, and received tribute from outlying chieftaincies. Age-based regiments served as warriors for the king and continue to serve in a variety of ways today. Much of the old system prevails in today's Swaziland. Cultural revitalization of many of these elements can still be found among the Zulu as part of this numerically powerful group's attempt to exercise power and influence in modern South Africa.

BANTU SPEAKERS IN BROADER ETHNOLINGUISTIC CONTEXT

The Bantu are a major subgroup of the Niger-Congo language family. This latter is the numerically largest and geographically most widespread linguistic group in Africa, covering most of sub-Saharan Africa except for the Horn and central portions of the Sudan. The Niger-Congo grouping relates the Bantu-speaking peoples of the Congo basin and southeast Africa historically and culturally to the dense population of West Africa, from which area the former group migrated, beginning a few centuries before Christ. Noting the common heritage, historian E. Murphy (1972: 179) observes, "The Bantu-speaking peoples share with their West African cousins common fundamental attitudes about God, religion, kinship, the nature of the world, and life."

There are many similarities between Bantu and West African health beliefs as well, as numerous examples in this book illustrate. In a classic assessment of human personality, Kluckhohn and Murray (1949:35) observed that "Every man is in certain respects like all other men, like some other men, like no other man." It may be useful to remind ourselves that all ethnolinguistic groups are like all other groups, like some other groups, like no other groups. It is the "some other groups" that is the source of much confusion, because there are many levels at which traits can be compared.

It may be useful to picture an inverted pyramid with horizontal bands labeled, descending from the top, All people, Africans, Niger-Congo speakers, Bantus, etc., and then think of what outstanding traits can be found at each level. For example, the Zulu are like all other groups (what Kroeber called "cultural universals") in that they marry, have families, live in settlements, have religious beliefs, have incest taboos, etc. The Zulu are like all Africans at a slightly restricted level of generality, like all Niger-Congo speakers with regard to somewhat fewer traits, and like all Bantu—and then southern Bantu—speakers with regard to still fewer traits. They are like all Nguni speakers in traits pertaining to animal husbandry (especially cattle keeping), marriage and kinship patterns (polygynous, patrilineal, patrilocal, patriarchal), settlement pattern (dispersed kraals), and others listed above. They share some distinctive traits with other groups classified as "Nguni proper" that distinguish this cluster from the Ndebele and Ngoni clusters. Finally, in some respects, the Zulu, like all human groups, are unique.

The question is not whether it is legitimate to generalize from one human group to another. We must generalize if we are to have a science of culture, of which medical anthropology is a subdiscipline.

METHODOLOGICAL SUMMARY

My own research in Swaziland, South Africa, Mozambique, and Zambia was in all cases applied and related to public health intervention objectives—mostly connected with childhood diarrhea and sexually transmitted diseases—rather than to theoretical or other academic issues. A general summary of these methods follows. It should be recognized that cultural data pertaining to meaning were sought, therefore statistically based random selection of respondents or informants was not appropriate, even if it had been feasible. As Handwerker and Wozniak (1997:874) have concluded, "The socially constructed nature of cultural phenomena makes the classical sampling criterion of independent case selection not only impossible to attain but also undesirable." In most cases, we sought representative experts or insiders who could explain locally constructed health knowledge systems, keeping in mind that there are variations in the systems and divergent viewpoints.

Swaziland

I went to Swaziland in 1981 to serve as an anthropologist on the USAID-funded Rural Water-Borne Disease Control Project. The project called for a knowledge, attitudes, and practices (KAP) survey relating to water and sanitation. The primary objective of the project was to discover how rural Swazis understood schistosomiasis as well as cholera and other diarrheal illness. However, I had the latitude to develop other research so that culturally appropriate interventions could be designed and implemented, especially for health education. In addition to conducting a standard KAP survey related to water and sanitation, I and my Swazi assistants carried out ethnomedical research with traditional healers using survey methods, key informant interviews, and participant observation. Between August 1982 and January 1983, my research assistants interviewed 144 traditional healers (herbalists, diviner mediums, and faith healers). I supplemented this with in-depth interviews with healers who were particularly candid and forthcoming and/or who possessed special knowledge (Green 1987).

These interviews began in 1981 before the healer survey and continued until the end of my full-time work in Swaziland in 1985. They have continued intermittently since then during return trips that I made as a consultant to that country, sometimes for as long as six weeks. Research in Swaziland also included considerable participant observation with traditional healers, chiefs, and other knowledgeable elders. All applied research was funded by USAID.

Mozambique

Research in Mozambique took place between 1991 and 1995, amounting to 20 months in-country, most of which was related to ethnomedical research and the development of health education strategies based on this research. I was assisted by Mozambican researchers who conducted semistructured, key-informant interviews in local languages. We worked primarily in Manica Province in central Mozambique (1991–92), Inhambane Province in the south (1994–95), and Nampula Province in the north (1995). We conducted additional formal focus group discussions (FGDs) in Manica, but gave these up in favor of adding structured group discussions focused on ethnomedicine to the curriculum of workshops for traditional healers.

Formal FGDs often produced stilted, stereotypical information of the sort healers imagined would please the FGD moderators—in other words, they resembled survey results in Africa when the subject matter is personal and private and when those seen to represent the government or the biomedical viewpoint are known to have strong, partisan views. On the other hand, once trust had developed after a few days in a workshop and healers were comfortable, informal discussion could produce valid and useful findings.

Some 275 Mozambican traditional healers were interviewed altogether in the three provinces mentioned. I designed all instruments, interpreted all findings, and conducted some interviews personally in each province in Portuguese, the national language. The applied research was funded by the Swiss Development Cooperation, the European Commission, and USAID.

South Africa

I worked intermittently in South Africa between 1992 and 1994 as a consultant to an AIDS/STD prevention program funded jointly by the AIDS Control and Prevention (AIDSCAP) project (funded by USAID and administered by Family Health International) and the AIDS Communication (AIDSCOM) project (also funded by USAID but administered by the Academy for Educational Development). (Since 1994, the program has been run by AIDSCAP alone.) Because of the Mozambique Minister of Health's experience of working colloboratively with traditional healers in AIDS prevention, AIDSCAP was amenable to trying this approach in

South Africa. Research consisted of in-depth interviews and reinterviews with healers, informal FGDs during week-long workshops, and some quick surveys of the pretest/posttest type to determine levels of knowledge and familiarity before and after workshops. A more comprehensive survey was conducted in 1993 with 70 workshop-exposed traditional healers who represented a national sample of such healers. Findings from South Africa have been already been reported in detail (Green 1994a), and I will only refer to them briefly here.

Zambia

In early 1995, I was asked to evaluate a collaborative program involving traditional healers in Zambia. The program was known as the Morehouse School of Medicine/Zambia AIDS Prevention Project (shortened here to Morehouse/Tulane AIDS project; Tulane University was a partner in the project and study). Among its accomplishments at the time was a Targeted Intervention Research (TIR) survey among a relatively large random sample (440) of Zambians. A subsample of (formal sector) health workers was also interviewed, but not traditional healers. I recommended that the TIR questionnaire be modified somewhat and that a sample of 81 traditional healers also be interviewed. This was done.

My involvement with the healer TIR was in general design, modifying the instrument, and analyzing and interpreting the findings (along with Masauso Nzima, who was principal investigator of the general TIR). The Morehouse/Tulane AIDS project allowed me to further analyze data from the general TIR and to publish it in this book. Chapter Five contains findings from both TIR surveys that relate to sexually transmitted diseases, including AIDS. Chapter Six contains TIR (and other) findings about malaria, tuberculosis, schistosomiasis, and other infectious diseases. In addition to these surveys, I spent three weeks in Zambia in April 1995 conducting interviews with traditional healers, health workers, and other informants and observing a workshop for healers on AIDS and STDs.

WHY SEEK ETHNOMEDICAL INFORMATION FROM TRADITIONAL HEALERS?

One occasionally hears that anthropologists have a bias in favor of traditional healers. It might be worthwhile to explore this, given the extent to which healers have contributed information for this book. First, a note on terminology. It has been argued that "traditional healer" is a misnomer because healers are not strictly traditional; they are adaptive and ever-changing. However, I will use the term because African healers themselves tend to prefer it over alternative terms that have been proposed and it is the preferred term in public health. Perhaps "indigenous ethnomedical practitioners" or "autochthonous practitioners of ethnoiatrics" might be more accurate, but a simple, generic term is needed and traditional healer is already widely used. African healers also like "traditional medical practitioner," but this is longer by one word, and some doctors oppose using the word "medical" in association with traditional healers.

But what of the alleged prohealer bias? Philip Singer, himself an anthropologist, has commented that

> Medical anthropologists have always had a love affair with traditional "alternative" healers in third-world countries. We have seen them as delivering some health services to the people most in need but least served by Western-trained physicians. We have also been reluctant to criticize any of these traditional healers because of our holistic approach which holds that each member of society has a role to play. (1986:29)[2]

I agree with this and could even add other reasons for this fondness. Anthropologists tend to be advocates for the poor and dispossessed. We are romantics who distrust Western urban technological society and feel alienated from it. The prospect of spending a couple of years immersed in a peasant or tribal society, making disparaging comments about civilization, is a strong pull for many of us. And who better represents an alternative to impersonal, Western technological mass society than traditional healers? Besides, they tend to be the local intellectuals; they are people we can talk with. We can float our pet theories with them, and they might well understand and improve on these, however scant their formal education.

In his 1976 presidential address to the 75th Anniversary Meeting of the American Anthropological Association, Walter Goldschmidt suggested that anthropologists tend to possess certain core characteristics rooted deep in our collective psyche. We are mistrustful of all sources of power, influence, and wealth. We loathe authority—indeed, we often shrink from the prospect of finding ourselves in positions of authority. Our escapist tendencies find expression in xenophilia—the romanticization of all

29

things foreign and exotic. This may help explain our love affair with traditional and alternative healing systems.

That said, and returning to the issues here, are there any reasons to interview traditional healers rather than those who consult them? There are several.

First, from my earliest work in Swaziland, I found that most information derived from health surveys, particularly if it sought to answer the "why" questions, was superficial at best and often of dubious validity. For this reason, I turned to in-depth interviews with traditional healers. I found the resulting information to be of much higher quality.

Second, so little was known about indigenous knowledge, beliefs, and behavior related to diarrheal and other illness at the time that only qualitative, anthropological research methods were appropriate. The same was true in Mozambique; moreover, traditional healers were the immediate group with whom we collaborated directly there in our program of reducing morbidity and mortality associated with diarrheal disease, AIDS, and STDs. Therefore, we needed to understand how they perceive illness.

Third, healers presumably represent the beliefs of clients who consult them and they are often better able than their clients to explain such beliefs, both because of their specialized knowledge and because their status in the community makes them less likely to be intimidated by an interviewer. Mitchell (1973) has measured the tendency in Africa for respondents of lower status than interviewers to be less cooperative than respondents of higher status. In my experience, traditional healers— who are regarded as being of high status by themselves and others—tend to be cooperative with researchers in part because they feel secure in their status. On the other hand, healing knowledge is considered sacred and secret in much of Africa. Some healers feel constrained by their empowering spirits to reveal information regarded as secret.

Finally, healers and laypersons seem to share essentially the same ethnomedical models in Africa, even if healers have deeper knowledge of the models and can (or are willing to) explain them better to anthropologists and others. Boster and Johnson (1989) have investigated whether people classify the natural world on the basis of form or function. (Function in this context relates to adaptive value, to human intentions, to classification serving some human need or end.) Based on their American study of how college students and expert fishermen classify fish, Boster and Johnson (1989:872) found that novices classify on the basis of form (similar to the scientific basis, morphology), while experts classify as much by function as by form. Cognitive psychologists have likewise found that experts and novices differ in the basis of classification, along the same lines as the fish study: Experts look beyond outward appearances to function, often utilitarian function such as whether the fish is good to eat. Or they use behavioral criteria for animals rather than their appearance. Such consideration of function requires more specialized knowledge than laypersons possess. This raises the question of whether laypersons and traditional healers classify (or interpret) illness cause in the same way. Perhaps traditional healers, as experts, consider factors unknown to laypersons.

Typically, African healers possess deeper knowledge about the cause of locally recognized illnesses than do those who consult them, a point often made by laypersons when interviewed. But this does not mean that the illness explanatory models differ substantially in their essential features. Studies in Africa in which both healers and their clients were interviewed and the results compared support this (Warren 1979:39–41; Bishaw 1989; de Sousa 1991:62, 73; Reis 1994:S40; Green and Nzima 1995; Nzima 1995). I will support this assertion with examples when I discuss findings from Zambia, below. Apart from healers being a good source of ethnomedical information, they can also have a potential role in health education and other interventions in the interest of improving public health. This is discussed throughout the book, but first let us return to the question posed earlier: How do Africans interpret illness, contagious or otherwise?

GENERAL CHARACTERIZATIONS OF AFRICAN HEALTH BELIEFS

Anthropologists tend to regard the cause attributed to illness as the key to understanding indigenous theories of illness and the independent variable that determines other elements of the health system. Foster (1976) decries a pre-1970s period of "grossly descriptive" medical anthropology in which lists of illnesses and treatments took precedence over interpretation and synthesis. He argues that "the most important fact about an illness in most medical systems is not the underlying pathological process but *the underlying cause*" (p. 774, emphasis added), a point advanced many years earlier by one of the first medically trained anthropologists,

W.H.R. Rivers (1924). Foster (1983:20) argues that an understanding of the cause of illness is necessary to understand treatment, prevention, and other aspects of health-related behavior. This may be a characteristic of folk or non-Western health systems. Glick (1967:36) observes that "whereas in Western medicine causation has no essential relationship to socio-cultural context, in most other medical systems causation and context are so intimately linked as to be the ethnographer's principal concern." Lieban (1977:23) concurs: "In most indigenous medical systems the primary consideration in the diagnosis of the disease is its cause."

This doesn't mean that verbalized statements about etiology are always good predictors of behavior, especially if such statements are elicited in formal survey or focus group contexts. Examples can always be found of incongruence between statements and behavior (Rubel and Hass 1996: 123). Nor does it mean that cause is the only factor in etiologic models or in decisions regarding treatment choice. Yet, even Yoder, an anthropologist who argues that "principles of causality are but one aspect of the process of naming and classifying disease," concedes that "notions of causality are crucial, however, in the choice of therapy, for they establish limits within which the appropriate therapy is chosen" (1981:241; see also de Zoysa et al. 1984; Kendall et al. 1984). The perceived degree of illness severity (personal vulnerability) and a variety of economic, and other material, including environmental factors are also important, but not, I argue, usually as important as causation beliefs for broadly predicting treatment choices, at least in Africa.

Recent anthropological studies that take a comprehensive approach to building decision models intended to predict health behavior still find great predictive power in the attributed cause of illness. For example, in their study of Mexican mothers, Ryan and Martínez (1996) found "a strong association between belief in *empacho* [the sticking of food on the stomach or intestines] and the use of treatments that involved physical manipulation or use of purgatives" (p. 54).

I am not implying that determining the cause of illness occurs by some simple, automatic, unambiguous process. Those who describe the "quest for therapy" in both rural and urban Africa make the point that nowadays especially, there are a number of therapeutic alternatives open to someone who is ill (Janzen 1978; Fierman 1981). Family members, friends, neighbors, and elders of the community, as well as a variety of indigenous healers may be consulted or may offer an opinion anyway. The

32

availability of Western-style biomedicine, religious faith healing, and—at least in some larger cities—the newer alternative therapies (e.g., homeopathy, osteopathy, and acupuncture) complicates this process further. Anthropologists often speak of "patterns of resort" when describing therapy-seeking behavior. For example, Cosminsky and Scrimshaw (1980:275) observe that although there is great variation and back and forth in such health behavior in Guatemala, "The trend is to begin with low cost or home remedies and move to more expensive resources as the course of the illness proceeds and becomes more serious," a pattern that holds for Africa, too.

Anthropologists generally consider therapy seekers "to be rational decision makers whose knowledge and resources affect their choices" (Ryan and Martínez 1996:47). Economic and other infrastructural factors (Harris 1979) are often invoked to explain health decision making without resort to cognition, or to cognition alone.

I believe that although economic and other material factors are important and to some degree determining, there are usually a number of factors that the health care seeker is consciously thinking about. Based on my studies of sexually transmitted illnesses in Africa, I think that once symptoms of this sort appear, there follows a rational calculation in the mind of the afflicted. If we could conduct a content analysis of this mind, we would find considerations such as recognition and classification of the illness (symptoms, signs, probable cause); severity and treatability; shame or embarrassment over the possible social response to the illness; fear of the reaction of the spouse or sexual partner; availability of effective home remedies (herbal or pharmaceutical); distance to nearest folk or bio-medical healers; cost of transportation; cost of therapies; time lost from productive activities, and so on. And these may be only the initial considerations. If first-stage therapies fail, all of the foregoing including assessment of probable cause are subject to reconsideration and reinterpretation.

Keeping therapy resort and the variety of competing therapies in mind, the focus of this book is on indigenous, traditional healing systems —using the somewhat controversial word traditional in full recognition that indigenous African healing systems are dynamic, adaptive, ever-changing systems, open to the accommodation of therapeutic pluralism (Janzen 1981:189). Many of the nonanthropologist, medically trained researchers and commentators cited in this book use a traditional-modern medicine distinction, so it seems necessary to adopt such language. If I use the word indigenous, it is to emphasize a local system as it is today, realizing that it has probably adopted substantial nontraditional elements in recent years.

It is also necessary to comment on the natural-supernatural dichotomy that appears in older anthropological literature and is still found in popular accounts—and some professional accounts—of African health systems. Most anthropologists have abandoned these terms in favor of personalistic and naturalistic, or impersonal explanations. Foster (1976) provides good definitions of these terms:

> A personalistic medical system is one in which disease is explained as due to the *active, purposeful intervention* of an *agent*, who may be human (a witch or sorcerer), nonhuman (a ghost, an ancestor, an evil spirit), or supernatural (a deity or other very powerful being). The sick person literally is a victim, the object of aggression or punishment directed specifically against him, for reasons that concern him alone. Personalistic causality allows little room for accident or change; in fact, for some peoples the statement is made by anthropologists who have studied them that *all* illness and death are believed to stem from the acts of the agent.
>
> In contrast to personalistic systems, naturalistic systems explain illness in impersonal, systemic terms. Disease is thought to stem, not from the machinations of an angry being, but rather from *natural forces or conditions* such as cold, heat, winds, dampness, and, above all, by an upset in the balance of the basic body elements. In naturalistic systems, health conforms to an *equilibrium* model: When the humors, the yin and yang, or the Ayurvedic *dosha* are in balance appropriate to the age and condition of the individual, in his or her natural and social environment, health results. Causality concepts explain or account for the upsets in this balance that trigger illness. (p. 775)

Foster begins this seminal paper with the observation that anthropologists tend to generalize about indigenous (tribal, folk, peasant, etc.) medical systems based on what they have learned about a single indigenous society (the one they know best). I suggest that Foster himself may have fallen into this trap a bit in his emphasis on humoral or other equilibrium models of health. The equilibrium model is important in Latin America, the area Foster knows best, but it is only one model of the naturalistic system in Africa, and not the most important one, as we shall see.

34

AFRICAN ETIOLOGY

Foster (1983:20) suggests that most of Africa is characterized by personalistic explanations. And, based on his analysis of a global sample of societies described below, Murdock (1980:48) likewise concluded that "supernatural" etiology predominates in Africa, particularly what he calls mystical retribution and sorcery. Many other anthropologists, not to mention scholars of other disciplines, missionaries, travelers, government administrators (pre- and postcolonial, foreign and African), doctors and health officials, and development professionals, have been more direct in characterizing African health beliefs as operating primarily, or solely, in the domain of witchcraft, sorcery, and/or spirits.

E. E. Evans-Pritchard (1937:67), in a classic of African medical anthropology, reported that the Azande attributed nearly all sickness, whatever the nature, to witchcraft or sorcery. Even if a careful reading of this highly influential work shows that the Zande recognized a "hierarchy of resort ranging from simple to serious, with recourse first to 'empirical' and then to 'magical' intervention," as Janzen (1981) notes, it is nevertheless true that a majority of scholars of Africa believe Evans-Pritchard to have said that "African causation of illness and misfortune is primarily due to witchcraft only" (pp. 188–189).

A generation after Evans-Pritchard's work, a leading symbolic anthropologist, Victor Turner, commented that the Ndembu (of Zambia) "are obsessively logical" when it comes to their illness beliefs, "though on the basis of mystical premises" (Turner 1967, quoted in Hahn 1995:16). Turner believed these premises to be personalistic ("generated or evoked and directed by conscious agents" [Turner 1967:300]) rather than impersonal.

One need only browse the stacks of a good university library in the area of African ethnomedicine and count the number of books with words like witchcraft, sorcery, magic, wizardry, and spirits in their titles for evidence of the predominant illness construct that is associated with Africans. Indeed, African anthropologists and medical specialists have often reached the same conclusion as Foster and Evans-Pritchard, as shown in examples in a later section.

What about variation within Africa? H. K. Schneider attempted to contrast what he called two of the great traditions of Africa, the West African and the Bantu. Fate is a central theme among West Africans, which—among the Yoruba at least—is closely related to relations one maintains with the high god Elegba or Eshu. Misfortune is related to fate and the unpredictability of Eshu, for these presumably representative West Africans. For Bantu speakers, "vital force" is a central concept. It refers to something that all beings, living or dead, have in varying degrees. Schneider (1981) observes that

> In contrast to West Africans, then, when misfortune afflicts a man it is never due to fate but always to the machinations of another person who attempts to increase his vital force at the expense of the victim. . . . To a Bantu, nothing happens by accident. Even if a man seemingly injures himself, as by falling out of a tree, he immediately suspects either an ancestor or another person as being the ultimate cause. (p. 190)

If this is true, Bantu speakers should be even more inclined toward personalistic explanations for illness—a type of misfortune—than West Africans. If we find that this has been exaggerated, and that naturalistic beliefs (including pollution) are actually important central themes in Bantu thought, then the broad characterizations of African thought as being personalistic are even less defensible.

Caldwell and Caldwell (1994) are among many influential applied scholars of various disciplines who perpetuate the idea that personalistic models of illness and misfortune predominate in sub-Saharan Africa. This impression may be reinforced by superficial responses to health survey questions, as, for example, in a recent study in Cameroon: "The immunization campaign was further hindered by resilient cultural beliefs about disease causation. Seventy-two percent of respondents stated that childhood mortality is a result of witchcraft or God's will" (Azevedo et al. 1991). As shown below, witchcraft and God's will are, in fact, two very different ways of thinking; the latter usually refers to natural causation. Survey findings seem to indicate that personalistic explanations are far more important than surveys suggest because survey respondents are often reluctant to be candid and forthcoming about beliefs they fear may meet with scorn and ridicule from interviewers.

Africans in the medical profession not infrequently characterize ethnomedical beliefs as supernatural and may be even more likely to condemn or devalue them than do foreign health professionals. I have quoted Motlana (Freeman and Motsei 1992:1186) characterizing African medicine as "superstition, meaningless pseudo-psychological mumbo-jumbo, which is positively harmful." Asuni (1979) has also written in this vein. Ajai (1990) says, "The practitioners of traditional medicine believe that diseases are caused by supernatural forces, the displeasure of ancestral gods, evil spirits, black magic, or spirit possession. . . . Occultism is an essential part of traditional medicine just like witchcraft and wizardry" (p. 685). The remainder of this article, which appears in *Medicine and Law*, is replete with language such as "gross negligence" and "the endangerment of the lives of citizens by untrained quacks."

TYPOLOGIES OF AFRICAN ILLNESS

A number of anthropologists have developed typologies that seek to characterize African health belief systems in terms of causal theories of illness. Some derive their typology from intensive study of a single society, while others generalize to a broad region based on a review of the ethnographic literature. Let us first review G. P. Murdock's typology of illness. It is based on a global sample of societies and is one of the most comprehensive typologies extant.

Murdock's Global Typology of Illness

Murdock's typology is based on an ethnographic survey of indigenous etiological notions of theories in 139 randomly selected societies of the world, 43 of them in Africa (Murdock 1980). The major division is into natural and supernatural theories of illness causation, the former predominating in a very small number of societies. Natural theories are subdivided into five subtypes: infection, stress, organic deterioration, accidents, and overt human aggression. Supernatural causation is subdivided into three broad categories: mystical causation (which is impersonal), animistic causation, and magical causation. Mystical causation is subdivided into four subtypes: fate, ominous sensations, contagion, and mystical retribution. Animistic causation has only one subtype: spirit aggression. Magical causation has two subtypes: sorcery and witchcraft. This is summarized in Figure 1.

Of interest to our discussion is infection, the first type under theories of natural causation. This is defined as "invasion of the victim's body by noxious microorganisms, with particular but not exclusive reference to the germ theory of disease" (Murdock 1980:9). Murdock notes that

37

For only 31 other societies do the sources mention theories of this type as of even minor consequence, and in most of them the infection organisms resemble worms or tiny insects rather than germs. The small number of societies reported to accept a theory of infection reflects both the recency of its scientific recognition and the very limited range of its diffusion. (p. 9)

	Type		Subtype
N			
a	Infection		
t	Stress		
u	Organic deterioration		
r	Accidents		
a	Human aggression		
l			
S			
u	Mystical	————————>	Fate
p		————————>	Ominous sensations
e		————————>	Contagion
r		————————>	Mystical retribution
n			
a	Magical	————————>	Witchcraft
t		————————>	Sorcery
u			
r	Animistic	————————>	Spirit aggression
a			
l			

Figure 1. Murdock's typology of illness.

Note the implication that ideas of noxious microorganisms arose because of the diffusion of Western biomedical thinking, rather than spontaneously in local societies. But why couldn't the idea arise independently? A Ghanaian villager told a colleague of mine that germs can be seen when one holds up a jar of dirty water to the sunlight and looks carefully (Warren, personal communication). No matter that he was probably seeing larvae; this may provide a clue to the rise of the "insects" and "worms" of naturalistic infection. It would be very easy to discern a cause-and-effect relationship between drinking water with tiny creatures and becoming ill not long afterward. Belief in tiny worms or insects that carry illness might well have developed before the introduction of Western biomedicine. Body lice or ticks could be another origin of indigenous germ ideas. Indeed, Europeans possessed ideas similar to those described by Murdock and detailed below from African research findings, prior to the rise of modern germ theory (see Chapter Seven).

According to Murdock's survey, infection illness theory is predominant only for the Japanese. But concepts of small or unseen insects or worms that carry illness are found in many parts of Africa. Examples of such illness agents from my own research include *kadoyo* among the Bemba; *iciwane* among the Zulu; *liciwane* among the Swazi; *atchi-koko* among the Macua of northern Mozambique; *khoma* among the Shona of central Mozambique, and—taking an example from others' research in West Africa—*kokoro* among the Yoruba of Nigeria (Foster et al. 1996).

Note that Asuni (1979), a Nigerian medical doctor, has written that infection and germs are "alien concepts" for Nigerian traditional healers. The insects and worms of naturalistic infection theory may be an unfamiliar idiom for educated Africans as well as for outsiders. Whether researchers are African or foreign, one finds these concepts, along with the dirt and heat of pollution belief, showing up in the miscellaneous, unclassifiable, "other" response category in African surveys (e.g., Oyebolo 1980; Freund 1989). This illustrates the need for an analytic framework like indigenous contagion theory.

As discussed in later chapters, these microorganismic agents may relate to agents of impurity (e.g., dirt) found in African pollution belief complexes, and they may possess mystical-seeming attributes. Yet it seems that those who become ill from contact with insects or worms are not singled out by spirits or sorcerers; the process is impersonal and therefore naturalistic. It may be useful to refer to such ethnomedical theory as naturalistic infection, following Murdock, to distinguish it from conventional biomedical germ theory.

Also of interest in Murdock's scheme is subtype 3, under theories of mystical causation: contagion. This is defined as "coming into contact with some purportedly polluting object, substance, or person" (Murdock 1980:18). Anthropologists often refer to this contagious process as pollution. Note Murdock's classification of pollution as supernatural, a viewpoint I contest below. Murdock (1980) continues,

> This mystical cause, which roughly parallels the natural cause of infection is attested for forty-nine societies. In one, Thonga, it is reported to be a major though not the predominant cause of illness. Among a variety of sources of contagion by far the most widespread are (1) menstrual blood or a menstruating woman; and (2) the corpse of a deceased person or some object associated therewith. The former preponderates in North America; the latter, in Africa. (p. 18; parens added)

The next subtype, mystical retribution, is defined as "acts in violation of some taboo or moral injunction when conceived as causing illness directly rather than through the mediation of some offended or punitive supernatural being" (Murdock 1980:18). This is supposed to be the predominant theory of the Thonga of Mozambique and South Africa (with contagion being perhaps the next most important theory).

Only 9 of 43, or 21% of randomly selected societies of Africa, are said to believe in mystical contagion as an illness cause—and contagion is said to be important only among the Thonga. However, southern Africa is underrepresented in the sample, especially when compared to West Africa. Other than the Bushmen, Hottentots, and Ovimbundu (Angola), the Thonga are the only "tribe" south of Tanzania and the Congo forest. Since the great majority of the population of southern Africa is Bantu speaking, there should have been more Bantu groups in the sample if the area is to be accurately represented.

This skewing of African societies has helped obscure the importance of both pollution and broader ideas about contagion. Furthermore, judging by the work of D. M. Warren (1979) and other authorities on West Africa (Iwu, personal communication), Murdock may have overlooked and underreported the prevalence of "mystical contagion" for Africa as a whole. He seems to have overlooked pollution of environments by various contaminants, a belief prominent among the Zulu and Thonga or Tsonga (see Chapter Two) and found in many parts of Africa.

In any case, interesting issues arise from Murdock's typology. First, infection is considered naturalistic, and the implication is that this theory may have arisen from direct or indirect influence of modern medicines. Infection, however, whatever its origin, contains mystical elements, by Murdock's own definition. Contagion, though, is considered mystical and is classified as supernatural. As we will see, there are societies in southern Africa, such as the Bemba and Thonga, where Murdock's

40

infection and contagion seem to be inextricably part of the same indigenous theoretical system. Further, the Thonga are said to be one of the few societies (21% of the sample) for whom mystical retribution is the predominant theory of illness (Murdock 1980:18).

For Murdock, menstrual blood and corpses are, respectively, the two most common agents of illness he calls contagion, a subtype of mystical illness. In Africa, both of these are believed to be highly polluting, although the source of pollution seems to be death rather than a corpse. Contact with strange places and foreigners, and with a range of contaminants and poisons in the environment, may also be considered polluting.

Although I differ with Murdock on some taxonomic points, and some quite well-documented illness theories seem to have been overlooked (e.g., inherited illness), his typology is a useful framework for discussion and analysis of the ethnomedical findings discussed in this book.

AN OVERVIEW OF ETIOLOGY IN AFRICAN SOCIETIES

As noted in the Introduction, anthropologists recently have given greater attention to naturalistic ethnomedical beliefs in Africa. This seems due, in part, to the increased participation of applied anthropologists in public health-oriented infectious disease programs in less-developed countries. Following are overviews from the ethnographic literature of African ethnomedical systems. I chose these examples because they shed light on the place and importance of naturalistic beliefs and because they were based on longer-term ethnographic studies rather than sample surveys. Here, we will only look at societies that lie outside of central and southern Bantu-speaking areas; in the next chapter, I present more detailed descriptions of ethnomedical systems in these areas. And in Chapter Seven, I describe what researchers have found specifically about contagious illness theories in tradition-based societies around the world.

Anthropologists often distinguish between the immediate (proximate) and ultimate cause of illness, or between the instrumental, efficient, and ultimate causes. The point is often made that if an illness considered natural does not respond to usual therapies, then another cause, likely to be personalistic, is suspected. It is also frequently noted that there may be competing theories about the cause of an illness within the same group of specialists or laypersons. However, I don't think either of these make our search for etiologic patterns fruitless. What most indigenous people believe about an illness *under normal circumstances* still has consequences, including behavior predictability with regard to prevention and treatment (indigenous and/or biomedical). This may be especially true for the more routine, less exotic etiologic notions associated with more immediate causation. Ngokwey (1988:798) has observed that instrumental causes are likely to involve ideas about contagion and infection. In fact, levels of illness causation are important in understanding the history of Western medicine. As noted by a medical historian:

> Classical philosophy and epistemology made available to medicine an elaborate structure of explanation involving a hierarchy of causes. First or primary causes were cosmological or divine . . . immediate causes related primarily to the more local environment or experiences of the diseased person. . . . They could include factors such as diet, emotion (stress), or exposure to weather, but also injury, poisons, or other more specific agents of disease. (Pelling 1993:312)

The rise of scientific medicine can be regarded as a process of suspending discussion of, or refusing to consider or debate, primary causes of disease and instead focusing on immediate causes, clues to which often arose in common-sense observations of contagious diseases (Pelling 1993:312).

We turn now to some general characterizations of African ethnomedical systems.

Shambaa and Sukuma (Tanzania)

Steven Fierman (1981) conducted an ethnographic study in a Shambaa village in northeastern Tanzania. He found that there are five categories of illness causation, even if these do not form a conscious system or folk theory with which all Shambaa would necessarily agree. They are: illness of God; illness that people bring on themselves through accident or neglect (for example, a child becomes sick if given inadequate or poor quality food); illness from sorcery; illness from spirits (*majini*); and illness caused by acts of an individual's moral will, such as swearing oaths that result in illness. For the Shambaa and many other Africans, "illnesses of God" does not mean God caused, as, for example, a means of punishment, but refers to those "that simply happen, with no moral cause. The causation of illnesses of God is close in its implications to the

English term 'natural,' meaning related to general principles of the behavior of things, as opposed to the artificial intervention of one's fellow men or women" (Fierman 1981:355).

These etiologic categories are recognized as permeable and sometimes overlapping. Fierman (1981:355) makes the point that sorcery and spirits comprise two separate causal categories, yet a single type of spirit is created and sent by sorcerers, a belief my colleagues and I encountered among the Macua of northern Mozambique. As another example of category permeability, purification rites may relate to witchcraft or spirits as well as to pollution beliefs.

Marlene Reid conducted a 13-month ethnographic study among the Sukuma. She identified three main imputed causes of illness: nature, sorcery, and ancestors (1982:132). Naturally caused illnesses included those that were minor and transitory such as colds, fevers, sores, and stomachaches. More serious communicable diseases such as smallpox, chickenpox, and measles were believed brought by the wind or air. Traditional healers sometimes gave medicines to prevent these. Illnesses present from birth, such as childhood epilepsy, were also considered naturally caused. Reid (p. 133) makes the important observation (discussed in Chapter Eight) that illnesses that affect a whole village, or most people at one time, were not considered as being caused by sorcery or ancestors.

Sorcery-caused illnesses "were usually those that had symptoms related to swellings and internal pain; [that] is, that could not seem to be touched from the outside or explicitly described" (Reid 1982:133). Unusual pregnancy, childbirth complications, impotence, and sterility might also be interpreted as due to sorcery. Ancestor-caused illness seemed to be classifiable as mental illness; those characterized by "lack of energy . . . talking wildly, running about, or sitting in a stupor. . . . Illnesses characterized by prolonged lack of interest and participation in daily activities along with other emotional manifestations" (p. 137).

Ibo and Yoruba (Nigeria)

A medical sociologist provides an overview of Ibo health beliefs, "not as a visiting white anthropologist . . . but as an Ibo with a strong background of traditional medicine in my family" (Ezeabasili 1982:17). He identifies three basic causes of illness: natural, witchcraft and sorcery, and mystically caused, due mainly to the neglect of ancestor spirits but also including taboo violation or reincarnation by the spirit of someone who was sickly when previously alive. Natural causes include breezes, winds, and/or entities that are carried by these. Examples of naturally caused illness are convulsions in children, cough, yaws, and scabies as well as epidemic illness such as smallpox. Contagious disease seems by this account to be considered natural rather than "preternatural" (the author's alternative term) or personalistic in nature. Wind/breeze illness may be referred to as "illness in the air" in southern Africa, and it appears to be a major subtype of environmental dangers, discussed more fully in the next chapter.

A paper on Yoruba concepts of health by ethnoscientists Foster et al. (1996) describes insects (according to the authors, equivalent to germs) and filth as the major immediate causes of illness. The paper focuses on the fundamental concept of *imótótó* in traditional Yoruba understanding of health and well-being. This term translates as cleanliness and proper sanitary behavior. Many examples are provided of how this concept underlies behavior such as disposal of human waste, use of soap and cleansing agents, sweeping and use of refuse dumps, bathing and hand-washing, use of chewing sticks, etc. The authors note that

> Studies of the Yoruba and other African peoples have often overemphasized magic and witchcraft in explanations of disease etiology. While nonempirical factors do find their way into Yoruba medical philosophy, empirical causation similar to that of allopathic medicine is integral to Yoruba medical philosophy. (p. 28)

Cokwe (Zaire)

Yoder (1981:241) reports that among the Cokwe, "one finds three different conceptual categories of medical causality: diseases of God, diseases caused by sorcery, and diseases caused by displeased ancestors. All illness episodes fall into one of these three categories," even if the categories overlap one another and there is flexibility in interpretation of cause. As with some other ethnographers of central and eastern Africa, Yoder describes diseases of God as those "which have an impersonal cause which arise from events in the natural world" (p. 241). He then attempts to determine in a general way which type of illness explanation is the most frequent. Working with a list of the 75 local "main diseases," he found out from interviewing an unspecified number of traditional healers that "most of these diseases had natural or impersonal causes, some could have either personal or impersonal causes, and a few were always ascribed to personal (ancestor or sorcery) activity" (pp. 241–242).

Yoder (1981:241) makes the point that I underscore in this book, namely that "in Africa scholars have long been interested in why people consider many diseases are caused by spirits, ancestors, or sorcery. Other kinds of causal explanation have received far less attention."

Kikuyu (Kenya)

Another African scholar attempted to quantify the relative importance of various illness causal categories based on a survey of Kikuyu diviners. Like Yoder for the Cokwe, Kimani (1981:337) reports that "Kikuyu diviners tend to rank the physical causes (natural or God given) highest compared to witchcraft, taboos and other cultural beliefs. Ancestral forces rank second." Table 1 summarizes the rank order of causal explanations for illness and misfortune, according to Kimani's findings.

Table 1

Ranking of Importance of Illness Causal Categories among Kikuyu Diviners

Causal Explanations	Frequency Rank	Illness, Misfortune Examples
Natural or God given	1	pneumonia, malaria, coughs, asthma
Ancestral forces	2	infertility, madness
Negligence of calling	3	madness, chronic poverty, calamities
Evil eye and sorcery	4	instant death
Spirits, witchcraft	5	madness
Breach of taboos, curse, dishonest and immoral behavior	5	tuberculosis, leprosy, madness
Heredity	6	otitis media, syphilis
Others (individual weakness, lack of resistance, infected food, lack of respect for elders)	7	most contagious diseases (e.g., tuberculosis, asthma)

It seems that "spirits and witchcraft" and "breach of taboos, curse, dishonest and immoral behavior" tie for fifth place. In any case, the personalistic explanations given so much prominence by most anthropologists not to mention popular writers, namely witchcraft, sorcery, and evil or avenging spirits, appear to be of relatively little importance among Kikuyu diviners. My experience among Nguni-speaking and other southern Bantu suggests that diviners tend to diagnose personalistic causes more often than herbalists or other practitioners or laypersons. One often consults a diviner only after routine treatment has failed and a condition is both serious and persistent. Clients may expect to hear personalistic explanations at this stage. Diviners are often considered specialists and consultants in ultimate causation. Perhaps the proportion of personalistic explanations found by Kimani would be even smaller had herbalists and laypersons been interviewed or observed.

Note that tuberculosis is listed as an example twice, once in association with breach of taboos (which overlaps with pollution, according to Murdock [1980]) and once with other origins, one of which components is "lack of resistance." Note, too, that heredity is ranked as the sixth most common causal explanation, yet Murdock does not mention this in his global typology of illness theories. There is relatively little mention of heredity in the ethnomedical literature on Africa, but I have heard this referred to often by healers and laypersons alike. Survey results from Zambia show that some illnesses are regarded as "inborn," meaning that they are inherited and are not transmissible or perhaps even preventable. One Zambian healer specifically commented that unlike the case with a syphilis-like syndrome (believed caused by an insect or dirt), "there's nothing like dirt or insects in the blood" with *ibele* (genital warts), believed to be inborn. *Ibele* is clearly distinct from personalistic illness since there seems to be no deliberate victimization.

While Kimani calls attention to both the importance and the specific contexts of naturalistic causes including heredity, she, like so many other observers, makes no direct reference to pollution or contaminating processes.

Sidama (Ethiopia)

Norbert Vecchiato (1998) reports that Sidama ethnomedical theories of illness "can be sub-divided into the naturalistic and supernaturalistic" (p. 253) Balance and equilibrium are basic to conceptions of health (*keranchimma*). Balance is thought to be maintained through watchfulness over one's physiological cycles (digestion, evacuation, "blood levels"); guarded interaction with natural forces; quality of personal acts; harmony with other people; and ritual propitiation of, and magical control over, supernatural forces (i.e., God, spirits, sorcery, and the evil eye).

Vecchiato (1998) observes that most infectious diseases are explained naturally, even though their treatment may involve magical remedies:

> For instance, malaria is mainly thought to be triggered by inhaling the pollen of blooming maize, but it may also be ascribed to exposure to bad weather. Additionally, following pan-Ethiopian beliefs, hepatitis is often thought to be caused by contact with bat droppings, although some informants thought that hepatitis may ensue following excessive ingestion of sugar cane or that it may be related to excessive blood in one's body. Similarly, tuberculosis is generally associated with overworking, fatigue, and undernutrition. (pp. 253–254)

Vecchiato (1990) also reported survey findings from the Sidama a few years earlier, noting that "most respondents failed to acknowledge the Anopheline mosquitoes as a potential source of ill health" in the case of malaria (p. 385). Although etiologic beliefs could be judged inaccurate by biomedical standards, these infectious diseases are thought to be caused by something in the environment (malaria and hepatitis) or a weakening of the body (tuberculosis). Both explanations are not far removed from the biomedical model; they are certainly closer than personalistic theories would be. For example, the Sidama are correct in looking to the environment to understand the cause of malaria. Anopheline mosquitoes may be the vector, but they require stagnant pools of water, rainwater, and hot weather to form and replenish these. These conditons are features of certain environments and not of others.

EVIDENCE FROM ETHNOVETERINARY MEDICINE

Findings from the emerging subdiscipline of ethnoveterinary medicine suggest that human and animal ethnomedicine share common beliefs about the range and nature of causal categories of illness. In their review of ethnoveterinary etiological beliefs, McCorkle and Mathias-Mundy (1992:60) observe that "two broad types of ethnomedical aetiologies can be distinguished: natural and supernatural," with those seen as "transmissible, chronic and curable/preventable" being defined as naturalistic.

Humoral pathology, or hot/cold balance, is also considered naturalistic. Although livestock is certainly believed susceptible to witchcraft or sorcery, the review of these authors documents a great many biomedically sound treatments and preventive measures, based usually on naturalistic or impersonal theories of illness. So,

> African herding strategies often reflect a highly sophisticated understanding of contagion and immune responses. For example, Fulani may move upwind of herds infected with FMD (foot and mouth disease) in order to avoid contagion; or they may move downwind so as to expose their animals to FMD, knowing that a mild case confers immunity. Only after an outbreak of FMD in Britain in the early 1970s did Western veterinary science discover that the FMD virus could be transmitted aerially over great distances, as from France to Britain. . . . Yet many pastoral groups of Africa have long known that wind or "odours" can carry this and other contagious diseases. (McCorkle and Mathias-Mundy 1992:67)

In fact, belief in airborne illness—contagious illness in the form of unseen agents of illness carried in the air or wind (i.e., "environmental dangers")—is widespread in Africa, as discussed further below.

WHAT DOES NATURALLY CAUSED MEAN?

Because of lack of agreement over what constitutes natural causes in the context of African medicine, it is worth reviewing the various ways this has been interpreted by anthropologists and others. Several years ago, this topic was discussed at a conference of experts in African ethnomedicine; their viewpoints were later published (Janzen and Prins 1981). Several meanings of natural or nature emerged in this context, which I will summarize: (1) The word nature can be used in the sense of those things that are evident; (2) Nature can refer to the existing phenomena that are around us, things that are part of one's natural environment; (3) There is the special conception of nature as somehow rule- or law-bound and thus impartial; (4) Natural can refer to illnesses that just happen, rather than happen as a result of human or spirit intervention; (5) "Illness of God" is a type of natural causation, at least according to some conference participants (e.g., Fierman, Yoder, and Kimani); (6) Some anthropologists have used the word natural as a residual category when there is no apparent human or spirit intervention; (7) Natural may be used when "the relationship between cause and illness—in time or space, or an interior relationship—is seen in a material sense" (Janzen and Prins 1981:431); and (8) Natural may denote "illnesses . . . that have to do with common sense. . . . It's when people have a sense of losing control on a technical level that they begin to look for a wider causal explanatory theory, and they look then to the social and the moral domain" (pp. 429–431). The point was reiterated that "any instance of illness can be 'natural' or 'unnatural' depending upon the circumstances of the illness" (p. 430).

The natural/nonnatural dichotomy seems a "rather old and basic characteristic of thought in Bantu-speaking societies" that was present at the time of first contact with Europeans (Janzen and Prins 1981:430). As Janzen and Prins observe:

> [The dichotomy] is part of a very resilient dimension of African medicine and therefore it reflects the sophistication and the depth of this framework that appears to have survived many attempts at change and reformulation; it seems to offer practitioners as well as philosophers and laymen a way of accounting for an entire universe of issues, namely misfortune or ambiguity. If you don't, or can't, explain it on one side of the dichotomy, you can always go to the other side. It's a completely adequate universe of explanations at a quite abstract level. (p. 430)

At the end of their analysis of conference findings about natural causation, the editors of the proceedings quote Zemplini:

> Do we have the right to speak of "natural cause" in African medical systems? If . . . we do not have a theory of natural causation, as we have a theory of supernatural causation, is it conceivable to speak of natural causes without having a theory of natural causation? . . . My question, more precisely, is to know if we have the right to speak of, to use the term, "natural cause," there where we do not have a *theory* of natural cause? (Janzen and Prins 1981:431)

When Zemplini comments that we have a theory of supernatural causation, he seems to mean that researchers have for years contributed to an etic or outside-scientific theory that purports to explain indigenous, ethnomedical (emic) theories of this sort, namely magic, witchcraft, sorcery, and related belief complexes involving various types of spirits. In this sense, do we then have a theory of natural causation? Perhaps not, but the attempt by the 1981 conference participants to define and delineate natural causation is certainly a first step. I hope to further this development by proposing that naturalistic infection, pollution, and environmental dangers (and possibly mystical retribution) are part of a widespread, emic theory of illness in Africa and other regions that can serve as a useful framework for analyzing ethnomedical findings and perhaps for predicting certain health-related behaviors.

IS POLLUTION BELIEF NATURAL OR SUPERNATURAL?

An analysis of pollution illness may appear to reveal sufficient mystical elements to disqualify the illness as fully naturalistic. Yet African pollution models are naturalistic in several important ways. First, they share with natural causation the important quality of impartiality. Equally important, both pollution and naturalistic infection involve unseen agents that may cause illness in anyone who comes into contact with such agents. The tiny or unseen agents of naturalistic infection (insects or worms) have already been discussed; they closely resemble the infectious disease agents of biomedicine. Agents of pollution illness are conceived as dangerous essences such as impurity, filth, or dirt (sometimes "dangerous dirt"); menstrual blood and other reproductive and bodily fluids; and death. In southern Africa, such essences may be called heat (e.g., among the Tsonga and Sotho), darkness (e.g., among the Zulu), or "shadow of death" (e.g., among the Macua).

These essences appear mystical as they are unseen and often do not conform to natural or empirically verifiable laws. On the other hand, they may represent a symbolic representation of empirically verifiable relationships. I have already quoted Victor Turner's comment that the Ndembu "are obsessively logical" when it comes to their illness beliefs, "though on the basis of mystical premises. . . ." But are African indigenous premises really or always mystical? Can they not represent observed cause-and-effect relationships in the observable, material world? People considered healthy have physical contact with people sick in certain ways, after which the well people become sick in the same way. Part of Lele (Central Bantu speakers in Zaire) pollution theory is that excessive promiscuity in a woman causes barrenness (Douglas 1963:123). Epidemiology recognizes that promiscuity (we now use the less-loaded term multipartnerism) can lead to STDs, which can result in barrenness. Is this Lele belief therefore more mystical or rational?

Peter Morely (1978:2) defines "non-supernatural disease etiologies" as "those based wholly on observed cause-and-effect relationships regardless of the accuracy of the observations made." It seems to me that pollution theory, like folk germ theory, meets this definition for the most part, although "based wholly" is a bit exacting. Perhaps when discussing indigenous contagion beliefs we could revise this to read: "Pollution and related ICT etiologies are based at least partially on observed cause-and-effect relationships, many or most of which are accurate in the sense that they describe empirically verifiable relationships. In any case, they are impersonal."

More specifically, to the extent that African pollution theory is associated with what we biomedically define as communicable disease, the indigenous theory behind local illness tends to be mostly based—or premised—on observed cause-and-effect relationships. It is essentially naturalistic. The theory appears mystical or supernatural to outsiders because of the unfamiliar, highly symbolic idiom in which it is expressed. Douglas (1963:9) characterizes pollution belief as "a complex algebra which takes into account many variables," and as a "symbolic language capable of very fine degrees of differentiation." Further, these symbols are deeply imbedded in the total system of ideas characteristic of a particular culture and their interpretation by outsiders can only be made "in reference to a total structure of thought" (Douglas 1963:41). Maybe this is true for a full, exhaustive interpretation, but I believe that enough of the essentials of a particular pollution belief system can be learned, and *compared between societies*, to make investigations into these systems worthwhile for both anthropology and public health.

In fact, Douglas, as an academic anthropologist interested in symbolic theory, regrets that

Comparative religion has always been bedeviled by medical materialism. Some argue that even the most exotic of ancient rites have a sound hygienic basis. . . . It is true that there can be a marvelous correspondence between the avoidance of contagious disease and ritual avoidance. . . . So it has been argued that their rule of washing before eating may have given the Jews immunity in plagues. But it is one thing to point out the side benefits of ritual actions, and another thing to be content with using the by-products as a sufficient explanation. Even if some of Moses's dietary rules were hygienically beneficial it is a pity to treat him as an enlightened public health administrator, rather than a spiritual leader. (1992 [1966]:29)

Douglas notes that she has no objection to medical materialism—a term coined by William James—"unless it excludes other approaches" (Douglas 1992 [1966]:32). I agree. My idea of pollution and related ICT explanations as representative of observed cause-and-effect relationships in the domain of health (subdomain of infectious diseases) is no doubt reductionistic and certainly is less than the whole story. Complex symbolic constructs, especially if near-universal (such as taboos about menstrual blood), arise for more reasons than health or hygiene.

My purpose is not to challenge other theories of the origin and persistence of pollution belief or to discuss some of the more theoretical formulations of pollution belief in other parts of the world. But I do want to give pollution and related contagion theories their rightful place in ethnomedicine and to emphasize what indigenous African medicine has in common with Western medicine, with a view toward developing effective public health approaches. This seems warranted after examination of ethnomedical findings about contagious disease in Africa and elsewhere.

There are a number of reasons why African pollution theory has been overlooked by anthropologists.[3] One reason may be because of its somewhat ambiguous position vis-à-vis the natural/nonnatural or natural/supernatural dichotomy, which is central to Bantu thought and to which anthropologists have attributed much importance. Pollution seems to straddle both sides of the dichotomy. Like people considered polluted, pollution itself is "betwixt and between" a cherished categorical distinction of anthropologists and Africans alike; it is liminal and ambiguous.

This ambiguity goes beyond Africa. For many years, anthropologists have used the *Outline of Cultural Materials* (Murdock et al. 1961) as a checklist of the diverse material and nonmaterial elements of culture. It attempts to be comprehensive, listing and coding numerically everything associated with human beings in all their cultural variation. "Pollution or contagion" is listed under "supernatural causation of disease" under the general heading "Theory of Disease."

I noted above that Murdock also classifies contagion as a type of mystical causation in his global survey of illness beliefs, while infection is considered a type of natural causation when it involves beliefs in germ-like "noxious microorganisms" that invade the body, carrying illness (Murdock 1980:9, 18). It seems that, for Murdock, when pollution involves illness-carrying forces or essences such as heat or darkness, it is mystical; when it involves germ-like ideas, it is natural. Africans do not appear to make these distinctions. In Zambia and elsewhere, the "insects" of infection may arise from the "filth" of pollution. In fact, ethnographic evidence strongly suggests that pollution beliefs should be classified and recognized as essentially naturalistic, or naturalistic with mystical symbolic overtones. Support for this view is found in Chapter Seven, where we consider historical models of contagious disease in Europe.

ARE BELIEFS IN WITCHCRAFT AND SORCERY DECREASING?

So far, I have not factored in such important considerations as urbanization, modernization, and cultural change in general. Do witchcraft and sorcery beliefs become less important and less frequent as Africans modernize, urbanize, and become better educated? Anthropologists are divided about this. Some, such as Mitchell (1965), believed so; others, like Marwick (1970), argued that such beliefs increase. In his more recent summary of this debate, Swantz (1990) notes that if witchcraft and sorcery accusations are a reflection of interpersonal tensions,

> Shouldn't the urban "modernization" processes which cause social strain because of employment and position competition, martial and sexual relationships, business competition, and inter-tribal relationships result in the increase of witchcraft accusations in urban society? If the sources of interpersonal conflict which lead to witchcraft accusations have increased in the cities, then on theoretical grounds the frequency of witchcraft accusations should be on the increase. (pp. 98–102)

Swantz, who conducted research among traditional healers in Dar es Salaam in the early 1970s, estimated that 5,000 cases related to witchcraft and sorcery were brought to healers in this city daily, accounting for 43 out of 100 cases of illness or misfortune brought to traditional healers (1990:91–100).

Reliance on indigenous medicine has generally not declined in Africa with urbanization, even when it competes directly with free medical services, according to Swantz and others (e.g., Bibeau et al. 1980:8; Fassin and Fassin 1988). From my research in Swaziland and Mozambique, I have seen no evidence that indigenous healers either decline in numbers as people migrate to cities, or—as recently averred by two researchers in Ghana—that their practices become more biomedical in

53

nature and "spiritual elements of treatment are abandoned" (le Grand and Wondergem 1990:28). I would say that witchcraft and other personalistic beliefs are not declining, or not declining much, with modernization; it is just that they are typically not found in association with contagious or infectious illness.

In the next chapter, I look at ethnomedical theories among Bantu speakers in southern Africa for evidence and a framework to analyze indigenous contagion theory and related topics.

NOTES

1. Bridewealth is the current preferred term for bride-price, and it refers to gifts made by the bridegroom and his kinsmen to the father and kinsmen of the bride. Bride-service denotes service or labor in lieu of tangible gifts.

2. Jarvis (in Wu 1995:173) likewise accuses proponents of herbal medicine as having "a love affair with nature . . . seeing it only as benign and benevolent without looking at the dangerous side."

3. The leading scholar of African pollution studies, Mary Douglas, agrees with this assessment, and is herself somewhat at a loss to explain why pollution beliefs have been overlooked. She wrote to me: "It is really a rare thing for me in the last 30 years to get correspondence about pollution in Africa. You ask me why no one talks about it, and so do I" (Douglas, personal communication).

CHAPTER TWO

POLLUTION AND OTHER CONTAGION BELIEFS
AMONG BANTU SPEAKERS

I will present a brief historical review of ethnographic reports of illness causation in southern Africa, searching especially for evidence of indigenous contagion beliefs. Before the first generation of professional anthropologists in this region were trained by Radcliffe-Brown and Malinowski—making them part of the so-called British School—work was done there by of one of the best amateur ethnographers, Swiss Protestant missionary to Mozambique, Henri Junod. His work among the Thonga and Ronga began in 1889.

Junod's classic, *The Life of a South African Tribe*, was published in 1926 (reprinted 1962). Recall that Murdock in his ethnographic survey reported that the Thonga were the only group in Africa for whom contagion, a "mystical cause, which roughly parallels the natural cause of infection," was "a major though not the predominant cause of illness" (Murdock 1980:18).

Junod (1962a [1926]:152–153) spoke of "dangerous impurity" that "contaminates" objects, individuals, and whole villages, requiring complex rites of purification. For example, he mentions the "extreme danger attached to the defilement which accompanies death. This uncleanness contaminates the community and can only be removed by collective purification." In another section, Junod (p. 187) mentions that a wife is considered taboo during her menstrual period, meaning that no sexual relations are allowed. During this time, she must avoid any physical contact with her husband, even indirect contact (e.g., by handling his food). Junod also reported that, "A woman who has had a miscarriage is impure for three months at least" (p. 192).

In his second volume, Junod comments: "As regards the causes of diseases, Thongas are groping in the grossest superstition." He then describes how traditional healers largely ignore physical symptoms and instead throw divining bones to determine cause: "There are three great causes of disease: the spirits of the gods, the wizards and the *makhumo*, defilement from death or from impure persons. A fourth less common cause is Heaven. The bones will reveal by the way in which they fall which is the one to be combated" (Junod 1962b [1926]:474).

Junod later defines *makhumo* more broadly as "the contamination of death, or the defilement resulting from contact with a woman in a state of physiological impurity." Junod describes avoidance behavior associated with pollution beliefs; for example, one must not eat from the plate of, or wear clothes from, a person who dies from (or has) an illness considered contagious (1962b [1926]:476–477).

Beliefs of this sort surface in modern-day "KAP" (knowledge, attitudes, and practices) surveys intended to gauge the accuracy of knowledge about how HIV spreads. Health educators usually classify answers about the virus spreading through casual contact merely as an incorrect answer, as evidence of lack of education, without realizing that belief in such mechanisms of contagion are part of a far broader contagious belief pattern that predates the introduction of scientific education, not to mention AIDS. Moreover, these beliefs may be medically sound and function to protect public health in the case of tuberculosis and other serious infectious diseases that have been endemic far longer than AIDS.

Under a section called sexual rites of purification, Junod (1962b [1926]:152) characterizes impurity in a different way, as a curse or malediction as well as a dangerous, impure quality associated with death. He tells us the term *ndjaka* refers to:

The frightful malediction accompanying death. It is something which kills a great many men. . . . This malediction or dangerous impurity contaminates objects, which must be cleansed by the sprinkling (*phunga*) as we have seen; but it affects still more deeply the village as a whole. (During periods of mourning) . . . all sexual relations (are) forbidden. Why? Because the village (is) in a state of contamination. . . . It cannot return to the ordinary course of life without a special collective purification. (p. 153)

I confess that I had not read Junod until I had worked in Mozambique for several months. I had already been struck with my own insight that: (1) Pollution beliefs were very important in at least the south and central parts of the country; and (2) Illnesses believed caused by pollution seem to be those biomedically classified as infectious and contagious. I might have reached this conclusion earlier had I read Junod sooner. Some 85 years ago, he described consumption (tuberculosis) as being caused by "the contamination of death, or the defilement resulting from contact with a woman in a state of physiological impurity" (1962b [1926]:465–476).

In addition to describing the nature and types of pollution recognized among the Thonga, Junod was one of the first—if not the first—to describe belief in an internal, invisible snake, an idea that, in at least one form, seems intimately associated with pollution beliefs (see Chapter Three).

Another Christian missionary/ethnographer, Dora Earthy, worked a few hundred kilometers to the north of Junod's area, among the Lenge. They are part of the Chopi cluster of the Shona/Thonga subgroup of Bantu speakers, according to Murdock (1959), and were and are found in what is today Gaza Province, Mozambique. Earthy's ethnographic account, *Valenge Women: The Social and Economic Life of the Valenge Women of Portuguese East Africa* (1968 [1933]), is based on residence and fieldwork conducted between 1917 and 1930, overlapping with Junod's period of work. Earthy felt that as a woman, she had special access to the world of women that, implicitly, might have been denied Junod.

There is nothing in the index of Earthy's book under pollution, contamination, dirt, impurity, defilement, purity, or cleanliness, but manifestations of underlying concern with pollution abound. For example, a pregnant woman must travel with her own sleeping mat, lest she defile another person's mat (Earthy 1968 [1933]:65). Earthy speaks of taboos associated with pollution caused by the blood of giving birth and notes that newborns are immediately fed a bit of blood from their severed umbilical cord to prevent convulsions or epileptic fits in later life (pp. 69, 153). Further, she provides a substantial list of taboos associated with menstruation, all involving the woman avoiding contact with objects that men might have contact with. A menstruating woman must also stay clear of cattle for the same reason (pp. 109–110). Earthy also describes rites of purification in various sections, including those intended to "cleanse defilement from death" (see, e.g., pp. 154–155, 162).

In addition, Earthy (1968 [1933]:62) describes a bodily force known as *nyakwadi*, which "arranges the menses" and is ruler of all body functions. This form of the "internal snake" concept seems to be closely associated with pollution beliefs, and is taken up as a separate topic in Chapter Three. In spite of the foregoing, Earthy says this about illness causality: "Diseases are generally attributed to the action of magic, practiced either by the man's enemies or a sorcerer (*muloyi*)" (p. 153).

Two contemporaries of Junod, E. W. Smith and A. M. Dale, began to work in the former northern Rhodesia in 1902. Elizabeth Colson referred to their 1920 ethnography, *The Ila-Speaking Peoples of Northern Rhodesia*, as "one of the great classics of African ethnography." The authors summarized what they learned about Ila theory of disease causation:

> Disease is regarded as something almost material which can be passed from one person to another and got rid of by washing or other means. Some diseases come through contact, more or less intimate, with certain dangerous things: things dangerous because of some maleficent quality inherent in them. (Smith and Dale 1968 [1920]:244)

Examples of dangerous things are certain animals, dirt, menstruating women, and fetuses. Smith and Dale (1968 [1920]:244) imply that contact accounts for most illness. Other causes described briefly are witchcraft, breaking taboos, natural causes (one example is "exposure to the sun"), ancestral spirits and ghosts, and those ascribed to God, especially in cases of virulent disease and plagues. Note that breaking taboos often relates to pollution in southern Africa and that illness ascribed to God is often deemed impersonal and natural. There is even a hint that contagious diseases tend to be understood naturalistically.

The wonder is that anthropologists did not pick up on hints from amateur ethnographers like Junod, Smith, and Dale about the significance of contact or defilement illnesses—for years to come.[1] Perhaps later anthropologists were reacting to nineteenth-century evolutionary theories of religion, advanced by Sir James Frazer and Robertson Smith, in which the relationship between beliefs in the sacred/holy and pollution/impurity were viewed as a way to classify religions on a scale of primitive to advanced: "If primitive, then rules of holiness and rules of uncleanness were indistinguishable; if advanced then rules of uncleanness disappeared from religion. They were relegated to the kitchen and bathroom and to municipal sanitation, nothing to do with religion" (Douglas 1992 [1966]: 11). For Robertson Smith, pollution was a major component of taboo beliefs, which was characterized as "magical superstition based on mere terror"—the exemplary expression of the primitive, savage, and irrational (Douglas 1975:55–58).

Or perhaps it is because, as Schneider (1981:181) reminds us, English-speaking anthropologists have, in general, neglected African belief systems in favor of social processes (with exceptions such as Evans-Pritchard, Turner, and Douglas). French sociologist Durkheim (1961 [1912, 1947 ed.]), in his *Elementary Forms of Religious Life*, advanced the idea that there are two forms of contagion: one related to the origin of primitive hygiene and one intrinsic to ideas about the sacred (Douglas 1975:49). Durkheim, van Gennep, and others showed how pollution rules often protect the social order, or social structure, from change, outsiders, and insider deviants—anything that would threaten the structure as it is.

Whatever the reason, words like pollution, although used by Frazer, seem rarely to have been used by the early English-speaking ethnographers in Africa, whether amateur or professional. Some described beliefs and behavior of this sort under the rubric of taboo. For example, Radcliffe-Brown dealt with taboo in his 1939 Frazier Lecture (Radcliffe-Brown 1952:133–152). His emphasis was on the "failure to observe rules of ritual avoidance" rather than on contact, although in discussions about Africa he uses as examples coming into contact with a corpse or menstrual blood (p. 136). Such contact, or failure to observe rules, results in attribution of an "undesirable ritual status," known as *thahu* (which only coincidentally rhymes with taboo) among the Kikuyu. A person who is *thahu* must be ritually purified.

Returning to southern Africa, Winifred Hoernlé, along with Isaac Schapera, Audrey Richards, and Eileen Krige, were among the first trained anthropologists in the region. They were all South Africans.

Hoernlé wrote a chapter in a widely read anthology (Schapera 1946 [1937]), reviewing what was known then about "magic and medicine." She draws on Junod and the few others who had done missionary, medical, and/or ethnographic fieldwork at that time. She notes that "some diseases come from 'defilement'," which can come from contact with childbirth or with "blackness" (the Zulu word *umnyama* is also translated as "darkness." The implication is that the source is death). A very few illnesses such as coughs, colds, fevers, and rheumatism were recognized as natural. "Others are sent by the spirits for neglect of custom. . . . But most diseases, especially if the onset is sudden or if they are long continued, are believed to be caused by sorcerers or witches" (Hoernlé 1946 [1937]:227).

Audrey Richards (1970 [1935]) spoke for many anthropologists of the day with her observation:

> We know that primitive peoples are alike in their almost universal belief that death and disaster are due to supernatural agencies. They differ, on the other hand, greatly as to the proportion of human ills which they attribute to hostile fellow beings with supernatural powers and that which they believe to be inflicted by supernatural beings, angry spirits and the like, themselves. (p. 170)

Writing years later about the Bemba of then northern Rhodesia, Richards (1956:28) reported that they attribute both blessings and misfortunes to either supernatural agencies or "impersonal magic forces, good or evil." These impersonal forces often relate to sexual intercourse or blood, particularly menstrual blood. Regarding the first, Richards notes:

> Sex relations according to Bemba dogma make a couple "hot." In this state it is dangerous for them to approach the ancestral spirits in any rite of prayer or sacrifice. And any chief or headman who attempted to perform such a ceremony without purification would run the risk of bringing disaster on his district. . . . Parents who do not purify themselves after intercourse run the risk of killing their children by accidentally touching the family hearth. Adulterers are more dangerous still, as they cannot purify themselves since the necessary rite can only be carried out by husband and wife. (p. 30)

Several examples are given of dangers believed to result from contact with menstrual blood (e.g., "a girl who allowed a drop of blood to fall on her husband's bed or who washed in the stream where others washed is thought to threaten illness to those near her" [p. 32]). Although death pollution is not called that in this book, Richards reports that those who have killed (people or lions) also become "hot" and "must not eat cooked food without purification" (p. 33). Of all these pollution dangers, Richards notes, "it is difficult to exaggerate the strength of these beliefs, or the extent to which they affect daily life" (p. 33).

Isaac Schapera's fieldwork among the Kgatla also began in the 1930s. The Kgatla are part of the broader group of Tswana found in today's Botswana and parts of South Africa. Although I cannot find use of the term pollution, nor an analysis of such a domain of thought as something distinct from other illness ctiologies, Schapera—like Krige and Richards—nevertheless described a process of contagion beliefs and behavior that related to major sources of pollution recognized in Africa: death, women's reproductive fluids including menstrual blood, and contact with strangers as when traveling or working far from home.

> The restrictions on sexual intercourse are associated with the idea that at certain times a person's blood becomes "hot," and until he has "cooled down," he is in a condition harmful to others with whom he comes into very close contact. Both men and women . . . are "hot" immediately after intercourse. . . . Widows and widowers are also "hot" for about a year after their bereavement. A woman is "hot" during her menstrual periods, during pregnancy (especially in the early stages), and immediately after childbirth. If she has aborted, she is "hot" until she menstruates again. . . . People are said to be "hot" when they have just returned from a long journey, from a funeral, or from visiting a newly-confined mother; a doctor is "hot" for two or three days after one of his patients has died; and a woman is "hot" if she has during the course of the day been mixing earth or smearing the walls and floors of her compound. (Schapera 1940:194–195)

In most cases of "hotness," "if the person affected indulges in coitus before 'cooling down,' his partner in the act will be stricken with disease and may even die" (Schapera 1940:194–195). We see that pollution or "heat" results from contact with menstrual blood, reproductive fluids, death, and strange places. We will return to this Tswana evidence below, when discussing traditional beliefs about promiscuity.

Eileen Krige is perhaps the first professional anthropologist to publish widely on the Zulu. Although she devotes little space to etiology in her chapter on medicine in her ethnography, she gives the impression that illness causation is a matter of wizardry, witch's familiars, poisonings, reanimated corpses, and the like, at one point stating, "The direct cause of an illness is very often the black arts and machinations of a wizard" (Krige 1950 [1936]:327). Illness causation by ancestor spirits is also mentioned. Although there is no specific mention of pollution or contamination in her sections on health, like Schapera, Krige describes the basic belief system elsewhere in her ethnography:

> It is a general rule in Zulu society that when anyone is ill or wounded, no "unclean" person may come to see him, even if he is a close relative or the wife, lest the wounds become poisoned. "Unclean" people include menstruating women, pregnant women, women with young children . . . , people who have had sexual connection . . . , people who have recently been to a burial, have handled a dead body or had anything to do with a corpse. To sleep with a woman renders a man unclean, even if no actual connection takes place. (p. 82)

In an earlier publication, and generalizing about the southern Bantu, Krige (1946:108) reiterates her comments about the defiling and contagious nature of menstrual blood, as well as "any irregularity in childbearing, such as the birth of twins, an abortion, or a miscarriage." The act of sexual intercourse itself is defiling, presumably because contact with women's reproductive fluids is considered polluting: "If the sex act is a powerful means for good, it is at the same time considered to be full of dangers. It brings in its train a certain 'uncleanness' or defilement which may prevent the healing of wounds and the recovery of sick people" (p. 108). She notes that due to dangers of defilement, sexual intercourse is taboo for those undergoing circumcision ceremonies or warriors in time of war (p. 108).

From the foregoing, we see that while there has been very little direct mention of pollution, contamination, or other contagion-like theories of illness in Africa as a whole, there has been a fair amount of description of beliefs in defilement and the danger of contact with death, menstrual blood, and the like in southern Africa, even if the significance of these beliefs in broader ethnomedical thought or general cosmology may have been unexplored. Perhaps some of this was due to the style of the time.

In discussing the anthropologists of the 1930s, Kuper (1973:94) notes that scholars like Schapera and Hoernlé wrote "long, discursive books" in which they "did not abstract. Principles of social organization were shown immanent in concrete activities, rather than as forming systems which could be comprehended." This may partly explain why we see no real analysis of pollution or contagion as a distinctive ethnomedical domain. Yet Junod, Smith, and Dale predate professional anthropology in the region and they provided some useful hints and clues. Moreover, the nonabstracting first generation of anthropologists managed to analyze witchcraft and sorcery as causal theories that served various social and psychological functions.[2]

In the 1970s, a British-trained ethnographer, Harriet Ngubane, herself a Zulu, did a study of Zulu ethnomedicine. Although she apparently did not attempt to measure the relative importance of the four main types of illness causation that she identified (natural causes, sorcery, ancestors, and pollution), she discussed pollution beliefs in detail and she called them just that. Largely on the basis of this work, Hammond-Tooke wrote (1989:92) that the Zulu appear to have "the most developed conceptual system" related to pollution in South Africa.

Before she discussed pollution proper, Ngubane wrote a section on ecology and health in her chapter "Natural Causes of Illness." This refers first of all to the balance or adaptation achieved between living beings and their environment:

> Zulu believe that there is a special relationship between a person and his environment. . . . The people in any particular region are adjusted to their surroundings; but should they go to a completely different region they would become ill, not being adapted to the new atmospheric and environmental conditions" (1977:24).

Before continuing with the quote, it should be noted that there is an empirical basis for this belief. Epidemiologists have found that when people migrate to or within malarial zones, their lack of resistance to local strains of malaria in the new environment makes them more vulnerable to malarial sickness than indigenous people—those adapted to atmospheric and environmental conditions, in Ngubane's language. Living conditions among migrants also tend to be below the prevailing standard, allowing increased exposure to infected mosquitoes and other disease vectors (Oaks et al. 1991:261–262). Note, too, that the notion that strangers pollute is found elsewhere, for example, Papua New Guinea (Hughes 1991), and that this has been interpreted as a cultural adaptation that preserves the purity of a value system or social order, overcomes contradictions within a social system, etc. (Rosen 1973). To continue:

> Zulu also believe that, when moving, both men and animals leave behind something of themselves, and absorb something of the atmosphere through which they move. . . . What is left behind in motion is known as *umkhondo* (track). Because neither men nor animals are restricted to a particular region, when they return from distant parts markedly different from Natal and Zululand, they bring back foreign elements that they have absorbed in their travels. Some wild animals and birds are reputed to travel long distances and on their return may introduce something foreign. (Ngubane 1977:24–25)

Ngubane notes that a variety of illnesses are attributed to contact with, or absorption of, dangerous environmental essences. Contact can even occur while not quite touching: "The action of contracting a disease by stepping over dangerous tracks is known as *umeqo*." Among environmental dangers are fumes of strong (traditional) medicines and discarded elements of illness that have been removed from a patient. The latter are believed to be a kind of "material substance; having been discarded it may hover around in the atmosphere or remain localized until it attaches itself to someone else" (Ngubane 1977:26). There may also be undesirable substances of this or other kinds left along roads, especially crossroads, by travelers. Whatever the source,

> the environment progressively becomes riddled with dangers. In order to survive despite these dangers, everyone must be frequently strengthened to develop and maintain resistance. In other words everyone must establish and maintain a form of balance with his surroundings. (p. 26)

Note that illness contracted from the environment is impersonal, fulfilling a key requirement for naturalistic illness, and that we encounter the notion of resistance with this type of illness. Ngubane explains:

> Some people are considered much more vulnerable than others to environmental dangers. These are: infants, strangers in the territory, people who have allowed a long stretch of time to elapse between treatments, and finally persons who are considered polluted. . . . People in a state of pollution include, for instance, the bereaved, the newly-delivered mother,

the homicide, and menstruating women. All these are considered vulnerable to environmental disease. (pp. 28–29)

Environmental dangers are considered "the primary cause of a wide variety of illnesses, some minor, others fatal" (p. 29). Examples are serious childhood illnesses that may result in death, including diarrhea ("green diarrhoea and white-coated tongue"). Ngubane mentions rash from contact with nettle as an example of a nonserious environmental illness. Note that both seem biomedically classifiable as contagious conditions involving contact. Contact is either with a pathogen, in the case of diarrhea, or with a toxic plant, in the case of nettle.

In my own fieldwork in Swaziland, two of the most serious childhood diarrheas, *umphezulu* (also called *inyoni*, which Ngubane mentions as an example of an environmental illness) and *kuhabula*, are attributed exactly to such environmental dangers (Green 1985). *Umphezulu*, characterized by greenish diarrhea, is contracted in utero and results from the behavior of the mother while pregnant.

Specifically, *umphezulu* is caused by: (1) a pregnant woman passing through an area where lightning has recently struck or crossing over a place where enemies have deliberately spread harmful medicines; (2) a pregnant woman failing to keep her head covered at all times. A child gets *kuhabula* by accidental inhalation of the smoke or invisible vapors of herbal medicines (sometimes mixed with dried animal skins) used to protect clan members against a variety of health dangers in the environment. I discuss the concept of airborne illness among the Swazi and other groups in Chapter Six, but it is important to understand beliefs about the role of the environment and the general natural context of contagious illness before looking more closely at pollution.

Honwana (1994) finds the same basic pattern among the Mozambican Tsonga that Ngubane described: Environments become polluted by a number of contaminants such as "foreign essences," "traces" of foreign people, "discarded elements" of illness that have been removed, as well as medicines and poisons of sorcery found in the atmosphere against which Tsonga have no immunity. Purification rituals are required to treat pollution of this sort. Clearly, we see in environmental dangers a model that explains contagious illness and conditions, that is impersonal, and that may relate to pollution, just as naturalistic infection sometimes relates to pollution. "Illness of the air" or wind is a major subtype of environmental danger.

Returning to pollution beliefs proper among the Zulu, Ngubane (1977:77) tells us that pollution is seen as a "mystical force," usually associated with women. It is referred to as darkness (*umnyama*) and it is conceptualized as a mystical force that diminishes resistance to disease and creates conditions of poor luck, misfortune, "disagreeableness" and "repulsiveness." "In its worst form *umnyama* is contagious" (1977:78). Babies become contaminated easily because of pollution the mother absorbs from the environment and passes through her breast milk.

Contact with death, especially if direct, is highly polluting: "Persons who actually handle the corpse, or who help with the burial in any way, are considered more polluted than people who are merely present at the burial" (Ngubane 1977:81). Homicide is even worse for the Zulu: "Taking a human life adds another dimension to the degree of pollution: in addition to the pollution that arises from death as from catastrophic death, the killer himself is polluted in a special way. His intention is not important. . . . He is polluted as long as he takes a human life" (p. 81).

Polluted persons are considered socially marginal, in part because they are in a dangerous state, one that could contaminate others within range. "A person who because of her polluted state withdraws from society is expected among other things to be soft spoken, control her emotions, and avoid sexual intercourse" (Ngubane 1977: 82). Ngubane remarks that diviners, who are usually female, remain permanently in a marginal state. "This is expressed by her attire, more particularly the white strips of goat skin strapped crossways over her breast" (p. 88).

Pollution seems to occur innocently and accidentally, that is, by mere contact with a person, place or essence; it is seldom regarded as resulting from a deliberate action. "A person is not polluted because she has 'sinned,' but she 'sins' and is automatically punishable if she does not observe a proper behavior pattern when she is polluted" (Ngubane 1977:97). In this regard, pollution is like what Murdock calls mystical retribution, referring to automatic punishment for violation of a taboo, unmediated by a spirit or person.

Ngubane illuminates some differences between pollution illness and ancestor illness:

With punishment administered by the ancestors on the descendants . . . the sinner is not often personally affected, but someone close to him is, as, for instance, when a child or wife falls ill as a result of transgressions of a father or a husband, or when all the inmates of a homestead experience various misfortunes because one of them has angered the ancestors. In addition, the ancestral wrath operates only in cases of violation of proper behavior towards members of the descent group. (1977:98)

This sort of punishment is open to "manipulation" (although "supplication" might be more apt) to avoid it:

By contrast, the "mystical force" is not open to any manipulation. The breach of proper behavior by the polluted is not only automatically punishable, but once administered it cannot be reversed. The "mystical force" is concerned with the well-being of the whole society, and it operates in situations closely connected with procreation. Its sanctions therefore guarantee the continuity of the society and the replacement of generations. (Ngubane 1977:98)

John Janzen, a contemporary anthropologist whose major fieldwork has been in the Congo (formerly Zaire), has come to appreciate the importance of pollution and purity beliefs. Instead of characterizing illness and misfortune in terms of witchcraft and spirits, he describes underlying concepts of health ("wellness") and well-being that find expression in ritual and ceremony among southern and central Bantu speakers.

In his semantic analysis of "verbs of well-being and affliction," Janzen observes that, "purity and pollution codes are known to be widespread in Bantu Africa, but only few studies have elaborated them in any detail." He describes three basic symbolic constructs of Bantu speakers, expressed as dichotomies: purity/pollution, balance/imbalance, and cool/hot. Balance refers to the maintenance of harmonious relations with nature, society, and the spirit world; its absence connotes disfavor of spirits, withdrawal of ancestral protection. Coolness does not refer to hot/cold humoral theory but "is a quintessential quality of the ancestors, and their presence is usually invoked to end the 'hotness' of strained relationships, witchcraft and pollution" (Janzen 1989:234; see also Janzen 1981, 1982, 1986).

IS THERE A DOMINANT CAUSAL THEORY AMONG BANTU SPEAKERS?

Having reviewed the evidence of pollution and related contagious beliefs in southern Africa, we might wonder where these fit in importance and comparison with other etiologic domains. A leading contemporary South African anthropologist, David Hammond-Tooke (1989), has generalized about etiological beliefs in that country and has characterized the "traditional world-view of South African Bantu-speakers" as falling into "four broadly-defined sets of theories purporting to explain illness and misfortune" (p. 46) among the four major ethnolinguistic groups of South Africa: Nguni, Sotho, Venda, and Tsonga. Note that these groups extend into some neighboring countries such as Zimbabwe, Mozambique, Botswana, Lesotho, and Swaziland so that any generalization about these groups should hold for a region broader than South Africa itself. The four identified theories are: (1) witchcraft; (2) spirits, ancestors; (3) Supreme Being; and (4) pollution. If we take witchcraft to include sorcery and Supreme Being to include what others call natural causes, then South African ethnomedicine seems little different from other parts of sub-Saharan Africa, except for the inclusion of pollution. Note that no humoral hot-cold thinking is mentioned.

Hammond-Tooke believes that witchcraft and sorcery is "by far the commonest basis for the diagnosis of major illness and misfortune" (1989:89) in South Africa, and he even attempted a rough empirical measure of this hypothesis. He examined 100 cases of misfortune among a Xhosa population (Bhaca) and found that 73% were explained in witchcraft-sorcery terms (Hammond-Tooke (1970:29, 1989:89). Only 44% of urban dwellers gave such explanations, suggesting that personalistic explanations decline with urbanization. It is possible that Hammond-Tooke might have reached his conclusion about the primacy of witchcraft and sorcery years before this attempt at measurement. In 1962 he noted, "The great majority of cases of sickness and death are believed to be the work of sorcerers or witches . . . or sent by the ancestors" (p. 265).

Since the Venda have not yet been mentioned, and they represent one of the four major ethnolinguistic groups of South Africa, let me cite another South African ethnographer, Hugh Stayt. Of Venda causal theories of illness Stayt writes, "Although certain epidemics and illnesses, such as malaria or pneumonia, are cured by specific methods of medicinal or external treatment, the BaVenda attribute nearly all diseases either to the evil influence of the ancestor spirits or to witchcraft" (1968:267). Stayt gives us apparent examples of exceptions of diseases that are widespread, important, often fatal, and in my experience, usually believed to result from naturalistic contagion.

Turning to the Shona of Zimbabwe, Gelfand et al. (1985:70) report that traditional healers believe that the cause of an illness must be determined before attempting treatment. A survey of 250 urban and 49 rural patients of traditional healers showed that about 28% of illnesses were attributed to witchcraft, about 17% to ancestors, and about 6% to angry or foreign spirits. What of the remaining 49%? Natural causes are specified most often, but there is no specific discussion of pollution beliefs. I suggest this is because such beliefs have not been specifically researched or disaggregated from natural causes.

Gelfand et al. (1985: 85–86, 94) list a number of purgative and emetic herbs used by the Shona, presumably for conditions in addition to diarrhea. Such medicines are usually used for pollution-type conditions in southern Africa. In fact, Hammond-Tooke (1989: 93–94) suggests that use of enemas and emetics be taken as a measure of the importance of pollution beliefs in a society. He notes that this is the "technique *par excellence*" used by the Zulus to expel pollution (p. 93). This seems a reasonable, useful hypothesis.

In an earlier paper, Gelfand—while asserting that supernaturalism dominates etiological thinking among the Shona—cites an intriguing example of Shona powers of naturalistic observation related to what Smith and Dale called contact diseases:

> An excellent example of preventive medicine amongst the traditional African is afforded by their [*sic*] practice of variolation. As in Europe, the idea of this must have been based upon empiricism, noticing the spread of the disease by contact. This interesting procedure in which material from the pustule is rubbed into the scarified skin of a non-sufferer, must have followed the observation that a contact might contract a mild form of the disease and so develop what we refer to as a state of immunity. (Gelfand 1980:5)

It would be intriguing to hear an explanation from Gelfand's informants of the theory underlying this practice. Incidentally, vaccination with

cowpox in eighteenth-century Europe developed from popular observation, rather than from physicians or scientists (Pelling 1993:320).

We see that Hammond-Tooke is in respected company in thinking that
witchcraft beliefs predominate in southern Africa. At least he recognizes
pollution as one of four basic etiologic theories in southern Africa; a
great many anthropologists have overlooked it entirely. Most anthropologists working in southern Africa and reviewed here believe—or report—
that supernatural or personalistic explanations predominate in causal
theories of illness. Pollution beliefs were well described by some of the
early amateur missionary-ethnographers working in southern Africa, even
if the actual term was not used and its significance was underappreciated.
In any case, many later anthropologists seemed to have overlooked it.

On the basis of my own applied fieldwork among several southern and
central Bantu societies, I believe that pollution and related contagion
beliefs are far more important than the literature suggests, with the exceptions mentioned (Douglas, Ngubane, Janzen, and Hammond-Tooke).
These beliefs are particularly important in connection with contagious
diseases, as amateur ethnographers Smith and Dale suggested more than
75 years ago in their observation that "virulent disease and plagues"
somehow belong in the realm of naturalistic explanation.

Maybe my view is skewed because of the nature of much of the
research reviewed here. Diarrhea and STDs both involve bodily fluids
and discharges related to digestion and procreation, which can be polluting due to their power to "symbolize social relations and social processes" (Douglas 1992 [1966]:125). On the other hand, the view of
anthropologists who emphasize the importance of witchcraft and sorcery
may be skewed. Hammond-Tooke agrees that pollution-related beliefs
have been underresearched. So it seems prudent to await the needed
research before concluding that witchcraft beliefs predominate in illness/
misfortune explanations for South African or southern Bantu speakers.

SUPPORT FROM RESEARCH IN WEST AFRICA

I strongly suspect that exaggeration of supernaturalism and exotification
of indigenous health beliefs have also occurred outside southern and
central Africa. While conducting long-term ethnographic fieldwork among
the Bono of Ghana, D. M. Warren did an emic analysis of 742 non-
synonymous illness lexemes related to 392 locally recognized illnesses.

The Bono themselves classify illness into the broad categories of naturally caused (*mogya mu yadee*) and spiritually caused (*sunsum mu yadee*), even if there may be some gray area between these. Of the 392 illnesses, 268 (68%) were found to be naturally caused. Most illnesses considered contagious were classified this way, although there may be extenuating circumstances: "If the disease is contagious but the victim is not aware of any contact, if the victim is suffering from stress due to the transgression of a cultural norm and if the disease is considered serious . . . or is deforming . . . , then it will be classified as a spiritually caused disease" (Warren 1979a:39).

Of the 268 naturally caused illnesses, analysis of "disease causation lexemes" showed that the most common citations were "impure blood" (117), "dirty blood" (26), "dirt" (22), and "insects" (16). Animals, worms, and other organisms are also mentioned. Again, this is the familiar lexicon of ICT, of pollution and naturalistic infection. Analysis of spiritually caused disease lexemes showed "witch power used for evil" (91 citations), "diseases inherited through the matriclan" (21), "medicine used for evil" (19), and "the devil and evil spiritual beings" (14). Incidentally, findings were "surprisingly consistent" between diverse groups of Bono informants: traditional healers, older-generation villagers, students, and hospital workers (Warren 1979a:39–41).

Warren (1974) created considerable controversy among anthropologists when he reported finding that most illnesses in a well-researched area of Ghana were considered to be naturally caused. Anthropological fieldwork was done in the same area some 20 years later, and the field worker found evidence to support Warren's conclusion, although he commented that this could be partly the result of recent changes due to influence of biomedical concepts (Ventevogel 1992:32).

Turning to a recent West African study, Ryan and his assistants visited 88 randomly selected compounds over a five-month period in a Kom-speaking area of Cameroon, collecting data on the treatments associated with 429 nonchronic illness episodes (Ryan 1998). Ryan was interested in the beliefs and behaviors of laypersons (caretakers) rather than traditional healers. He and his assistants asked about cause for each illness episode:

In 38% of cases, caretakers attributed the primary cause to climatic changes (e.g., too much sun or dust, or seasonal transitions). They also attributed illnesses to overwork (8%), to illnesses having crossed from a previous illness (8%), to bad food (5%), to accidents (4%), and to other idiosyncratic causes (10%). In 26% of the cases, people simply said they didn't know what brought the illnesses.

In no case did informants directly attribute the illness to witchcraft or social transgressions. Wombong residents tend to associate witchcraft and social transgressions with either chronic illness or illnesses where otherwise healthy adults get sick and die suddenly. (p. 215)

Judging by these findings, perhaps the issue is largely one of whether we are considering acute or chronic illness. Many or most contagious illnesses can be considered acute, and at least in a given manifestation, and therefore not in the domain of witchcraft and sorcery, for the Kom and perhaps other Africans. Although Africans and virtually all people distinguish illnesses on the basis of their severity (Weller 1984; Ryan 1998), this may not be equivalent to the Western biomedical distinction between chronic and acute. Illnesses like tuberculosis, malaria, and AIDS are hardly considered acute in biomedicine, yet I find that these fit the naturalistic, indigenous contagion theory profile I am discussing here.

A RECENT CRITIQUE OF AFRICAN NATURALISM

Before I conclude this section, I must deal with the arguments of a contemporary anthropologist, Robert Pool. He believes that a number of recent anthropologists have found *too much* naturalistic thought in African etiology, when in fact, "in the final instance, everything boils down to witchcraft" (Pool 1994a:12). Pool agrees that Evans-Pritchard influenced generations of anthropologists in his classic *Witchcraft, Oracles and Magic among the Azande* (1937). But he shows that this discussion of witchcraft and illness is full of inconsistencies. Sometimes Evans-Pritchard seems to be saying that Azande believe that *all* illness is caused by witchcraft, other times he contradicts this. Nevertheless, in the end, Pool concludes that the usual interpretation is the right one: That is in fact what Evans-Pritchard meant. No doubt Pool would think Janzen (1981) was wrong in suggesting that Evans-Pritchard was misinterpreted, that Janzen is a revisionist.

Pool further says that some anthropologists find evidence of natural etiologies only when they press Africans for explanations of things they are not used to explaining. Pool (1994a) even questions the value of investigating etiology, observing from his own fieldwork in western Cameroon that, "Wimbum do not discuss minor self-limiting or easily treatable ailments in aetiological terms. When I push them for an explanation they say that they 'have no cause' or 'just happen'" (p. 12). This, of course, is part of the defining language of natural causation, as we have seen and as we shall see in later chapters.

Pool suggests that anthropologists who find naturalistic thinking among Africans are projecting or imposing their own "biomedically determined constructs" on Africans. Perhaps Pool does not recognize the implication here: If an explanation sounds naturalistic or scientific, it must be of Western, scientific origin. But why can't nonpersonalistic explanations of illness be of indigenous, African origin? Westerners seem to have trouble conceding this possibility.

Pool also criticizes anthropologists who analyze medical systems as something distinct from the broader domain of general misfortune. In other words, if we try to separate out medical systems from the broader domain of misfortune, we have distorted reality, violated the holism in African thought; illness and misfortune are part of a single domain of thought. A full examination of misfortune, Pool believes, would surely produce much evidence of supernatural, personalistic, and specifically witchcraft thinking. I'm sure this is true, just as an anthropologist from Mars studying Americans would find much evidence of religion if not magic in a broader study of misfortune as perceived by Americans. The term itself implies forces beyond human control, fate. But this does not mean that Africans understand all illness as witchcraft caused. Pool asks:

> After all, why study *medical* systems? All this talk of medical systems, medical knowledge, medical behaviour, medical situations, behaviour related to health and illness . . . flows from a biomedically determined and basically practical interest in disease and health care. That health workers in Africa focus their attention on such matters is understandable, but why should ethnographic enquiry be limited to a domain which has been defined beforehand: a medical system, consisting of naturalistic aetiology, disease and health care behaviour? . . . By focusing on the "practical," "natural," "empirical," and "behavioural" aspects of disease they automatically exclude the "supernatural" and "ritual" aspects of illness . . . as well as other non-illness misfortunes, thus not only creating an indigenous medical domain but also reducing it to a somewhat inferior version of biomedicine.

Indigenous conceptions of illness, and concomitant practical behaviour, are thus narrowed down (naturalised and separated from other non-disease misfortune, their "supernatural" aspect being either purged or socialised). This thereby brings them into line with biomedical conceptions of disease, based ultimately on positivistic assumptions about the nature of physical reality, thus making anthropological interpretations more acceptable to biomedical health workers. (1994a:15)

Thus far, we have discussed the many anthropologists who maintain(ed) with Evans-Pritchard that Africans believed that most illness is supernaturally or personalistically caused. So it is ironic to find a contemporary anthropologist who characterizes practical-minded, positivist anthropologists as constituting a new paradigm that sees naturalistic thought in every African utterance related to health, and a paradigm that needs deconstructing. I believe that naturalistic thinking can be found by anthropologists in African ethnomedical thought because it is really there, not because we naturalize indigenous perceptions to suit our paradigms. Perhaps there was less naturalistic etiology before the influence of Western biomedicine, except that early ethnographers such as Junod, Smith, and Dale described this as very important in the societies they studied over longer periods than do most of today's anthropologists.

As to the charge that reports of naturalistic ethnomedical belief make anthropological interpretations more acceptable to biomedical health workers, I think the issue is not so much anthropological interpretations, but African health models themselves. Officials in African health ministries often view traditional medicine as dangerous and socially devisive. In this view, traditional medicine and its practitioners reinforce and perpetuate superstitions and belief in witchcraft, along with irrational and unnecessary fears and anxieties—not to mention witchcraft accusations and reprisals against innocent victims of such accusations. Traditional health beliefs are said to impede acceptance of scientific thinking and perpetuate magical thinking (Asuni 1979; Velimirovic 1984). If this view is justified, African postindependence government policies of ignoring, discouraging, or suppressing traditional medicine make sense.

But if there is much in African medicine that is rational, empirically based, and naturalistic—even if expressed in idioms unfamiliar in the West—then it cannot be dismissed so easily. Let me reiterate a point made in the introduction: My primary motive for writing this book is not to criticize anthropologists and others for exaggerating supernaturalism.

74

It is to show that Africans understand contagious disease (but not necessarily other conditions of illness and misfortune) in ways that are in some fundamental ways not very different from Western biomedicine. It is to show that there is sufficient common ground between the two systems to develop public health approaches that can build on and even incorporate elements of indigenous contagion theory. This seems preferable to the current official or unofficial policy of ignoring or confronting indigenous health beliefs. If this is construed as a bias toward the practical, the useful, the life-saving, so be it. I leave postmodernist epistemological musings to others. Perhaps it was these musings that led Pool to conclude that "the Wimbum do not have a medical system" (1994a:17) and neither, presumably, do other Africans.

No doubt I am not doing justice to the intellectually stimulating but essentially elitist academic argument that Pool presents. I agree with Pool that anthropologists and other social scientists unavoidably restrict and distort reality when they "discover" and describe social or cognitive systems, and that there is greater variability in systems than anthropologists and others usually acknowledge. But that does not mean that there are no systems. As Warren (1995:873) notes in his review of Pool's book (1994b), "There will always be variability in every system but there are also parameters and limits for each system, often with differing degrees of fuzzy edges." If social systems are nonexistent and/or unknowable, then there is no social science and Pool and I are in the wrong business. As Young (1998) recently noted, postmodernist anthropologists see ethnography and indeed science as the root of all evil; they ultimately fall into the trap of cultural solipsism.

A CLOSER LOOK AT
INDIGENOUS CONTAGION BELIEFS

Thus far, we have seen that in many parts of Africa, health-related causality concepts can be found that are nonpersonalistic in character. These include the concepts that anthropologists classify as naturalistic, for example, indigenous germ theories (naturalistic infection), heredity, God's will, organic deterioration, dangerous environments, trauma, and accidents as well as pollution or contagion. A few anthropologists have even suggested that naturalistic theories predominate in explanations of illness and misfortune in some African societies. However, I have found no one who has claimed predominance of pollution beliefs for any African society; indeed most anthropologists reviewed in Chapter One never directly mentioned this domain of thought.

Among those who have discussed pollution, there seems to be general agreement that it represents a form of impersonal causation that is distinct from attribution of illness to spirits, witches, sorcerers, or ancestors. But there is no consensus that pollution should be classified as naturalistic. As noted above, Richards (1956) characterized pollution, without using that term, as an impersonal but magical force for the Bemba. Ngubane (1977: 77) described pollution as a "mystical force" for the Zulu, usually associated with women. Yet pollution, Ngubane explained, occurs through an impersonal process; victims are not singled out for illness or misfortune by a human or superhuman force. Still, pollution can involve punishment for the Zulu. Ngubane (p. 97) describes a process of punishment if a person in a polluted state "does not observe a proper behavior pattern when she is polluted." However, this punishment is considered automatic (taboo breach—>result) and not open to manipulation or supplication, as is the case with personalistic conditions. In sum, there seem to be enough exceptions to the personalistic pattern that it may not be justified to call pollution a mystical force.

Ngubane (1977) also tells us that pollution is "conceptualized as a mystical force which diminishes resistance to disease" (p. 77). Note that the link between pollution and illness here seems *indirect*: Pollution diminishes resistance, then illness ensues. My findings suggest that pollution also causes illness directly, through direct physical contact. This is exactly what Smith and Dale (1968 [1920]:244) found in the former northern Rhodesia in the early 1900s, as reviewed above.

Therefore, we can define pollution as a process that involves direct or indirect contact with a substance or essence considered dangerous because it is unclean or impure. Contact may be through a person, place, or thing, although perhaps it is usually a person. Unlike victims of witchcraft, sorcery, magic, or spirit-caused illness, people are not deliberately singled out by a superhuman force. Pollution refers to an impartial, impersonal process of contagion: Anyone coming into contact with the unclean, dangerous substance becomes contagious, vulnerable to illness or misfortune, and/or actually ill. While polluted, people find themselves in "dangerous states," often through no fault of their own, that put them in a socially marginal condition (in part because they are contagious), subject to various taboos, "particularly concerning sexual intercourse" (Hammond-Tooke 1989:91). Such people also become socially marginalized until they become cleansed or purified.

When illness results from contact with a tiny, invisible organism usually described as an insect or worm, rather than an unclean or impure essence, the etiological theory is classifiable as indigenous germ theory, or naturalistic infection. The process is similar to pollution in that contact leads impersonally to illness (but not to misfortune, it seems). But indigenous germ theory seems less concerned with taboo violation and avoidance behavior. And because agents of illness resemble those of biomedical germ theory, and do not possess the mystical-seeming attributes of heat, darkness or "shadow of death," this etiologic theory seems more naturalistic than pollution theory. Clearly, though, they have much in common. For example, dirt or filth, code words for the impure state of pollution, can also be found in explanations of indigenous germ theory. The insect of germ theory in Zambia is sometimes described as originating from filth, as noted above. It therefore seems justified to regard both theories as components of a broader theory of illness through contagion. The same is true of environmental dangers, which, as we saw earlier, also relates to pollution and attempts to explain contagious illness in an impersonal manner. It therefore seems justified to regard these three interrelated, etiologic theories as part of a single, broader construct that is essentially naturalistic because it is impersonal in all its manifestations.

Forces of contagion also seem impervious to supplication or manipulation. Either a person must accept contagious illness as an unavoidable part of the human condition, or he or she might prevent this by such mundane actions as cautious behavior or taking medicine. There is ethnographic evidence for both responses. The former is less well documented, but researchers working in Africa have encountered the view that malaria and even STDs are "but another tribulation of a hard life" (Caldwell and Caldwell 1994:204; see also Inhorn and Brown 1998). Other naturalistic illness causation theories, with which ICT shares essential features, include explanations involving personal hygiene, diet, heredity, trauma, lifestyle, aging, overdose or toxic reaction to medicines, exposure to the elements, and the like (discussed further in Chapter Six). It may be useful to summarize in graphic form what indigenous contagion consists of and what associated code words are found with each constituent theory (see Table 2).

Table 2
Elements of Indigenous Contagion Theory

Naturalistic Infection, or "Germ Theory"	Pollution	Environmental Dangers
Characteristic Concepts and Code Words		
insects worms tiny animals	dirt impurity contamination heat darkness shadow of death bad blood ──────── Reference to common "pollutant," i.e., death, menstrual blood, other bodily fluids or discharges. Contact with foreign people and environments.	illness in the air wind, breeze, or dust dangerous elements in the wind or air traces, tracks vapors, fumes poisons in environment or atmosphere discarded elements
Characteristic Treatments		
Killing the "noxious microorganism." Search and destroy.	Purging, enemas, purification rites, washing, burying, fumigation. Usually involves quarantine.	often similar to pollution treatment

A CLOSER LOOK AT POLLUTION

Pollution beliefs are highly developed among Nguni speakers (e.g., the Zulu), for whom pollution is related to menstruation, miscarriage, the death of a husband or child, and sexual intercourse, the last said to generate "dangerous heat" (Schapera 1940:194–195; Richards 1956; Ngubane 1977; Hammond-Tooke 1989:92). Sources of pollution for the Tsonga include menstrual blood and birth-related bodily fluids, death including abortion and miscarriage, the birth of twins, sickness itself, and physical contact with a new environment (Junod 1962b [1926]; Green 1994b; Honwana 1994). Regarding the last, about which there is comparatively little in the literature, Honwana (1994 and personal communication) reports that the Tsonga believe that "traces" of people remain in the environments in which they lived.

Going to a new area leads to pollution by exposure to these traces or foreign essences, to medicines and poisons against which Tsonga have no immunity, and to discarded elements of illness. Both labor migration and war have thrust many Tsonga into foreign environments. Exposure to a combat zone should be doubly polluting because contact with death is a major source of contamination for a great many African people. In any case, Honwana reports that men returning from war and work in the South African mines must undergo a purification ceremony before they can be reintegrated into society. Indeed, there is a protective ritual that is performed before people depart for a foreign environment. In terms of my ICT construct, pollution from exposure to foreign environments represents the border area between pollution and dangerous environments, and the evidence just reviewed provides further evidence of the permeability of boundaries separating the constituent models of ICT.

I have also found illicit sexual acts, such as adultery, to be considered highly polluting among the Tsonga as well as the Shona and Bemba. As already noted, anthropologists have reported this among other Bantu speakers (Schapera 1940; Richards 1956).

In his summary of pollution beliefs in southern Africa, Hammond-Tooke (1989) tells us that sources of pollution for the Tsonga (Thonga) are menstrual blood, the *lochia* (abortion?), death, the birth of twins, and sickness itself. Among the Venda, pollution is characterized as dirt and various purifications are associated with birth (especially of twins), abortion, things that must be done after illness, after crime, and after a burial. Data are a bit more extensive for the Sotho and Nguni. Pollution among the Nguni is related to menstruation, miscarriage, the death of a husband or child, and something that occurs after sexual intercourse and before the woman washes. Pollution is sometimes described as "heat" by Zulus. Sexual intercourse is said to generate dangerous heat, as does anger. People in a state of heat are not only dangerous to other people since they are contagious, they can also pass darkness or dirt on to cattle, and they can depotentize medicine and food.

Hammond-Tooke (1981b:15–16) also relates pollution concepts with the Sotho ethnomedical concept of heat. The Kgatla term *go fisa* (heat) can be used to refer to states of physical health such as fever or depressed fontanel. The Kgatla believe it is caused by a variety of polluting contacts, such as with corpses or less directly with close kinsmen of the recently deceased; with a woman in an "unusual" sexual state; or with a traveler. Yet Hammond-Tooke (1981a:) notes the distinctiveness of pollution beliefs among the Sotho-speaking Kgatla: "This complex of beliefs is clearly analytically separate from that concerning ancestors or witches. Firstly, it does not involve the actions of intelligences, whether human or 'spiritual.' Secondly, there seems to be little, if any, association with morality" (p. 112).

He suggests that the Kgatla concept of pollution is better understood as "impersonal causation," as distinct from the "typical African theory of causation, which sees misfortunes in terms of the actions of ancestors and witches, especially the latter" (Hammond-Tooke 1981b:16, 21). He describes a Kgatla "pollution complex," wherein contamination occurs through "no fault of one's own," an idea supported by Mary Douglas's work among the Lele of the (now Democratic Republic of) Congo. Douglas notes that Lele rules of pollution do not depend on intention but only "whether a forbidden contact has taken place or not" (Douglas 1992 [1966]:155), just as Ngubane (1977:81) found among the Zulu. Finally, Hammond-Tooke (1981b) suggests that Bantu-speaking societies may differ in their emphasis, so to speak, of certain elements of pollution theory: "Just as the Zulu have a minor pollution category of heat, complementary to the major category of darkness, so the Kgatla have darkness as (a) secondary form of pollution to their heat" (p. 15).

Let us look closer at people finding themselves in dangerous, polluted states through no fault of their own. Is this always the case with pollution illness? Pollution beliefs may develop at least in part as a means of social control, especially in relation to rules governing sexual intercourse. Few areas of behavior are more socially disruptive than illicit intercourse, including: sex with kinsmen (incest), with nonspouses (adultery), with women not of one's own generation, with menstruating women, with widows or women who have miscarried or aborted, or with women during period of postpartum taboo in which a baby is already nursing. Some such behavior, especially the first two or three examples, threaten the social fabric itself, the foundations of the social structure. The indigenous causal chain of intercourse pollution and its resolution appears to be something like:

violation of intercourse rule → polluted state symbolizing social marginality → social opprobrium → application of medicine or ritual of purification → return to former social status (ritual of aggregation) → reinforcement of social rule → restoration of social harmony, social maintenance.

A person might bring pollution on himself, through careless or deliberate behavior. Mary Douglas (1992 [1966]) thinks the carelessness possibility more common, noting:

> A polluting person is always in the wrong. He has developed some wrong condition or simply crossed some line which should not have been crossed and this displacement unleashes danger from someone . . . pollution can be committed intentionally, but intention is irrelevant to its effect—it is more likely to happen inadvertently. (p. 113)

My research on sexual behavior and intercourse pollution suggests that there may be a deliberate decision to misbehave on the part of someone who feels above the rules of society. In this case, pollution might result from something like hubris: I know I should not have sex with my neighbor's wife but I want to and maybe I can get away with it. Here we see deliberate rule violation leading to impersonal consequence. Perhaps what this means, at least in a structural-functional framework, is that no one can violate certain social rules without serious consequence. Incest, adultery, and other rules governing sexual behavior have great potential for social disruption if ignored. Pollution might function to remind members of the social group that no one is above the social rules that have developed in the interest of preserving and perpetuating the social group. Those who disrupt society by flaunting its rules must be removed from society for a period, they must be marginalized, made into social lepers, any contact with whom would be dangerous to others.

Indeed, *any* sexual intercourse may be considered dangerous and at least potentially polluting, as in the discussion of "dangerous heat" above. Among the Lele, "Sexual activity was held to be in itself dangerous, not for the partners to it, but dangerous for the weak and the sick. Anyone coming fresh from sexual intercourse should avoid the sick, lest by the indirect contact their fever should increase" (Douglas 1992 [1966]:151). Douglas relates the presence of this belief with the lack of formal legal institutions in small-scale societies, noting, "Sex is likely to be pollution-free in a society where sexual roles are enforced directly. In such a case anyone who threatens to deviate would be promptly punished with physical force. This supposes an administrative efficiency and consensus which are rare anywhere and especially in primitive societies" (p. 141).

It may be that pollution resulting from sexual intercourse—or at least certain types of intercourse—ought to be regarded as a special type, or subtype, of pollution in at least some societies. In the case of intercourse pollution, the transgressor of social rules may know what he or she is doing, therefore this is not the inadvertent or no-fault situation that characterizes many pollution-related illnesses. One may decide to transgress social rules governing intercourse with a widow, a kinsman, a menstruating women, a nursing mother, or a prostitute who may be polluted in multiple ways. Evidence that this is an emic distinction within pollution models can be found among the Tsonga, who seem to use "heat" to designate sex-pollution, and "darkness" for death-pollution. And the Lele of Congo distinguish a syndrome called *hanga*, which Douglas (1992 [1966]:123, 206) trans-lates as "sex pollution."

Another domain of human experience with great potential for social disruption is death. Indeed, we may find that association with death is at least as polluting as participation in incest and adultery. Among the Sotho, contact with death causes *fisa* (heat, confounding the general-izability of Tsonga pollution classification), and it may result from actual contact with a corpse to a variety of indirect contacts such as being a close relative of someone who dies. A miscarriage (or abortion?), especially when the fetus is improperly buried, is so polluting that it affects whole societies (Hammond-Tooke 1989:94–95). But death-related pollution seems not to involve deliberate rule violation, other than in cases of murder, although recall that the Zulu believe that deliberate murder and accidental homicide are both equally polluting (Ngubane 1977;81).

There are other sources of pollution in southern Africa, for example, menstruation, initiation rites, or the birth of twins, that involve no intention, but are just ordinary, unavoidable human experience. In any case, it is never easy to reduce human behavior to neat, discrete categories.

WHY HAVE POLLUTION BELIEFS BEEN OVERLOOKED?

Clearly, pollution beliefs are widespread and important in at least southern and central parts of sub-Saharan Africa, yet they have been largely overlooked by anthropologists and others. Since these beliefs are found in ethnomedical systems in many other parts of the world, notably the Indian subcontinent, it is especially surprising that there has been so little mention of these in association with Africa. I proposed several possible reasons for the neglect of pollution by anthropologists and others in Chapter One (e.g., deemphasis of African belief systems in favor of social processes by English-speaking scholars; pollution beliefs may have been less important in the past). However, no single explanation seems to adequately account for such serious oversight. Here I propose a number of other possible reasons.

Pollution beliefs may have been overlooked due to excessive interest by Western researchers in studying exotic areas of belief ("culture-bound syndromes") such as witchcraft, sorcery, and spirit possession. I have borrowed Goldschmidt's term xenophilia—the romanticization of all things foreign and exotic—to partially account for overemphasis on supernaturalism in descriptions of African health beliefs. A number of anthropologists are as guilty of xenophilia as explorers, adventurers, missionaries, big game hunters, and journalists. The more exotic seeming one's fieldwork and research findings are, the more interesting and appealing they are to students, colleagues, and the reading public. Books sell, students are attracted to classes, lecture offers increase. A Mozambican anthropologist commented to me that whenever one of her University of London professors gave a lecture on witchcraft or sorcery, the auditorium would be full. She wondered what size crowd a talk on ritual pollution would draw.

The tendency to sensationalize indigenous medicine is not peculiar to anthropologists or even to Westerners. For example, Gumede (1990:38), an African medical doctor and presumed expert on African medicine, perpetuates the idea that illness is always "unnatural" among "Africans" (he generalizes to the continent from, essentially, Nguni-speaking South Africa). Gumede asserts that diarrhea with blood and mucous in the stool, tuberculosis, and venereal disease are all caused by witchcraft and sorcery. In sum, "Disease is a man-made phenomenon through the agency of a spirit, or disease may follow a visitation from the ancestral spirits as punishment for failure to fulfill certain obligatory customary rites due to the departed" (1990:41). This is especially surprising coming from a Zulu, among whom pollution beliefs are highly developed, according to Ngubane and Hammond-Tooke.

In a later chapter in his book on traditional healers, Gumede quotes an article in *Social Science and Medicine* that some African illnesses may be regarded as naturally caused. He seems to accept this and gives *umkhuhlane* (which he translates minimally as colds) as an example—the only one, it seems. He might have quoted an earlier article of my own, published in that same journal:

> Suffice it to say here that for most Swazis, illness is believed to be caused by sorcery—i.e., the deliberate use of spells and medicines for harmful medicines—or less commonly by ancestral displeasure resulting in the withdrawal of spiritual protection. A relatively small number of illnesses such as colds, flu, and simple diarrhea are regarded as ordinary or naturally occurring. These are collectively known as *umkhuhlane*. (Green 1985:278)

I admit that I, too, missed the significance of pollution as well as naturalistic infection beliefs among the Swazi during my applied ethnomedical research in the early 1980s (I did write about environmental dangers). I remember puzzling over findings about contagion beliefs attributed to dangerous things in the physical environment and the air, not knowing quite how to interpret these. At the time, I had little training in medical anthropology, although more of this might not have helped.[3]

Why isn't more attention given to pollution beliefs? I offer this hypothesis: Pollution beliefs have been overlooked because they do not fit into the accepted, "personalistic" paradigm of African illness explanation. Researchers trained in this paradigm do not expect to find, and therefore do not find, evidence of impersonally caused illness.

Let me continue to speculate and submit several more possible explanations as explicit, testable hypotheses. Note that some of the hypotheses about pollution also pertain to other components of indigenous contagion theory. Pollution beliefs have been overlooked because:

- They are of a relatively mundane yet complex nature and are associated with reproductive bodily fluids and therefore to the world of women. There are access barriers to this world for male anthropologists. It may be no accident that the few anthropologists who emphasized African pollution beliefs in their fieldwork tend to be women (e.g., Douglas, Ngubane, Gotlieb).

- Pollution is in a somewhat ambiguous position in relation to the natural/nonnatural or natural/supernatural dichotomy, which is especially central in Bantu thought and to which anthropologists have given much importance. Pollution has features of both natural and supernatural; it straddles the dichotomy. Yet pollution occurs impersonally.
- Parts of the indigenous system can be confused with a faulty interpretation of the biomedical model.
- The first anthropologists in Africa were generalists, not medical anthropologists, and it seems that pollution beliefs are relatively contained within the domain of health (or health/good fortune). Witchcraft and sorcery may be more pervasive in the broader realm of social relations, including politics, economics, and religion.[4]
- They form a complex, symbol-laden whole, an understanding and decoding of which requires analysis on many levels.

Perhaps a problem in terminology has contributed to the obscurity of what I call pollution. This term is conspicuously absent between pollen analysis and poltergeist in dictionaries and encyclopedias of anthropology, at least those compiled by men (e.g., Winick 1956; Davies 1972; Hunter and Whitten 1975). However, one compiled by a woman (Seymour-Smith 1986:227–228) devotes a few hundred words to pollution, although these focus solely on India, mostly in the context of caste. Likewise, a search of the key-word "pollution" in health science databases yields information on environmental pollution in the modern, Western sense. Perhaps if there were another unambiguous and generally accepted anthropological term, the idea of pollution might appear in the literature more often.

All of the foregoing may have contributed to the marginalization or obscurity of the phenomenon of pollution in Africa, but even taken altogether they still—to me—don't fully explain how a central ethnomedical etiological concept could be so overlooked.

Are pollution ethnomedical models increasing or decreasing in importance in southern Africa? Ethnobotanist A. B. Cunningham believes that illnesses attributed to pollution are increasing with urbanization, at least among the Zulu whose ethnomedical practices he has studied extensively. He found that the largest volumes of herbal medicines for sale in Natal were enemas or emetics used in cleansing the body of pollutants encountered in the crowded, stressful, and highly competitive urban environment (Cunningham 1993 and personal communication). The implication is that pollution beliefs increase with urbanization. Cunningham believes this is because there are more opportunities for exposure to pollutants in the urban environment. We might hypothesize that, if true, this Zulu belief expresses in the idiom of pollution the epidemiologically recognized causal relationship between concentration of population and rise in infectious diseases.

Janzen (1981) reminds us that African healing systems, although they contain self-validating internal logic, are open systems amenable to change. In discussing Buxton's (1973) *Religion and Healing in Mandari*, he expresses the point well:

> The philosophy on which rests Mandari medicine has certain basic assumptions which however, do not constitute a tight unified whole. It has a number of symbolic centers, inner cores with a high degree of stability. Change of the core is very slow, and there is emotional resistance to it. However, on the periphery, new ideas and practices are adopted, checked, confirmed or rejected. Continuing attachment to symbolic centers can well be combined with acceptance on the periphery of revised extraneous elements, even including a gradual widening of the recognition of empirical causation. Folk medicine and scientific medicine then begin to exist side by side. (Janzen 1981:189)

So it may be with pollution beliefs, naturalistic infection, and environmental dangers. Perhaps ICT has become more related to empirical causation; perhaps the insect/worm theory developed this way and has merged with darkness, heat, and dirt beliefs. In any case, those involved in public health should respect the symbolic centers and adopt the idiom of pollution and naturalistic infection in attempts to reach people in culturally meaningful ways.

Janzen (1981) discusses the integration between Kongo ethnomedical and Western biomedical systems from his own fieldwork. The Kongo system has integrated elements of biomedicine in the treatment of illnesses thought to be natural. "(African diviners) are impressed with the direct cures of biomedicine for smallpox, bilharzia, sleeping sickness, parasites, malaria and others which their traditional pharmacopeia handled less well" (p. 192). But not all of these illnesses may have been regarded as natural in the past: "It is true that a host of diseases such as fevers, infections, and pathologies once dealt with in terms of human causation have now, with greater scientific knowledge in the Kongo community, come to be dealt with as natural causation" (p. 192).

We should consider also that pollution and related ICT models are inherently compatible with biomedicine in several ways and may already have been influenced by it in the adoption or at least adaptation of beliefs in microorganisms of contagion, that is, in the tiny insects or worms that carry contagious illness. Moreover, as Janzen has observed, pollution and purity are religious as well as health-related concepts, and Christian missionaries have adopted this vocabulary and, in parts of Zaire/Congo at least, equated purity with Christian "grace" (Janzen 1989:234). The rise of syncretistic Zionist churches in southern Africa—now the largest church in South Africa—and their use of the color white and other symbols of purity suggest that they are well aware of how to respect and build on the symbolic centers of existing belief systems of the majority population.

NOTES

1. Missionary and amateur anthropologist A. T. Bryant did not describe a process of pollution or ritual contamination in his book on Zulu health practices (Bryant 1966 [1909]), although these beliefs are highly developed among the Zulu.

2. Most of these theories seem to have been formulated in the 1940s or 1950s (e.g., J. D. Krige 1946; Schapera 1940).

3. I have already reviewed a number of etiological typologies by anthropologists pertaining to Africa including southern Africa, and pollution beliefs are seldom mentioned. Further exposure to the findings and theories of anthropologists and other scholars might have reinforced my mind-set that lurking beneath the most innocent explanations of illness in Africa lay superstitions about witchcraft and spirits.

4. I am indebted to Josefa Marrato for this insight.

CHAPTER THREE

RESISTANCE TO ILLNESS AND THE INTERNAL SNAKE CONCEPT[1]

Before looking at my research findings that support the hypothesis that there is a widespread yet overlooked indigenous construct explaining contagion, let us turn to a belief complex that sheds further light on pollution and related contagion beliefs and behavior.

In parts of southern and east Africa, there is an apparently widespread belief in the existence of an invisible, internal snake. It is often described as a power or force of some kind that dwells in the stomach but that can move throughout the upper body. It is designated by the local term for snake (*nyoka* in Shona and Tsonga and other languages; other variants include *Nyowa, ndjoka, ndzoka, nyoga, inyoka,* and *Nyakwadi*). Less often, a local word for worm is used, perhaps signaling a different concept. If a comprehensive treatment of this subject exists in the anthropological or related literature, I have been unable to find it. Indeed, there seems to be little published on the subject at all. Yet, the invisible snake concept appears to be both widespread and of fundamental significance for an anthropological understanding of illness causality beliefs that relate to diverse illnesses and conditions affecting both children and adults. These illnesses and conditions include diarrhea and other stomach conditions, sexually transmitted illnesses, epileptic and other convulsions, mental retardation, growth abnormalities, digestion, helminthic infections, fecundity, prenatal development and childbirth, and barrenness.

This chapter summarizes findings from my research and program experience in Mozambique and elsewhere in southern Africa (see Methodological Summary section, Chapter One), as well as findings from the literature about internal snake or worm ideas in Africa. To bring some order to such diverse findings, they are organized chronologically, the earliest first. There are some minor exceptions to this, in the interest of presenting the findings from several Mozambican societies in the same subsection. In my view, the internal snake is a cultural metaphor that reflects pollution and contagion ideas, as well as related concepts such as respect for natural bodily processes, physiological homeostasis, and resistance to disease.

I also review a number of studies from the literature, each with their own objectives and methodologies. Their findings, along with mine, are uneven in details and sometimes contradictory, a point I take up later in the chapter. Although there seems to be little literature on internal or invisible snakes, there is a fair amount from Mozambique, much of it unpublished. This country encompasses a great deal of vertical or north-south territory, cutting across a number of ethnolinguistic zones or belts. The various ethnic groups of Mozambique are closely related to groups in contiguous countries—South Africa, Swaziland, Zimbabwe, Zambia, Malawi, and Tanzania—which indicates the cultural diversity found within Mozambique. It also suggests that invisible snake beliefs found in Mozambique ought to be present among linguistically related groups in neighboring countries. Limited research findings presented below confirm this.

THE SNAKE IN THE STOMACH: SUMMARY OF FINDINGS

I have already introduced the pollution (defilement) views of the missionary and respected amateur anthropologist Henri Junod in Chapter

Two. Based on research conducted early in the twentieth century, Junod describes a condition that "might be gastritis, congestion of the liver, or dysentery" and notes:

> We should often be wholly at a loss how to prescribe were it not for the highly picturesque, and often particularly appropriate, imagery used by the patients, or by their friends, in describing the various symptoms; for instance when a sufferer from "inside trouble" says that "it bites" (*luma*), we know that it is a case of intestinal colic. But it becomes somewhat puzzling when a patient declares that he suffers from an intestinal worm which passes from his stomach into his neck and returns through his lungs, when it does not happen to take a fancy to remain in his head! (Junod 1962b [1926]:474)

In a footnote, Junod mentions the diarrhea-related syndrome *tinyokana* (sing. *nyokana*). He interprets this syndrome as "tapeworm and the lumbric," but comments that Thonga see these "little snakes" as necessary for digestion. If Western medicine drives the tapeworm out, this is bad—as illustrated by one old woman who asked for another, traditional medicine to prevent all worms from escaping. Junod comments, "Some of them must remain in her body (otherwise, quoting the woman) 'who would eat (her) food afterward'" (1962b [1926]:474).

The missionary anthropologist E. D. Earthy worked among the Lenge in Gaza, north of Junod's area in Mozambique, between 1917 and 1930. She, too, provides findings on an invisible snake, introducing the subject much as Junod did: "And here I must describe the strange concept of *Nyakwadi*":

> Inside every person lives *Nyakwadi*, in the form of a snake. *Nyakwadi* lives in front (apparently just above the abdomen). If *Nyakwadi* leaves the front and goes round to the back of a person, it is a sign that both will die. Also if *Nyakwadi*'s eyes look to the back instead of to the side of a person *Nyakwadi* dies and the person, too. (Earthy 1968 [1933]:62)

She notes further, "*Nyakwadi* . . . moulds the child from the day of its inception. . . . It is *Nyakwadi* who pushes the child out when it is ready to be born." The investigator was told that "*Nyakwadi* arranged the menses and . . . *Nyakwadi* was ruler of all body functions." Furthermore the snake is essential to life; "If a person dies his *Nyakwadi* dies and is buried with him" (Earthy 1968 [1933]:63).

Based on fieldwork among the Sotho-speaking Lovedu of the Trans-vaal (South Africa) a half-century ago, anthropologists Krige and Krige speak of an "internal snake believed to be intimately bound up with fecundity and childbirth. Every one is said to have a snake in his stomach." They continue:

> It is not a real snake, yet it is conceived of as having a head and of being able to crawl up to a man's neck (causing what we call indigestion) and running back again when he coughs. When a person has stomach-ache it is often said, "The snake is biting," while dysentery is referred to as "red" or "white snake," according to the stage of the disease. The most important function of this snake, and one that forms a common subject of con-versation in connection with barrenness, is, however, its reproductive one. It is believed that semen comes from a man's snake; if his snake is "no good," a child will not be born. The snake of a woman is sometimes identified with the womb and for conception it is necessary that this snake should accept the semen. (Krige and Krige 1943:212)

The Kriges go on to say a bit more about the internal snake as it relates to human reproduction.

In a book that seeks to identify patterns underlying health beliefs in southern Africa, W. D. Hammond-Tooke (1989:55) discusses the Kriges' findings under a heading of Traditional Ideas about Anatomy and Physi-ology, rather than in an immediately preceding section on Life Force and Personality. As I argue below, the internal or invisible snake may indeed be conceived as life force with a personality. Elsewhere, Hammond-Tooke (1989:80) suggests that "a snake in the belly" can be a distinguish-ing characteristic of witches in South Africa. This notion may come from the report of Booyens, which suggests that the Tswana of South Africa associate serious diarrheal illness with the concept of an "intestinal snake" called *kokwana*. According to Booyens (1989:11), "It is said that the snake, 'sent' to the child through witchcraft, 'eats' the child's food and the child itself." The internal snake concept that emerges here appears as something evil, a weapon of sorcery or witchcraft. Indeed, snakes occupy a place in African cosmology as witches' familiars, manifestations of ancestor and other spirits, and adjuncts to rainmaking and other rituals. This helps obscure the internal snake-pollution association for researchers.

When my colleagues and I first encountered the belief in central Mozambique of a snake that dwelt in the stomach, called *nyoka*, we were conducting ethnomedical research on child diarrhea (Green et al. 1991: 12–13; Green et al. 1993:267–268; Green et al. 1994). As we began to discuss our earliest findings with local health workers, we were told that *nyoka* represented a crude understanding on the part of uneducated people of the role of the human intestines and/or of parasitic worms that could be seen in the feces of infected people. Findings by Maina-Ahlberg (1979) and Yoder (1981) suggest that ideas of snake-like creatures in the stomach may be related to intestinal worms elsewhere in Africa. This seemed plausible, yet the traditional healers with whom we were conducting in-depth interviews specifically denied it.

Other health workers thought *nyoka* was somehow related to sorcery. Informants also denied that. (Our sample of 104 healer informants represented not only Shona speakers, but speakers of the Ndau, Manica, Sena, and Ute languages as well.) After a series of repeat interviews specifically on *nyoka*, it emerged that this snake is conceived of as an invisible force that somehow demands purity of the body it inhabits. If contaminants enter the body, the *nyoka* reacts with displeasure, causing pain and discomfort. It is referred to as if it has a personality somewhat independent of the body it inhabits; for example, it may be angry or calm. A useful English translation of the concept might therefore be Guardian of Bodily Purity. *Nyoka* may be thought of as a symbolic expression of the need to respect the human body—even as a personified immune system. We further found:

> All people are born with a *nyoka* and it remains within the body until death. *Nyoka* can move up and down in the body from the area of the heart to the abdomen. *Nyoka* is not visible, even if one cuts open a body. Its existence is confirmed through bodily sensations when it is disturbed. For example, if "dirt," spoiled food or bad medicine enters the body, *nyoka* may contract and cause cramps, or it can make noises of complaint in the stomach. *Nyoka* cleanses the body by means of diarrhea, which like menstruation is seen as a natural function of ridding the body of impurities—a view of diarrhea that conforms to current biomedical thinking. (Green et al. 1994:13)

As *nyoka* is regarded as a force that ensures purity, it was not surprising to learn that it was associated with menstruation, reflecting the common belief among Africans that menstrual blood is highly polluting. When "dirt" accumulates in a woman's body, her *nyoka* twists and turns in discomfort and irritation, which are felt in cramps that precede menstruation. Such cramps are taken as evidence that the *nyoka* is preparing to expel accumulated impurities from the body through the menstrual process.

Another focus of our ethnomedical research in central Mozambique concerned STDs, or illnesses believed associated with sexual intercourse or genito-urinary symptoms. Menstrual pollution played a role here. If a man has intercourse with a woman while she is menstruating, he becomes contaminated with the impurities her *nyoka* is in the process of expelling and he develops a disease known as *nyoka khundu*. If a man does not treat this *nyoka khundu*, not only will he remain sick, but at the moment of conceiving a child with a woman, the unborn child's *nyoka* will be negatively affected. When the child is born, it will not only have symptoms of *nyoka khundu*; it will also be susceptible to various other illnesses.

About the same time as we were conducting our fieldwork in central Mozambique, other studies in connection with two separate theses were concluded. One was on mental retardation and the other was on diarrheal disease; both were conducted primarily among Tsonga speakers in Maputo Province. Marrato (1991) and de Sousa (1991) encountered belief in a snake or worm that lived in the stomach or intestines, the movements of which related to the production of convulsions and diarrhea, as well as to mental development of the child. Fieldwork in both studies was based on in-depth, anthropological type interviews with traditional healers and their clients (mothers).

In 1992, a thesis in medical geography appeared, based on fieldwork in southern Mozambique, on the Ronga-speaking island of Inhaca (Gibbs 1992). A finding of interest here is that *nyoka* is "a basic traditional concept," explaining disease causation. *Nyoka* is said to dwell in all people. It can be bad (i.e., cause illness); yet it serves to "give life" and one cannot survive without it (p. 31). When food is eaten, the chief *nyoka* either accepts the food, "putting it toward the life-giving force within the body," or it rejects it, in which case it is converted to poison. This poison makes people ill. There is medicine that "kills the poison" and changes the *nyoka* in a way such that it stops making poison (Gibbs 1992:32).

According to Gibbs, there is belief among Ronga traditional healers that *nyoka* is related to worms that are visible when they leave the body. This is explained as the *nyoka* "becoming many" in order to make much poison. Medicine, in the form of store-bought (anthelminthic) syrup, can expel the worms. However, in the words of a diviner, echoing Junod's informant around a century earlier, "some must stay in—if they all come out you can't live" (Gibbs 1992:33). Gibbs further comments that Ronga laypersons cannot—or at least do not—give explanations such as the foregoing. They may talk in a general way about *nyokas*, but they refer more detailed questions to traditional healers, sometimes saying: "Only the *nyangas* can know such things."

My colleagues and I conducted interviews on childhood diarrhea with 109 Macua traditional healers in another northern Mozambique province, Nampula.[2] We encountered the idea of an illness-associated worm (*mihaco*) that becomes visible when expelled from the body through diarrhea or vomiting. *Mihaco* seems to have no positive (i.e., protective, health-promoting, cleansing) function; instead it provokes anemia, diarrhea, other illnesses. It "eats" or "sucks up" a person's blood and "weakens the body"; it "bites until it causes death." There was disagreement about whether everyone is born with these worms or still has them in adulthood. One healer said, "Some you are born with; others you catch from outside." Not surprisingly, the aim of therapy is to kill or expel the worm(s). Only one out of the sample of healers had a different opinion, commenting: "It is necessary to have *mihacos* in order to live. . . . There are some who only live in the stomach and do no harm."

In an ethnomedical study of seizures, loss of consciousness, and convulsions in Swaziland, Reis (1994:S40) mentions a snake in the stomach that causes convulsions by raising itself in the body. Reis notes that the Swazi interpretation of this seems to relate to a naturalistic or impersonal cause rather than a personalistic one. A study of epilepsy among Tsonga speakers of southern Mozambique that relied on traditional healer informants (Panizzo 1994) also found that an internal snake, *nyoka*, was causally involved in seizures and convulsions, and that these were related to the local illness *nyokane* (see Epilepsy section, Chapter Eight).

In 1993, I interviewed traditional healers and health workers from many parts of South Africa in connection with evaluation of a collaborative program in AIDS (Green and Zokwe 1993). I used the opportunity to do some brief interviews on internal snakes. According to my co-investigator, a Xhosa with considerable knowledge of that group's traditions, all children are born with a snake in their stomach. If a child has diarrhea or bites itself (wanting blood), it must be treated to "calm its *nyoka*." These symptoms also mean it is time to have an animal sacrificed for the child, which will let its *nyoka* know it's being recognized and appeased. Later in the life cycle, during certain ceremonies where traditional brew is being taken, one must take a little brew for one's *nyoka*. On a superficial level, *nyoka* can refer to tapeworm. "But this is the kind of distorted interpretation Xhosas might give whites" to hide their culture from probing and unsympathetic outsiders. *Nyoka* is a dangerous force until it is "developed" and calmed ("settled") and turned into a positive force of health. It is like a special soul. It has a personality.

My informant was emphatic that *nyoka* is not something bad nor something that should or could be removed. A Pedi traditional healer endorsed the foregoing description as true for the Pedi as well as the Xhosa. She maintained that Zulus understand *nyoka* in the same way, "unless they've forgotten it."

During an informal group discussion on *nyoka* involving six traditional healers (five Xhosas and one Zulu), all agreed that everyone is born with a *nyoka*. It is created at the moment a man's sperm fertilizes a woman. *Nyoka* must be "developed" in order to "nurture" it and make it calm. Zulus were said to begin to nurture the *nyoka* prenatally; Xhosas wait until the child is born. The *nyoka* tends to be reincarnated and carry traits patrilineally, therefore if a father—or even a mother—is unhealthy at the time of conception, the baby will be born unhealthy and must be treated at once. Later, if a child's fontanel is depressed, its *nyoka* is said to be thirsty. It must be given medicine to relieve the thirst. The *nyoka* may at times pull a baby's fontanel down.

According to the six South African healers, at the time of death the *nyoka* partly stays with the corpse (requiring special rituals if the person dies violently or away from home); partly becomes reincarnated; and partly becomes a fully participating and useful ancestor spirit after some 20–30 years. There seems to be a transitional period during which the *nyoka* learns how to be an ancestor spirit. In this last depiction, *nyoka* seems to resemble or be part of the "multiple soul" concept found in many parts of Africa.

Late in 1993, I trained a group of interviewers in anthropological research methods in Tanzania. The interviewers were from diverse parts of that country, yet many were familiar with a belief in an internal snake in their home areas. Some used the term *nzoka*. However, they were unsure whether the snake was essentially a destructive, negative force or something related to maintenance of one's health. This question was answered for at least one Tanzanian society when I subsequently discovered a study mentioning *nzoka* beliefs among the Sukuma in Tanzania:

> Each person was born with an *nzoka* (literally "snake") in his stomach. If he listened well to his *nzoka*, he could avoid sickness. If he was about to eat something and his *nzoka* started to grumble and growl, it was warning him that that particular food would be disagreeable. If he went ahead and ate it, the *nzoka* would have to vomit or defecate into the person's body, making the person feel sick. Some of the things an *nzoka* might object to were dirty food, leftover food, foods that should not have been mixed together. . . . The hot sun could irritate the *nzoka*, causing it to vomit poison into the person's body. Sickness was not the same in everyone because the likes and dislikes of peoples' *nzoka* differed. One man likened this to modern health beliefs by saying that modern health practitioners believed that people differ in their response to disease and treatment because of the differences in blood. The Sukuma believed, he said, it was a difference in *nzoka*. (Reid 1982:131–132)

During my fieldwork in Swaziland (1981–85 and periodically later), I overlooked the significance of the internal snake. However, from limited interviews with (nonhealer) elders in Swaziland in 1994 I learned that all children are born with worms (*tilo*) in their stomach. These grow into a snake (*inyoka*), described as a kind of invisible master of the body. *Inyoka* keeps the person healthy; one must have it to be alive ("Once it comes out you are dead"). When someone is hungry, his *inyoka* makes noise ("krrro-krrro-krrro!").[3] When taking food that does not agree with *inyoka*, it dispels it through vomit. One elder said, "It helps analyze the food and put the dirty things outside (the body). . . . The *inyoka* instructs you in what it needs." Another commented, "This *inyoka* instructs you in what it needs. Some call it appetite." Thus, in Swaziland the snake seems to represent an ethnophysiological concept of digestion and appetite, an essentially positive force.

Also in 1994, I conducted brief research focused on childhood diarrhea and STDs in Inhambane Province in southern Mozambique but north of Inhaca island and Gaza already referred to. I interviewed 7 traditional healers and participated in a week-long discussion with 33 healers in the course of a collaborative workshop. My Mozambican colleagues had just conducted interviews with local healers over a several week period. The healers spoke Tsonga or related dialects such as Chitwa or Bithonga.

According to healers in Inhambane, the most important locally recognized children's illness is *nyokani* (mentioned by Junod some 80 years earlier). A child may inherit a quality or condition from its mother and thus be born with this illness, the symptoms being foam in the baby's mouth as well as vomiting, fits, convulsions, and diarrhea. Another type of *nyokani* can result from a child being left on the ground, allowing "dirt" to enter the child via its anus. Although *nyokani* involves more symptoms than diarrhea, one healer commented, "*Nyokani* is the mother of all diarrheas." Once diagnosed, treatment of *nyokani* must begin immediately, continue for two–three weeks and be coordinated with the phases of the moon.

As the name suggests, *nyokani* is related to *nyoka*. The first is an illness, whereas the second, according to our Inhambane informants, is something that all children are born with inside them that grows as the child grows. There are said to be two *nyokas*, one male and one female. *Nyoka* may "eat the energy" of a child's food. It may provoke diarrhea, vomiting, or fatigue. One healer said traditional medicine must be given to the child to kill the male *nyoka*, which, in turn, will cause the female *nyoka* to die. Other healers described somewhat different treatment approaches, but seemed to agree that the aim of treatment is for the *nyoka* to be expelled through defecation. According to some, the purpose of the medicine is to slice the *nyoka* up into small pieces, which then come out a bit at a time and are visible. Still other healers denied there can be any external or visible evidence of *nyoka*.

After the week-long workshop for traditional healers in Inhambane, I tried to reconcile some of the apparent inconsistencies between accounts of *nyoka* among speakers of Tsonga-related dialects in southern Mozambique. Is *nyoka* a force to be nurtured and strengthened? Or is it something bad that should be killed and expelled? With these questions in mind, I interviewed two traditional healers from Inhambane who had moved to the Maputo area, one a Chopi and the other a Tsonga. They both agreed that all people are born with a *nyoka*. If it becomes disturbed, it manifests itself as the disease *nyokani*. The attacks of this illness are related to the phases of the moon. The purpose of therapy is to kill or expel the *nyoka*. However, this does not pertain to the "beneficial *nyoka*." This *nyoka* was said to be essential in the maintenance of health; indeed, a person cannot live without it. It turns bad or becomes agitated or angry if one eats food that disagrees with it. *Nyokas* have their own food preferences: "My *nyoka* might like a food that your *nyoka* hates." The Tsonga healer volunteered that "good hygiene" is needed to keep *nyoka* undisturbed. When I asked for examples, both healers said that sur-roundings, including latrines, kitchens, and cooking utensils, must be kept clean and free of flies. A *nyoka* may be happy or angry, depending on the purity and cleanliness of the body. An unhappy *nyoka* makes noises in the stomach. There is treatment to "clean out the dirt from the stomach," which pleases the *nyoka*.

I interviewed a small number of traditional healers and health workers in a Bemba-speaking area of Zambia in early 1995. I encountered belief in *nsoka*, which means snake but in the context of an entity dwelling within the stomach and seems to refer to ordinary worms—visible when outside the human body—that cause symptoms of illness. Not everyone has these worms. Those who do, suffer from an illness called *insokanda*, believed caused by eating impure food or drinking dirty water although it can sometimes be caused by sorcery. It is considered contagious. Bemba healers provide medicines to expel the *nsoka* and thereby cure *insokanda*.

Finally, a study from Ethiopia was published in 1998 on worm/snake beliefs among the Sidama, a Cushitic-speaking people in southern Ethiopia. The basic Sidama concept of *hamosho* is described as follows:

A fundamental Sidama concept postulates that every human being is born with *hamasho* and that a man born without *hamasho* cannot survive. The main function of *hamasho* is to digest food, which is thought to be carried out through five main states: (1) receive food that reaches the stomach; (2) crush it into a fine poultice; (3) separate good and bad food substances; (4) transmit nutrients to heart, liver, and lungs; and (5) pass the rest to the lower intestines to be later transformed into excreta and evacuated. The digestive properties of *hamasho* are considered vital. (Vecchiato 1998:254)

When *hamosho* is "satisfied" by being fed good-quality food, digestion proceeds normally; "conversely, an unhappy or famished *hamosho* will rebel and cause ill health" (Vecchiato 1998:255). As with *nyoka* beliefs, Sidama consider stomach cramps, diarrhea, and gas pains to be manifestations of *hamosho*'s displeasure. Although this description, which derives in part from ethnographic interviews with traditional healers, makes no specific mention of pollution concepts, we see parallels with *nyoka* concepts of purity (of food), personification of an internal snake/worm, and the need to satisfy and keep alive a stomach-dwelling creature so that it can perform life-sustaining functions.

SUMMARY OF SNAKE FINDINGS AND DISCUSSION

Based on published and unpublished sources, and on my own fieldwork, belief in an internal snake can be found along a strip of southern and east Africa extending at least from the southern cape of South Africa (Xhosa) to Ethiopia in the north. Janzen (1989:243) suggests that this generally coastal area may represent a meaningful cultural area, somewhat distinct in health beliefs and ritual practice from other Bantu-speaking zones. No doubt a more exhaustive literature search would unearth additional references and a more accurate map could be constructed. For example, the worm or snake ethnophysical concept has been noted in the Congo (Yoder 1981:239; Janzen, personal communication).

There may be significant belief differences among societies in southern Africa about the nature of the internal snake. Researchers need to determine if the internal snake is conceived as a positive force, a neutral ethnophysiological concept, an expression of witchcraft, or something that may be both positive and harmful, depending on conditions. Other questions include: Must one always have one or more snakes in the body to remain alive? Is the snake essential to life and health—or is it a consumer of vital energy and/or a major source of illness? When the snake relates to the objective of therapy, is the aim to: (1) kill or expel it or "cut it into pieces"; (2) strengthen or nourish it; or (3) "calm" or "cool" it? Are there medicines to strengthen the *nyoka* of children? Is the concept related to purity or pollution-prevention? Future research should determine whether any differences in beliefs are actual or due to differences in research methods and resulting data validity, to institutionalized prevarication (as my Xhosa informant suggests), or to varying levels of causal explanations.

According to my own and others' findings, traditional healers may give deeper, more detailed explanations than do laypeople regarding complex concepts such as *nyoka*. The topic might be guarded or taboo. Earthy (1968 [1933]:63) wrote of the Valenge: "The young people are not usually taught about *Nyakwadi*, though they overhear their elders talking."

In Reis's Swazi study, patients of traditional healers were found to be less certain than healers in their explanations of causes of seizures, although they offered "the same variation in etiological concepts" (Reis 1994:S40). This argues for anthropological, rather than survey, methods and specifically for in-depth interviews with traditional healers.

Returning to the internal snake, although researchers such as Booyens and Hammond-Tooke have suggested this is related to witch-craft, it appears to be quite the opposite for most (but not all) of the societies reviewed. The internal snake emerges as a positive, albeit dangerous, force. Reviewing the essential qualities of the internal snake in many of the societies for which we have information, we see it is a force that performs vital digestion functions; it requires cleanliness and purity of body; it reacts to the introduction of dirt or impure, spoiled foods by provoking various bodily discharges such as diarrhea and vomiting as well as grumbling in the stomach; it guards the body against impurities or what Shona healers called "contamination"; and it requires clean surroundings external to the body.

My hypothesis is that the internal snake is conceived as a protective life force when it is invisible under all circumstances; it is an ethno-physiological concept related to digestion and stomach disorder when it is conceived as a worm (less often, a snake or grown-up worm) that becomes visible outside the human body. These two roles are not mutually exclusive since even as a protective life force, the invisible snake seems to regulate diet and digestion.

CLEANING OUT THE BODY

I have already metnioned Hammond-Tooke's (1989:93) observation that where we find use of enemas and emetics, we are probably dealing with pollution beliefs. This seems a reasonable hypothesis, so let us consider these practices among the Zulu—which he singles out—as well as other groups in the region.

Enemas and emetics are used by the Zulu for a wide range of conditions, including diarrhea and stomach disorders, menstrual problems, barrenness, chest problems, nausea, general debility, and/or "body pain believed to result from excessive accumulation of gall . . ." (Ngubane 1977:107–108). Medical missionary A. T. Bryant, working among Zulus at the turn of the last century, reported that treatment of malaria was "with emetics and purgatives" in order to "rid the system of its excessive accumulation of bile" (1966 [1909]:54).

Based on fieldwork on the 1930s, Hoernlé (1946 [1937]), reported that Zulus make a broad distinction between "(black medicines), which are very powerful and work mostly as purgatives . . . (and are) thought to take away the 'blackness,' the evil . . . ," and "white medicines, which are soothing and purifying in their effects and are always used to settle the body after the use of the black medicines" (p. 229). Recall that *umnyama*, "blackness" (or "darkness"), is the Zulu code word for pollution (Ngubane 1977).

I have already mentioned the ethnobotanical survey of traditional herbal medicines sold in Natal, a predominantly Zulu area, in which it was found that

> The largest volumes of herbal medicines for sale . . . were the four major categories of mixed species: *ubulawu* (1,966 bags/yr), *intelezi* (1,924 bags/yr), *ikhubalo* (1,883 bags/yr), and *imbiza* (1,211 bags/yr. (All of these) are used in cleansing the body of "pollutants" encountered in the crowded, stressful and highly competitive urban environment through enemas . . . or emetics. (Cunningham 1993 and personal communication)

Cunningham notes, "A valuable feature of market surveys is that they provide a record of health concerns unbiased by reluctance on the part of respondents or patients to reveal what they might be reluctant to discuss with staff of a hospital" (personal communication). It is rare to have this sort of ethnobotanical corroboration for hypotheses pertaining to ethnomedical beliefs; data of this sort for the other societies we are considering would be most useful.

Based on my five years of fieldwork in Swaziland between 1981 and 1992, I found enemas and emetics used widely among the Swazi for diarrheal and other stomach-centered illness (for prevention as well as treatment), including ridding the body of "bile"; for sexually transmitted illness such as *gcunsula* (probably syphilis), *idrop* (probably gonorrhea), *imbune, lugola, tilonza,* and *timvilapo*; to prepare a woman for childbirth; to cleanse impurities from an initiate diviner-medium in order to prepare for revelatory dreams, visions, and spirit possession (see Janzen 1989:233); and to treat a variety of illness such as madness (*tilwane*), poisoning (*sidliso*), harmful spells (e.g., *umklwebho*), bilharzia (*umthundungati*), sterility, impotence, headaches, and influenza.

Even "Zionist" Christian faith healers (*baprofeti*) may use holy water to administer enemas. Some prominent traditional healers list enemas (*kucatseka*) and purgatives (*kuhlanta*) as being generally their most common treatment method. Yet these practices are not only in the hands of traditional healers; Swazis appear to rely often on purgative self-treatment for common conditions. Washing the external body with special purifying medicines, a process known as *kugeza*, is another commonly used method of treatment related to pollution/purity beliefs (Green 1992).

What of the relative importance of witchcraft and pollution beliefs in Swaziland? I have written about this:

> The concepts of purity and contamination appear central in diarrheal disease. Of two major forms of serious child diarrhea, *kuhabula* is believed caused by contamination when a ritually unprotected child inhales dangerous medicinal vapors; and *umphezulu* results from the exposure of the pregnant mother to mystical environmental contaminants. One less common form of *umphezulu* is due to a type of sorcery that relies on physical contact—a type of contamination—of a pregnant women with deliberately placed harmful medicines. In all cases of *umphezulu*, the immediate cause of the diarrhea is in utero contamination of the child due to circumstances affecting its mother. (Green 1985:280–281; Green et al. 1994:17)

The Tsonga and Batwa also administer enemas and emetics for diarrhea and other children's illness such as *chicuna* and *zombo*. In such cases, my healer informants in Inhambane Province, Mozambique, report that they must first "remove the dirt" from the child's stomach with an enema, and then restore the child's strength with another medicine. A frequently encountered ultimate cause of childhood diarrhea is adultery, a belief found in many parts of Africa (Hogle and Prins 1991a). Either the father commits adultery and then touches the child, thereby passing contamination in the form of "heat" to the child; or the mother commits adultery and passes "contaminated breast milk" to the child through nursing. Purgative teas may also be used for childhood diarrheas. Tsonga healers further report that the dirt of a sexually transmitted illness such as *chicasameti* can be passed to another person during intercourse, unless first removed by enema.

Turning to the Shona of Mozambique, they appear not to rely on enemas and emetics, Hammond-Tooke's measure of the importance of pollution beliefs, in treating diarrheal disease. But pollution beliefs seem clearly to predominate over witchcraft beliefs in two presumably representative areas of ethnomedicine: diarrheal and sexually transmitted illness. During two months of data gathering in Manica Province, Mozambique, my colleagues and I only encountered one type of diarrheal illness whose etiology involved an evil or avenging spirit. There were likewise only one or two references to witchcraft in descriptions of the more serious diarrheas. The great majority of diarrheal illness was attributed to naturalistic causes, especially pollution (Green et al. 1994: 17). In any case, we only asked about purgatives and emetics in connection with diarrhea. Gelfand et al. (1985:85–86, 94) list a number of purgative and emetic herbs used by the neighboring Shona of Zimbabwe, in association with a range of illnesses.

Sexually transmitted illnesses (STIs) seem to be interpreted by Shona speakers in ways similar to diarrheal disease. Shona traditional healers recognize two broad categories of STIs: *siki* and *nyoka*-related conditions. The former seem to correspond with the more serious common STDs of Western biomedicine—syphilis, gonorrhea, chlamydia, and chancroid—and are believed to be caused by a common invisible, microscopic agent (*khoma*), or by direct contact with genital discharges that contain *khoma*. *Khoma* is conceptualized as a type of dirt that is contagious. This dirt can, for example, be "eaten" by a fetus in the womb and cause death of the fetus. Some healers treat *siki* by removing and burying the illness; when a person later passes over the spot where it is buried, he or she can become contaminated. *Nyoka*-related illnesses seem to include less serious, perhaps self-limiting, genito-urinary infections. These are also understood in terms of traditional ideas of pollution, as might be expected from their association with the Guardian of Bodily Purity (Green et al. 1993:261).

Earlier I noted that Shona speakers in Zimbabwe seem to attribute many illnesses to natural causes and that they use many purgative and emetic herbal medicines (Gelfand et al. 1985:85–86, 94).

The Tsonga and related groups of Mozambique use enemas and emetics for diarrhea and other children's illness such as *chicuna* and *zombo*. In such cases, my healer informants in Inhambane Province, Mozambique, report that they must first "remove the dirt" from the child's stomach with an enema, and then restore the child's strength with another medicine.

These findings suggest that there is a relationship between use of enemas and emetics and presence and importance of pollution beliefs. There may be other indicators, for example, belief in an invisible, internal snake. Since there is so little about invisible snakes in the anthropological literature—and none that I know of in the public health literature—I close this chapter by offering the following hypotheses that emerge from the findings just presented:

1. Belief in an invisible, internal snake that protects the body it inhabits against impurity is a major expression, metaphor, or symbol of pollution belief. The presence of such belief is an indicator of the importance of pollution beliefs in that society.
2. If a guardian-type snake concept is found to be associated with a particular illness, the illness is probably related to pollution rather than to witchcraft, sorcery, spirits, or even natural causes.
3. The internal snake is conceived as a life force when it is invisible under all circumstances; it is an ethnophysiological concept related to digestion and stomach disorder when it is conceived as a worm (less often, a snake) that becomes visible outside the human body.

Finally, we might ask why a snake would emerge as a major symbol to express pollution beliefs? Based on her analysis of Beng (Ivory Coast) culture, symbolic anthropologist Alma Gottlieb suggested:

Certain distinguishing anatomical features of snakes suggest a liminal, "betwixt-and-between" status. These include their lack of limbs, their annual shedding of skin, and their fluid, slithering movements. Moreover, snakes are the one type of forest creature that do in fact move regularly from forest to village and back again. . . . We can hypothesize that the combination of these features makes snakes appropriate for carrying the symbolic weight of punishing transgressors against symbolic boundary maintenance. (1992:39–40)

Victor Turner also comments on the appropriateness of the snake in symbolizing liminal status, noting that "the snake appears to die, but only sheds its old skin and appears in a new one." It is this characteristic of "undoing, dissolution, decomposition . . . accompanied by processes of growth, transformation, and the reformulation of old elements in new patterns" that links snakes symbolically with people in marginal, liminal states (1967:99, 1987:9).

NOTES

1. Much of the material in this chapter appeared in Green (1997).

2. See Murdock's description of the "Yao cluster," summarized in Chapter One, for a quick ethnographic overview of the Macua (Murdock 1959:290–306). For more recent and detailed ethnographic background on the Macua, see Baptista (1989) and Martinez (1989).

3. A century earlier, an elderly Thonga described one of the sounds of *nyoka* as, "Pfie . . . pfie!" (Junod 1962b [1926]:474).

CHAPTER FOUR

CHILDHOOD DIARRHEA[1]

Indigenous beliefs about childhood diarrhea were introduced in a summary way in the last chapter. This chapter covers the findings of some applied research related to childhood diarrhea that I directed in two provinces in Mozambique, Manica and Nampula, as well as some unpublished findings from a survey in Zambia. I also examine indigenous beliefs related to the causes of diarrhea within the broader framework of analysis of ICT. Finally, I discuss the relevance of the ICT construct in light of evidence related to childhood diarrhea from elsewhere in Africa.

The main research objective of my colleagues and me in Mozambique was to discover and illuminate indigenous knowledge of diarrheal disease and the underlying explanatory theories that give meaning to what people observe when children become ill (Yoder 1991:46). We wanted to use these emic, explanatory models to: (1) develop health communications strategies with which to communicate preventive and promotive health messages; (2) develop ways to introduce recommendations likely to be accepted; and (3) make appropriate use of existing community resources, especially traditional healers (see Weiss 1988).

We attempted to discover explanatory models of childhood diarrhea through interviews with traditional healers. Some healers felt constrained by their empowering spirits not to reveal secret information to interviewers. We found that individual, in-depth interviews were the best way to overcome inhibitions and suspicions, especially when the purpose of the interviews was understood and approved by most healers.

Our main programmatic objective was to decrease morbidity and mortality from dehydration due to childhood diarrhea through promotion of oral rehydration. A basic premise of this collaborative program was that diarrhea/dehydration prevention efforts can take advantage of the prestige, credibility, widespread availability, and authority of traditional healers to promote behavior change and the adoption of new technology such as oral rehydration solution (ORS) among those who consult healers for diarrhea and related children's health problems.

BACKGROUND TO THE GEMT PROGRAM

At the time of Mozambique's independence from Portugal in 1975, the new government, led by the Frelimo party, embarked on a radical program to transform the country's economy and society as quickly as possible. Its goal was to create a modern, nontribal, nonracial, equitable nation, through "scientific socialism." The "traditionalism" of the various ethnolinguistic groups were thought of as obstacles to progress. Accordingly, there was an attempt to abolish traditional practices such as bride-price (*lobola*), polygamy, initiation rites, land tenure, and traditional healing practices. Traditional healers, spirit mediums, and cult leaders were discouraged—sometimes arrested, executed, or punished in other ways—as purveyors of "obscurantism" and superstition. Many went underground or simply continued to exercise power informally and behind the backs of government officials. Chiefs and other indigenous political leaders were also suppressed. The alienation of traditional and ritual leaders and healers was a significant factor in Frelimo's loss of political control of most of the geographic area of Mozambique (Hanlon 1990).

Until recently, policy decisions and program planning related to health and other sectors in Mozambique were made at the national level, then imposed from above on unquestioning provincial and district authorities, and ultimately on rural villagers or on the many dislocated people living in camps or periurban areas. This top-down approach meant that health programs were often ill-suited to the cultural or physical realities of Mozambicans, especially rural folk. It also had the effect of undermining self-reliance and fostering dependency.

Beginning in the mid-1980s, there was growing awareness within the ranks of the Mozambique government that ideology had led it to underestimate the power of tradition—indeed of culture. It did not go unnoticed that some of the early success of the rebel group Renamo could be attributed to its ability to manipulate traditional beliefs in such a way that people believed Renamo had won the approval of ancestor spirits as well as magical protection from local spirit-mediums (Wilson 1992). (Another reason for the group's success was the sheer ferocity and barbarity of its attacks on the civilian population.) By the 5th Frelimo Party Congress (1989), the government formally recognized the mistakes it had made in its zeal to radically transform Mozambican society. It looked for ways to ways to make itself more popular with the masses, especially since the multiparty elections held in 1994.

Late in 1990, I was asked by the Department of Traditional Medicine (or GEMT, to use the Portuguese acronym), a small unit within the Mozambique Ministry of Health, to help develop a policy regarding that country's traditional healers, and to advise on any necessary legislative modification. There was no legal recognition of healers by the Frelimo government, nor was there any program of cooperation or collaboration with the exception of some informal, uncoordinated local-level efforts on the part of a few health workers. On the contrary, intersectoral relations were among the worst in Africa. After making some policy and legislative recommendations, and with the support of my colleagues in the GEMT, I suggested that the government, through the Ministry of Health, demonstrate its new intentions by supporting a pilot collaborative program involving traditional healers.

It was not known what percentage of the population rely on traditional healers for childhood diarrhea treatments, in part because there had been virtually no rural-based surveys in the previous 15 years. Many Africanists accept 80% as a fair estimate of the proportion of sub-Saharan African populations that relies on traditional healers, even if many also visit hospitals (WHO 1976; Bichmann 1979; Oyebolo 1981). In Mozambique, the proportion may be higher because of the destruction by

Renamo insurgents of the government's rural health infrastructure (World Bank 1989).

Preliminary census work by the GEMT in Maputo and Manica Provinces suggested a traditional healer:population ratio of roughly 1:200. This estimate is comparable to those made elsewhere in Africa: 1:287 for Uganda (Hogle and Prins 1991b:29); 1:234, 1:575, or 1:260 for Zimbabwe (Gelfand et al. 1985); 1:200 for Lagos State, Nigeria (Green 1989); 1:100 for rural and urban Swaziland (Green and Makhubu 1984:1073); 1:407 (rural) or 1:280 (urban) for Ghana (Wondergem et al. 1989:24); roughly 1:200 for two periurban areas of Mozambique (Maputo and Manica Provinces) (Jurg et al. 1991); "conservative estimates" of 1:375 and 1:454 for two Dar es Salaam neighborhoods (Swantz 1990:13) and 1:60 for periurban Senegal (Fassin and Fassin 1988:354). With a national population of about 16 million, Mozambique should have approximately 80,000 healers. The physician: population ratio in Mozambique is about 1:50,000, with some 52% of doctors concentrated in the capital city. It was recognized that cooperation with traditional healers could greatly extend government outreach to the rural population (Green et al. 1991).

Based partly on these statistics, the GEMT developed a plan for a collaborative program between the National Health Service and indigenous healers. Research was conducted in Manica Province in 1991 with focus on childhood diarrheal disease and sexually transmitted disease, including AIDS. One goal was to gather information adequate to develop culturally appropriate communication between government and traditional healers to improve intersectoral cooperation in disease prevention and treatment. Another goal was to show the value of rapid ethnomedical research to develop health education and public health interventions.

Diarrhea was an initial focus area of the program because it was and is a high-priority health concern and there seemed to be potential to have substantial health impact in the short to medium term. Moreover, there had been fruitful collaboration between modern and traditional health sectors in childhood diarrhea elsewhere in Africa (Green 1985; Hoff and Maseko 1986; Warren 1982, 1986, 1989; Tahzib 1988; Anokbonggo et al. 1990). One reason for selecting Manica Province for the model program is that the Beira Corridor (a narrow strip surrounding the highway from the port city of Beira to the Zimbabwe border) was relatively secure, allowing interviewers access to rural areas. Furthermore, traditional healers seemed relatively well organized in that province, greatly facilitating communication and the practical logistics of organizing a collaborative program.

The approach at the GEMT in the initial pilot area, and in several areas since, can be outlined as follows: We began with ethnomedical research focused on illness related to diarrhea. After reviewing and analyzing our findings, we sought to identify any common ground already existing between indigenous healing and biomedicine. We tried to build on this by finding the "fit" between what exists and what we wished to promote in the interest of public health. Our approach was to build on existing beliefs and practices, rather than to ignore or confront them.

Once research provided an ethnomedical base of information and common ground had been identified, and specific areas of existing beliefs and behavior had been targeted for encouragement or discouragement, we developed a communication strategy[2] that embodied these elements.

Our research methods are described in the Methodological Summary, Chapter One. They were basically semistructured, open-ended interviews and focus group discussions with traditional healers. Typical of applied research associated with international health programs, time and financial constraints limited us to methods characteristic of rapid assessment procedures or strategies (Scrimshaw and Hurtato 1987; Cernea 1990; Yoder 1991) or rapid ethnographic assessment (Bentley et al. 1988).

Recall from Chapter One that the Shona/Thonga cluster occupies a geographical position between the Central Bantu to the north and west, and the Nguni to the south (Murdock 1959:374–380). Healers in our sample came from several ethnolinguistic groups related to the Shona language (chiShona): chiUte, chiNdau, chiManica, and chiSena. To simplify, I refer to Shona-speaking healers in this chapter. Two basic types of specialists were found, the herbalist and the diviner-medium. The latter also uses herbs but additionally works closely with ancestral and other spirits believed to assist in diagnosis, in determining treatment, and in treatment itself. Many healers professed specialties in both areas and so may use two or more names to describe their specialties.

LOCAL DIARRHEA TAXONOMIES

A variety of illnesses characterized by frequent, loose, watery stools were described by Manica healers. The illnesses were said to be very common, especially among children. Focus group participants cited between two and four of the locally recognized diarrheas—including those with symptoms biomedically recognized as dehydration—as the most common serious health problems afflicting children in the area. The focus of individual interviews was on childhood diarrheas.

On the basis of the interviews, we created composite profiles of several locally recognized diarrheal diseases. While the profiles are useful in obtaining an overview of the diseases, it must be recognized that they mask conceptional differences between language groups, areas, and individual practitioners. The differences add to the difficulty of designing a health communication strategy involving healers—indeed a fair amount of focus group time was devoted to clearing up differences and finding points of agreement among the healers themselves. Healers in Manica, as elsewhere in Africa, do not ordinarily share secret knowledge with other healers. This means that they may never have been exposed to anything like a composite profile of locally recognized diseases in their own areas, and they may disagree with details of symptoms or recommended treatments. The spelling of all terms in local dialects of chiShona relies on the Portuguese orthography used by interviewers.

Manyoka

Manyoka is a general term for diarrhea. If the term is unqualified, it refers to the simple, common, nondangerous type. *Nyoka kusorora* refers specifically to simple diarrhea. It is a condition of both children and adults and it is believed caused by eating bad food or drinking bad water. It may also be associated with the rainy season, playing in a dirty area, bad hygiene, flies that alight from mangoes, "bad eating habits," and "bad hygiene." In children, additional causes offered include giving a young child coarse-grained porridge or too much water.

Healers began discussions of *manyoka* by referring to a snake (*nyoka*, singular of *manyoka*) believed to inhabit the sufferer's stomach. As discussed in Chapter Three, the *nyoka* reacts to dirt or impurities introduced into the body by causing diarrhea, which flushes the dirt out of the body. Various qualifiers were added to the general term *nyoka* to denote specific diarrheal illnesses. *Manyoka ekufambissa* is associated with a child cutting its first teeth. *Nyoka dzo kusorora* was said to be caused by neglect of tradition. *Manyoka kuhambisa asinadriru* seemed to involve an avenging spirit entering a child to seek compensation for a past homicide committed by a kinsman. However, most explanations for simple diarrhea seemed naturalistic.

During discussions of *manyoka*, more serious symptoms—such as vomiting, blood in diarrhea, appetite loss, or constant thirst—were sometimes described. Used in this sense, *manyoka* probably does not denote simple diarrhea but is instead a generic reference to all diarrheas. The causes of such *manyoka* syndromes usually go beyond food and hygiene and refer to "contamination," taboo violation, or other such causes.

Phiringaniso

The diarrhea was described as frequent and watery in this children's illness. There may be vomiting, sunken fontanel, and dry, wrinkled skin. The cause of this illness was attributed to violation of the norms of sexual behavior. It usually seems to be provoked by a man having extramarital intercourse while his child is still breastfeeding, then coming home and touching his child before washing. The child becomes "contaminated" and soon after exhibits watery diarrhea. The mother might also cause this diarrhea in her child by having extramarital sexual relations. In both cases, the more immediate cause of the symptoms is the disturbed *nyoka*. *Phiringaniso* was described as being different from and more serious than diarrheas resulting from bad food or water.

Chinhamukaka

The main symptoms of *chinhamukaka* are whitish, milky diarrhea frequently accompanied by vomiting. The vomit may also be milky. This illness was said to occur in the summer, and some healers related it to a child's exposure to heat. Some informants mentioned depressed fontanel, sunken eyes, skin that has lost elasticity, and lack of urine production—all dehydration symptoms according to biomedicine. Its cause is said to be a mother stepping in milk expressed from the breast of a woman who has had a miscarriage. The mother's breast milk becomes contaminated, and she passes this on to her nursing child, who develops diarrhea. Several other causes were described (e.g., a child being exposed to "heat," either directly by the sun or via "hot" or contaminated breast milk; a child drinking too much water; a child drinking breast milk when its mother is pregnant again; a child ingesting "dirt"; or a child's *nyoka* being disturbed). Some healers cited more than one cause.

Chikahara

This term appears to be used to refer either to an illness or simply to the symptom of a depressed fontanel in a child. In any case, *chikahara* denotes, or is identified by, a sunken fontanel. Another dehydration symptom associated with this syndrome may be a sunken roof of the mouth. There may be high fever as well. However, most healers seemed not to associate the fontanel symptom with diarrhea, a common phenomenon in traditional medical systems worldwide. Still, *chikahara* was recognized as being life threatening. Children were said to be born with this illness. The immediate cause of sunken fontanel was said to be the child's *nyoka* contracting or pulling downward, which also pulls down the fontanel. The *nyoka*'s action is considered a reaction to contamination, or pollution.

Chikamba

Symptoms of *chikamba* include greenish diarrhea and a lump or pain in the left side of a child's waist. Healers in two of three districts cited depressed fontanel as a primary symptom; some believed *chikamba* unrelated to diarrhea. A child is believed to be born with *chikamba*. The ultimate cause is that one of the parents slept with a partner outside of the marriage. If it is the father, and he sleeps with his wife before purifying himself, his semen will carry a contaminating agent to his wife's womb. The woman's next child will be born with this contamination and will eventually fall ill. As an inherited illness, *chikamba* is not considered contagious.

Ntsanganiko

Symptoms of *ntsanganiko* include chronic diarrhea mixed or streaked with blood, weight loss, and fever. As noted by Nichter (1991), indigenous terms for bloody diarrhea exist in many cultures, and usually refer to dysentery. *Ntsanganiko* is almost always a child's illness. Newborns are said to die within two–three days if it is not treated. Like *phiringaniso*, *ntsanganiko* is said to be provoked by the behavior of the

114

parents of a child, in this case failure to perform funeral rituals for a family member. Some healers commented that such failure is an example of Mozambicans trying to act "too modern." A second explanation held that if a nonkin person visits someone where there has been a death within the family, the visitor should take preventive medicine to combat contamination from the death. Failure to do so results in members of the visitor's family falling ill with *ntsanganiko*. A diviner-medium commented wistfully that many traditions are neglected nowadays and that hospital medicine cannot treat conditions that result from such neglect.

Kuamwissira

This is a childhood diarrhea provoked by nursing a child with milk believed to be spoiled or contaminated by a mother's new pregnancy. Some healers described the diarrhea as milky or mucousy. Some mentioned the dehydration symptom of dry, wrinkled skin.

Nyongo

Children with *nyongo* are said to have greenish or very white eyes, in addition to the symptom of diarrhea. There is also brown mucous in their vomit. It is often seen during spring when many green leaves are eaten. Another cause is when fear becomes "stuck in the child's stomach." In the latter case, a healer gives medicine to make the child vomit.

Other Syndromes

Occasional mention was also made of "simple diarrhea" and cholera, using their Portuguese names. These names were recorded only near the provincial capital, Chimoio. Cholera was described as a serious type of diarrhea characterized by vomiting and diarrhea, and perhaps by pain and "heat in the stomach." Its cause was said to be spirits bringing bad luck or revenge. Its treatment was similar to other diarrheas and involves cutting roots, boiling them in water, and giving the decoction to drink.

DISCUSSION

By the standards of indigenous African medicine, Manica healers recognize a relatively large number of childhood diarrheas. By comparison, there are only three major types of childhood diarrhea (including fontanel syndrome) in Swaziland (Green 1985), five among the Baganda (Hogle and Prins 1991b), and five in Lubumbashi, Zaire (Yoder et al. nd). Few societies anywhere appear to exceed eight ethnomedical categories of diarrhea (Yoder 1991:49).

According to some (but not all) Manica healers, the aim of treatment in common or simple diarrhea is to stop the symptom of diarrhea, whereas in all more serious syndromes such as *chinamukaka, phiringaniso, chikahara,* and *chikamba,* the aim of treatment is to "calm the *nyoka*" of the sufferer. Others claim that all diarrheas should be stopped, although some note that the best way to accomplish this is to calm the *nyoka*. Stopping the diarrhea appears inconsistent with the belief that diarrhea serves the useful purpose of ridding the body of impurities or "contamination." That medicines are used with this avowed purpose probably reflects healers' ambivalence toward the symptom of diarrhea: It is good that impurities are leaving the body, yet diarrhea is dangerous. The same ambivalence can be found in modern biomedicine. Diarrhea is seen as flushing toxins from the body, yet a variety of largely ineffective remedies intended to stop diarrhea by retarding peristalsis still are used and are even recommended by pharmacists and prescribed by doctors.

Little variation was found in the basic approach to treating diarrhea, either between healers, by ethnolinguistic group, or by specific type of diarrhea. Herbs (usually roots, the part of a plant most commonly used in southern Africa) are boiled to make decoctions or cold-water solutions, then given as teas. A decoction might be mixed with porridge and given to a child. Some treatments also involve rituals intended to reconcile an adulterer with his or her spouse, to decontaminate a mother's milk, or— infrequently mentioned—to expel harmful spirits. A major difference between traditional and modern treatments is that the former attempts to go beyond symptomatic cure and uses a form of sociotherapy to rectify a problem in family relations that may be viewed as the underlying cause of a child's illness. Since these deeper causes often relate to correct and moral behavior of the parents, and since improvements in these areas probably contribute to domestic harmony, we viewed ritual treatment as holistic treatment complementary to symptomatic therapy.

One intended effect of herbal treatments is to stop or "slow" the diarrhea. The herbs may contain tannins, which retard peristalsis in the bowel. Purgatives and enemas seem not to be used for diarrhea. One healer explained that there is no need to increase the flow of diarrhea by putting more liquids in the child's mouth or by performing an enema. As mentioned in Chapters One and Two, the use of enemas and emetics can be taken as a measure of the presence, and perhaps importance, of pollution beliefs.

Dietary and water restrictions during childhood diarrhea episodes are often said to have "serious health consequences" in Africa (see, e.g., Ekanem and Akitoye 1990). Manica healers claimed not to give much specific dietary advice regarding the sick child. Since the quality and purity of a mother's milk is of such importance in locally recognized diarrheas, healers are more inclined to give dietary advice to mothers, for example, avoiding bitter food or alcoholic beverages while their child has *manyoka*. For the older sick child, most healers seem to advise maintaining normal levels of feeding.

However, some nutritional and general advice seems to be of considerable negative health consequence, especially if it reflects the beliefs and actual practices of mothers of children with diarrhea. For example, healers often advise mothers to allow less food and liquid into the child because—as several noted—the less that goes in, the less comes out in diarrhea. For this reason, healers were nearly unanimous in prescribing only small amounts of fine-grained, nonwatery porridge for children with diarrhea. Porridges are made from sorghum for babies during their first six months, and maize for older babies, or when sorghum is not available. Other porridges are used as vehicles for introducing herbal medicines into the child. They are made from the same grains but are relatively dry and only small portions are given. There seems to be a notion that these porridges "clean" or wash out the child's insides.

Most healers said they do not ordinarily give water to children in the first four months, and they are sparing with liquids when medicinal herbs are given. Some healers specifically mentioned that water is bad for infants—or for older babies in more than very small quantities. In his study of childhood diarrhea among Tsonga speakers in southern Mozambique, de Sousa (1991:77) found that mothers "drastically reduce water intake" of children with diarrhea. Still, a few Manica healers reported giving or recommending rice water as a remedy for diarrhea.

Most healers also spoke of a traditional prohibition against giving salt to a child before the eighth month, or before its first teeth appear. Salt was believed to be harmful to babies, even to contaminate them. Some

117

healers said that salt interferes with traditional medicines; others claimed that the ancestors forbid salt for young children. Our interviewers did not follow up on the notion of salt contaminating, but further to the south, de Sousa (1991:78–79) encountered the belief among Tsonga-speaking healers and mothers alike that salt "absorbs" misfortune and the contamination of death. In any case, prohibition against salt for babies greatly complicates attempts to promote adding sugar or salt to drinks or porridges already in use, for homemade rehydration. Only a very few Shona healers claimed they added a small amount of sugar and salt, sometimes with lemon juice, to porridges intended for children with diarrhea.

In another finding related to both diet and infants' immunity to infections, a mother's colostrum appears to be regarded as dirty (a possible code term for pollution) or spoiled and bad for the nursing infant; therefore, it is discarded. The infant does not nurse until the mother's breast is "cleaned" and cleaner-appearing milk emerges. Only one relatively better-educated healer claimed that colostrum was good for babies because it was "full of vitamins." It should be noted that aversion to colostrum is common in many developing countries (Edgerton 1992).

Traditional healers in Manica did not recognize a syndrome equivalent to what modern biomedicine calls dehydration. Many individual symptoms of dehydration were recognized, but not necessarily in association with diarrhea. A depressed fontanel in a child is biomedically recognized as a sign of dehydration. Kay (1993) calls the sunken fontanel syndrome culturally interpreted rather than culture bound and provides names for this in a couple of dozen widespread languages. We encountered various names for sunken fontanel, the most common being *chikahara* or *chipande*.

Beliefs expressed about this syndrome by Manica healers in individual interviews included, in order of frequency: It is a symptom of the disease *chikamba*; it is a sign of *any* serious illness; it is something that provokes diarrhea or fever; it is something unrelated to diarrhea; it means that the pulse can be felt in a child's chest, and this is a signal that death is approaching; it is a sign that the *nyoka* is pulling inward and downward; and it is a symptom accompanying serious diarrhea. It became apparent during focus group discussions that virtually all healers agree that a child's *nyoka* can and does pull the fontanel inward or downward. However, a healer might not volunteer such information in an interview

118

context, depending on the wording of a question and on whether the person inquiring seems to the healer to understand and sympathize with the concept of *nyoka*.

Sunken eyes, dry skin or skin that has lost elasticity, and lack of urine production are other dehydration symptoms that are linked with *phiringaniso* or *chinamukaka*, and not necessarily with the fontanel syndrome.

"Lack of blood" and "lack of water" (in Portuguese: *falta de sangue, falta de agua*) are concepts that arose in discussions with healers in the context of childhood diarrhea (see Pillsbury [1978:126–127] for discussion of similar concepts in North Africa). Although the former might seem to refer to anemia, the two phrases appear to mean the same thing for most healers. They refer to a condition that occurs when all traditional methods have failed and a child still has diarrhea. The child then develops symptoms such as whiteness of palms and soles, white eyes, swelling in limbs, loss of appetite, loss of skin elasticity, general weakness, and thirst. These symptoms are interpreted as resulting from the child being without water. Healers noted that they can give a child water, but this will just swell up his stomach: "It won't be enough." The child must be taken to a hospital quickly, where doctors "will put water" (or "blood") into the child by needle in the arm. Some healers said that If lack of water occurs at night, one can give a boiled water, sugar, and salt mixture, but the child must still be taken to the hospital. The foregoing may reflect the impact of government health education efforts at explaining dehydration and promoting ORS.

In spite of the ability of some healers to provide such explanations, there was no evidence of ORS packets in use, or even much knowledge of ORS other than some awareness that it is used in hospitals. Of 48 traditional healers who commented on ORS, 38 had heard of it and 10 had not. Of the 38, 15 expressed a generally positive attitude toward ORS; 14 were negative; 1 expressed no opinion; and 8 said it sometimes works and sometimes fails. Of these 8, 5 commented that ORS does not work if bad spirits are involved in the disease or its cure, and 2 mentioned it does not work for *phiringaniso*.

Most traditional healers who recognized ORS thought it was a remedy for diarrhea rather than dehydration. Several had tried it on children in their own families and found it not only failed to stop the diarrhea, it actually increased the flow. One healer knew a packet of ORS is mixed

119

with one liter of boiled water and that the solution can be used for one day only. A more urbanized healer claimed he knew how to mix sugar and salt solution himself.

CAUSES AND PREVENTION OF DIARRHEA AS UNDERSTOOD BY HEALERS

A variety of causal factors emerged in discussion about locally recognized diarrheas. These include: a nursing mother's milk becoming contaminated; wrongful or neglectful behavior on the part of the child's parents; consumption of dirty water, badly prepared food, spoiled food, etc.; exposure to sun or heat; stepping in contaminated milk; a child drinking too much water or salt—or an infant consuming any salt; disturbing the *nyoka*; bad hygiene; a new pregnancy (because the mother's milk becomes spoiled); resuming sexual relations after a postpartum taboo period but before performing a special ceremony; the parents of a child failing to perform a mortuary ceremony after the death of a kinsman or neglecting other traditions.

During two months of data gathering, only one type of diarrhea was mentioned whose etiology involved an evil or avenging spirit, and its existence was only discovered by probing. There were likewise only one or two references to witchcraft in descriptions of the more serious diarrheas. It is true that Mozambican healers are wary about revealing beliefs about spirits, sorcery, or witchcraft to those perceived as government authorities because of the government's earlier attempts to suppress just such beliefs. One healer explained that evil spirits exist, but they do not provoke diarrhea directly. Instead, they prevent curative medicines from working, and this is why rituals to expel spirits may be required. It is possible that this way of regarding—or explaining—the role of harmful spirits protects healers from the intrusions of disapproving outsiders. But, from the evidence here and elsewhere in the region, I do not believe that childhood diarrhea is commonly interpreted in terms of witchcraft, sorcery, spirits, and the like.

Manica healers appeared to think in terms of successive levels of explanation, with more fundamental causes underlying more immediate causes. For example, the cause of simple diarrhea (*nyoka dzo kusorora*) might be bad food or dirty water. If symptoms persist in spite of treatment for *manyoka*, the condition might be rediagnosed as something with a deeper, more serious cause, such as *phiringaniso*. In the latter case, the cause is believed to be adultery, and treatment incorporates the ritual purification of the sick child's parents. However, multilevel causal explanations seem to exist even in the absence of persistent symptoms and rediagnosis. In fact, with exposure of healers to modern biomedical ideas, additional explanatory levels may be added by healers to accommodate foreign concepts, a point that has been made by Pillsbury (1978:28).

Thinking that reflects differing levels of abstraction can, of course, be found in biomedicine as well, especially in public health. Scientific explanations for a case of dysentery might point initially to an infective microbe as the immediate cause. But at successive degrees of abstraction, the cause of the illness may be described as fecal contamination of food, the prevalence of flies, a lack of toilets, an unsanitary environment, lack of education, poverty in general, or a lack of political will to allocate more resources to education or alleviation of poverty. What is different in this regard between a diagnostician trained in indigenous medicine and one trained in public health is the focus and content of causal explanations, not the use of levels.

Reviewing our findings on diarrhea causation, pollution, or contamination as healers called it, appears to be the broadest, even if not always the most fundamental, explanatory principle in local etiologies of diarrhea. The notion that pathology in social relations leads to illness—characteristic of African thought—is also evident in Manica but is secondary to notions relating to pollution. We found that transgression of rules regarding sexual behavior (such as committing adultery) is a source of social strife believed to lead to various diarrheas afflicting children. However, social strife is not seen as directly causing illness such as diarrhea; it is mediated by a process of contamination. One such diarrhea, *phiringaniso*, is attributed to a man having intercourse "outside the home" (a norm transgression and source of social strife) while his child is still breastfeeding, then touching his child before washing or decontaminating himself. For at least some healers, the contamination caused by wrongful behavior can be transmitted by the father's semen to his wife, after which the next child will be born with the same contaminant. The child's *nyoka* will know this and will sooner or later react with diarrhea or other symptoms. Viewed thusly, some serious childhood diarrheas are congenital.

Diarrheas not related to pollution belief are, for the most part, classifiable as naturalistic, including the notion that some conditions can be inherited. Witchcraft, sorcery, and spirits seem to be involved only rarely.

The concept of *nyoka* relates to concern with contamination and serves to unify the various causes and levels of explanation. Diarrhea itself is referred to by the plural form of *nyoka*, and the term contamination was often used by healers in explaining various diarrheas. For example, we were told that a child's porridge made from maize should be beaten on a traditional grinding stone, or pounded in a mortar while still in the maize leaves, because pounding it directly in the mortar contaminates it.

Whether diarrhea is attributed to diet, environment, social relations, taboo violation, death in the family or vicinity, miscarriage, or a new pregnancy, it is always the *nyoka*, the Guardian of Bodily Purity, that reacts by provoking diarrhea and related symptoms, warning that there needs to be expulsion of impurities and subsequent purification. Pollution is thus a central ethnomedical symbolic or metaphoric construct in that it seems to influence other constructs, yet is not necessarily influenced in the same manner by what may be referred to as secondary constructs. Transgression of norms and neglect of tradition seem to qualify as secondary constructs in the context of our research because they do not relate directly to one another other than when mediated by pollution. Note that pollution beliefs may be closely associated with childhood diarrhea in other traditional societies outside Africa (see Chapter Seven).

It would be most useful to learn from mothers (or child caretakers) how notions of contamination enter into the decision-making process of where to take a child with various diarrheal symptoms. Our findings derived from healers show that therapeutic interventions link closely to ideas of contamination. As noted above, a principal, general aim of treatment is to "calm the *nyoka*." Explanations of the purpose of treatment for specific diarrheas often refer to contamination. For example, the herbs used for *chikamba* are said to "clean the dirt" out of the child caused by parental adultery. In the case of *chinamukaka*, the mother's breast milk is decontaminated in addition to treatment of the child.

CHILDHOOD DIARRHEA AMONG THE MACUA

The GEMT developed a similar collaborative program involving healers and diarrhea prevention in Nampula Province, northern Mozambique.[3] My colleagues and I gathered ethnomedical data among Macua traditional healers, using research methods similar to those used in Manica (see Chapter One). In this section, I review research findings to shed further light on the central topics of this book.

The Macua are part of the Yao cluster of the Central Bantu (Murdock 1959: 290–306). They live in dispersed homesteads or small hamlets and recognize matrilineal descent (see Central Bantu section, Chapter One). They number over seven million in Mozambique at present and are predominantly Muslim.

More than 20 diarrheal syndromes were mentioned during systematic interviews with healers in Nampula, well over the norm for Africa, as noted earlier. It almost seemed that each traditional healer had his or her own names for diarrhea that few, if any, other healers shared. This made it difficult to identify common diarrheas and construct a composite profile of each. During a May 1995 workshop for Macua healers in Nampula, some two months after the initial interviews, it developed that many of the indigenous names for diarrheas collected earlier were names of symptoms or names of other children's illnesses in which diarrhea might be a symptom. It also appeared that some illness names were dialectical variants of the same illness. Therefore, an attempt was made to classify variants together and to check that the symptoms seemed to point to essentially the same condition. In intensive group discussions, Nampula healers unanimously agreed on four basic names representing distinct childhood diarrheas. These are:

1. *Oporar, Ohara, Ovialua*, characterized as simple diarrhea. This can be a generic term when there are no special symptom characteristics. It can also refer to the diarrhea that babies get during teething, or to watery feces without blood or mucous symptoms.
2. *Muacharia, Muanan'luku, Muanan'hama*, characterized as diarrhea with blood and mucous.
3. *Omtupha Mwana, Wacia*, characterized as diarrhea with white-streaked mucous.
4. *Mavuca*, characterized as liquid feces with white-streaked mucous (more liquid than #3, it seems).

A variety of causes are attributed to childhood diarrhea in Nampula, representing the five broad domains of illness or misfortune causality found in at least southern Africa and discussed earlier: natural causes, witchcraft and sorcery, pollution, and evil/avenging or ancestral spirits. But the causes most commonly encountered are classifiable as either natural or pollution, the latter often associated with or resulting from violation of social norms. Natural causes include inappropriate or spoiled food, lack of hygiene, bad or contaminated water, dirt in various forms, or worms in the stomach. Natural diarrhea can also result from teething in babies, measles, or other conditions. Ideas that parallel germ or helminthic infection theory sometimes arose, reflected in statements such as "(It) comes from drinking water with little worms that multiply in the stomach." Macua healers recognized naturalistic infection in the form of "noxious microorganism" (Murdock's term), which they call *atchi-koko*. This was translated into Portuguese as "tiny worm" that carries illness. *Atchi-koko* also proved essential in understanding indigenous STD beliefs (see Chapter Five).

Diarrhea from pollution may occur if a parent commits adultery and then touches his or her child before being ritually cleansed. Or it may occur through contact with menstrual blood, such as when a menstruating woman touches a newborn child. It may result from parents resuming sexual relations after a period of ritually prescribed abstinence, prior to taking the proper medicines. What these examples have in common is contact with an essence or substance considered dirty or dangerous, resulting in illness. In these pollution-related diarrheas, it is the parents who have contact with the pollutant, and the innocent child who suffers the consequence.

Contact with pollutants can occur during sexual intercourse, when male and female essential fluids commingle, providing an etiological link between STIs and child diarrheas. One cannot fail to see the link with morality, sexual behavior norms, and social control in this interpretation of childhood diarrhea: If someone commits adultery, he or she not only risks becoming ill, but one or more children can become ill as well, through parent-child contact. This may occur more often through mother-child contact since there is more opportunity for this than for father-child contact. In one type of diarrhea, for example, "(a) mother passes this illness to (the) child through breastfeeding or blood circulation." We see in this statement notions of contaminated blood and breast milk.

A third causal category, sorcery/witchcraft, was encountered only very occasionally, such as when a respondent told us that *oporar* is caused by "someone putting a poisonous medicine in water"; or when another said a variant of *muacharia* is caused by "sorcery from envy, or personal struggles between family members or neighbors" (Green et al. 1995a:34).

SUNKEN FONTANEL

The fontanel is called by several local names: *esulo*; *esuloy eronela*; *thomela* or *inthoci*. A syndrome of depressed or sunken fontanel is not well recognized; perhaps swollen fontanel is more recognized. One healer specified that the Macua terms (above) refer only to the fontanel, not to any irregularities pertaining to it. In any case, fontanel irregularity or abnormality are recognized by some healers and associated with fever and headaches. It appears to be recognized more as something to do with the head than with diarrhea. A minority of healers associated fontanel conditions directly with diarrhea. Some healers who said the fontanel was just a natural phenomenon may have been referring to changes and eventual closure of the fontanel, which indeed are part of a baby's development.

When asked what caused a depressed fontanel, several healers simply said that it was natural. Other representative answers include:

"It is caused by child's first teeth and associated with crying from this discomfort."

"(It is) associated with fever, diarrhea and headache."

"It's caused by teething and ripeness of the head(?)."

"It has no cause (it is a natural part of growth?)."

"It's caused by badly prepared food."

"It is caused by diarrhea with yellowish feces and associated with red, yellow, or swollen eyes (malnutrition symptom?)."

"It's caused by headaches."

"I don't know cause, I know only the treatment—vaccination."

"(It) appears when a baby has a hot body (*oviha eruthu*) or hot head (fever)."

"(It is) caused by any disease."

"It's caused by illness of the head with fever; the fontanel swells and becomes abnormal. It means the child is very sick."

"It means the child is not growing properly."

"It is a matter of God, it is not related to anything."

"When the child has fever and refuses the breast."

"Constipation."

"There is no relationship between depressed fontanel and diarrhea."

125

"(It's due to) headache caused by *jini* (spirits))."
"Fontanel provokes headaches, fever, difficulty in breathing."
"(It's caused by) leaving the baby alone to cry."
"Jumping the child."

Except for one answer that referred to *jini* spirits, we see classic Bantu speakers' expressions of natural causation (no cause, God, teething, association with other symptoms, diet). Jumping the child may refer to death pollution resulting from violating mourning rules (see below).

We next asked about treatment of the fontanel. The answers of a number of traditional healers suggest that conditions of the fontanel are thought to be secondary or incidental to fever, headache, or certain types of diarrhea. Therefore, treatment is directed to the conditions considered primary. Answers included: giving medicine to drink or to bathe the baby in (the head or the whole body); rubbing a rock on the baby's mouth and fontanel; "painting" the fontanel with a stone to strengthen the baby; rubbing or scrubbing the fontanel with a medicine from roots or leaves; administering a vaccination from a root medicine on both ears and on the nape of neck; giving a boiled root decoction to discharge the "high tension"; and chewing a medicine then spitting it on the fontanel. One healer mentioned ORS in this connection. Another said fontanel problems are serious and babies should be sent to the hospital for treatment.

In general, we see that a connection between diarrheal disease, dehydration, and actions needed to remedy dehydration is weak or nonexistent. For treatment of child diarrheas, various roots (occasionally leaves) are boiled, and a decoction is drunk. The intended purpose may be to clean out the stomach or intestines, or to clean out worms. In the latter case, the treatment objective may be to see the expelled worms in vomit or feces. The whole body may be washed in the medicine, especially if body sores are part of the symptoms.

Sometimes these medicines are given in porridge form, perhaps with a pinch of salt. Decoctions are often taken three times a day. Some syndromes may be treated by means of vaccination; its purpose may be to make the illness "disappear." Sometimes roots are placed on burning coals and the resulting smoke is inhaled or may be used to fumigate the anus. Roots may be ground on a stone and the resulting medicine applied directly to parts of the body with swelling. Parents may have to abstain from sexual activity, although if the child becomes worse, they may be "required" to resume intercourse.

Cures recommended by Islamic healers might be used in addition to, or instead of, the foregoing. For example, a healer might write words from the Koran, put the paper containing them in water, and have the patient drink the solution.

ARE DIARRHEAL ILLNESSES PREVENTABLE?

We asked Macua healers if they thought diarrheal illnesses were preventable. Prevention often was taken by traditional healers to refer to medicines, amulets, and the like. A number of informants told us that soon after birth, all babies are treated to prevent all illnesses, including diarrhea. The treatment is called *omuaculela muana*. It consists of roots or leaves, and the preparations are used for drinking and bathing the baby. With at least one such preparation, the mother and child both drink the medicine. Informants also reported that a certain root may be used in a medicine to vaccinate the child.

Diarrhea may also be prevented by avoiding foods that cause diarrhea. At least one type is preventable by parents refraining from intercourse. To prevent *mavuca*, a medicine prepared by a traditional healer is expressed on the umbilicus of a baby by the child's father. About one-third of the traditional healers said there are no ways to prevent childhood diarrheas, or at least no way other than avoiding the bad foods that cause diarrhea and protecting the mother's milk.

SOME MACUA POLLUTION BELIEFS

As elsewhere in Africa, Macuas believe death is a mystically polluting force. Recall that Murdock (1980:18) defines contagion as "coming into contact with some purportedly polluting object, substance, or person," and he notes that in Africa, the polluting object is most likely to be a corpse or death itself. Among the Macua, *eruku* or *erungu* means shadow as well as personal vital force or spirit, soul or aura. In a recently dead person, *eruku* is called "the shadow of death." *Eruku* seems equivalent to heat or darkness in that it can pollute through contact. The Macua term *phunho* may be used for the name of the medicine and treatment for contamination by Shadow of Death. *Majini* (spirits of human origin) may be present at funerals and contact with these can also pollute.

After the funeral of a person who dies from tuberculosis, all who participated in the funeral must be purified of death pollution. The possibility of pollution from death is serious and omnipresent until proper funeral rites have been performed and the shadow becomes a useful ancestor spirit (*munepa*). Before this, people can become ill or unlucky by merely being in the place of the shadow of death, such as at a funeral. As in many other parts of Africa, a woman considered polluted by the death of a husband or child cannot prepare or serve food to others lest they become ill from indirect contact with death.

Eruku is something like a dangerous spirit, not because of destructive or evil intent on its part, but simply because it is in a dangerous, transitional state between life and realm of the ancestors. One can become ill by merely being in a certain place and thereby be exposed to eruku. All funeral participants must therefore be purified, especially if they have touched the corpse or dug the grave. All this describes the domain of pollution, but the lexicon, symbolism, and metaphor used by the Macua may seem to be that of spirits instead of the impersonal heat or darkness found among the Tsonga and Nguni.

Parents who have sex after the death of a close kinsman are said to engage in "jumping the hair," or jumping ahead of the shaved-head mourning period. Death pollution will affect the next baby: The mother will abort it or else it will die soon after birth.

Macua healers understand dirt as an agent of diarrheal and other illnesses. "Dirt" refers to a state of ritual uncleanliness as well as filth in a more ordinary sense. The term is used in both these ways by the Sotho, Zulu, Shona, Bemba, Nyanja, Tsonga, Swazi, and other regional societies.

LOOKING BEYOND MOZAMBIQUE

How characteristic of sub-Saharan Africa are Shona or Macua beliefs about childhood diarrhea? A survey of ethnomedical literature on childhood diarrhea suggests that most African etiologic belief about diarrhea is naturalistic and ICT related. Childhood diarrhea is usually believed caused by eating bad or incompatible food, breastfeeding under certain conditions, teething, parents having sex with other partners, bad water, and poor hygiene. For example, a survey of traditional healers' beliefs

128

about diarrhea in Zambia (Freund 1989) showed that a plurality of healers (41%) said that diarrhea is caused by a miscellaneous category characterized by words such as "air" and "worms" (code words for pollution or indigenous germ theory), followed by "bad food" (16%), breastfeeding from a pregnant mother (13%), parents having sex with other partners (10%), witchcraft (5%), bad water (3%), and poor hygiene (2%).

Following are some unpublished findings from the Targeted Intervention Research (TIR) survey in Zambia that I describe in some detail in Chapter Six. This was based on a random sample of Zambians in two provinces, one where Bemba is the major language, the other where Nyanja predominates. I was involved in the analysis of the findings to follow, and I both designed and analyzed findings from a parallel TIR survey of Zambian traditional healers.

Among Nyanja speakers, *kutulula* was used as a general term for diarrhea; among Bemba speakers, the term was *Ukupolomya*. Symptoms referred to among both groups were passing watery stools, passing stools often, stomach pains, weakness. Associated symptoms include fever, vomiting, becoming thin, loss of appetite, and loss of water. Bemba and Nyanja terms were provided for more serious or specialized types of diarrheal illness, such as diarrhea with blood or mucous in the stool. Some used English disease names such as dysentery and cholera.

Diarrhea was described by both Bemba and Nyanja speakers as a serious illness that affects men, women and children. Some commented that diarrhea can be fatal. Most Nyanja speakers thought the cause of diarrhea to be eating or drinking contaminated, dirty, or rotten food or water. In the words of representative respondents:

"Diarrhea is caused by eating dirty food."
"(It is) caused by the kind/type of food that one eats like vegetables and dirty surroundings."
"The causes of the illness are flies and toilets which are dirty with germs. The transmission is by eating food which flies have made dirty. Also living in a dirty house with dust."
"Drinking dirty contaminated water, eating bad food."
"(It is) transmitted (by) flies which sit on stools which have been left in the open and then go and sit on food."
"Eating something rotten."
"Eating food without washing one's hands after using the toilet."
"Diarrhea is caused by eating bad food, food that has gone bad, uncovered

food because dirty flies sit on the food, lack of personal hygiene. It is not transmitted from one person to the other."

"(It's caused by) dirty water, eating leftover foods."

"(It) can be caused by passing where a sick person had left human waste and also by flies."

"If someone who is purging leaves the feces on the toilet then someone steps on them, he is likely to get the disease. This illness can also be brought about by flies in the sense that if flies sit on the feces/stool, it takes some germs and if it sits on food (person gets sick)."

"(Cholera) is caused by germs. It is waterborne. Transmitted through drinking dirty water, untreated water and eating dirty food."

For those who distinguished transmission from cause, several said that diarrhea is transmitted by flies that have come into contact with exposed stools or with germs contained there, and then touch or contaminate food. Some believed that diarrhea cannot be transmitted from one person to another, at least among adults.

In my own interviews of healers and laypersons in Zambia in 1995, I discovered belief in noxious worms (rather than a protective snake) in the stomach, apparently similar to what Macua healers believe (above). The term *njoka* in Nyanja, or *nsoka* in Bemba, refer more to a worm than a snake, one that only some sick people have in their stomach. Not all people have the worm; it is rather uncommon. It may result from contact with dirty water or bad food, or it may be sent by an evil or jealous person. In either case, it is always considered bad. An illness, *insokanda*, results from the presence of the worm. Patients are given medicines to expel the worm; sometimes a traditional healer sucks it out.

A number of respondents suggested ways to prevent diarrhea that reflect modern health education messages, although they are also compatible with pollution and related ICT beliefs (e.g., boiling drinking water, keeping the house properly, and general cleanliness; cleaning the surroundings where food is taken or eaten; washing hands after using the toilet). In the early 1980s, some of my Swazi informants insisted that their ancestors knew about washing hands before preparing meals and after the toilet long before the Europeans came. This might be so. A study of hand washing in Botswana found a major reason people do this even today is to "remove contamination or 'dirt,'" sources of both being described as blood, pus, and other bodily fluids (Kaltenthaler and Drasar

1996a:77). Contamination is a code word pointing to pollution beliefs, and bodily fluids are common pollutants.

Returning to Africa as a whole, in a useful survey of traditional diagnoses and theories of diarrhea causation throughout Africa, Hogle and Prins (1991a) found a wide-seeming range of explanation, yet these were groupable under categories such as "foods as contributing causes," "bad maternal milk" (a pollution concept), "God-given," and "parental sexual transgressions," with personalistic causes invoked only infrequently. A childhood diarrhea study based on both focus groups and survey methods conducted by Yoder (1995:233–245) found a range of naturalistic and specifically indigenous contagion ideas used to explain causes of a variety of symptomatically differentiated diarrheas. These causes include: germs, worms, unripe fruit, bad or spoiled foods, food that is too sweet, dirty or unboiled water, teething, worries, negligence, measles, letting a child crawl without any clothes, not enough water in the body, heat from the sun, and bottle feeding. Some diarrheas were said to "come from the wind" or from a bad wind, signaling its contagious nature, according to Swahili informants. There were several mentions of a child being born with illness. There appears to have been only one mention of sorcery (and none of witchcraft or evil spirits).

De Zoysa et al. (1984) quantified answers about the cause of various childhood diarrheas in a survey in Zimbabwe (n = 402) and found that 76% of the diarrheas were attributed to natural causes, 15% to "social and spiritual causes," and 8% to a combination of the two. Another study of diarrhea in two sites, southeast Ivory Coast and northern Togo, found that "the descriptions of symptoms provided by mothers usually correspond to biomedical terms, and supernatural causes are not usually assumed for it [diarrhea]" (Guillaume and Rey 1988). A study in northwestern Ethiopia reported that most mothers believed that diarrhea is caused by the will of God, a common way Africans refer to illnesses that are unavoidable and natural (Sircar and Dagnow 1988).

On the other hand, a study of diarrhea among the Tswana by Booyens—the same researcher mentioned in Chapter Three who interpreted the internal snake as witchcraft—seems to challenge the etiologic picture of diarrhea presented here. He observes that there are three basic types of child diarrhea: sorcery-caused, ancestor-sent, and naturally caused. Booyens, in his English abstract of his Afrikaans article (1989), notes, "Within this general aetiological frame, serious diarrhoeal disease of infants is usually seen as sorcery related" (p. 11). Contact of infants with people regarded as ritually polluted is seen as a major causal agency. It is conceptualized as infants being "stepped upon" by "tracks." It would appear that this researcher confuses pollution with sorcery, since contact with ritually polluted people is offered as an example of causation in the context of sorcery. And then there is the clue from mention of "tracks." As we saw in Chapter Two, a track is called *umkhondo* in Zulu, and it refers to something left behind by people and animals, something that is distinctive to a particular environment to which local creatures adapt. Honwana (1994) also describes this belief among the Tsonga. Exposure to "foreign" tracks to which people are not adapted can cause illness, a belief classifiable as environmental dangers, a component of ICT.

Apart from his example of sorcery, Booyens (1989) mentions intestinal snake (*kokwana*) as another cause attributed by the Tswana to serious diarrheal illness. He interprets this as witchcraft. There is no need to repeat the arguments of Chapter Three on how to interpret the internal snake concept—there are two basic ways. I have no first-hand research experience among the Tswana. However, I have found that belief in an internal, invisible snake among southern Bantu speakers is often associated with pollution ideas. I therefore feel safe in suggesting that Tswana snake beliefs associated with childhood diarrhea might also be related to pollution rather than to witchcraft.

It appears that when researchers encounter exotic findings about tracks, internal snakes, mystical-seeming heat or darkness, etc., they tend to classify these according to the prevailing interpretive framework— which in the case of Africa is personalistic. If ICT were better understood, researchers would see that "contact of infants with people regarded as ritually polluted" (Booyens 1989:11) is probably less likely to be an example of sorcery than of indigenous contagion theory. In Chapter Seven, I give examples of researchers in Latin America who have difficulty interpreting and classifying indigenous etiological findings pertaining to winds, dirt, tiny animals, volcanic ashes in the air, and "hot milk" within the prevailing ethnomedical framework of humoral theory. I suggest that these findings also point to ICT.

NOTES

1. This chapter draws on findings published in Green et al. (1994).

2. I use the term "communication strategy" rather than "health education" or "training" because the latter terms are condescending, implying that healers are somehow deficient in knowledge—that once they are trained (as if remedially) by some method only we can recommend, they can be enlightened and their practice improved. This, of course, is presumptuous, paternalistic, and arrogant, and it ignores the great extent to which healers can educate and enlighten biomedical health workers—and the extent to which healers are already providing help to their clients.

3. For the full research report, see Green et al. (1995a).

CHAPTER FIVE

SEXUALLY TRANSMITTED DISEASES AND AIDS

This chapter focuses on another subgroup of infectious contagious diseases with which I have ample research experience: sexually transmitted diseases, including AIDS. Following anthropological convention, I make a distinction between STD and STI (sexually transmitted disease/illness). The former denote biomedical constructs, whereas the latter denote indigenous, emic, or folk concepts (Hahn 1984). Syphilis is an STD, whereas *chimanga* (see below) is an STI. A possible confusion nowadays is that STIs may be used in public health discourse to denote sexually transmitted infection(s), which, of course, is a biomedical construct.

I first report findings from applied research in two areas of Mozambique and then from two areas of Zambia. Following that is a summary and analysis of all STI findings in the context of indigenous contagion theory and related issues central to this book.

The stated objective of the GEMT's AIDS prevention program in Mozambique was to reduce the spread of HIV not only by promoting responsible sexual behavior and condom usage but also by treating and preventing standard STDs. Although the GEMT program objectives were fully consistent with Mozambique's National AIDS Program, only the GEMT program sought to achieve these objectives through active collaboration with traditional healers. We sought to take advantage of the prestige, credibility, widespread availability, and authority of traditional healers to promote behavior change and the adoption of new technology such as condoms among those who consult healers for STIs and other illnesses.

Some research has suggested that traditional healers see and attempt to treat many or most of the STD cases in southern Africa, if not all of Africa (Good 1987; Green 1994a; Nzima 1995:3). A broad program objective was to reduce STD incidence and thereby HIV seropositivity by means of behavior change on the part of traditional healers (in their treatment and referral practices) and—through them—their clients. Another was to promote reduction of sexual partners by reinforcing indigenous beliefs about the dangers of indiscriminate sex with strangers.

In sub-Saharan Africa, HIV is transmitted primarily through heterosexual intercourse, infecting women as often as men. Africa is also characterized by high incidence and prevalence of standard STDs such as gonorrhea, syphilis, chlamydia, and chancroid. The program with which I was involved in Mozambique began in late 1990, by which time the causal relationship between at least the ulcerative STDs—notably genital ulcer disease or chancroid, and syphilis—and HIV infection was quite well established. Such STDs enhance the efficiency of HIV transmission. Yet no one could say how much reduction in this type of STDs would result in how much reduction in HIV infection rates. Since then, it has been found that even nonulcerative STDs such as gonorrhea and chlamydia somehow facilitate HIV transmission during sexual intercourse (see, e.g., Wasserheit 1992:69). At least one researcher, however, believes this is most likely to occur if partners already have immune systems weakened by concomitant infections of the sort that are common in Africa (malaria, anemia from malaria, schistosomiasis, helminthic infections, etc.), even among the urban and more affluent (Root-Bernstein 1993).

This means that all STDs need to be reduced (all infectious disease ought to be reduced if Root-Bernstein is right) if HIV transmission is to be curtailed. We wished to reduce STD incidence by working with traditional healers, even if we did not know exactly how to do this. Our program was therefore different from other AIDS prevention programs in Africa, which emphasized promotion of condoms. We also planned to promote condoms but did not expect their widespread adoption since this had not occurred in African countries with far higher HIV seropositivity than Mozambique (e.g., Uganda, Zambia), where there had been strong condom promotion for years.

Few AIDS prevention programs emphasized the STD reduction approach in 1990–91. Such approaches are now more common. A highly influential study in Tanzania published in *The Lancet* in 1995 showed a 42% reduction in HIV incidence as a result of improved STD case management in clinics in a rural area of Tanzania. "Condom use with sex partners other than their spouse was reported by only 2.4% of men . . . and 2.3% of women. . . . Only three individuals reported regular use of condoms" (Grosskurth et al. 1995: 534). One has to wonder: If we can reduce HIV by 42% by aggressively treating STDs *in clinics*, which is an improvement over business as usual, how much greater impact might we have if we included traditional healers in our treatment effort since they already see most of the STD patients?

For now, let us turn to findings about STIs in the site of our pilot program, Manica Province, a Shona-speaking area of Mozambique. I will not repeat the general discussion about methods, choice of program site, etc., since this has been covered.

RESEARCH FINDINGS ABOUT STIs IN MANICA

The ethnomedical research required for the GEMT's program could not be accomplished through sample surveys. Virtually nothing was known at the time from research about indigenous Mozambican theories and healing practices related to STIs. Our research was highly exploratory in nature and related to complex beliefs and behaviors that Africans, including Mozambicans, tend to keep secret from those who may hold unsympathetic or even derisive views (such as government interviewers). We therefore relied primarily on what might be characterized as the traditional anthropological method of in-depth, key-informant interviews, supplemented by focus group discussions.

For purposes of nosological translation of STIs to STDs, clinical symptoms for major STDs found in Africa are summarized here from a standard handbook for Tanzanian health workers (*Communicable Diseases*, African Medical and Research Council, Nairobi, 1978),[1] and from Jones and Wasserheit (1991).

REVIEW OF CLINICAL SYMPTOMS

- Gonorrhea: Initial symptoms are painful urination usually followed by thick, yellow, purulent discharge from the urethra. In females, the urethra is short and urethritis is often not noticed.
- Chlamydia: Symptoms are similar to those of gonorrhea, but infections tend to be less acute and milder. Women are usually infected at the endocervix, urethra, or both. Infection of the endocervix may produce no symptoms but inflammation of the cervix is often present and there may be a discharge. The most common symptom among women is a burning sensation while urinating. With men, symptoms are usually present seven–ten days after infection and consist of burning sensation during urination and a discharge.
- Syphilis: Primary syphilis is characterized by a hard chancre, a single, painless ulcer on the genitals or elsewhere (lips, tongue, breasts); even when not treated it will heal spontaneously in a few weeks. The lymph glands are bilaterally enlarged but not painful. Secondary syphilis appears four–six weeks after the primary infection as a generalized secondary eruption (symmetrical rashes that do not itch), often accompanied by mild constitutional symptoms.
- Chancroid: An ulcer develops on the skin of the penis three–five days after sexual contact. The ulcer can enlarge in every direction. New ulcers often develop from the initial one. They are painful and soft on palpation. In most cases only one side is affected. The chancroid sore is painful and soft, as distinct from the syphilis sore, which is painless and hard.
- Papillomaviruses: A genital papillomavirus infection may result in (i) no obvious lesions, (ii) a small papule or bump (flat *Condylomata*), (iii) an exophytic genital wart with spikelike projections (*Condylomata acuminata*), or (iv) eventually a cancer (most often cervical). Most persons with genital or perianal warts have no symptoms and are mainly concerned about the appearance of the warts. In men they are usually located on the penis, scrotum, or urethra, while in women they are located on the labia, introitus, vagina, and cervix. They are

found in the perianal area in both sexes (Jones and Wasserheit 1991:25). Genital warts may also be due to *Condylomata acuminata.*

SIKI ILLNESSES

According to our research findings, Manica traditional healers recognize two broad categories of illnesses believed to be sexually transmitted: *siki* and *nyoka* related. A generic term, *siki*, exists in several Shona dialects to designate more serious sexually transmitted illnesses. A few older healers suggested that the term *siki* may derive from the English word sick and may have been borrowed from the Shona of neighboring Zimbabwe, where English is the official language. Such derivation might lend credence to the local belief (found elsewhere in Africa) that syphilis and gonorrhea were first introduced by Europeans. The *siki* illnesses known as *chimanga, chicazamentu, mula, songeia, chikeke,* and *gobela* seem to correspond to the more serious and common biomedically recognized STDs: syphilis, gonorrhea, chancroid, and chlamydia, which are also the STDs that facilitate the transmission of HIV. *Siki* illnesses were uniformly described as "adult diseases," meaning they are not found in children before the age of intercourse. They are characterized by either painful urination and a milky discharge (*chicazamentu, songeia*) or by various types of genital sores or boils (*chimanga, chikeke, gobela,* or *keni*). A syndrome characterized by painful genital ulcers (*mula*) is distinguished from this latter group. *Siki* illnesses are usually said to be more common in men than women (Green et al. 1993).

Siki illnesses are believed to be caused by a common tiny, invisible, animate illness agent (*khoma*) or by direct contact with pus or other genital discharges (sometimes called dirt) that contain *khoma*. Different illnesses are carried by different *khomas*, so the word must be regarded as generic. *Khoma* was sometimes translated as a tiny worm or insect. One healer conversant in biomedical concepts explained that *khoma* was like a microbe.

Note that only a century ago, Western medical science was uncertain whether different STDs had different *khomas*: "Some medical writers claim that there is but one poison, and that the varieties of venereal affections are simply modifications of one disease, while others believe that these several affections are due to different poisons, and, therefore, are distinct diseases" (Pierce 1889:873).

Manica healers are not unlike biomedical physicians in their treatment of *siki* illnesses: They introduce a medicine into the body to kill or neutralize the specific illness-causing *khoma*. Special roots are boiled, after which the decoction is cooled and given to the patient to drink. In another type of medicine, certain leaves are crushed or ground, then the resulting juice is drunk. Some medicines are applied directly to genital sores. Treatment takes about one week and is usually accomplished in the patient's own home.

NYOKA-RELATED STIs

The concept of *nyoka* has been discussed in Chapter Three. Recall that Shona healers described it as a protective force that demands that the body it inhabits be kept free of impurities or contaminants lest the *nyoka* reacts with displeasure, causing pain and discomfort. Manica healers described two sexually transmitted illnesses associated with this complex concept: *nyoka kundu*, which affects men, and *nyoka dzoni*, which affects women. A woman who has sex with a man who has *nyoka kundu* is said to contract the female disease *nyoka dzoni*, and vice-versa, through a process described as contamination. *Nyoka dzoni* can also be caught by stepping in urine or feces contaminated by the male disease.

Some healers also described congenital transmission. If a man does not treat his *nyoka kundu* with indigenous medicines, not only will he remain sick, but at the moment of conceiving a child with a woman, the unborn child's *nyoka* will be contaminated or polluted. When such a child is born, it will not only have symptoms of the disease *nyoka kundu*, it will also be susceptible to various other diseases, healers explained. In biomedical terms, the child will have poor resistance, or a weak immune system. A mother also passes her illness on to her unborn daughter if she does not treat her *nyoka dzoni*.

The symptoms of *nyoka* illnesses are diverse and include a variety of seemingly less serious and possibly self-limiting genito-urinary infections and conditions such as nonspecific urethritis, yeast infections, prostate infections, and trichomonas. Among these are conditions that, according to biomedicine, may not be sexually transmitted but nevertheless affect the genital or lower abdominal area.

HEALERS' UNDERSTANDING OF AIDS

We also asked healers about AIDS. Findings here support those of KAP surveys in Mozambique and elsewhere in Africa. Although all traditional healers had heard of AIDS (SIDA in Portuguese) in 1991, most claimed to know little about it beyond what they had heard and understood from the radio (e.g., that it is incurable, fatal, and sexually transmitted). A second source of information after radio was other people. A majority believed they had neither seen nor treated this disease and that it is new to Mozambique.

A few healers seemed to confuse AIDS with familiar STIs—even referring to it as a *siki* disease—perhaps because they had heard that it is sexually transmitted. These healers claimed that AIDS is not really a new disease; it is the familiar STI *songeia*, or perhaps *chimanga*. Therefore, they felt, there are a variety of familiar medicines to cure or prevent the disease, a belief found elsewhere in Africa (Ingstad 1990:34; Staugaard 1991; Scheinman et al. 1992). At least one other healer thought AIDS is different from traditional STIs, although there are indigenous medicines to cure it. In short, some healers claimed they could treat—and have cured—what they believe to be AIDS. Healers reported that patients might come to them and announce that they have AIDS, in contrast to the traditional diagnosis carried out by a healer assisted by spirits.

Some healers believed that AIDS is highly contagious and is characterized by progressive weakness, sores on the body, appetite loss, prolonged diarrhea, emaciation, and coughing. There appeared to be only very general understanding of how AIDS is transmitted. Several forms of casual contact were mentioned as means of transmission, such as people eating together. Some healers mentioned extramarital sex and noted its increase in modern times. A few healers said it is better to prevent than try to cure AIDS, even mentioning the use of condoms.

STIs IN THE CONTEXT
OF INDIGENOUS CONTAGION THEORY

In an earlier analysis of these STI findings, I and my colleagues concluded that *siki* illnesses were understood "in much the way biomedicine understands common STDs"; in other words, what we found seemed to be a naturalist explanation influenced by biomedical thinking. We suggested that *nyoka* illnesses were believed caused by pollution (Green et al. 1993:271). My thinking was doubtless influenced by the absence of supernatural elements such as witchcraft and sorcery in our findings, elements that anthropologists (and others) are of a mind-set to discover. When I reanalyzed the findings from Shona healers after three years of additional research and program experience with traditional healers in southern Africa (including two additional regions of Mozambique), I found evidence that *all* STIs are understood to some extent as being caused by pollution as well as by naturalistic infection.

Consider the supporting evidence for the conclusion about pollution in the section to follow. We found no evidence among Manica healers of personalistic etiologies of STIs or of theories that STIs are caused by witchcraft, sorcery, or spirits of any kind. If we take Hammond-Tooke's typology as comprehensive, we are left with either natural causes or pollution beliefs—and I have argued that the latter are naturalistic because they are an example of impersonal causation.

BODILY FLUIDS AND CONTAGION

Bodily essences such as blood, pus, and female bodily fluids such as menstrual blood and vaginal fluids are commonly conceived as potent and dangerous in many parts of Africa. As noted, illnesses involving bodily fluids and discharges related to digestion and procreation tend to be seen as pollution illnesses, according to Douglas (1992 [1966]:125). STDs/STIs meet this criterion since they involve boils, pus, and related unsightly, malodorous, milky discharges. Then there is blood: It appears that a quality of the blood determines susceptibility to at least some *siki* illnesses, and it is the blood that healers attempt to fortify with medicine to prevent *siki*. Among the nearby Tsonga, Zulu, and Bemba, one's blood can become "bad" or "dirty" or "weak" from having intercourse with too many partners, or through association with death or other polluting influences or contacts (Schapera 1940: 194–195; Green et al. 1995b; Nzima 1995), propositions with which Shona healers would probably agree. Some Manica healers said that *siki* can result when people whose "blood doesn't mix" have intercourse.

Sexual intercourse is regarded as involving the mixing of menstrual blood with sperm. According to Shona belief, sperm can carry pollution

142

to the *nyoka* of the unborn child and thereby determine that child's future health. Shona women appear to be able to catch *nyoka dzoni* from contact with the menstrual blood of another woman with the illness (e.g., by stepping in the place where such a woman has bathed). Thus, menstrual blood, or an agent carried by it, is considered an agent of contagion. As we know, menstrual blood and death are the two most common agents of pollution in Africa, and probably worldwide (Murdock 1980:18).

We also find terms that constitute what we might call the lexicon of pollution, namely those that translate as dirt, filth, impurity, and contamination as well as their opposites, cleanliness and purity. In the words of a Shona healer, "The reason the baby dies inside a woman with *chimanga* is that there is something dirty inside her uterus, and the fetus eats this dirt and then dies." Another explained that if *songeia* (a *siki* illness) remains untreated, the "impurity goes inside the stomach and causes internal abscesses." Still another explained that syphilis-like *chimanga* can be transmitted through contact with the "dirt of the illness" by wearing the clothes of or stepping in the urine of a person with *chimanga*. Some healers described this dirt as something in an infected person's urine, others described it as little insects, linking pollution beliefs with the insects of naturalistic infection. Furthermore, *mula* (chancroid or genital ulcers) can be caused by bad hygiene, specifically by not washing after sexual intercourse. Treatment of several *siki* STIs is aimed at "pulling out the dirt."

A woman with gonorrhea-like *chicazamentu* can be without symptoms (i.e., in a latent stage) for a year because the dirt is said to hide or remain in her menstrual blood. Several healers commented or implied that *chicazamentu* is not as bad for women as for men, because the dirt comes out little by little during menstruation. It might take a year for this natural self-cleansing process. The implication is that *chicazamentu* may be self-limiting in women. At least one healer stated this explicitly. With treatment, the dirt of *chicazamentu* also washes out of the body through urination. One way of preventing *songeia* is to drink a concoction that makes a man or woman urinate right after intercourse "to eliminate possible dirt which could cause the illness." (Note that pus discharges may be referred to as dirt or filth.) Others differentiated the two (e.g., one healer spoke of "pus and the dirt of sex").

"Contamination," an African code word for pollution, was used frequently when healers discussed any STIs. For example, healers reported that women with *chimanga* will contaminate their babies; that menstruating women will contaminate their sexual partners; that physical contact with "tiny animals" from a "contaminated person" will make another person sick with the same illness; that treatment of *chimanga* requires medicines to make both the mother and father "clean" so that they won't contaminate the fetus in the mother's womb; that the STI-transmitted sores of a contaminated baby are difficult to cure; that *chicazamentu* results when someone has contact with the clothes of the contaminated person, or steps in that person's urine, or steps on that person's "little animals" (another word for insects or worms [i.e., naturalistic infection]).

Reference to *nyoka* is another indicator of pollution. In addition to what we have called *nyoka* illness, *siki* STIs may also be linked to *nyoka* symptoms. A disturbed *nyoka* or one "in a bad position" or one that "pulls down" can be part of the cause of certain *siki* symptoms, according to informants. In the words of one healer: "The origin of *chimanga* is *nyoka*."

Evidence for pollution belief can also be found in treatment of STIs. Some Manica healers reported that they remove a *siki* illness and bury it. When a person passes over the spot where the illness is buried, he can become infected. As noted, burying the source of pollution is a common health-related practice in Africa, according to Douglas (1992 [1966]). Pollution illnesses are also conceived as being highly contagious. This is not so with illnesses caused by witchcraft, sorcery, or spirits in which cases only a specific individual—usually not others in the area—is thought to be targeted for misfortune by a superhuman being or force.

To interject an interesting comparison, Khmer (Cambodian) AIDS and STI beliefs are curiously parallel to those found in southern Africa (see Chapter Seven). AIDS is thought to be so contaminating that those who die of it are not cremated in the usual Buddhist ritual,

> but, instead, must be buried usually in extremely great haste and some distance from the village, with no participation by Buddhist monks. This goes far beyond a question of following the Southeast Asian practice following inauspicious death, in which people fear attack by the spirit of the deceased, but it is a clear expression of the fear that the AIDS will pass from the bone through the air, in the case of cremation, or the soil, in the case of burial, and contaminate the neighbourhood. (Eisenbruch 1998b)

SEXUALLY TRANSMITTED ILLNESS AMONG THE MACUA

In this section I discuss the STD/AIDS findings of the GEMT research described in Chapter Four. The research methods were similar to those used in Manica Province and are outlined in Chapter One. I and my colleagues first elicited from healers a free listing of illnesses related to symptoms of the genital area. The illnesses are listed here, with summary comments about attributed symptoms, causes, and treatment. Our focus was on STIs that were cited by the largest number of respondents and corresponded with the standard STDs of public health concern in Africa: syphilis, gonorrhea, chancroid/ GUD (genital ulcer disease). We turn now to the composite profiles of Macua STIs. The first two illnesses were by far the most frequently cited.

1. *Ekkissinono, equissonyonyo, kassinono,* or *kassinyonyo.*[2] This STI is characterized by pain or difficulty in urination, frequent urination, (white) pus discharge (sometimes blood), itch at end of penis, pain in stomach, genital pain, stains, hair loss, red sores on genitals. Men and women are affected in roughly equal numbers—"one contaminates the other"—although one informant thought it more present among women because a lone male can sleep with a lot of women and spread it that way. Its cause was said to be sex with an infected person; sex with a woman whose menstrual period ended less than 24 hours previously; sex with a widow prior to treatment (purification); sex with a family member or with any "contaminated person."

2. *Mussekeneke (mussequeneque).* This is characterized by sores in or on the genitals; blood in the urine; white or milky genital discharge in both men and women; sores on penis and on vagina; genital swelling; bad smell; hair loss. It affects men and women equally. It is caused by sex with an infected or contaminated person.

3. *Mula.* Characterized by genital sores which can burst and discharge pus, swelling in groin. This is translated by local health workers as GUD or chancroid. The immediate cause of *mula* is intercourse with a contaminated person. A baby can also catch this illness while still in mother's womb. A child can also catch *mula* by urinating where a dog has urinated.

4. *Ehire.* Characterized by swollen legs and sometimes sterility. Symptoms may affect men more than women, who are "carriers." The causes are said to be intercourse with a widow in one's family;

transgressing a social rule about sleeping with the spouse of a dead uncle or with someone in one's own lineage; or sex with a menstruating woman.

5. *Namuili.* Characterized by swelling or edema or abscess in genital area. Its cause is sex with a contaminated person.

6. *Yiri* ("incest"). Characterized by pain in bladder. The cause is said to be violation of the incest taboo, specifically sex with a mother, father, a matrilineal aunt or uncle; brother or sister.

7. *Ethogo.* Characterized by sore/boils on genitals, anus, and whole body. Also by "stains on the body" and hair loss. The cause is as with most Macua STIs: sex with a contaminated partner.

Other syndromes were only mentioned once or twice by healers. One such was *okala ovenya*, a woman's illness characterized by vaginal hemorrhage, perhaps abortion or miscarriage, and "pain in the lower intestine." It is caused by a woman engaging in sex after having an abortion, "before being purified." If a woman obeys traditional prohibitions and lets two menstrual cycles pass before resuming sex, she won't get this illness. Another is *chipata*, which is characterized by swollen testicles (perhaps hydrocele). It is also believed caused by a man having sex with a menstruating women.

Treatment of *mussekeneke* consists of boiling roots and giving the resulting decoction to a patient to drink in order to "provoke frequent urination and thus clean out the filth (pus) and thus cure the patient." Salt may be added to the decoction; a patient may also bathe in or inhale medicines. To "clean" or "purify" are words used to describe the treatment of virtually all Macua STIs. In the case of an STI exhibiting genital sores or ulcers (*mussekeneke, mula, ethogo*), root medicine may be applied directly to the sores or ulcers. Some healers use the sap from a tree that resembles the patient's discharge visible in the urine. Often a patient is required to refrain from sex until cured, which is said to take three–four days for most STIs. Some healers mentioned that the partner of the patient must be treated too.

Another illness related to intercourse is *mahithé* (in Portuguese, *sombra do morto* [shadow of death]), which, as noted above, is metaphoric of death pollution. *Mahithé* is characterized by emaciation, wasting, and stomach pains. It is fatal if untreated, especially in men, although it is said to affect men and women equally. It is caused by having sex with a widow or widower before "shaving the head and

146

washing," which one must do within three–six days after death of spouse. For treatment, an elder man or woman must shave the head of the patient early in the morning. Leaves are prepared and the patient bathed, and all members of the family except the patient must eat a specially prepared meal. Instead, the patient must eat *nyema* beans on the same day. His normal diet can resume on the following day. To prevent violation of this rule, one normally shaves the head of the widow(er) early and "bathes in order to pull out the shadow of death" from the wife or husband.

This illness is of interest because it clearly illustrates beliefs about death pollution, it introduces a vivid metaphor of pollution (shadow of death) comparable to "darkness" or "heat," and it may shed light on beliefs surrounding AIDS. This STI seems parallel to *kaliondeonde* in Zambia (see below), which has similar wasting symptoms, is believed to result from death pollution, is considered fatal, and was translated by Zambian informants or interviewers as AIDS.

THE CAUSE OF STIs

In general, Macua healers attributed causes of STIs to either "catching it from an infected partner" or violating local rules of sexual conduct (e.g., having sex with a widow, with a woman who has aborted or miscarried, with a menstruating woman, or with someone who has been "contaminated" [their term] by the death of a close relative—all before undergoing a purification ceremony). A related contamination belief is that one can get *kassinyonyo* by urinating at a crossroads where a dog has urinated. Broadly speaking, the causes of STIs may be classified as naturalistic and specifically pollution related.

However, naturalistic infection was also encountered. It is of methodological interest that no named germ-like agent of pollution resulting from sexual intercourse emerged during fieldwork. However, just before a May 1995 workshop for Macua healers in Nampula, the concept of *atchi-koko* emerged during intensive group discussions that attempted to define the common ground between Macua and biomedical theories of sickness. *Achi-koko* was said to carry STIs from a contaminated person to his or her partner. This term refers to a tiny, unseen organism that lives in the blood and carries illness. Macua healers translated *atchi-koko* into Portuguese as *bichinho*, meaning a tiny worm. Clearly, it parallels *akashishi* among the Bemba of Zambia; *iciwane* among the Zulu; *liciwane* among the Swazi; and *khoma* among the Shona. In other words, it is the worm or insect of Murdock's naturalistic infection.

Atchi-koko has some special characteristics that distinguish it from germ or STD bacterium. For example it seems more contagious than most bacteria or viruses. According to informants, it can climb up the "bridge" formed by a stream of urine when someone urinates onto a puddle of urine left by a dog carrying *atchi-koko*. Like some STD bacteria, It can also be passed from a sick or infected mother to her child, an idea also expressed about the parallel concept of *khoma* among the Shona.

Whether belief in "noxious microorganisms" (as Murdock calls the agents of naturalistic infection) arose spontaneously or because of diffusion of Western biomedical thinking, it seems now to be imbedded in indigenous Macua beliefs, at least about STIs. It did not arise in connection with diarrheal illness. However, due to the rapid nature of our research, other investigators should look for *atchi-koko*, or something like it, in connection with other illnesses deemed contagious. In our STD/AIDS prevention communications strategy for Macua healers, we suggested that *atchi-koko* and dirt can be avoided during sexual intercourse if a condom is used.

SEXUALLY TRANSMITTED ILLNESSES IN ZAMBIA

This section focuses on an ethnomedical research and health intervention program related to AIDS and STDs in two pilot areas of Zambia. The research and intervention were funded by USAID through the Morehouse/ Tulane AIDS Prevention Project, one component of which focused on traditional healers and designed along the lines of the GEMT's AIDS/STD program in Mozambique (Green 1995).

As a first stage of the Morehouse/Tulane project, a TIR survey was conducted in 1994, based on a random sample of 440 Zambians. It was recognized that traditional healers ought to have been included in the original TIR, as expert informants about indigenous health related beliefs and practices. However, the TIR instrument was borrowed from the global AIDSCAP project, and there was no provision for traditional healers even though there were special forms for biomedical health workers. When I first became involved with the Morehouse/Tulane project as a consultant, I suggested adding interviews with traditional healers to the TIR data; the program staff and USAID/Zambia readily agreed. I worked with the field supervisor of the first TIR, Masauso Nzima, and developed a modified interview schedule. In mid-1995, 81 traditional healers were interviewed in four Copperbelt towns, having been randomly selected from lists of healers provided by two traditional healer associations in the region. Interviews were conducted for the most part by the same interviewers who had worked in the first, general TIR. Thus, we have findings from a general TIR and what I will call a healer TIR.

It is unusual for a study of this sort to have such a large random sample taken from the general population (most of whom admit they consult traditional healers) *and* a fairly large sample of traditional healers themselves. It seems to be the only TIR to date that offers such findings (others have been conducted in Malawi, Ethiopia, Senegal, South Africa, Swaziland, and perhaps elsewhere). The two types of data provide an unusual opportunity to compare self-reported information with groups very familiar with one another, and it helps answer criticisms raised by some skeptics that neither group can be relied on to provide valid answers to questions pertaining to an area of life thought to be kept secret from outsiders.

Comparing findings from the two surveys, it can be seen that laypersons are more likely than traditional healers to say "don't know" or an illness "just comes," or to deliberately give a biomedically pitched answer to a question on illness causality. This argues for not excluding traditional healers, even if they are not part of a project's direct target audience (if the study is applied), which in the case of the Morehouse/Tulane project they were. Recall from Chapter Two that Pool (1994a:12) interprets the frequent "don't know" or "it has no cause" answers to questions about illness causation as evidence that etiology is not important for Africans, a conclusion I disagree with.

Several nonhealer respondents said they are Christians so they only believe in modern medicine; their answers are accordingly tailored to what they think is biomedically acceptable. This is a variant of the tendency of rural—or poor, relatively powerless—Africans to tell well-dressed interviewers who represent the power elite what they think the interviewers want to hear. It does not necessarily mean that the respondents do not (also) believe in traditional medicine or consult healers.

Note also that some illnesses not considered STDs may be thought to be caused by sexual intercourse, at least some of the time. Quite a number of respondents saw a direct connection between tuberculosis and AIDS, even regarding them as the same disease. Of course, there is some basis for this view in Africa. Others believe urinary schistosomiasis to be caused or transmitted by sexual intercourse. These illnesses are discussed in Chapter Six.

SUMMARY OF FINDINGS ABOUT ADULT ILLNESSES

Findings reported in this chapter and part of the next derive from in-depth interviews with randomly selected respondents in Cimwemwe district, a predominantly Bemba-speaking area, and with randomly selected respondents in Chawama district, a predominantly Nyanja-speaking area. They also derive from interviews with a sample of 81 traditional healers in the Copperbelt area. The healers sample consisted of men and women, diviner-mediums, and herbalists. Perhaps because the Copperbelt is a relatively wealthy area with job opportunities in the mines and therefore many immigrants, traditional healers were from a variety of ethnolinguistic groups. The main group self-identified was Tumbuka, followed by Ngoni, Namwanga, Bemba, Lozi, Kaonde, Kunda, Chewa, Tabwa, Bisa/Lala, Kalinda, Shona, Lamba, Aushi, and Namwanga. This ethnic heterogeneity seems desirable from the viewpoint of identifying broad, regional patterns of ethnomedicine. Bemba illness terminology was used by most or all informants. Many illness names vary around the same root words among Bantu-speaking groups within a given region.

When healers were asked to name illnesses affecting people "in the nether area," the most frequently cited were: *akaswende* (the symptoms of which resemble gonorrhea), *akasele* (resembling syphilis), and *bola-bola* (resembling chancroid). Sometimes AIDS or HIV were mentioned. Next often in frequency of response was *ibele* or *tumukolwe* (vaginal warts). Less frequently mentioned were *mukolwe, umukunko, ulushinga, ubusako, icipelo* (resembling hernia); *insula* (swelling of testicles); *akankulila* (shrinking of testicles into the abdomen); *amabolo ukufimba* (swelling of the testicles); *ubusako, ulusula, ikando,* and *mukunko* (prolonged menstrual period); *icambu;* and *ubwamba ukukanaima.*

150

English names were often given in association with the four most common STIs (i.e., gonorrhea for *akaswende*; syphilis for *akasele*, chancroid for *bolabola*, and warts for *ibele* or *tumukolwe*). This does not mean that these STIs correspond symptomatically to the STDs of biomedicine in an exact way. Occasionally, an informant or interviewer translated *akasele* as gonorrhea rather than syphilis. This may be because of disagreement and/or confusion over STI symptoms as well as actual overlap between the biomedically recognized symptoms of gonorrhea and syphilis. It is also possible that symptoms of chlamydia are subsumed under *akaswende*; we should not assume from the present studies that Zambian healers simply do not recognize chlamydia. A major factor here is that compared to gonorrhea, chlamydia is not nearly as well recognized—or mentioned—by Zambian doctors and nurses. Traditional healers may well have never heard of this STD.

For each STI, a composite profile of causes, symptoms, and other characteristics has been constructed from reviewing all answers to survey questions and generalizing from the majority of answers in both the general and healer TIRs. One-time or idiosyncratic answers (e.g., *bolabola* is characterized by "blood . . . in the eyes and fingers") are generally not part of a profile. We turn now to the composite profiles of Zambian STIs, based on findings from the two TIRs.

GONORRHEA-LIKE ILLNESSES

From Cimwemwe and the Copperbelt, a gonorrhea-like illness is called *akasele*, less often *utulonda* or by the English term "leaking" (or *linkin'gi*). The primary symptom is pus discharge, or leaking, from the penis. Other symptoms include itching of the penis or vagina, stomach pains, genital sores, fever, blood discharge from genitals, "rash or pimples develop all over the body," pain when urinating, difficulty in urinating, vaginal discharge with bad odor, backache, abdominal pain, diarrhea, weakness, loss of appetite, and loss of weight.

One layman gave the order of symptoms as: (1) itching, (then) a small sore appears on the penis three–seven days after sex. It disappears without treatment and appears later; (2) sores spread around the penis; (3) pus discharge; (4) pain when urinating; (5) diarrhea; and (6) fever. A few others gave variants of this. Note that these and other informants

151

mentioned genital sore(s) as a symptom of *akasele,* and some mentioned a blood discharge or blood in the urine. These symptoms suggest syphilis, chancroid, or urinary schistosomiasis. Certainly there is overlap between the symptoms of *akasele* and *akaswende*, the STI considered next. Some informants commented that the symptoms of both STIs were very similar. And some noted that the illness is more serious in women because they can be without symptoms, therefore the illness is "difficult to notice." This conforms with the biomedical view.

Informants in Chawama referred to the same illness variously as *kasele*, also *chinzonono*, leaking, *linkin'gi*, and "drop."[3] Outstanding symptoms were pus discharge from the penis or vagina (leaking) and pain in urination. Some mentioned difficulty in urinating; fever; pain in the groin, abdominal, or waist area; and blood in the urine or discharge. A few mentioned genital sores or ulcers.

Representative causes of *akasele*, offered by respondents in the Bemba-speaking area, include:

"dirt (not washing our private parts) and mixing of blood."

"sleeping with a woman attending her monthly period."

"Insects found in the vagina of a woman . . . as the result of not being hygienic."

"At times, the germs (insect) can be gotten if you sit on the pus from a sick person."

"stepping where one with the disease dropped pus or urinated."

"too many sexual partners and (sharing the) same toilet with a sick person."

"germs and dirtiness of a woman who does not wash her privates."

"All these diseases come as a result of having sexual intercourse with an infected person. They are caused by *utushishi* [body insect] found in the water of the woman's vagina."

"Dirt is the major contributor. Having sex with many sexual partners may also cause it. Mixing of blood."

"casual sex and nothing else."

"The illness is caused by a germ. This germ results from dirty which comes as a result of having sex with different people without bathing." ["Dirty" is often used as a noun in Zambian English.]

Respondents in Chawama agreed with those in Cimwemwe. For most, the cause of *kasele*, *chinzonono*, etc., was "having sexual intercourse with a partner who is infected." Others said having too many sexual partners or sleeping with prostitutes or "sugar daddies." Some spoke of dirt found in vaginas as the cause, others referred to a tiny insect. Witchcraft was rarely mentioned or implied. Other representative or illuminating comments include:

"Menstrual discharge causes *chinzonono*."
"If a woman sleeps with two men and she didn't wash the dirt from the first man, then the mixture of semen can cause the illness leaking."
"I don't know the insect."
"(The cause is) dirt from women who do not bathe."
"If germs go down they eat you up."
"It destroys the intestines."

Virtually all respondents in both provinces said that the gonorrhea-type STI affects both men and women. Most believe it can cause infertility, and that it must manifest symptoms, at least in men. Most said the illness is serious, although not as serious as AIDS.

Regarding prevention, a few said that condoms are useful, but others denied this. One Chewa man said, "Semen causes *chinzonono*. Thus, when you have a condom on and semen (is) collected, the semen goes up the urethra and then it rots to cause *chinzonono* [gonorrhea]. This was a personal experience." Others said *chinzonono* can be prevented by not having many sexual partners. A number of respondents mentioned taking herbs or capsules before having sex with someone who might already be infected. The latter probably refers to antibiotics; this practice is known to exacerbate antimicrobial resistance. Several informants commented on ways to prevent STIs:

"(It) can be prevented if only women learn to clean themselves after sex."
"It can't be prevented especially (by) we who drink beer."
"(It can be prevented) by taking herbs before meeting a woman to have sex."
"by taking capsules or tablets in advance for prevention."

"Tattooing" (vaccination with indigenous medicine) was mentioned by several as a traditional means of STI prevention.

It appears that treatment with traditional medicine is thought to be effective because it "finishes" the illness and "cleans" the body or system. Some lay informants agreed with the comment of one informant, "At the hospital (*kasele*) doesn't get completely cured." Variants of this comment were made often by traditional healers. Some lay informants viewed traditional medicine as a necessary complement to hospital treatment; one said, "*Akasele* can be cured, if you go to the hospital early, finish your treatment and then go to the African doctor who will give you medicine that will make you vomit and diarrhea. It cleans your stomach and the disease comes out."

Other lay informants had higher opinions of hospital treatment. One said: "The hospital is better than the African doctor because they first examine you before giving you medicine." Actually, evidence from the healer TIR suggests that some 70% of healers perform physical examinations for STIs.

CHANCROID-LIKE ILLNESS: *BOLABOLA*

Symptoms of *bolabola* are similar to the STD chancroid. The name *bolabola* seems not to vary from group to group in Zambia, apparently because *bola* comes from the English "boil" or "ball" and is descriptive of symptoms. In Chawama, symptoms of *bolabola* include swollen groin and a sore or ulcer in the genital region that bursts at a later stage and produces pus. Another symptom is "walking with legs apart" due to the pain of brushing against the ulcer in the groin. Other symptoms include ulcers on the penis, thinning of hair, and slimming. This last was designated as a late-stage symptom, and might suggest evidence of local recognition of a close relationship found between chancroid and AIDS (Caldwell and Caldwell 1994:204).

As causes of *bolabola*, respondents spoke of *tudoyo* (insects) and dirt, as with the other two common STIs and AIDS. Contact with menstrual discharge or other vaginal liquid was also a cause, and was related to dirt and sometimes insects. Respondents also mentioned as causes sleeping around, sex with too many people, and prostitution, as with other STIs.

The illness, and sometimes the insect, was said to "eat up" veins or intestines inside a person. Several informants commented that *bolabola* can cause infertility. *Bolabola* was said to be prevented by not having many sexual partners, or by using medicinal protection from a traditional healer. In the latter case, a person believed protected "can sleep with any infected person" without danger.

154

Informants in Cimwemwe described *bolabola* symptoms as swelling, ulcer(s), or bubo(es) in the groin or genital area which swell further and eventually burst. There is also pain when urinating, "failure to walk properly," and pus discharge at a later stage. Attributed causes are also much the same as those offered in Chawama:

"when you have sexual intercourse with too many partners."

"using same toilet with some affected person; (using) the same bedding, not washing your penis, and through sexual intercourse."

"*Bola-Bola*/chancroid could be transmitted by sitting on the pus left by the sufferer."

"*Akaswende* and *bolabola* are caused by dirt on the private parts of male and female (not washing our bodies), causing a germ."

"An insect which is found in the semen of an infected men." [This remark was from a woman respondent.]

"(It is from) sex with an infected person. A person who is carrying this body insect.

"This illness can affect both men and women because the insects that cause *bolabola* are found in both sex organs."

"I only know that there are some minute parasites that cause this disease and the same applies to all three diseases [STIs] we are discussing."

Note that insects and dirt seem linked. One Bemba-speaking respondent explained that *bolabola* is "caused by the insects found in the sex organs of a man or woman. The insects come as the result of not cleaning the sex organs after intercourse."

According to respondents in both Chawama and Cimwemwe, *bolabola* is considered easily treatable by traditional or modern medicine. It is not viewed as very serious if treated early. Traditional treatment consists of drinking a decoction made from roots, which expels the illness or illness agent. We found an idea already encountered in Mozambique, namely that drinking herbal medicine "makes the disease pass through urine."

Like other local STIs, *bolabola* is considered preventable by use of traditional medicines, by avoiding sex with too many partners or risky partners (those with the illness or with dirt or insects), or perhaps by use of condoms. As with answers to questions about AIDS and other locally recognized STIs, it is not known how sincere answers are about the value of condoms—considering the very low condom prevalence rate in Zambia (roughly 2% in 1994–95). At best, expressions about the value of

155

condoms would come from something heard on the radio or at a clinic, rather than arising from personal experience.

Another STI, *indangili*, was also mentioned by a few Bemba-speaking respondents. It too "has ulcers or sores in the genital area as one of its symptoms. The other symptoms are itching and fever." One respondent described a syndrome more like "crabs" or at least one that begins that way: "*Indangili* is caused by insects that live in the hair that grows around the genital areas and armpits. If not noticed very quickly they eat up the hair roots and lay their eggs in the holes. If they become too many they start eating up the skin which later on become sores and they keep on becoming big sores." I offer this description of genital lice as an example of how the idea of tiny STI-carrying insects might have arisen independently of Western biomedicine, along with the example of larvae in dirty water mentioned earlier.

SYPHILIS-LIKE ILLNESS
(*KASWENDE* IN NYANJA; *AKASWENDE* IN BEMBA)

In Chawama, symptoms of *kaswende* were said to be genital sores, fever, pus discharge, pain in urination, itching, abdominal pain, and swollen testicle. Note the confusion between a syphilis-like and a gonorrhea-like illness. Some even spoke of "walking, legs apart" and large genital ulcers which later burst, symptoms more associated with *bolabola*/chancroid. Syphilis and chancroid symptoms are therefore also sometimes confused, if we use STD symptoms as the yardstick. Even traditional healers failed to mention the painless sore which is the defining characteristic of syphilis.

In Cimwemwe, symptoms of *akaswende* were virtually the same: genital sores, fever, pus discharge. Again, we see symptom overlap between a syphilis-like and a gonorrhea-like illness. One informant commented that *akaswende* and *bolabola* are the same illness. Attributed causes of *akaswende*, sometimes called syphilis by respondents, look much the same as those we have already encountered for *akasele* and *bolabola*:

"from sleeping with an infected woman."
"Menstrual discharges cause syphilis; having sex with a woman who doesn't wash her discharges nicely."

"Sharing clothes (especially pants) with an infected person."
"Akaswende and *bolabola* are caused by dirt on the private parts of male and female."
"(It is) caused by *utushishi* (insects)."
"(It is) caused by *utushishi* germs that eat away the skin."
"These diseases (*akaswende, akasele, bolabola*) are caused by certain living organisms that live in the human blood (*utushishi*)."
"dirt found in private parts of women."

Among Bemba-speaking respondents, insect and dirt were the immediate causes attributed to *akaswende,* and promiscuity or multiple sexual partners were given as less immediate causes. Still less immediate seems to be violation of taboos governing sexual behavior (e.g., having sex with a menstruating woman or one who has had a recent association with death).

Like the other Zambian STIs, *akaswende* is believed able to cause infertility, destroy or "eat up" the intestines, and perhaps destroy the sex organs. An informant in Cimwemwe commented on the pain and isolation of an *akaswende* sufferer: "A person is always in pain and feels he is neglected by fellow friends. At times he feels mentally disturbed."

Akaswende can be prevented by taking traditional medicine in advance or by "drinking the yellow and black capsule." A behavioral method is to refrain from sexual intercourse with those "who have too many sexual partners" or "who patronize bars." A few respondents mentioned condoms or fidelity (e.g., "In certain [circumstances], [*akaswende*] could be prevented by use of condoms and sticking to one sexual partner and by the traditional healers who use selected roots [for drinking])."

Indigenous and modern treatments were both mentioned, and supporters of both were found among laypersons. One critic of indigenous treatment commented that some people die from traditional treatment "because there is no proper dosage in the medication of African doctors."

OTHER ILLNESSES WITH GENITO-URINARY SYMPTOMS

A number of other locally recognized illness were mentioned with genito-urinary symptoms or that affect the "nether" or "shyness" areas of the body or the reproductive system. Instead of discussing all of these, I will present beliefs about causation of some of the more frequently mentioned illnesses. This should assist our understanding the etiology of contagious

157

illness, in part by contrasting them with illnesses considered noncontagious.

Genital warts are called *nkombola*, *Ibele ibele*, or *akamukolwe* in Chawama and Cimwemwe. Comments about causation are of interest:

> "Polyps/warts just come, they have no cause. . . . It's not a serious disease."
> "The causes of *akamukolwe* are natural" [i.e., there are no known causes].
> "I don't really know what the cause of *nkombola* is."
> "(It) can be treated by a traditional healer."
> "They just come."
> "(They) cannot be prevented because the illness has no cause."
> "It is caused by *tushishi* (insects)."
> "It just comes on its own."
> "*Akamukolwe* is an illness that is not transmitted by any means."

The most frequent comment was that warts just come, and therefore have no cause. Insects or germs were seldom mentioned, nor was witchcraft, sorcery, spirits, magic, or taboo violation.

Other, nongenito-urinary illnesses were identified that "cannot be transmitted," that are not contagious. These may be inherited (one is born with the condition) or they "just happen—they have no cause." Illnesses of this sort include anemia, diarrhea in adults or ordinary diarrhea, swollen feet or legs, some types of headache or stomachache, "paralysis on one side of the body" (stroke?), "aching bones," and "ordinary cough (not tuberculosis/*ichifuba*)." Of swollen feet/legs, someone mentioned a characteristic of hereditary illness: "We are born with this illness, therefore cannot be transmitted to the other person." But another respondent said the cause of this syndrome was "stepping on African medicine," a reference to sorcery. Other illnesses or conditions not considered transmitted are those caused by injury or trauma (e.g., backache caused by "doing work while you are bent over").

Interviewers encountered a woman's illness in Cimwemwe called *kusuma amenshi*. Its main symptom appears to be a painless, watery vaginal discharge. "The only problem is that the person with the disease feels shy (with) other people because of her condition." The cause of this illness was said to be dirt:

> If the woman does not clean herself properly then she will have this disease. This disease is also believed to be caused by "Juju," that is, if a

woman flirts with another woman's husband, then the woman whose husband is going out would practice some African medicine on her as punishment.

A women's genito-urinary or menstrual syndrome called *ikando* was described in Cimwemwe. Its symptoms were "pain when attending monthly period, perhaps vomiting, small sores in the genital areas, failure to pass urine, and pain in urination. In describing its cause, some informants said *ikando* has no cause, it simply "affects the unfortunate ones." A minority view was that *ikando* could be transmitted nonsexually (e.g., "[It can be] transmitted by wearing outfits of the infected"). However, most claimed that *ikando* "cannot be prevented by any means as it has no cause," and most believed that this illness can be treated only by "African medicines and not Western medicine."

It is common in southern Africa to encounter a men's genito-urinary or testicular syndrome characterized by swollen testicles. This may be hydrocele or another condition of scrotal mass, which relates to hernia or trauma or which perhaps is congenital. Hydrocele is not biomedically regarded as sexually transmitted. In Cimwemwe, *insula* symptoms were described as swelling of testicles, pain in the testicles, abnormal appearance of the testicles, not walking properly, "change in step when walking," fever, pain in the veins, and hardness of the stomach. This apparently noncontagious syndrome is etiologically different from the major STIs we have considered. Some representative comments:

"It is not transmitted in any way, it just comes."

"(It is) a result of witchcraft. This illness cannot be transmitted from one person to another because it comes as a result of witchcraft."

"Swollen testicles . . . only start on their own and they can never be transmitted from one person to the other."

"(It has) no cause; this disease is not transmitted."

"Witches put people in this pain. The disease is not transmitted to another person through sexual intercourse, but witches do this."

"(It) can be caused by using dirty water."

"Swollen testicles can never be prevented as they just start on their own and may at times stop on their own."

We again see evidence that an illness usually attributed to witchcraft and sorcery illness *is not* seen as contagious. In fact, this is logical: In illnesses or conditions of this type, an individual is deliberately targeted for misfortune. Recall from Chapter One, part of Foster's (1976:775) definition of a personalistic illness is that "The sick person literally is a victim, the object of aggression or punishment directed specifically against him, for reasons that concern him alone. Personalistic causality allows little room for accident."

AIDS

Among Bemba-speaking respondents, AIDS is called *Kalombo Mwane*, *ukondoloka* ("slim disease") or as *akashishi*, which, as already noted, means small insect or simply agent of illness transmission. A few said AIDS is known as *kaliondeonde*, an illness caused by death pollution and considered untreatable by hospital medicine. This illness is characterized by diarrhea, loss of weight (or slimming), fever and any type of prolonged illnesses. In other words, this illness was described in a way that accurately reflects the profile of AIDS as it is manifest in Africa.

Other symptoms mentioned include, in rough order of importance, loss of hair, hair turning light colored, vomiting, tuberculosis (*ichifuba*; see Chapter Six), body weakness, rash, sweating, cough, headache, malaria, shivering, being sickly, sores that do not heal, and loss of appetite (note that all symptoms are accurate for AIDS). Some respondents drew a parallel between AIDS and tuberculosis symptoms; others saw even more of a connection, saying the two diseases are causally connected (which in Africa is often true.) The great majority did not believe it possible to have AIDS without symptoms, although one respondent said "AIDS is so serious because symptoms come too late when the illness has (already) advanced." Another said, "It's possible to have AIDS without having symptoms, until ones goes to the hospital and they are tested to have the disease AIDS." Asked about the order in which symptoms appear, one respondent said, "You cannot tell which sign comes first because the person can sometimes have so many diseases at once."

The main cause of AIDS was said to be having sex with someone infected with AIDS. Some respondents also mentioned blood transfusion and syringes. Some referred to mechanisms more related to indigenous causality concepts, notably pollution (e.g., "sleeping with someone who has aborted without being cleansed"). Others mentioned forms of casual contact commonly mentioned all over the world (e.g., kissing, bites from bed bugs, sharing clothing or used razor blades, etc.). At least one respondent mentioned witchcraft as a cause, but most saw AIDS as a new disease best understood biomedically, or as a variant of other, familiar STIs caused by sexual misconduct or more immediately by insects or dirt. Representative comments include:

"This illness is caused by an unknown insect. It is transmitted through sexual intercourse."

"AIDS is caused by *tushishi* (insect).

"(AIDS is caused by) *akashishi* [insects] that moves in the blood, and stays in the *mumenshi* [semen] of the men and women."

"It results from a man having sex with a woman who has just aborted; treatment consists of 'cleansing the whole body.'"

"AIDS is caused by women."

"(AIDS) is caused by prostitution."

"(AIDS is caused) by adultery."

"(AIDS is caused) by having sexual intercourse with a lot of women who may be infected."

"(Some) who drink a lot of *kachasu* [locally brewed gin] get this disease of slimming after (drinking) for a long time without proper diet."

"(It is) caused by *kashishi* that eats the genital area."

"(It is) caused by syringes that have been used by someone with the disease."

"(It is) an illness of shyness—one becomes a laughing stock in the society."

Most respondents reported that AIDS is serious, fatal, and incurable. Some said that traditional healers can treat it even if they cannot cure it (an opinion shared by the WHO). A few believed that healers can cure AIDS. Respondents were divided over whether AIDS causes or is related to infertility. In one detailed answer, the respondent commented, "Apart from causing infertility, AIDS causes death and suffering among parents, relatives of the diseased person in terms of taking care of the sick, providing moral and financial support."

Among Nyanja-speaking respondents in Chawama, AIDS is conceived in very much the same way as in Cimwemwe: It is caused by an insect (*kadoyo*) or by dirt and it is transmitted by having sex with someone who has the insect, dirt, or virus. Other biomedically taught causes such as unsterile needles and blood transfusions were also mentioned. The role of blood or contaminated blood seems understood, although sometimes it is not clear whether the biomedical or indigenous pollution model is

161

being expressed (e.g., in the comment, "If someone has a bleeding sore and an AIDS patient has a bleeding sore and their bleeding sores meet, then the one who is not a patient will suffer from it"). The symptoms mentioned are also essentially the same in the two provinces: wasting (slimming), chronic diarrhea, and respiratory problems characteristic of tuberculosis. Some thought the symptoms of AIDS could be absent or subdued, as in this comment: "(The man with AIDS) is not sick but will be finishing bit by bit."

On a behavioral level, AIDS was thought to be caused by "having sex just with anyone," prostitution, too much sex, or "promiscuity." Prevention was thought to be possible by either avoiding sex or using condoms, or—in some cases—avoiding casual contact believed to account for AIDS transmission (sharing razors or clothes, "barber shops not using spirits," etc.). Others spoke of preventing AIDS by sticking to one sexual partner, "conducting yourself well," or "not having sex just with anyone, in any way."

About treatment, most respondents expressed something like this comment: "Both the (doctor) and the traditional healer have failed to cure this disease (AIDS)." Most felt the illness can also be spread to unborn children as well as sexual partners: "When the woman is pregnant, all the three people will die, the child, the mother, and the father."

DISCUSSION OF STI CAUSATION THEORIES

The language and imagery of ritual impurity or pollution are evident among both laypersons and traditional healers, although healers are often better able—or more ready—to explain indigenous concepts. It can be seen that hygiene, moral restraint, and taboo observance helps maintain purity; lack of these lead to contact with dangerous substances such as reproductive fluids or death, and hence to STIs including AIDS. There is also frequent reference to illness-carrying insects, evidence of indigenous germ theory or naturalistic infection.

For most healers, the immediate cause of *akaswende, akasele,* and *bolabola* is *utushishi,* an agent of illness translated as "insect" or "bacteria." Those who mentioned the STI *tumukolwe* said it is also (immediately) caused by an *utushishi.* This illness agent is believed to reside in sperm, vaginal fluid, and the blood of both men and women.

Healers might refer to an STI sufferer having "contaminated blood." Sometimes a healer will say these illnesses are "found in either the penis or the vagina," without being more specific. It seems that each STI has its own distinctive *utushishi* (e.g., a healer speaks of "the *utushishi* that can cause *bolabola*," or a layman characterizes the identity of the "insect" causing AIDS as "unknown.") In this regard, *utushishi* is equivalent to the STI-causing *khoma* of the Shona-speaking traditional healers of Mozambique, who speak of it in exactly the same way.

Illness from *utushishi* is contracted primarily from sexual intercourse, although for many or most healers it can also result from contact with clothing or toilets "carelessly used by a patient" with an STI. One can get *tumukolwe* by "stepping on medicine that someone who had this illness had washed off," by wearing the pants of a sufferer, by "stepping on infected urine with bare feet," or "being near an infected person and getting his or her sweat or smell." Healers with more biomedical awareness or education deny that STDs (rather than STIs) such as syphilis or chancroid or AIDs can be transmitted by casual contact. In the words of one, "It is not true that (these three illnesses) can be transmitted by exchanging clothes and/or sharing the same toilet or any other . . . means. Only sexual intercourse." However, most healers seem to believe that STIs can be transmitted by what we call casual contact.

Some healers said that the three or four common STIs are all caused by dirt or dirty, code words of pollution. One elaborated: "In men the dirty that causes gonorrhoea is carried in the sperm while in women the dirty is carried in the vaginal fluid. This dirty is also found in the blood. The dirty is transmitted because there's an exchange of blood, vaginal fluid, and sperm during sexual contact."

At times, dirt seems a simple concept, something that results from mere lack of hygiene. At one level this is true. But it is more than the equivalent concept in English, it is something that results from violation of moral codes and taboos. Both notions can be inferred from the following quote from a healer: "Gonorrhea is caused by dirt. This dirt comes when a woman is having sexual intercourse with different men and not washing the vagina. Different sperms form dirt that cause gonorrhea."

One healer referred to "insects that are dirty and deadly," again linking the two concepts, dirt and insect. Even more tellingly, another healer referred to bubos being caused by "dirty water that is inside the private parts (and) changes into (an) insect." One healer tried to translate the local illness agent into the biomedical analogue: "The dirty on the sex organs develops into a germ that may either cause gonorrhea, syphilis, or chancroid." Thus, dirt underlies and gives rise to insect or germ. In any case, the two concepts seem to be directly and causally related.

Another healer said "Each illness has an 'egg of illness'" (*utumani twabulwele*), apparently another expression of the idea of a tiny, invisible illness agent. Some healers used the English medical terminology of germs or bacteria instead of insect or dirt. Several healers referred to the pus of STIs as an element of dirt or as something the insect secretes or transmits and that is contagious, accounting for transmission of an STI through casual contact. One healer said this holds true for gonorrhea and syphilis, "but not chancroid because there's no insect in the pus from buboes." For some, pus seemed synonymous with dirt or dirty.

Only one healer claimed that gonorrhea and syphilis are caused by witchcraft. This healer actually described a process more like sorcery with impersonal, unsorcery-like elements: A poison is left at a crossroad where a victim (intended?) can walk by and catch the illness from contact with the poison. This sounds like an example of an ICT-type environmental danger found at crossroads, as described by Ngubane (1977:26). In fact, in relating the transmission of these same STIs, the same healer described a more direct pollution process: "Through having sex, the dirty from an infected person together with the infected blood can easily be deposited either in the man or woman once there is this exchange of blood with an infected blood."

What we might call the intermediate causes of STIs includes sexual intercourse with a person with a particular *utushishi* or type of dirt. More broadly speaking, STIs are caused by having certain types of prohibited sex, or sex with prohibited persons, or sex with persons considered in a polluted state such as menstruating women, widows, or women who have suffered a death in the immediate family. STIs can also be caused by having sex with those who have many partners, with strangers, or with those who do not wash themselves or practice genital hygiene. Sex with too many people or with strangers (including prostitutes) is dangerous because these people might carry the insects or dirt of an STI; they might be in a polluted state.

It is noteworthy that several other, less common and perhaps less serious illnesses "affecting the nether area" such as *mukunko* (prolonged menstrual period) and *mukolwe* (vaginal warts), are transmitted through the impersonal process characteristic of pollution. For example, these illnesses can be contracted by passing by a "road junction which was being used by the patient to bathe so that she gets rid of the illness." Or they can be contracted by touching a plate handled by a patient. *Ulushinga* is likewise unrelated to witchcraft, sorcery, or spirits, but to pollution concepts. It is: "mainly caused by dirt. Mothers don't know how to clean the genital organs of their babies. This (breaks into) the passage where urine has to pass and eventually develops into an illness. Even older people who don't clean genital organs develop the same problem."

Some illnesses, such as *ibele* (genital warts), are believed to be transmitted through breastfeeding. Some believe that illnesses such as *ibele* and *ubwamba ukukanaima* are congenital or inborn illnesses that "follow the blood line for a certain clan." An inborn illness is considered distinct from other types of illness, including those caused by pollution. One healer specifically commented that unlike syphilis, "There's nothing like dirty or insects in the blood" with *ibebe*. Furthermore, *ibele* is not contagious and cannot be transmitted through sexual intercourse. *Ibele* was also described by a healer as "naturally caused" (equivalent to "it comes on its own"), which for Zambian healers and their patients (judging by the STD TIR) means that these illnesses are not considered contagious. On the other hand, there may be a link between hereditary and pollution illnesses. The illness described as prolonged menstrual periods was described as "caused by the 'dirty water' that some people inherit from their parents who had earlier on suffered from an STD." Dirty water refers presumably to body fluids carrying an agent of infection or pollution.

Elderly men can also get genital warts from contact with the "medicines women insert in their vaginas . . . to please men during sexual intercourse." These medicines are probably vaginal tightening agents, abrasives or irritants used in Zambia and elsewhere in the region. These are considered risk factors in the transmission of HIV (Brown et al. 1993).

TREATMENT

As discussed in Chapter One, "The therapies found in every society stem largely from prevailing causality beliefs, which form the rationale for treatment" (Foster 1983:17–24). Foster suggests that the world can be divided into: (1) places that recognize the equilibrium model, where patients believe they know what has happened to them (e.g., too much "cold" food); and (2) places that follow personalistic explanations of illness, where a practitioner with supernatural powers is needed to divine the ultimate cause and to determine how to placate or overcome the supernatural agent. In (1), self-diagnosis is the rule and self-treatment is common, although traditional healers may also be sought for herbs, massages, and other treatments in line with equilibrium theory. If we take the equilibrium model to mean naturalistic or impersonal causation rather than being only one expression of this, and if we accept pollution beliefs in southern Africa to be an example of impersonal and at least quasi-naturalistic causation, is Foster's hypothesis validated by the treatment of STIs in Zambia?

According to the two TIR surveys, all STIs (and diarrheas) seem to be regarded as treatable and curable, although some have heard—and seem to agree—that the new disease AIDS is not. Zambian traditional healers are allopaths in their treatment of the common STIs: The main objective of treatment is to kill an infective micro-organism (insect, dirt, bacteria, virus), or expel it from the body or blood. As is characteristic of healers in the broader region, they use herbal decoctions (teas, or, less often, herbs mixed in porridge) made from boiled roots. These might have the effect of purgatives or emetics, especially if they are supposed to expel dirt. Some medicine is said to make the illness insect leave the body through frequent urination, a finding we encountered in Mozambique. Other treatment objectives include cleaning the blood, healing wounds, or making specific symptoms disappear such as warts, ulcers, sores, or other visible skin symptoms. STIs featuring sores or ulcers may be treated topically with poultices made with powdered roots. For STIs with warts or growths, these might be cut out and/or the patient may be asked to sit in a container of water with crushed medicinal roots.

Sometimes the treatment objective is described as "cleansing the body" or "purifying the blood." One healer explained, "In the case of chancroid the aim is to neutralize the pus and purify the dirt that is found in the blood. The nerves become normal again. In the case of gonorrhea and syphilis, the *tushishi* are killed completely and the blood purified." Whatever the treatment choice, clearly there is a logical connection between this and the "mystical premise" (or identified cause) proposed or diagnosed.

Although most herbal medicines were described as taken orally, some healers used herbal suppositories or "put powdered roots in the anus." Medicine was also introduced through "tattoos" around the waist and elsewhere. These are actually small incisions made with a razor blade; herbal paste is then rubbed into the incisions. For example, for *bolabola*: "I burn the medicine to get the charcoal which I crush to powder and make tattoos on the parts affected and I also give (medicine) for drinking over a two-week period." This same process is called *kugata* among the Swazi and Zulu, and the burned powder is called *insiti*. In some African countries, this treatment is referred to as traditional vaccination, although the purpose is usually curative rather than preventive.

Zambian healers appeared quite open about the roots they use, considering how secretive such knowledge is supposed to be traditionally. Some healers expressed to me their strong desire to have curative roots for STIs analyzed by hospitals to prove their efficacy to doubting doctors.

CHOICE IN STD TREATMENT
AND FAITH IN TRADITIONAL MEDICINE

A majority of lay respondents said that traditional healers are able to cure the major STIs; this response was elicited from a random sample of Zambians, reflecting normal variations in income, education, and occupation. Even educated respondents expressed faith in traditional treatment. When asked about the causes of *akasele* and *akaswende*, one man in Cimwemwe correctly named the genus and species of the bacteria that cause gonorrhea and syphilis. As for treatment, he commented, "those treated with Western medicines are not completely cured because the same illness affects them again, and in case of *akasele*, it causes infertility. But traditional medicines cure both illnesses completely . . . hence traditional medicines are the best."

In fact, a number of laypersons and virtually all healers expressed the view that hospital medicines only alleviate symptoms and do not do the full job of killing or expelling the agent of illness; symptoms will return unless indigenous medicine is used. In evaluating this attitude, it should be remembered that there is considerable antimicrobial resistance to common STDs in countries like Zambia, perhaps especially with gonorrhea and chancroid. Even when antibiotics could be effective, patients may not take the full course for various reasons. Moreover, hospitals may

167

run out of antibiotics, or dilute them to make them go farther. This, in combination with antibiotic resistance, means that modern antibiotics may be as ineffective as they appear to many Zambians.

Apart from *materia medica*, respondents generally saw traditional healers as more sympathetic, more likely to keep confidences, and more accessible than modern health workers, which parallels exactly the findings of the Malawi TIR (Helitzer-Allen and Allen 1992:30). Clinics are regarded as busy, impersonal, and very public places to be seen waiting in a queue when one has an embarrassing condition.

Of course, research must be done to determine whether healers can successfully treat any STDs with their indigenous medicine. Until this is accomplished, we cannot responsibly develop a strategy designed to influence treatment behavior. If healers *cannot* treat STDs successfully, then the emphasis must be either on influencing healers to refer their patients to clinics, *or* to think about involving healers in syndrome-based treatment with antibiotics, at least on a pilot or cooperating basis. By the latter I mean that healers who have attended AIDS/STD workshops could cooperate with a biomedically trained clinician in syndrome-based treatment, perhaps at the healer's place of business.

On the other hand, if healers are found to be able to cure some STDs, we need to first determine which ones. This outcome would obviously change a general strategy of somehow influencing clients of traditional healers to report to clinics instead of to healers—a difficult task under the best of circumstances.

Note the crucial role of belief in the cause of STIs: Many Zambians prefer traditional healers over hospitals and clinics not only because of some of the "cultural" reasons such as feeling comfortable, but because they believe modern biomedicine cannot actually kill the agent causing the STI—it can only alleviate symptoms. Thus, the detail with which the STI cause is discussed in this book is justified by its crucial role in understanding—and perhaps influencing—choice of treatment.

BLOOD CONCEPTS

Our Zambian findings suggest areas deserving further investigation. We have already encountered the notion of diminished resistance to illness—including pollution-related illness in some Bantu-speaking societies. Whether this is expressed as *nyoka* (Shona) or strong/weak blood (Zulu), it resembles the biomedical idea of an immune system. Strong blood and weak blood are concepts that also arose in our Zambian research. Strong blood refers both to potency and to resistance to sickness. However, according to a colleague working in AIDS prevention with healers in Uganda (King, personal communication), "Strong blood usually relates to someone who may be infected with HIV and has not come down with symptoms, or to someone whose children all resemble him/her rather than the other parent." This concept should be explored further through in-depth research. Is there a link between strong/weak blood and the bio-medical concept of the immune system? How widespread is the concept? Are there contradictory meanings, depending on group? Could these concepts be used in explaining biomedical concepts of both AIDS and STDs to both traditional healers and to laypersons? Could such concepts be used in mass media AIDS education?

Bad or dirty blood seems to be a related indigenous concept. As in other societies that neighbor Zambia, STIs and perhaps AIDS are con-ceived as illnesses involving blood that becomes bad, dirty, or impure from excessive "mixing" or contact with "strange blood" through sexual contact. In his pioneer fieldwork among the Kgatla (Tswana) of Botswana, Schapera (1940:196) reported that: "A woman promiscuous in her sexual favors will likewise acquire 'bad hips,' through the accu-mulation in her body of the 'bloods' of many different men. 'These bloods fight one another, they do not agree, and they poison the woman's body.' The condition is held to be contagious."

In a later publication, Schapera (1978:174) refers to "pre-marital promiscuity" among the Kgatla, noting, "If a girl had many lovers her womb became spoiled, because the different 'bloods' ejaculated into her 'disagreed' with one another."

Returning to the earlier work, Schapera (1940) reported that syphilis was widespread in the 1930s and was "recognized as a distinctive dis-ease": "But, although its connection with sexual life is well known, it is not held to result from 'hot blood.' In fact, according to some informants, many people do not regard it as contagious, and have little hesitation im sleeping with persons infected with it" (p. 196). On the other hand, there were many remedies for "bad hips," whose symptoms Schapera thought "are almost certainly those of gonorrhea," noting, "These remedies are designed in most cases to 'purify' the blood and so remove the infection" (p. 196).

Although we cannot know for sure what Tswana informants of the 1930s meant when they spoke of syphilis, at least one major class of STIs was apparently seen as a contagious, pollution-type illness very similar to those STIs I and my colleagues have investigated in southern Africa. For example, during workshops for South African traditional healers representing all major, local ethnic groups except, as it happens, the Tswana, healers were in general agreement that one's blood "gets dirty" from having too many sexual partners. Moreover, one can get STIs from "mixing blood from different sex partners."

Several informants in the Zambian general TIR expressed the same view: STIs result from too many partners and a resulting excess of "mixing of blood" or "mixture of semen." This mixing spreads "dirt" or STI agents. Consider a fairly typical comment from Cimwemwe: "*Akaswende* and *bolabola* (are) caused by dirt and mixture of blood from too many sexual partners." Although dirt may be conceived as resulting from simple lack of hygiene, it may have another dimension, relating it to lack of moral behavior. Recall the healer who commented, "Different sperms form dirt which cause gonorrhea." Or the Cewa man who said, "If a woman sleeps with two men and she didn't wash the dirt from the first man, then the mixture of semen can cause the illness 'leaking'." A respondent in Cimwemwe commented about syphilis-resembling *akasele*:

> This is a disease that is caused by dirty blood. When a man meets a woman during sexual intercourse, there is a point where a man actually touches to reach the climax. This is the point where the sperms are ejected into the womb. At this point, blood is exchanged and if this blood is dirty, the man will come out with it and the same blood will stick on the skin of the man. Once it is kept there for sometime, it will form some pimples and later cause a sore.

Blood of this sort is believed to be contagious, or to carry contagious agents of illness. In the words of a different Cimwemwe informant also describing *akasele*: "(It) can be transmitted by stepping on the blood or touching the blood . . . passed out by a sick person."

It would seem that strategies for culturally appropriate and effective ways of introducing and promoting condoms could be based in part on the concept of bad or dirty blood. Among the elements of a condom-promotion strategy: (1) AIDS or HIV (and perhaps some other STDs) seem to be understood as a disease of bad blood; (2) People must avoid contact with one another's blood; and (3) People with HIV/AIDS (or perhaps certain other STIs) and their sexual partners must use a condom in order to avoid contact with "impure blood."

During discussions with South African healers in a 1992 AIDS prevention workshop, some important information arose about condoms and entry points for their promotion. Several healers explained that it is not traditional for a healer to advise a patient to refrain from intercourse while the patient is undergoing treatment for an STI or another illness. A husband may react negatively if his wife is advised by a healer to refrain from intercourse during her treatment. Intercourse with a condom is preferable to refraining from sex altogether, and a husband can understand that bad blood will not be transferred to him by his wife if he uses a condom. Note that healers at the workshop stressed the notion of bad or impure blood—in fact, AIDS seemed to be understood more or less accurately as a disease of bad blood, which for healers explained why people must avoid direct blood-to-blood contact (Green et al. 1992:38).

In view of the importance of this regionwide concept, there should be more qualitative research on the concept of bad or dirty blood so as to refine general communication strategies between traditional healers and health care personnel, as well as specific strategies for the promotion of condoms and sticking to one partner. AIDS educators could usefully adopt the language of "mixing of blood" without compromising medical facts or public health in any way. After all, what is HIV infection but the transmission of an illness agent from one person's blood to another?

GENERAL CONCLUSIONS

STI etiologic beliefs among Zambians and Mozambicans emphasize two major components of ICT: naturalistic infection and pollution. Clearly, such etiology represents an area of potential interface between indigenous and cosmopolitan medicine. Both agree that the cause of sexually transmitted illness is impersonal and, in fact, relates to conditions that may be modifiable, such as avoiding sex with strangers or contamination/infection with an unseen agent of illness that can be sexually transmitted. Both are concerned with prevention of contact with agents of illness whether these are conceived as agents of pollution, or as microbes. Both agree on the role of cleanliness and general hygiene (the maintenance of purity and the avoidance of dirt). Both agree generally on the role of blood: Traditional

171

healers sometimes referred to STIs as well as AIDS as a condition of bad or impure blood. Certainly the admonition that people must avoid contact with the blood of a person with AIDS makes sense to traditional healers.

Foster (1983:21) tells us that indigenous preventive measures, like treatment, are always in conformity with prevailing beliefs about illness causality, therefore these practices may not be biomedically effective as preventions. In Africa, prevention may take the form of medicines used in a variety of ways including immunizations, as well as sacrifices and offerings, the wearing of amulets to ward off evil, and "the observance of prohibitions and taboos and a number of rituals including bodily hygiene" (Koumare 1983:27).

Prevention is the foundation of public health in general and AIDS programs in particular. Yet Africans are often thought to be fatalistic—to not believe that prevention of illness and misfortune is possible. This is only partially true. Of the four categories of illness causation in southern Africa (spirit-sent, witchcraft and sorcery, pollution, and natural causes), those considered naturally caused are usually thought to be unpreventable because they "have no cause." Illness believed due to witchcraft, sorcery, or spirits cannot be prevented because superhuman will cannot be thwarted by mere human effort. For contagious, pollution-related illnesses, on the other hand, prevention may relate to agents of pollution or to actual medicines intended to provide protection against future opportunities for contact with dangerous contaminants. Or prevention may depend on certain types of behavior. Recognition of this was basic to communication strategies I recommended to the AIDS/STD projects in both Zambia and Mozambique.

Prevention is essentially the same for all STDs, therefore AIDS/STD preventive education in both countries can make the same pitch for STIs. Furthermore, the cause of all STDs is, biomedically speaking, essentially a tiny, unseen organism, even if distinctions are made between bacteria, viruses, and protozoa. The Africans interviewed believed the immediate cause or agent of STIs to be tiny, unseen agents of illnesses characterized as insects or minuscule animals—much the same as germs, even if some more elaborate processes involving pollution and taboo violation beliefs are part of the broader etiology of STIs. The point is that biomedicine and indigenous medicine already agree on the agent and means of prevention: These tiny organisms carrying STIs or STDs should not be transmitted from person to person.

172

There is also considerable agreement between public health and indigenous beliefs about the role of behavior in prevention of STIs/STDs, including AIDS. An objective of the Morehouse/Tulane project was to enlist the help of indigenous healers in promoting reduction of the number of sexual partners one has, or in the popular phrase, "sticking to one partner." Zambian and Mozambican healers already interpreted locally recognized STIs as resulting from a violation of the codes that govern proper sexual behavior, and they recognized that sexual intercourse outside of marriage poses dangerous risks of illness. Some Zambian healers commented to me that they felt encouraged and vindicated to learn that their own governments as well as the international community *also* wish to warn people against having sex with "just anyone," with too many people, with strangers, with prostitutes.

These are actual examples of STI prevention given by both traditional healers and their clients on behavioral ways to avoid STIs, just as an illness like bilharzia can be prevented by avoiding swimming in dirty water. It is not of great health education consequence that these examples of indigenous preventive methods are based on exotic-seeming premises related to pollution (e.g., sex with strangers is dangerous because one never knows if the partner is contaminated with menstrual blood or a recent association with death). The message remains the same: To be safe, one must remain faithful to one's partner.

BELIEFS AND ATTITUDES ABOUT CONDOMS

Traditional healers were skeptical about condoms. Many believed condoms are of limited usefulness because they can burst or fall off, an obstacle to condom use cited in a great many parts of Africa. One Zambian healer said, "The condom does not cover all the penis hence leaving a certain area exposed to insects." There is truth to this—a fact that many Western professionals who promote condoms are unaware of. Chancroid is very common in Africa and it is possibly the most important STD that increases the risk of HIV transmission yet it is not preventable —at least fully preventable—by condom use (Jones and Wasserheit 1991). Nor are venereal warts fully preventable by condoms.

The views of African healers are similar to African and American church leaders, many of whom see condoms and their promotion as contributing to trends toward sexual experimentation among teenagers and

173

promiscuity in general. In the words of one healer, "Advertising condoms is like supporting casual sex instead of scaring people about AIDS."

In spite of all the cultural barriers to condom acceptance, and in light of the above comments about agreement over the causal agents of STIs and STDs, condoms *can* be described and promoted as something that can effectively serve as a barrier to the transmission of "dirt" and "insects," as these are locally understood. In a collaborative workshop for traditional healers in South Africa in which I was involved, there seemed to be a breakthrough in understanding condoms when there was in-depth discussion about whether or not condoms could prevent "heat," one of the agents of STI transmission along with dirt (Green et al. 1992). It was essential in this case that AIDS educators used the terms and symbols already understood by traditional healers, which some skeptics might consider a major and perhaps dangerous "concession to traditional beliefs." Yet, indigenous symbols and metaphors tend to inspire some degree of awe, whereas the flat, sterile message of modern health education tends to inspire yawns. We ought to be considering which is more likely to motivate behavioral change.

IS SEXUAL BEHAVIOR CHANGING
IN AREAS OF HIGH HIV PREVALENCE?

Consider that: (1) Years of condom promotion has yielded so few results in Zambia or elsewhere in Africa; (2) STD and HIV incidence has been declining in Uganda, and, to some extent, in at least parts of Tanzania (Pool et al. 1996; World Bank 1997:92–93). Continued low overall condom prevalence suggests that we must look elsewhere—such as reduction of the number of sexual partners—for part of the explanation for these changes. Evidence can be found in the Zambian TIR of behavior change in the direction of reduction of sexual partners, on the part of those with STD experience. The following comments from male respondents were offered in response to a variety of questions in the general TIR, not just ones that asks specifically about behavior change, so many of them can be considered spontaneous. Comments in quotes are from respondents; those not in quotes are from their interviewers.

> He stopped picking girls from streets [and] bars and he uses condoms. He has lately become very faithful to his wife.

174

"Yes, my behaviour completely changed after undergoing all those pains, I hated most women because I thought that they all might be carrying the insect."

He never dreamed of having sex with anyone apart from his trusted girlfriend.

He terminated the relationship with his girlfriend and stopped playing with friends who like casual sex.

Mr N. has terminated the relationship with his girlfriend because she is a prostitute—she gave him STD. He avoids friends who like casual sex, and he always uses condoms. He keeps himself safe for fear of contracting AIDS.

"My mother . . . condemned me very much; she told me to stay away from girls as they might bring my death. My girl never even wished to talk to me again." [This man confesses that he never had knowledge about the existence of STDs, and he has sworn not to go to bed with any lady apart from the one he intends to marry (his trusted girlfriend). He promised never to use a condom (with her). It is not 100% protective.]

He stopped casual sex or even just having one sex partner. He said he will wait until he marries.

In 1993, during a short-term assignment in Uganda, I found anecdotal evidence that people were starting to change their behavior from fear of AIDS. One heard that growing numbers of women were refusing to have sex and that men were often choosing monogamy, fidelity, or at least partner reduction rather than sex with outside partners, even with condoms. Significant decreases in STD infection rates seemed to support that something was happening. But self-reported and possibly exaggerated condom use rates among men remained at a low 2%–2.5%, so changes in STD incidence seemed unrelated to condoms. (This would be true even if some men used condoms in "high-risk" encounters. With such high HIV prevalence in the general population, a great many encounters would be high risk). Many health professionals working in HIV/AIDS prevention doubted or rejected the new STD incidence findings, reasoning that condom user rates would have to be higher for STD incidence to decline.

What these health experts forgot is that the HIV/AIDS prevention message was and is more than "use a condom." The full message has been something like,

Don't have sex before marriage; remain a virgin until marriage [in the euphemistic language of AIDS programs, young people should postpone their "coital debut"]. If you cannot do this, then at least remain faithful to your partner. After marriage, be faithful to your partner. If you cannot be faithful to spouse or regular partner, you risk getting a disease, perhaps AIDS, so protect yourself by: (1) having as few partners as possible; and (2) always using a condom.

This has been dubbed the ABC approach to AIDS prevention: *A*bstinence; *B*e faithful; use a *C*ondom. Condom only becomes necessary when abstinence and fidelity fail. Yet they are an appealing technical fix for USAID, UNAIDS, and other major players in AIDS prevention (Rotello 1997:188–189). They involve a product, the United States makes the product, cost-effective contraceptive social marketing (CSM) programs can be used to promote condoms for AIDS prevention just as it has successfully promoted contraceptives for family planning, and condoms allow for some fairly clear-cut measures that can be used as "performance indicators" in AIDS programs (namely condom sales and condom use as reflected in prevalence surveys). Programs in behavior change are more complicated and offer fewer clear-cut measures of effectiveness.

Whatever the reasons, HIV/AIDS programs have often been narrowly focused on condom promotion, to the exclusion of other possibilities. It took years and countless studies before STD treatment became a standard approach to HIV prevention. Several studies have suggested that STD treatment is in fact more cost effective than condom promotion, and because it is also a technological solution that relies on U.S. (or another developed country's) technology and drugs, there may now be a danger that AIDS programs will all jump on this bandwagon and again neglect behavior change.

Certainly, most AIDS programs have to date failed to give adequate attention to the option of partner reduction or fidelity, even though this may be the only part of AIDS prevention that churches, traditional healers, schools, and other conservative authorities are willing to participate in. The most recent statement of the World Bank on global AIDS (World Bank 1997) reasserts that condoms are the best and most cost-effective means of HIV prevention, surpassing STD treatment. Behavior change of the partner-reduction fidelity sort is given inadequate mention as a possible means of prevention.

Moreover, most AIDS prevention programs appear to lack baseline data on number of sexual partners (as distinct from contact with commercial sex workers) in most parts of the world. USAID and UNAIDS have taken steps to remedy this. Percentage of partner reduction became Indicator #1 under the new Strategic Objectives of USAID's HIV/AIDS program (Sept. 1996 Revision [internal working paper]); it is also now a key performance indicator used by UNAIDS.

Since my work in Uganda and Zambia, evidence has emerged of behavior change in the direction of fidelity and monogamy. A study of 1,545 randomly selected men and women in Jinja district, Uganda, found that 34% of men and 18% of women had had sex with a "nonregular sexual partner" in 1990, compared to only 12.7% of men and 4.3% of women in the 12 months before being interviewed five years later (Asiimwe-Okiror 1995).

A study in Tanzania presents evidence of "a substantial change in sexual behaviour" due primarily to fear of AIDS. "Respondents preferred partner reduction, and in particular sticking to one partner, to condom use" (Pool et al. 1996:203). And in a survey of nearly 1,100 women in Zimbabwe, Simon et al. (1998:325) found that "Most of the women interviewed (76%) said they knew someone who had died or was sick with AIDS." As a result, "44% (485/1093) of women aged 15–49 years reported taking action to avoid HIV-1 infection. [Twenty-four percent] reported abstinence (14% of 20–49 year-olds), 24% monogamy, 7% condom use, 2% had avoided beer halls, and 4% reported other actions." Note that there were seven times more abstinence-monogamy answers as condom answers. Regarding overall condom use, this study showed that 4% of women reported using condoms as a family planning method and 3% used them "for other reasons" such as preventing AIDS and/or STDs (Simon et al. 1998:327).

It appears that after years of neglect (perhaps cynicism about Africans changing their "multipartneristic" sexual behavior), we can expect more research and program attention to changes in sexual behavior. Evaluation of USAID's AIDS prevention efforts between 1990 and 1996 showed that behavior change was its least successful area of accomplishment; it was recommended that more effort be put into this intervention area (Pielemeier et al. 1996).

NOTES

I thank Josefa Marrato, Manuel Wilsonne, Annemarie Jurg, and Amando Dgedge for their help in the original research on which this analysis is based. Some of the STD/AIDS findings from Manica have been published (Green et al. 1993). Findings from Nampula Province, Mozambique, and Zambia have not been published.

1. Some Tanzanian STIs are very similar in name to Zambian STIs (e.g., *kaswende* is offered as the vernacular name for syphilis).

2. This appears to be related to the names of a gonorrhea-like syndrome recognized in neighboring societies, called *chinzonono* among the Nyaja of Zambia, and *chisonono* among chiCewa speakers in Malawi (Helitzer-Allen and Allen 1992).

3. "Drop" is used in Swaziland and a large part of South Africa to denote gonorrhea (Green 1994a:60).

CHAPTER SIX

MALARIA, TUBERCULOSIS, AND OTHER INFECTIOUS DISEASES

Thus far, we have looked in some detail at findings about sexually transmitted illness and diarrheal disease. This is because most of my own applied research has focused on these areas and because these sicknesses are also recent program priorities of USAID, the WHO, UNAIDS, UNICEF, the World Bank, and other major funders of applied health research in developing countries. However, other infectious diseases account for more morbidity and mortality than higher-profile diseases like AIDS—for example, malaria or tuberculosis. Indeed, some researchers are beginning to suspect that HIV infection through heterosexual intercourse is only possible in the presence of multiple infections from other infectious diseases. Here is an outline of the argument of biochemist Robert Root-Bernstein in his own words:

> HIV is not the whole story of AIDS . . . multiple immunosuppressive agents act synergistically with each other and HIV to create . . . a vicious

cycle . . . in which each new agent produces further immune suppression, allowing yet more infections to catch hold. . . . No one at risk for AIDS has a normal immune system to begin with. (1993:172)

Because of climate, environment, poor health services, and poverty, Root-Bernstein argues that Africans tend to carry around a great many more infections than the average Westerner. This includes viruses such as CMV, EBV, HSV1, HSV2, HBV (Mozambique is said to have the highest hepatitis B incidence in the world), HAV, and HTLV as well as various STDs (some of which are rare or absent in northern countries), a variety of helminthic infections, *E. coli*, *V. cholera*, malaria, tuberculosis, and many others. These various infections "insult" the immune system either directly or indirectly. An example of an indirect insult is malaria-causing anemia; anemia is very immunosuppressive. Indeed many antimalarial and antiparasitic drugs are also immunosuppressive (Root-Bernstein 1993:305). The dangerous synergy between AIDS and tuberculosis is so well established that a journal called *TB and HIV* was launched in 1994. Sickle cell anemia and other conditions common in Africans also require blood transfusions, itself either a direct risk for HIV infection or an indirect risk through its immunosuppressive effect. "Among the other factors chipping away at the immunological competence of central Africans is acute undernutrition or malnutrition, extremely prevalent in the developing countries where AIDS is epidemic" (Root-Bernstein 1993:307). Moreover,

> War creates havoc, all too often manifested in the disintegration of health care facilities, food distribution services, and agriculture. Tens of millions of refugees have been forced from their . . . African and Asian homes during the last decade. . . . Preventive public health services such as immunization and provision of potable drinking water were discontinued leaving huge populations susceptible to controllable infectious diseases and epidemics. . . . These conditions are not duplicated in any Western country. (p. 309)

I suppose the former Yugoslavia might have been mentioned in the last quote; nevertheless, all these conditions conspire to weaken immune systems of people in tropical Africa, possibly enabling heterosexual transmission of HIV. Many of the contributing conditions are also found among disadvantaged groups in Brazil, the Caribbean, India, mainland southeast Asia (especially Cambodia), and elsewhere. HIV infection is likewise growing rapidly in these areas, and much of the transmission is heterosexual, unlike western Europe, the United States, Canada, Australia, and New Zealand.

The reasons for this epidemiologic difference between sub-Saharan Africa and developed countries is no doubt even more complicated. Since Root-Bernstein propounded his theory of multiple insults to the immune system, it has been found that HIV-1 has various subtypes, or clades, that behave differently. Viral subtype B, characteristic of the United States, seems to seek as a point of bodily entry microscopic abrasions in the anal area, whereas subtypes A, C, and D, which predominate in Africa, seek epithelial langerhans' cells in vaginal (especially cervical) and oral mucous membranes (Soto-Ramirez et al. 1996). Still, it is not known how or why HIV-1 viral subtypes evolved in different ways. The role of other infectious disease in immunosuppression and susceptibility to HIV infection (and certainly the progression toward AIDS once people are infected) is not negated by the discovery of HIV-1 viral subtypes; it seems to me that Root-Bernstein's theory might help explain the conditions that account for their divergent evolution.

Infectious diseases like malaria and tuberculosis are of interest to us because: (1) They account for high morbidity and mortality in Africa (and other poor countries or other poor populations, worldwide), and they require culturally appropriate interventions; (2) They may increase susceptibility to HIV/AIDS; and (3) They illustrate the range and significance of ICT in southern Africa. What have ethnographers and others reported about Africans' understanding of contagious diseases like these?

W. D. Hammond-Tooke, whose ideas on the centrality of witchcraft beliefs have already been discussed, concluded in his early ethnographic fieldwork among the Bhaca that the cause of virtually all acute and chronic illness was believed to be magic, in the broad sense (1962:264). He noted that Bhaca (South Africa) recognition of contagion was barely developed; the only examples given were influenza; and, "If a person has a stomach-ache and lies on his stomach in a path, the next person who passes along that path will get it" (p. 264). We are told the Bhaca did not regard tuberculosis as contagious; it was considered hereditary and hopeless. Yet Hammond-Tooke quotes one or more informants as saying that if a man with tuberculosis has intercourse with his wife, "He will leave the sickness in her and it will be passed on to his children" (p. 265). This sounds to me very much like recognition of infection-contagion. Hammond-Tooke also quotes an informant who attributes the high incidence of tuberculosis to "the meeting of different tribes and nationalities" (p. 265), which also sounds like contagion belief, in fact, it sounds like an example of contact-with-strangers pollution, as described by Ngubane, Schapera, and others for southern African societies.

As noted in Chapter Two, amateur ethnographers Smith and Dale (1968 [1920]) suggested over 75 years ago that "virulent disease and plagues" somehow belong in the realm of naturalistic explanation in Zambia. Stayt (1968:267) also described belief among the Venda (South Africa) that "consumption" results from intercourse with a woman who has had an abortion: "Consumption (*lufhila*) is common and is the most dreaded of all diseases. It is thought that a woman who has had an abortion will infect any man who has sexual intercourse with her before she has gone through the necessary purification rites."

This is another way of referring to contact with death pollution. The author also discusses malaria in naturalistic terms but does not tell us the attributed cause. Nevertheless, treatment of malaria involves use of a vapor bath and "a strong emetic and purge," a common treatment for pollution illness. The attributed cause of pneumonia is likewise not given, yet treatment is "to draw out the evil and bury it in the ground" (Stayt 1968:270–271). Mary Douglas (1992 [1966]) has observed that rites of reversing, untying, burying, washing, erasing, and fumigating are the ways of "expunging" pollution in Lele society, and Hammond-Tooke, as already noted, suggests that purgatives and emetics are the treatment of choice for pollution illness.

W. D. Raymond, a government chemist in Dar es Salaam, wrote a series of articles on Tanganyikan indigenous *materia medica* between 1936 and 1938. He believed that the danger of infectious disease was well known, but that "the transmission of malaria through the mosquito was either not known or not accepted" (Raymond 1936, 1938, quoted in Beck 1981:70). A recent ethnomedical study of malaria in southern Ghana found that, although the role of the mosquito was generally not recognized, malaria is perceived as an environmentally related disease caused by excessive contact with heat from the sun, which upsets the equilibrium of the blood (Agyepong 1992).

A very recent study of malaria beliefs among Tanzanian traditional healers showed the following attributed causes, by number of healers:

mosquito bites (19); "small animals" in the mosquitoes (11); dirty water (4); bites by bugs, fleas, or ticks (3); staying in the sun (2); dirty environment (1); change of season (1); and witchcraft (1) (Gessler et al. 1995:123). There is clear evidence here of naturalism, including indigenous contagion theory and some evidence of biomedical concepts. One healer elaborated on indigenous germ theory, explaining that *vijidudu*, or "small animals" living in the abdomen, may become activated by excessive heat and then move through the blood to the brain, causing fever. Commenting in their own and several other African studies, Gessler et al. (1995:123) remark that malarial illness tends not to be understood as witchcraft related or supernaturally caused in any way.

A study of tuberculosis beliefs of Tswana traditional healers in Botswana showed that some consider tuberculosis to be naturalistic but contagious. Other explanations showed evidence of pollution beliefs. Tuberculosis was seen either as an indigenous illness called *tibamo* or as a European disease. It could have a number of causes, including being born face down. *Tibamo* was believed to be transmissible from a child to its parents if traditional medicines were not used at once. Further,

> The Botswana healers have a concept of contagion, more akin to "defilement," which can include droplet infection, but also includes transmission by walking on infected spittle. They believe that disease is associated with states of bad blood, which occur in pregnancy, menstruation, abortion or widowhood (since the spouse's blood had been mixed with that of the dead spouse during coitus). Those with good blood are not susceptible to catching disease. (Haram 1991:170)

We recognize the familiar idiom of pollution beliefs (e.g., "defilement," a term used by Junod more than 80 years ago in describing Tsonga pollution beliefs). We also recognize "bad blood" associated with menstrual blood and death (the latter expressed in abortion and widowhood). We even see evidence of indigenous immunity concepts in the idea that those with good blood are not susceptible to catching the illness. I think that any student of Health Education 101 (or Medical Anthropology 101) could design an approach that could make use of indigenous concepts such as defilement and good/bad blood. Further, any such design would be more effective than a "presentation of the facts" that would almost certainly rely on scientific terminology that would appear so alien to most Africans that tuberculosis might seem like a foreign illness that local people do not get and need not worry about.

INFECTIOUS DISEASES IN ZAMBIA

The purpose of the general Zambian TIR survey (of laypersons, not traditional healers; see Chapter Five) was to discover ethnomedical beliefs and practices related to illnesses considered causally connected to sexual intercourse. So as not to influence the choice of illnesses, respondents were initially asked to identify "the most common illnesses that affect adults in your area." This elicited some interesting information about malaria, cholera, tuberculosis, and other contagious diseases that are important because of their contribution to adult mortality and morbidity in Zambia and Africa. These data also shed light on pollution theory and show that STIs (including AIDS) and diarrheal illness are only two expressions of a broader theory of contagion found in southern Africa.

Findings reported in this section are from in-depth interviews with randomly selected respondents in Chawama district, a predominantly Nyanja-speaking area, and with randomly selected respondents in Cimwemwe district, a predominantly Bemba-speaking area. The illness or disease profiles are from notes taken directly from informants in the Zambian general TIR, organized by disease (if a biomedical term was used) or illness (if an indigenous name was used). Rather than fixing an arbitrary number of response categories and counting how many of which kind of response we see, I have tried to preserve the idiom of the respondent. Comments listed first were most representative—or encountered most frequently— and so on, in rough descending order of frequency. All quotes are set off by quotation marks. Bracketed comments are my own.

Malaria

We turn first to malaria TIR findings. Malaria is considered a serious, dangerous, potentially fatal sickness that affects men, women and children. It is said to cause great suffering. When respondents in both Chawama and Cimwemwe were asked in open-ended fashion to list and describe three "adult diseases," malaria was usually mentioned. This suggests that malaria is one of the top three health concerns for Zambians. In the words of one respondent, "Is there any person who has never suffered from malaria?" Although some respondents used the English disease term, both Bemba and Nyanja speakers used (*i*)*mpepo*, which seems to denote cold or cold air, or *ubulwele bwa mpepo*, or *mpepo mutupi* to refer to a syndrome that resembles malaria.

Among Bemba speakers, malaria symptoms mentioned were: headache, thirst, weakness in joints, body and eye pains, "hotness of the body," high temperature, feeling cold, and delirium ("shouting and behaving like a mad person"). Other symptoms were loss of appetite, "loss of blood" (a symptom said to appear only after one or two months), weight loss, vomiting, "purging," "mouth bitterness," "inability to work," and lack of strength and energy. One respondent said, "The person with this illness also becomes slim due to loss of appetite and blood." A few respondents explicitly associated malaria symptoms with AIDS. Most believed that one cannot have the sickness without symptoms; a few thought one could be without symptoms. The concept of latency emerged; one respondent saying, "An illness without symptoms does not mean that it is not serious because symptoms can show sooner or later." Another commented, "An illness without symptoms is much more serious because it causes much damage to the body before one knows that he or she is sick."

Among Nyanja speakers, malaria symptoms were described as consisting of: headache, thirst, weakness in joints, body and eye pains, feeling cold, shivering (*kunjenjemela*), and/or "feeling *mpepo* (cold) regardless of your coverings." Also loss of appetite, weight loss, "goose pimples," vomiting (*kuluka*), "inability to work," and lack of strength and energy. In the words of one respondent, "The temples are painful and the veins also swell. When one bends over, feels like the forehead is going to drop off." Most respondents believed that one cannot have the sickness without symptoms.

Bemba speakers and their neighbors had many ideas about malaria causation. Answers have been grouped around central ideas to help illuminate patterns of response.

Air, Weather, Insects

Bemba speakers said:

> "Malaria nowadays is transmitted from one person to the other like an airborne disease. It was not so in the past."

185

"Malaria is also transmitted through breathing contaminated air—air that has been breathed out by a person with malaria."

"The illnesses comes due to weather; others we just contract them."

"Malaria can also be transmitted in hot weather, like in tropical areas."

"(It is caused by) germs carried by flies."

"Malaria is caused by a parasite" [*akashishi*].

"Sometimes it is caused by change of weather, drinking contaminated water, and at times food. Sometimes it could be a symptom of an STD."

"Weather changes . . . caused by bathing in cold water, having no warm clothes."

"(Malaria is) caused by a mosquito bite, which bite contains impure fluids." [n.b.: pollution language]

"(Malaria) spreads through sleeping in the bed and sharing one blanket and using the same air for breathing."

"(It is) caused by drinking water from the well, water from the river, and through mosquito bites."

"This illness is caused by mosquito bites, for mosquitoes carry dirty fluids [pollution] especially in the rainy season, which they inject in people. Malaria is spread by air as in the case of an infected person spitting on the ground."

Several Nyanja speakers mentioned mosquitoes (e.g., "It comes by a bite from mosquitoes which have germs." "A mosquito can cause someone to get malaria, but not everyone."). Others commented that malaria is "caused by dust." Another said, "If one is in the same room with the one suffering from malaria and breathes the same air as that sick person, they can get malaria." Several mentioned or implied cold weather. (Cold weather probably refers to the rainy season when mosquitoes are more prevalent.) One respondent said, "Malaria and diarrhea are very common during the rainy season." Several commented that "[malaria] just comes," a typical statement of naturalistic causation. A few Nyanja respondents mentioned diet, specifically "eating small mangoes," as a cause.

Nyamongo (1998:203–204) found similar beliefs among the Abagusii of Kenya. Although some accepted the role of mosquitoes, a significant number of informants believed malaria can be caused by eating "sugary foods," like sugarcane or ripe bananas.

When Europeans began to travel and live in tropical countries in the seventeenth and eighteenth centuries and became exposed to malaria and other tropical diseases, "fluctuating and high temperatures, humidity, and the sun were seen to be the main factors that weakened the constitutions of European races and increased their vulnerability to disease," according to medical historian Worboys (1993:516). No doubt there was mutual influence between Europeans and Africans and other tropical peoples regarding theories of disease causation.

Dirt, Environment

Bemba speakers said the following:

"Using dirty utensils can lead to contracting malaria, also if you use the same toilets."

"This illness comes when a person does not bathe regularly because the pores on the skin close and the affected person starts shivering due to fever."

"Cerebral malaria can be transmitted through sharing the same bed with an affected person because the illness travels in air from the affected person to other people."

"When you are in the same house with malaria it can be transmitted to you."

One respondent said malaria is caused by "germs found in water." He elaborated, "(Malaria) can be prevented by drinking boiled water. But once some people get the illness, it becomes difficult for others to avoid it since the germs that cause the illness now travel in air. People do not choose the type of air to breathe. One breathes the air that has been breathed out by an infected person, [then] he or she gets the illness."

Nyanja speakers gave similar answers:

"It is caused by dirt."

"It is caused by heaping up rubbish and passing urine and feces anywhere other than the toilet where a mosquito can easily lay its eggs [and thereby multiply them]; a number of them will bite a person and cause malaria."

"It is caused by flies which are many, due to rubbish. People dump dirty all over the place."

"A person can get it through dirty drinking water."

Here is evidence of pollution beliefs (contact with dirty, bodily waste), and perhaps a garbled health message that combines the role of the mosquito with that of the fly in transmitting diarrheal disease. Etiologic ideas about illness in water seem classifiable under environmental dangers.

Biomedical Explanations

Several biomedical-sounding explanations were given by Bemba speakers:

> "It is caused by a parasite. This illness is transmitted by mosquitoes. There is no other cause apart from a parasite which is carried by mosquitoes. However, . . . some people believe witchcraft can also cause malaria. But the illness due to witchcraft only shows malaria symptoms, but clinical diagnosis shows malaria (to be) negative."
>
> "(One gets malaria) if you travel from one place to another and if you are bitten by a mosquito."

An interviewer recorded that a Bemba respondent "used to suspect that the cause of malaria is mostly change of habitation, but she now believes that mosquitoes can be the cause." Here we see evidence of schooling and/or health education, but a more traditional view still holds that malaria can result from contact with strangers and strange places—in other words, from traveling. As noted in Chapter Two, there is epidemiological evidence to support this view (Oaks et al. 1991). We also saw that exposure to strangers is considered a pollution risk factor in Mozambique and elsewhere in the region. Exposure to unfamiliar surroundings can also lead to illness of the environmental dangers sort described by Ngubane for the Zulu and by Honwana for the Tsonga.

Only two Bemba speakers alluded to personalistic causation, both saying that either witchcraft or mosquito bites can cause malaria.

Transmission

The TIR interview schedule asked respondents to distinguish between cause and transmission of illness. It is not clear how respondents understood this distinction. Some Nyanja speakers said the cause of malaria is cold weather or dirtiness, whereas transmission is by mosquitoes. Judging by the studies of malaria beliefs cited above, the role of the mosquito may well have been unknown in Zambia before the introduction of Western medicine—indeed, it was unknown to Western medicine before technical advances nearly a century ago led to the discovery of the rather complex etiology of this vector-borne disease. In any case, a number of Zambian lay and healer informants now seem to accept a role of mosquitoes or other insects in transmission, even if these have been integrated with older ideas about pollution and environmental dangers.

Informants also considered malaria to be highly contagious. Recall that some respondents thought one could catch malaria by breathing the same air as a sick person, or by sleeping in the same bed with a sufferer. And some thought malaria could spread from a sufferer to everyone in the same house, just like dysentery.

Let us pause to consider belief in airborne illness, a clear expression of our ICT component environmental dangers, and something commonly associated with contagious disease in Africa. "Illness in the air" or "airborne illness" (*mubulale muwamuwala*) appears to be an indigenous Bemba etiologic category, equivalent to airborne illness concepts elsewhere. For example, the Bambara of Mali seem to classify smallpox, measles, and other contagious illness as "wind illness" because only wind has sufficiently widespread contact with the body to cause outbreaks (Imperato 1974:15). Imperato suggests that wind is only the immediate or proximal cause of at least an epidemic of smallpox. The remoter or ultimate cause may be a sorcerer, witch, or diviner who is believed to initiate an epidemic. In our terms, smallpox is transmitted by wind and caused (at one level) by someone with ill intent.

Although I found evidence of belief in sorcerer's intent behind some airborne epidemics among the Swazi, this seemed to account for a minority of *tifo temoya* (illnesses of the air or wind). *Tifo temoya* is a general Swazi term denoting illnesses that are contracted through inhalation. In a survey that I directed of 144 Swazi traditional healers, we asked for examples of illnesses and conditions one gets from inhalation. Multiple responses were permitted and recorded. Thirty-eight cited evil spirits; 37 cited colds, flu, or asthma; 27 cited tuberculosis (*sifuba*); 25 cited severe headaches (malaria?); 16 cited stomachache; 16 cited a type of hysteria (*lihabiya*) attributed to sorcery; 14 cited a type of acute psychosis (*ufufunyane*); 13 cited bad dreams; 11 cited diarrhea; and 4 cited cholera (Green 1985:278).

In interpreting these findings, it is hard to know what do with "evil spirits," as this is usually considered a cause rather than an effect or outcome. Perhaps there was some communication difficulty between interviewers and healers.[1] In any case, out of 188 multiple answers, 120 (64%) seem to refer to conditions biomedically classifiable as contagious, infectious disease. (I assume severe headache in an endemic malaria zone—except for higher elevations—usually refers to malaria, and stomachache usually refers to syndromes involving infectious pathogens, given local conditions.)

In other words, airborne illness for the Swazi usually means contagious illness, and most of this illness is biomedically classifiable as such. Comments accompanying the above answers from five of the respondents help illuminate the concept of airborne diseases:

> *Tifo temoya* can move by air from one area to another. . . . You may hear old people say that there is a hot air coming from the east that will cause fever. Then after a while you will feel the fever. . . . Some *tifo temoya* are when the seasons change and you get the "flu." . . . These diseases mostly affect children. They are infectious diseases caused by witchcraft and the air can spread them to other people.

The last comment is odd in the context of the discussions in this book. Witchcraft is thought to be personalistic, misfortune targeting an individual. If it were in the air, it would sicken many. This comment reminds us that witchcraft is a complex metaphor; translations of this loaded term by informants may mislead outsiders including anthropologists. Janzen (personal communication) prefers to not use this term, but to translate the Bantu radical more directly as "power of words," or "words or thoughts in anger." Further, there may be differences of opinion among healers and laypersons about illness causation: Ethnoetiologic categories of witchcraft, natural causes, spirits, etc., may be permeable and overlapping among participants of an ethnomedical system themselves. Even if the ultimate cause of an illness is supernatural, the immediate cause may be impersonal and contagious, involving contact or absorption of illness carrying essences or agents, whether through touch or inhalation.

Returning to the Zambian malaria findings, the theme of contagion is found in several answers (e.g., "Once one suffers from malaria, then it means that everyone in that house will suffer from it"). Note the syncretism between the biomedical model and traditional pollution beliefs, as well as confusion over health education messages (e.g., preventing malaria by boiling water, "burying all the rubbish," "washing hands after visiting the toilet," "It is caused by flies, which are many due to rubbish. People dump dirt all over the place"). Sometimes a respondent offered a clear expression of the biomedical model: "Transmission . . . comes by a bite from mosquitoes which have . . . germs."

Prevention

Some Bemba speakers gave biomedically influenced examples of ways to prevent malaria:

> "It can be prevented by spraying medicine on stagnant water as this is the breeding grounds for mosquitoes. Tall grasses should be cut as they harbor mosquitoes."
>
> "This can be prevented as long as the grass is cut and spraying is being done regularly."
>
> "It . . . can be prevented by clearing pools and cutting the grass short."
>
> "by not staying where there are mosquitoes."
>
> "by medicine to kill the mosquitoes."
>
> "by using a mosquito net."

Others spoke of cleanliness, consistent with a pollution or naturalistic interpretation and/or with health education messages related to diarrheal disease (e.g., "[One must] clear the surroundings and bury the refuse"). Another said, "Usually (malaria) comes when you're not cleaning the surrounding(s) and when you do not make a drainage for stagnant water."

There was disagreement about prevention among Nyanja respondents. Some said they did not think malaria could be prevented. Others thought there was a traditional medicine for this purpose. More than one respondent (apparently attributing malaria to cold weather) said that malaria can be prevented by wearing warm clothes.

Note the role of cleanliness, antipollutants, or other naturalistic remedies in explanations that refer to mosquitoes or their habitat. Perhaps we needn't read pollution into these explanations at all, but should view them as indigenous naturalistic understandings or as evidence of confusion between public health preventive messages concerning fecal-oral diseases such as cholera and those concerning malaria. Although one sees evidence of pollution beliefs here and in many other parts of the findings on nondiarrheal, non-STD, contagious illness, it is also true that there is clear evidence of confusion over health education messages concerning different diseases. For example, messages about stagnant water and nonpotable water may be confused, as with the respondent who said, "When one goes to the village and drinks water from there, one can have malaria. Mosquito bites also cause malaria."

Some Nyanja informants seemed to combine the notion of cleanliness —the general remedy for pollution—with preventive measures recommended by public health, for example, "(Malaria, diarrhea, coughing, and "swelling of feet") can all be prevented (by) being clean, burying all water collecting points, cutting grass surrounding the houses and if possible spraying the rooms at night and using mosquito nets." Another reflected the same general view: "You can buy medicine to kill the mosquitoes. . . . (You can) use a mosquito net . . . (and) don't drink or eat dirty things."

South African traditional healers who were exposed to both AIDS prevention and tuberculosis prevention messages at the same workshop understandably confused means of transmission and prevention of the two diseases (Green 1994a:226).

Indigenous Versus Hospital Malaria Treatment

Some Bemba speakers thought modern medicine is superior to indigenous medicine, others thought both are effective. In the words of one, "This illness can be treated by both modern and traditional medical systems. In one traditional (treatment), a patient is covered in a blanket and then subjected to steam derived from boiling eucalyptus leaves. (Curing) the illness does not take more than one day after this treatment." Another commented, "it takes long to cure (about one month) and the affected person feels as if no one loves him/her in the world." Some respondents emphasized the value of treating malaria in the early stages.

Most Nyanja speakers said they thought malaria is best treated at the hospital, not by traditional healers (whereas traditional treatment was generally preferred for STIs). Others said both types of treatment are effective. In fact, some botanical medicines used by healers in the region have been found to be pharmacologically effective against malaria (Chhabra et al. 1990; Jurg et al. 1991b; Nat et al. 1991; Sofowora 1993), while there has been little if any ethnopharmacological evidence to suggest that local botanical medicines are effective against the pathogens of STDs—although this may be due to lack of research.

Tuberculosis

Tuberculosis, or the parallel indigenous syndrome *icifuba, cifuba*, or (*i*)*chifuba*, is one of the "adult illnesses" most commonly cited by informants. *Icifuba* and its cognates are translated as coughing, but like *sifuba* in Swazi/Zulu, it means chest or chest problem in both Bemba and

Nyanja. This illness is said to affect men, women, and children. Some respondents saw it as a fatal, incurable illness. Several informants, especially Nyanja speakers, associated tuberculosis with AIDS, noting that this association adds stigma and social rejection to an already unfortunate condition. Some commented that tuberculosis or *icifuba* could actually be a symptom of AIDS, or that it might only appear to be so because of the symptom of weight loss: "This illness makes a person slim because he/she loses appetite. One becomes a laughing stock as people start associating the patient with . . . AIDS."

The main symptoms described for tuberculosis or *icifuba* were prolonged and/or blood-producing cough, "weakness of the body," and loss of weight. Others mentioned fever, chest pains, backache, loss or thinning of hair, "hair like a baby," rash, and skin peeling from the legs. *Icifuba* can also occur without symptoms: "That which does not show symptoms is dangerous and more serious as it destroys the lungs before showing up. That which shows symptoms is less serious as the person affected can easily seek medical help or buy medicine from the shops. . . . Someone can have the illness but it disappears on its own after two to three days." A few Bemba speakers said that symptomless tuberculosis is that illness variety that occurs in the bones rather than in the blood.

The following representative causes of tuberculosis or *icifuba* were offered by Bemba speakers and their neighbors:

"TB is transmitted through sexual intercourse where one partner is affected."

"(It is caused by) dust, unwashed blankets, if rooms of the dwelling house are not always swept, and if there is no general surrounding cleanliness."

"*Icifuba* usually comes due to dust, wind and cold."

"Some suffer from TB after being bewitched, others just get (it). As for bronchitis we are born with it."

"*Icifuba* (coughing) is transmitted through bad air, dust and sharing the same bed with the affected person."

"(It is) transmitted through the air we breathe (or) drinking milk straight from the cow."

"Causes of *icifuba* are *ulukungu* (dust), *ukutalala* (coldness), and being bewitched. It is also transmitted *mumwela*. [Bemba: "in the air."]

"(It is transmitted) through the air we breath, (and) from milk."

"TB/AIDS of today is mainly transmitted through sexual intercourse. . . . Others, especially youngsters, who drink a lot of *kachasu* [locally brewed alcoholic drink] get this disease of slimming after taking the beer for a long time without proper diet."

"Germs, dust, breathing different sorts of air can cause *ichifuba*. TB can be transmitted through breathing contaminated air."

"through having sexual intercourse with a woman during her menstruation, and also there is ordinary cough that starts on its own."

"TB is transmitted through sexual intercourse where one partner is affected. It is also transmitted through kisses and eating at the same table with affected persons."

"This illness is transmitted through sharing cups when drinking beer and also breathing the same air with people who have the illness. This (is) possible because the germs can travel in air."

"When someone breathes air with dust, dust goes in the lungs and develops a germ which multiplies and affects the lungs . . . some people believe witchcraft also causes this illness."

"TB is an airborne disease, and it is transmitted from one person to the other through air. It is also transmitted through cups and careless spitting of sputum."

"TB is caused by smoking."

"Breathing different sorts of air can cause *ichifuba*. . . . (It) can be transmitted through breathing contaminated air."

The causes attributed by Nyanja speakers and their neighbors are similar:

"It is caused by dust (*kakungu*)."

"(It is caused by) breathing the coughed air that has been given out by an infected person."

"*Kuyenda yenda*" [being promiscuous].

"Coughing or TB is caused by dust, dirt, or if someone has aborted and has not been cleansed, it will bring a bad cough if they sleep with someone or if they cook for the family. The illness can also come if a woman who is menstruating puts salt in relish or if a woman who is not married has sex and cooks for the family. [nb: dust is a type of dirt]

"staying somewhere cold."

"People say it's caused by dust, but those are just speculations, we do not know the truth."

"dust, dirt, and cold."

"Cough is transmitted by sitting near someone with a cough."

194

Several respondents commented that this illness is transmitted through air (*mpepo*).

Some described cough rather than *cifuba*, *icifuba*, or (*i*)*chifuba*, but referred to chest pains, slimming, and other tuberculosis-like symptoms as well as coughing. Others used cough and *cifuba* interchangeably. Attributed causes of the indigenous syndrome cough resembled some of those for tuberculosis (e.g., "Cough is caused by dust [*kakungu*] . . . cough is transmitted through the air (*mpepo*). . . . When one person has a cough, everybody else in the house gets it"). Yet cough is distinguished from *cinfine*, translated as "common cold." And some commented that "cough . . . is very serious as it can lead to death." At least one informant changed cough to TB and *cifuba* during an interview.

One Nyanja speaker thought "cough-*cifuba*" was inherited ("inborn") and not transmissible (or preventable). But the symptoms described (chest congestion, noisy breathing that sounds like snoring, "breathing while the mouth is open," difficulty in breathing) might refer to syndromes other than tuberculosis. It was described as "not very serious." This and other evidence suggest that for some Zambians at least, "cough-*cifuba*" includes other respiratory syndromes less serious than tuberculosis.

Once again, there is evidence that an illness biomedically classified as infectious and contagious is interpreted for the most part as an impersonal illness related to germs, dirt, or dust; to air, wind, or dangerous environmental conditions; to sources of pollution such as death or menstrual blood; to sexual intercourse (or kissing); to diet or cleanliness; or to heredity. Only a very few respondents mentioned witchcraft.

A medical encyclopedia of 1925 described tuberculosis in language quite similar to this. First, some history of what was called consumption or phthisis:

> descriptions of (consumption) are found in the writings of classical authors, such as Laennec, who recognized that this and the various kindred conditions of other organs originated from the small tubercles. . . . These were then supposed to be impurities from the blood. About the year 980 A.D., Haly Abbas of Baghdad, and again, in 1779, Cullen, recognized the infectious nature of phthisis, but it was not until after the middle of the nineteenth century that it was proved. (Corish 1925:672)

According to this dated encyclopedia, the tubercle gains access to the body by two principal means: inhalation ("by far the most common channel"), or ingestion (drinking milk is mentioned). Regarding inhalation, "The sputum and other discharges from persons affected with phthisis are crowded with germs . . . and each of these bacilli, when dried and blown or carried about on dust, is capable of doing incalculable harm" (Corish 1925:673).

Prevention

Not surprisingly, Zambian ideas about prevention of tuberculosis or *icifuba* are related to attributed causes. For those who emphasized the role of dust, prevention might be "by growing a lot of trees in residential areas. Trees act as wind breakers and hence dust is stopped from spreading. . . .The ground should be watered every morning to avoid dust."

For those who cited sexual or other contact with infected people, "TB can be prevented by avoiding mixing with people who have lost weight, avoiding kisses and casual sex, wearing shoes to avoid stepping on *ifikola* (sputum)." Or if the cause was related to cleanliness, a representative answer was, "(It) can be prevented by means of being clean all the time." If the cause was related to smoking, "TB can be prevented by stopping smoking cigarettes." If related to cold weather, it can be prevented "by wearing warm clothes." Other preventive measures included boiling milk, having only one sexual partner, taking antimalaria pills, sleeping under a mosquito net, keeping surroundings clean, and keeping warm.

Some thought the illness unpreventable because it is in the air people must breathe. Overcrowded conditions—which is a factor in the spread of tuberculosis—may be implied in the comment, "There's too large a population using the same air." One Nyanja speaker said, "It cannot be prevented because it just comes."

The preferred treatment tended to be the hospital, although some endorsed traditional medicines. Some stated the belief that the illness becomes incurable if not treated in its early stages, and in a hospital. A few Bemba speakers thought some types of tuberculosis, such as the variety "in the bones" and without symptoms, "is a very serious illness as it has no cure and the affected person always dies."

Bilharzia (*Schistosomiasis haematobium*)

A syndrome characterized by blood in the urine (known as *umthundungati*, or *umfundzan-ngati* "blood-in-urine" in the Swazi language) seems to be widely recognized in southern Africa (e.g., Ndamba et al. 1994). This syndrome seems to be characterized in the same way by Bemba speakers, where it is called *ukusunda umulopa*. It is known as *lukozo* in Nyanja. For both groups, the main symptom is passing blood in the urine. Sometimes respondents insisted that this is the only symptom; several others mentioned additional symptoms such as weakness, pain or itching while urinating, urinating frequently, passing very yellow urine, or difficulty passing urine. These symptoms raise the possibility that one or more STDs or at least nonschistosomiasis genito-urinary conditions may be classified as *ukusunda umulopa*, *lukozo*, or even "bilharzia" by some Zambians. (Schistosomiasis tends to be known as bilharzia in England and its former colonies in Africa.) Since the out-standing symptoms are genito-urinary, it is not surprising that some in Africa including Zambia interpret the associated illness with sexual intercourse.

Most respondents thought this illness to be very serious, and virtually all thought that it always manifests symptoms, that it cannot be without symptoms, and that it affects both men and women. One Nyanja respondent mentioned a symptom that might suggest intestinal schisto-somiasis: "Bilharzia affects and damages the stomach." It is probable (and suggested by the Swazi findings presented below) that intestinal schisto-somiasis is usually thought of as an illness unrelated to the urinary variety, probably an illness classified as diarrheal or stomach related.

Nyanja speakers gave these representative answers about cause:

"playing in dirty stagnant water. (It is transmitted) through germs that enter the body from the water."

"Bilharzia is caused by drinking dirty/stagnant water."

"anybody either young or big playing in stagnant water that has urine in it." [This comment was made by a woman who said she had learned about bilharzia at school.]

"contaminated water at the well, or through dirty toilet, or water which is not chlorinated."

"as for bilharzia, people get ill because of dirtiness in either the water they are drinking or dirty toilets."

"Bilharzia is caused by drinking dirty/stagnant water."

"through drinking untreated water where there are germs; stepping where an affected person has urinated."

"drinking unclean water."

A few Nyanja speakers who identified drinking dirty water as the cause somewhat incongruously mentioned "avoiding swimming in stagnant water" as the appropriate prevention. This probably reflects awareness of contemporary health education messages about bilharzia.

Representative answers from Bemba speakers include:

"(You) get it from dirty water, stepping on water with bilharzia germ."

"It only occurs when you have sexual intercourse with too many partners."

"Dirty found in water, a germ, or *akashishi* [tiny illness-carrying insects] that caused the disease."

"An insect or germ found in dirty water bites a healthy person and they get bilharzia disease."

"Dirt causes this disease; an infected person urinates carelessly like in water, then other people may get infected . . . snails . . . caused by certain germs found in water . . . a small insect found in snails in the water."

As with other some illnesses considered to be sexually transmitted, one respondent thought *ukusunda umulopa* "destroys fertility" if left untreated. Others did not think so. One said, "Bilharzia does not cause infertility but if not cured on time may cause the penis to be weak."

With both groups, we see the familiar emphasis on dirt, illness-carrying insects, uncleanliness, and sexual intercourse. We also see evidence of health education in the mention of snails and water, even though many thought that contaminated water must be drunk to cause illness. Ways to prevent this illness included not drinking untreated water, not playing in stagnant water, and "keeping away from those who are sick." Three Nyanja speakers said *lukozo* cannot be prevented, "as this comes from God." As we have seen, this is a way of saying that the illness is natural as well as unavoidable. From the comments about cause and prevention, it appears that a schistosomiasis-like syndrome is classifiable as an ICT illness or other naturally caused illness.

For many respondents, bilharzia is associated with snails and malaria with mosquitoes, just as Zambians associate some forms of diarrhea with flies. A quick look at such findings might lead one to the conclusion that most Zambians, even those with little formal education, understand the cause of these infectious diseases in the modern, scientific way. But this is not the full story. Mosquitoes, snails, and flies—the vectors of certain infectious diseases—seem to represent concepts included relatively recently in the causal chain, elements superimposed on more traditional pollution-related beliefs about dirt, insects, and traditional processes and mechanisms of contamination.

Judging by the healer TIR findings on STIs (Chapter Five), traditional healers may be more likely than laypersons to remain traditionalists in illness interpretation, faithful to the elders—the spiritual advisers—who taught them about herbs and healing. They are more likely to remain loyal to interpretations uninfluenced by modern health education, except when they are trying to impress biomedical health personnel in the context of collaborative workshops or surveys. Of course, laypersons might show off their knowledge of modern medical knowledge in similar settings.

Treatment

Most respondents thought both hospital and traditional medicine can cure bilharzia, *ukusunda umulopa*, or *lukoza*. One who recommended hospital treatment said, "(It is) curable if you seek medicine in time." To gain a view of indigenous treatment, the following is an interviewer-constructed profile of a Nyanja woman who was treated by a local healer for bilharzia, based on a series of survey questions about health care service delivery:

1. Informant went to a traditional healer for treatment for bilharzia.
2. She chose the particular healer because he was near her home. The clinic was too far.
3. Anyone can receive treatment at the traditional healer's clinic, both men and women.
4. The treatment was free.
5. Informant went there on foot.
6. The traditional healer was very near, just a few meters away.
7. It took her about 15 minutes to get there.
8. She was seen just on arrival.
9. She was not seen by anyone else apart from the healer.
10. The waiting room was just an enclosure around the hut.
11. She was seen in an open space (within the enclosure).
12. She was only asked to explain the symptoms.
13. The healer told her to stop swimming in dirty water and gave her medicine (roots) to soak in water and drink.
14. The healer was friendly.

15. Informant said she was satisfied with the treatment she got because the disease didn't come back. She would still go back except now she lives far away from the particular healer.
16. Informant said she did not see anything wrong with the service.
17. Informant said both men and women were comfortable with the healer.
18. (There is) no need for a woman to get permission from her husband to visit the clinic (or healer).

We should not dismiss this patient's satisfaction with indigenous treatment as just psychological. There have been some studies of indigenous medicines used to treat *Schistosomiasis haematobium* infections in the region. For example, Ndamba et al. (1994) analyzed the most commonly used plants used by 286 traditional healers in Zimbabwe, 85% of them registered with the Zimbabwe National Traditional Healers' Association.

> The plant materials were prepared according to the guidelines of the traditional healers and their efficacy determined by administering the crude extracts orally to hamsters infected with *S. haematobium cercariae*. The results obtained suggested that plant extracts from *Abrus precatorius* (Leguminosae), *Pterocarpus angolensis* (Leguminosae), and *Ozoroa insignis* (Anacardiaceae)were lethal to adult schistosomes. (Ndamba et al. 1994:125)

Blood-in-Urine in Swaziland

It is illuminating to compare the above findings with those from another country in the region. The following information comes from my work in Swaziland (see Methodological Summary in Chapter One). In a survey of 144 traditional healers (herbalists, diviner mediums, and faith healers), and with 117 healers answering a question on *umthundungati* or bilharzia, 67 (57%) said they don't treat this illness, and 47 (43%) said they sometimes treat it. Most use *imbita* (an herbal decoction for drinking) to "kill the worms inside you" or "clean the insides or kidneys." It's often prescribed to be drunk over a period of several days.

One hundred forty-three answers (some multiple) were given in explaining the causes of this illness: 29 (20%) said it was contact with dirty, stagnant water, or water that has been urinated in; 29 (20%) said water with tiny creatures, worms, or snails; 22 (15%) didn't know or declined to comment; 20 (14%) said drinking unboiled, infested, or stagnant water; 17 (12%) simply said water (without specification); 8

(6%) said *likhubalo* (see below); 8 (6%) said *umklwebho* (a common type of sorcery); and 7% gave miscellaneous answers.

Representative direct quotes from surveyed healers about the cause of *umthundungati* or bilharzia include:

"It is caused by unmoving water."

"Bilharzia is caused by swimming in dirty water or walking in stagnant water."

"It is caused by tiny creatures found in dirty water."

"It's caused by swimming in dirty water that contains harmful creatures."

"When you drink dirty water mostly you are affected by bilharzia."

"My *gobela* [teacher, master healer] told me bilharzia is caused by snails in stagnant water."

"It's caused by small creatures found in stagnant water."

"I know it is caused by still water and when you swim into the dam water or if you bathe in it."

"It is caused by bathing or swimming in water that has small insect that cause bilharzia. Usually they are found in stagnant water."

"I am not sure what causes bilharzia. Some believe that when a person dances too much, he urinates blood."

"When we grew up they believed it was caused by crossing the fire. I do not think it is so in this day."

"They say it's caused by urinating in someone's urine."

"That disease called bilharzia is caused by stagnant water with some small worms. When they get in the stomach, they bite the inside of the stomach. They even get into the skin."

"The worms in stagnant rainwater get inside you and eat your veins."

"This disease you call bilharzia, we call *likhubalo* because the person urinates blood."

" Give medicines for cleaning the insides." [Several healers mentioned the aim of treatment is to "clean the insides or kidneys."]

"*Imbita* (herbal decoction) kills the worm inside."

One faith healer said he had "proved" that water is linked to bilharzia because he found that only those swimming in a certain pond nearly got blood in their urine. This is an example of the empirical, observation-based process of production of African health knowledge. It is not all derived from elders or dreams.

These findings from Swazi healers closely resemble those from laypersons in Zambia. We find the same range and type of answers referring to dirtiness, uncleanliness, illness-carrying snails, worms or insects, or drinking or exposure to contaminated water, with a few mentions of sexual intercourse or sorcery. We also see evidence of modern health education.

Critics of the approach of this book might argue that it is impossible to separate ethnomedical beliefs that are traditional from those that have been influenced—perhaps heavily so—by Western biomedical ideas and education. My response is that African ethnomedicine, like African religion, seems always to have been an open, changing, adaptive system that incorporates new ideas and beliefs even if it reworks them to suit existing beliefs. And, from a practical viewpoint, it does not matter how much biomedical ideas about, for example, microbes has influenced indigenous "germ" theories of unseen insects. What is important is the nature and content of the present belief system, however blended and syncretistic it might be. The fact that some Swazi *bogobela*—master healers who train initiates—teach that bilharzia is caused by snail-contaminated water only proves that new, foreign ideas have been adapted and adopted into the present etiological system by its most conservative and influential participants. It is the present belief system—not an imagined pure system of the past—that needs to be understood by those in public health who would influence popular health beliefs and practices in ways deemed compatible with public health.

In addition to the Swazi healer survey, I conducted in-depth interviews with traditional healers between 1981 and 1985. I came to know some of these 20-odd healers well; I interviewed some dozens of times and I was able to observe some in virtually all aspects of their healing practice. A few traditional healers had ideas about bilharzia that seem more personalistic. From a field note from an interview with a traditional healer named S. on 7/31/81, I recorded:

> When a healer mixes up powerful, dangerous, and "poisonous" herbs, especially those used in sorcery or to treat madness, special precautions must be taken to avoid contaminating the environment. A healer either mixes the medicines away from his home or, as S. advises, carefully burns around the area where the mixing took place. Otherwise, members of healer's family or innocent passersby will come into contact with the contamination when they pass the area where the mixing took place. They will then develop bilharzia symptoms.
>
> Is there another way to get (urinary) bilharzia? S. said it can be sent by an enemy in the form of *tilwane* (evil spirits or familiars). In this case,

treatment involves *kufutsa* (medicinal steam inhalation). For the environmental-contamination type, herbal medicine is taken orally, via enema, or through *kugata* (traditional vaccination). S. related that he has cured a number of patients of bilharzia, in fact his current apprentice had it when she arrived, and he was able to cure her. He admits, however, that some patients don't respond to treatment. (Green 1992)

Both of these theories seem unrelated in any direct way with biomedical concepts and health education messages. The first theory is classifiable as ICT, environmental dangers type, and the second as witchcraft/sorcery. The first type—which according to the Swazi healer survey as well as our Zambian data is more common—illustrates how innocent passersby become contaminated even though powerful, dangerous herbs are the sources of pollution rather than the more usual contact with death, menstrual blood, dirt, etc. Still, the illness is spread impersonally by mere contact with a substance or presence in a particular place rather than through deliberate targeting of a victim by a superhuman agent. Note also the enema treatment for environmental/contamination bilharzia, typical of pollution illness.

An herbalist informant told me that what Europeans call bilharzia is really *lukhuba*. He said it is due to natural causes and may be thought to have an epidemic character, especially if a number of children fall ill with this at the same time. If only one child gets it, it may be regarded as "sent" by enemies through sorcery. To treat *lukhuba*, there are herbs to "wash out" the system, taken orally or via enema.

A diviner-medium informant said that although *umthundungati* and bilharzia have identical symptoms, they aren't the same. Bilharzia is caused "by drinking certain types of water and a little creature gets inside you. *Umthundungati* is caused by being poisoned by someone" (i.e., sorcery).

Some healers believe that bilharzia is really the locally recognized syndrome *likhubalo*. This STI-type illness is believed to be caused by a possessive man who, with the help of a specialist, treats his wife with potent medicines believed to ensure fidelity. Subsequent lovers become victims of the man's revenge. Unless treated immediately, the lover dies suddenly, often after exhibiting the symptoms of blood in the urine, at the end of the penis, or from the nose. One rather educated healer explained to me that *likhubalo*, like what Europeans call bilharzia, can also involve blood in a man's urine, but only just before an adulterer drops dead from

203

the sorcerer's medicine. Thus, *likhubalo* may be considered acute, whereas bilharzia is chronic. A very similar syndrome is found in both Zimbabwe and central Mozambique, where it is called *rukawe, rikaho,* or *rikaho*. In Mozambique, this illness seems to be the only one related to sorcery, rather than ICT, and it is said to be comparatively rare.

Another of my healer informants told me that *likhubalo* and *umthundungati* have similar symptoms but different causes. *Likhubalo* is caused by a husband's jealousy or by being exposed to an area where a healer has been mixing medicines for "protecting" a wife with *likhubalo*. *Umthundungati* comes from two sources: stagnant water containing "little animals" that get inside you, or taking European pills.

At the time of our healer survey in Swaziland, there was some question about the existence of belief in something equivalent to waterborne disease, which was the focus—and part of the title—of our project. I quickly found that *air*borne disease (*tifo temoya*, discussed above) was an indigenous concept and one frequently referred to. I was less sure about water, partly because an equivalent phrase in the Swazi language (*tifo temanti*) never arose spontaneously. But in our survey of traditional healers, we asked which, if any, illnesses could be caused or transmitted by water. Whatever the degree of biomedical influence the answers reflect, bilharzia and its local analogues was the most frequently cited example (68/144 citations), followed by cholera (32) and stomachache or diarrhea (19); miscellaneous illnesses received only 1–3 citations.

Much of what we were measuring was biomedically influenced knowledge; 41 healers replied that they didn't know about these "doctors' matters" or that they didn't believe water causes illness (as long as water looks clean, there are no dead animals in it, etc.). But the same survey—plus some of my own in-depth interviews and observations—suggests that some healers at the time (the early 1980s) were being trained by their *bogobela* in biomedically influenced notions about bilharzia and its rather complicated cycle of transmission involving an intermediate vector. This may illustrate one way in which new medical ideas are incorporated into African ethnomedical systems. I wouldn't be surprised to learn that a greater number of Swazi traditional healers today have some notion that germs or unseen worms can be carried by water—even if it appears clean—and cause illness. If treatments to "clean out" the bodies of those who suffer from water- and germ-related illness seem unsuccessful, then healers (and patients) may suspect personalistic causation.

Epilepsy

Sometimes a syndrome not usually classified biomedically as communicable or infectious is believed by Africans to be contagious, in which case it appears often to be interpreted in an ICT framework. Before dismissing ethnomedical beliefs and practitioners as erroneous, it must be acknowledged that some epilepsy in Africa *is* contagious—or rather, some infectious, communicable diseases in Africa are manifest in epileptic-type seizures. For example, cysticercosis, a type of tapeworm infection, can cause epileptic seizures (Avode et al. 1996).

Let us look at some examples of African epilepsy models from the literature. For example, Awaritefe (1989) notes:

> It was found that most Nigerians, including some medical students, share the belief that epilepsy is contagious. They would therefore not eat, drink, or sleep in the same room with an epileptic, or touch him during his fit. The origin of the belief is now lost in obscurity, but traditional healers seem to be its current repository and propagators. The views of the latter are reinforced and sustained by people fleeing in panic from a patient experiencing a grand mal attack. (p. 449)

A survey about epilepsy, or at least seizures, was conducted in Tanzania with 3,256 heads of households (mean age 40.2 years, range 15–90 years; M/F ratio 1:1). Forty percent of respondents believed that epilepsy was infectious through physical contact, flatus, breath, excretions, or sharing food; 33.3% mentioned various causes including heredity, witchcraft, infection of the spinal cord, and hernia. There were a number of "I don't know" (Rwiza et al. 1993).

Reis (1993, 1994) notes that epilepsy is believed to be a contagious illness in many parts of Africa, but not in Swaziland. She admits that during her Swazi fieldwork she heard mention of a snake in the belly (the *nyoka* discussed in Chapter Three) and she may not have known what to make of this, concluding that epilepsy is mostly explained as caused by sorcery. Apart from *nyoka*, she describes one local type of epilepsy as resulting from breathing in *tinyamatane* from someone else's clan. I know from my ethnomedical research in Swaziland that this refers to clan-specific protective medicines and that people can become ill from exposure to *tinyamatane* from another's clan. This interpretation qualifies as *tifo temoya*, as the Swazi call airborne

205

illnesses, a major type of "environmental dangers," itself a major component of ICT.

Pertinent to the *nyoka* association, Marrato (1991:15–16) conducted a study of epilepsy among the Tsonga, who border the Swazi. Among the names of different types of epilepsy were terms denoting "big *nyoka*," "female *nyoka*," and two other types of snake in the stomach (a fifth type translates as "falling down"). As we have seen, *nyoka* among Nguni speakers and some of their neighbors is a symbolic expression of the need to respect the human body, specifically to protect it against the introduction of impurity. It is a central part of the pollution lexicon. Marrato (1991:15–16) also found that during a seizure Tsonga believe that "gases" that come from the rectum or mouth are thought to be contagious; a bystander can get one type of epilepsy illness from breathing the gases. This sounds like the reaction to epilepsy in Nigeria just cited, and it is further evidence that such syndromes may be understood in an ICT framework.

Yet not all seizures are thought of this way, as Reis observed of Swazi beliefs. Among the Tsonga, Marrato (1991) found that epileptic-like seizures are explained as "naturally caused" (*ntumbunuko*) by 30% of traditional healers, or caused by punishment from one's ancestors for bad behavior by 70% of healers. As a second answer, 20% gave *mpfukwa* (witchcraft and sorcery) as the cause.

FINDINGS FROM MALAWI

We now turn to findings from a study in Malawi that served as the model for the TIR in Zambia and other countries. In spite of this, it was called a focused ethnographic survey (FES), and it was funded under the AIDS Control and Prevention Project of USAID (Helitzer-Allen et al. 1996).

I had no involvement in this study and have only minimal first-hand knowledge of Malawi. However, there is no reason to suspect that Chewa and other Bantu-speaking groups there (Lomwe, Yao, Tumbuka, Ngoni) differ significantly in illness beliefs from neighboring groups in Zambia and Mozambique. The Chewa, who comprise perhaps 50% of Malawi, are part of the Maravi cluster of central Bantu, according to Murdock's (1959:294–295) classification. This cluster includes the Nyanja of Zambia, whose ethnomedical beliefs are discussed above, as well as the Sena and Nyasa of western Mozambique, geographically adjacent to the Shona. Thyolo district, where the survey was conducted, appears to be ethnically mixed, with Lomwe predominating in the survey. Other groups listed in the survey are: Ngoni, Yao, Nyanja, Mang'anja, Sena, and Makhokhola. The Lomwe are part of the Yao cluster that include the Macua, as already mentioned.

The principal investigators of the Malawi survey have allowed me to use the raw data from this study to look for evidence of pollution and other beliefs. I outline the methods and scope of this study by quoting from the final report (Helitzer-Allen and Allen 1992):

> An ethnographic research tool called a *Focused Ethnographic Study* (FES) was developed specifically to learn about community member's knowledge, beliefs and experience of illnesses transmitted through sexual intercourse . . . twelve sets of FES guides triangulate illness names, perceived symptoms, causes, appropriate health-seeking behavior, and treatment with reports of illness experiences.
>
> Malawian interviewers administered the FES in two Thyolo (district) villages over a one-month period. A total of 154 interviews were conducted with adult men and women using same sex interviewers. Using the first six guides, eighty-two (82) local illnesses were named. Lists of symptoms, causes, and sex affected were collected from key informants. From this list of illnesses, a group of twenty-one (21) core illnesses, believed to be transmitted through sexual intercourse, were selected for further study. In-depth interviews elicited more detailed information about personal experiences with these illnesses. (p. 1)

Unfortunately, there was insufficient time available to conduct in-depth interviews about malaria, bilharzia, cholera (or their indigenous counterparts), and other locally identified syndromes. But these data can shed light on the relative importance of naturalistic/personalistic ethnomedical beliefs and relevance of the ICT construct. Surveys—especially those reanalyzed by someone uninvolved in the study—are not the best way to discover ethnomedical beliefs and practices. Nevertheless, I have firsthand research experience with several neighboring central Bantu-speaking groups, and this helps in interpreting survey findings.

Moreover, there are certain strengths of the present survey: (1) Like the Zambian TIR, this study provides ethnomedical findings on a great many (82) illnesses affecting adults, many of which appear to be contagious, judging by associated symptoms; and (2) These findings can be used to challenge the argument that traditional healers and the average person in the same community may not or do not share the same ethnomedical beliefs. Of course, there are certainly times in reviewing these survey findings when one wants to ask, "Why? When? How? Please explain." Often respondents simply say they don't know the cause of an illness they have identified. No doubt this is easier than giving an answer that might be invalidated or held in low esteem—or not understood—by an interviewer. This might explain the relative lack of personalistic explanations. And if pollution beliefs are part of a "complex algebra of symbolic system deeply embedded in a particular society," as Douglas (1963) has said of the Lele of neighboring Zaire, it is likewise easier not to give an answer that might require a lot of further explanation. Furthermore, pollution beliefs tend to sound supernatural and superstitious to the educated outsider—even Murdock classified them as mystical contagion—so respondents might be as apt to withhold these ideas as comments about spirits or witches. Despite these weaknesses inherent in survey research, there is ample evidence of pollution belief and broader indigenous theory of contagion.

Since causal theories provide the key to understanding ethnomedical systems, it is useful to examine the complete list of causes attributed to adult illness as only a computer can compile, since a slight variation in the wording of an answer qualifies it as a separate answer (Helitzer-Allen and Allen 1992:24–26). The list offers insight into the range of causal theories and perhaps the relative importance of pollution, witchcraft/ sorcery, spirits, taboo violation, natural causes, etc., although the frequency of answers is not given. (However, it seems from the raw data that no answer was given more than four times.) Of course, we must not conclude too much from such a list. It is probable that causes related to witchcraft would be underreported in a formal, survey context.

I have attempted to categorize illness causes by the general type of causal theory the answer seems to represent. These categories parallel Murdock (1980) and other etiologic taxonomies I have described. If answers were ambiguous, category straddling or otherwise hard to classify, or if symptoms were listed as causes, I didn't try to categorize them. My intent was to discover broad patterns, especially of the relative importance of personalistic explanations compared to naturalistic and specifically ICT explanations. I also wanted to link types of causal explanation to broad categories of illness.

COMPLETE LIST OF CAUSES ATTRIBUTED TO "ADULT ILLNESSES" IN MALAWI

[Code: P = Pollution; T = Trauma; CHD = Cleanliness, hygiene, diet; ICT = Indigenous contagious theory; PER = Personalistic explanation; LA = Lifestyle or aging; E = Environmental[2]; OT = Overdose, toxic reaction; H = heredity; NU = Natural or unavoidable]

Abortion/stillbirth, discharge of blood/first sex outside home	P
Accidents	T
Adulterous man/preg. wife/unborn gets ill	P
Adultery	P
Adultery by man, day of child's funeral	P
Adultery by man, spell on woman, man ill	P
After delivery, sores in uterus	
Bad drinking water	CHD
Bad germs	ICT
Bathing in bad water	CHD
Bathing in infected waters	CHD
Bathing in water w/infected person's urine	P
Bathing in water w/snails in it	ICT
Being close to patient	ICT
Being hit on the back	T
Being inactive	LA
Blood clotting in body	
Body sore causes genitals to swell	
Born before full term	H
Born with it	H
Born with it (all females)	H
Born with it (some men)	H
Breathing air from infected person	ICT
Breathing bad air in dusty rooms	ICT
Bright sunlight	E
Carrying too much luggage on head	T
Childbirth (after)	
Coating of blood in body	ICT
Cold and damp weather	E
Contacting water w/snails w/bilharzia	ICT
Coughing	
Damp conditions	E
Does not know any cause	NU

Dreaming about illness, get it next day	
Drinking bilharzia-infected water	CHD
Drinking river water	CHD
Drinking river water w/bilharzia	CHD
Drinking too much *kachasu*	CHD
Drinking water w/snails in it	CHD
Drinking well water w/bilharzia	CHD
Due to leg injury	T
Dust blowing into eyes	ICT
Dusty wind	ICT
Eating food lacking vitamins	CHD
Eating food w/dust on it	CHD
Eating foods (esp. meat) unsuited to person	CHD
Eating raw tomatoes	CHD
Eating sweet potato leaves	CHD
Eating too many sweets	CHD
Eating unclean food	CHD
Epilepsy if neglected	
Failing to clean teeth	CHD
Fetus causes wounds in uterus	T
Fetus in spot too long, causes sores	T
Fighting	T
Flies bring from infected person's eyes	ICT
Flies transfer human waste to food	ICT
Food decays in teeth causing decay	CHD
Friction caused by moving	T
Germs in mouth after beer drinking	ICT
God's anger because of sinful behavior	PER
Heavy blows on back	T
Hit by rains	E
Hit during a fight	T
Improper disposal of afterbirth	P
Improper disposal of stillbirth	P
Inactive people	LA
Inherited	H
Inherited but develops later in life	H
Injury w/any vein connected to genitals	T
Intercourse/dead person's relative before funeral	P
Intercourse/many women their bloods clot	P
Intercourse/many women their bloods mix	P
Intercourse transmits AIDS germ	P

210

Intercourse: very active as youth	LA
Intercourse/woman/aborted discharging blood	P
Intercourse/woman/aborted still "hot"	P
Intercourse/woman/deliver discharging blood	P
Intercourse w/many women	P
Intercourse w/menstruating woman	P
Intercourse w/prostitutes	P
Intercourse w/woman aborted same day	P
Intercourse w/woman recently aborted	P
Intercourse w/woman recently gave birth	P
Intercourse w/woman recently miscarried	P
Intercourse w/infected person	P
Invisible germ bites person	ICT
Invisible leprosy	ICT
Lack of blood in body	
Lack of blood/water in body	
Lack of exercise	LA
Lack of vitamins	
Lice	ICT
Long walks for fat person	LA
Looking into infected person's eyes	ICT
Mauritians coming to Nchalo brought it	ICT
Menses blood clots in penis	P
Mosquitoes (bites from)	ICT
Mosquitoes during rainy season	ICT
Not cleaning teeth	CHD
Old age	LA
Opening bottles w/teeth	T
Overworking	T
Overworking in fields	T
Passed on to children	H
Person unused to work	LA
Poking eardrum w/stick to clean it	T
Poor blood circulation	LA
Poor diet	CHD
Pregnant woman overdose tablets to abort	T
Rubbing eyes w/dirty fingers	ICT
Running long distances	T
Scratched by a branch	T
Shaking head too much	T
Sleeping long hours	LA

Sore throat	
Splitting headache	
Sprinkling water over someone	
Starts on its own	NU
Starts when menstruation about to begin	P
Stepping over dead snail	P
Stepping over infected person's stool	P
Stepping over infected person's urine	P
Testicle breaks and dissolves	
Too much gas in bowels	
Too much sun	E
Too much walking in the sun	E
Too much worry	LA
Touching blood from warts	ICT
Trying food never had before	CHD
Twisting back ligaments	T
Unclean home	CHD
Unclean pubic hair	ICT
Uncovered food	CHD
Urinating on fire	ICT
Using herbs to make sexually active	OT
Using toothbrush of tooth decay victim	ICT
Using traditional herbs	OT
Uterus still contracting after delivery	
Very cold weather	E
Walking in rains	E
Walking long distances	LA
Water infected w/human waste	ICT
Well water during rainy season	ICT
Witchcraft	PER

CLASSIFICATION OF ILLNESS BY CAUSE

Pollution (part of ICT)	= 28
Other ICT	= 26
Cleanliness, hygiene, or diet	= 23
Trauma	= 19
Lifestyle, aging	= 11
Environmental	= 8
Heredity	= 7

Overdose, toxic reaction	=	2
Personalistic	=	2
Natural, unavoidable	=	2
Unclassifiable	=	16
Total causes	=	144

By now we are familiar with the idiom of pollution and recognize such phrases as "stepping over infected person's stool"; "intercourse with many women (and) their bloods mix"; "improper disposal of afterbirth"; "intercourse with a dead person's relative"; and "adultery by man (on the) day of child's funeral." These are sufficiently different from biomedically recognized processes of infection that they can be regarded as expressions of indigenous thought. Other expressions of indigenous contagion theory might reflect influence of modern health education (e.g., "using the tooth brush of a tooth decay victim" and "water infected with human waste"). However, both types of contagion belief are part of contemporary ethno-etiology. Both presumably motivate treatment and perhaps prevention or infection-avoidance behavior.

We see that at least 28 answers might be classified as reflecting pollution beliefs (fully 21 answers referred to sexual intercourse, adultery, or "sex outside of home"), and 26 seem to reflect other indigenous contagious theory such as illness in the air. There are also 23 explanations that refer to cleanliness, hygiene, or diet.

Although one might quibble about the classification of some individual answers, the general picture is indisputable: With only two answers that refer to witchcraft or God's will, and none that refer to spirits of any sort, it is safe to conclude that the great majority of causes attributed to the range of locally recognized illnesses are impersonal or naturalistic rather than personalistic. In the first category we can include physical trauma (e.g., "twisting back ligaments"), natural environmental causes such as hot or cold weather, physical symptoms leading to other symptoms, and heredity as well as ICT-pollution explanations.

There are many examples of naturalistic theories other than those related to pollution (e.g., "eating foods [especially meat] unsuited to a person" and "opening bottles with teeth" [leading to a syndrome called *kupweteka*, one of whose symptoms is "failing to eat hard foods," that is, sugarcane]). "Eating unclean food" suggests either naturalistic or specifically pollution thinking. The concepts of "lack of blood" and "lack of water" in the body were also found among the Shona and other groups

213

in Mozambique (Chapter Four). These conditions are thought to result from serious, persistent diarrhea—usually caused by pollution—leading to the development of symptoms such as whiteness of palms and soles, white eyes, edema in limbs, loss of appetite, loss of skin elasticity, general weakness, and thirst. These symptoms are interpreted as resulting from the child being without water or blood (Green et al. 1993; see Pillsbury 1978).

We also see evidence of modern biomedical concepts, such as bilharzia (*likozo*) being caused by little snails in stagnant water, or a malaria-like syndrome being cause by "mosquitoes during the rainy season." There were four mentions of germs. An answer like "breathing air from infected person" implies either naturalistic infection or modern germ theory. There was no specific mention of tiny, unseen worms, insects, or other exemplars of indigenous germ theory. There was one mention of an "invisible germ" that "bites (a) person," suggesting that respondents may translate the indigenous concept of invisible worm/insect into germ.

In sum, the findings reported here bolster the argument that magico-religious beliefs in African ethnomedicine have been exaggerated, while naturalistic including pollution beliefs have been underreported. Certainly these findings, like those reported elsewhere in this book, are at odds with Hammond-Tooke's findings (1989:89) from southern Bantu speakers that suggest 73% of cases of illness are explained in witchcraft-sorcery terms.

There is also a section on attributed causes of STIs. No conclusions are offered other than that "social causes" are mentioned prominently. All the sexual intercourse taboos common in southern Africa are listed: sex with prostitutes, sex outside of marriage, sex in connection with abortion or miscarriage or death, sex with multiple partners (leading to "mixing of blood"), sex during menstruation, aborted women who are "still hot," etc. Witchcraft, evil eye, jealousy, avenging spirits, and natural causes are also cited (Helitzer-Allen and Allen 1992: 24). The authors make the point that cause or etiology is complex, but "mode of transmission" is almost always understood to be due to sexual intercourse" (p. 36). The authors also felt they had insufficient time to adequately analyze their findings. They agree that ICT including pollution provides a useful framework for analysis of these data (Allen, personal communication).

Regarding therapy choice, one respondent is quoted as saying of STI patients, "In most cases they go to traditional healers because they are ashamed (when) with the Western doctors." The authors note that traditional healers seen as more sympathetic, more confidential, and more accessible than modern health workers (Helitzer-Allen and Allen 1992:30).

A urinary schistosomiasis-like syndrome called *likodzo* also emerged in the Malawi study. The most commonly cited symptoms were "pain in urination" (33.3%) and "urination of blood" or "pants stained with blood" (21.7%). The most common attributed causes were bathing in or drinking stagnant or "bad" water, or water with little snails (36.6%); sexual intercourse with an infected person or a menstruating woman (19.5%); and stepping over an infected person's urine or over a dead snail (14.6%). Only one informant cited witchcraft, compared to three who said people are born with *likodzo*. Again, we see that answers do not differ much when we compare findings between three countries in the region, and between answers given by traditional healers and laypersons. We also see again that local interpretation of an illness biomedically classified as infectious is squarely in the domain of indigenous contagion theory.

Incidentally, my research in several countries in Africa, including Liberia, suggest that people who cite sexual intercourse as the cause of illnesses that we gloss as schistosomiasis and tuberculosis would agree that it is not the act of intercourse itself that is dangerous; it is the opportunity for contact with illness-causing agents. Intercourse provides one point of contact for contamination or pollution between people, albeit a particularly potent and dangerous one because of the intimacy of the contact and the opportunity for direct exposure of men to women's reproductive fluids. Sexual intercourse is also a point of contact for nonpollution health threats such as medicines or spells (Ingstad 1990:33), as illustrated by Swazi beliefs about the sorcery illness *likhubalo*. Therefore, it is on the circumstances of intercourse, not the act itself, that many Africans focus in diagnosis and determination of appropriate therapies.

CONCLUSIONS FROM SOUTHERN AFRICA

We have looked at ethnomedical beliefs and some related practices associated with malaria, tuberculosis, and schistosomiasis and found that they tend to be interpreted in the framework of ICT. What about other contagious diseases? There has not been a great deal of ethnomedical studies of contagious disease beyond those covered, and a number that exist are not based on ethnography in any form but only on superficial, sample surveys, as we will see in the next chapter. In such surveys, researchers are basically looking for right/wrong answers, judging indigenous knowledge and beliefs against a rigid standard of biomedicine. However, some of the more qualitative, ethnographic studies yield data of interest to ICT. Studies of both types are reviewed in the next chapter, those pertaining to Africa as well as to other regions of the world.

NOTES

1. As Ngubane (1977:25) notes, the plural form of *moya* can mean spirits as well as air, wind, soul, or an amicable attribute of people, in the Zulu language, which is mutually intelligible with Swazi (siSwati). Perhaps interviewers added the modifier "evil" in their translation attempt. Then there is the siSwati word *tilwane*, which may have been used by healers and which can mean or refer to spirits, spirit familiars, mental illness, or even little animals such as bed bugs, fleas, or germs.

2. This refers to natural environmental factors rather than ICT-related "environmental dangers" factors as described by Ngubane and others.

CHAPTER SEVEN

INDIGENOUS CONTAGION THEORY IN BROADER PERSPECTIVE

In this chapter, I attempt to answer two questions. First, does it matter if illness is thought of in natural or personalistic terms? The answer to this leads to a discussion of how indigenous health beliefs and practices in developing countries (not just Africa) tend to be characterized by researchers who influence international health programs. Second, I try to determine if indigenous contagion theory, as described for many parts of Africa, is found in other parts of the world.

A NEGATIVE, DISMISSIVE, ETIC MIND-SET

To answer the first question, I begin with an observation or hypothesis that most anthropologists would agree with: Public health programs in developing countries (and among minority or foreign-born groups within developed countries) would be more effective if those who design and implement programs possessed an empirically based understanding of existing ethnomedical beliefs and practices and designed and implemented programs with these in mind (Airhihenbuwa 1991:156). This is especially true in the context of public health programs in which compliance with complex treatment regimes or adoption of new behaviors are desirable, as in many contagious and infectious diseases. To the extent that the domain of ethnomedicine is viewed as supernatural or personalistic, it has been easy for those involved in the serious business of saving lives in public health programs to dismiss ethnomedicine as "meaningless pseudo-psychological mumbo-jumbo, which is positively harmful" (Motlana, in Freeman and Motsei 1992:1186), and to proceed with health campaigns—as if they were driving a bulldozer that would plow under such superstitions to clear the way for science.

There is an assumption, easy to find in the medical literature, that the greater an individual's commitment to personalistic ethnomedical beliefs, the less likely it is that the person would adhere to biomedical treatment or be open to sound preventive strategies. Anthropologists McElroy and Townsend (1996:101) put it this way: "If evil eye, or witchcraft, or soul loss is a major component of a culture's explanatory model of illness, it is less likely that a person from that culture will believe that one can control disease through pragmatic, preventive measure." And if the prevailing belief in public health is that *most* illness is understood supernaturally by Africans or others, and this is bolstered by at least some anthropologists, the perhaps understandable tendency is to not make distinctions between domains within an indigenous health system, but to seek to replace all of it with Western biomedicine, through education at all levels. The characterization of African and other health systems as supernatural becomes a rationale for making no effort to understand, let alone accommodate, existing ethnomedical beliefs and practices.

Conversely, to the extent that an ethnomedical domain is naturalistic, it resembles the models of biomedicine and public health (which have different scopes and emphases), and it becomes more difficult to dismiss. In any case, ethnomedicine cannot be dismissed. Colonial regimes and authoritarian postindependence governments in Africa have failed in their attempts to do so. Therefore, public health programs must accept the prevailing ethnomedical system as a given and then find some way to work within it.

Whatever the nature of the overall system, if a particular ethnomedical domain is essentially naturalistic, such as we find in ICT, those involved in health programs should be better able to build on common ground that exists between the indigenous and biomedical models of illness, treatment, and prevention. This ought to result in interventions that are more culturally meaningful and therefore likely to influence behavior. It should galvanize the support of existing, indigenous health opinion leaders and practitioners, forging potentially powerful alliances in, for example, AIDS or childhood diarrhea prevention campaigns. More lives would be saved and more human suffering would be alleviated in return for the hundreds of millions of dollars that are now spent annually on international health programs (or "minority" health programs in developed countries).

But none of the foregoing is likely to happen any time soon. One need only survey the literature on ethnomedicine in a public or international context to discover Western medical ethnocentrism in one of its more extreme and harmful forms. The approach that emerges from such literature seems to be: Prove native health beliefs wrong (or childish) with superficial KAP surveys, then lead the natives out of darkness and get them to do what we want them to do, calling this "behavior change," "health facilities utilization," and "treatment compliance." There is little recognition or acknowledgement (aside from some anthropologists) of the fallibility and malleability of biomedical models of illness and of treatment regimens and of the fact that these models are themselves culturally constructed. Western treatment models of diarrhea 30 or so years ago were quite different from those that inform health programs today. Beliefs and practices marked "wrong" in a KAP survey then might be "right" today. Yet, public health zealots can be so sure that they are right, and that there is only one correct way, that they will quarantine or inoculate whole populations to "save" them, whatever the views of those they wish to save.

I conducted an extensive literature search primarily to test the relevance of the ICT analytic construct in developing countries outside Africa. While doing this, I also compiled evidence of the Western medical ethnocentric bias just described. Part of my search involved using key word combinations such as "infection and ethnomedicine" or "traditional healing and disease" and conducting global searches using databases such as Medline, Popline, and Sociofile. This exercise ought to generate a fairly representative and unbiased universe of abstracts that represent research related to ethnomedicine and infectious disease, producing studies that are multilingual, global, and multidisciplinary. It was essential to go beyond anthropology and consider the viewpoints of others who work in international health (public health professionals, clinicians, medical geographers, sociologists, etc.) because, among other reasons, anthropologists contribute only one (minority) voice among many in this field.

A great many of the journal articles—including a few from *Social Science and Medicine* and *Human Organization*, in which many anthropologists publish—depict ethnomedical beliefs and practices negatively, as obstacles to proper treatment and the adoption of approved behaviors. Articles more sympathetic to ethnomedicine tend to be based on longer-term fieldwork and to deal with more theoretical topics. It is not likely that these will be read by busy practitioners who design and implement health programs in developing countries. In other words, sympathetic, nonapplied ethnomedical literature seems to contribute less to prevailing views in international health than less-sympathetic, more applied, and less anthropological literature. The apparent dominant view appears to be supported by KAP survey reports of erroneous folk or tribal health beliefs and superstitions, along with suggestions of how to overcome, circumvent, or eradicate these.

For example, a study of conformity to tuberculosis treatment regimens in India found that (all emphases in this and the next two paragraphs are added): "Noncompliance was found related to poor socioeconomic conditions, *health-damaging beliefs*, lack of health information" (Barnhoorn and Adriaanse 1992). A study of schistosomiasis in Brazil found "a contradiction between *cultural values and habits* and conventional control measures, which has resulted in the disease continuing to be endemic, despite health education measures" (Noronha et al. 1995). A study entitled "Culture and 'Compliance' among Leprosy Patients in Pakistan" reported that "Many patients had initially consulted traditional healers . . . which resulted in lengthy delays before they were correctly diagnosed" (Mull et al. 1989). A study of mosquito-borne lymphatic filariasis transmission in southern Thailand noted that, "Results indicate that poor knowledge and lay, indigenous, traditional belief systems contribute to high risk behaviours, and inappropriate preventive, illness and treatment choice behaviours" (Rauyajin et al. 1995). A study in Zimbabwe concluded, "The findings show that *traditional explanations of an illness such as diarrhoea can inhibit health education campaigns against this disease which kills many children every year*" (Pitts et al.

220

1996:1223). A report about suspected toxic reactions to indigenous medicine in South African implies that death from poisoning often results from a visit to a traditional healer, and that "A great deal of secrecy still surrounds traditional medicine, *hampering rational therapy*" (Venter and Joubert 1988). The clear impression from such representative articles is that indigenous medicine is a barrier to effective treatment and can lead indirectly or directly to death.

Some studies are less alarmist yet still patronizing and dismissive of indigenous health knowledge (e.g., "Programs designed to encourage breastfeeding in the Philippines *must first address the tenacity of traditional health beliefs before any real progress can be made*" [Fernandez and Guthrie 1984]). A study of leprosy in Venezuela concluded that "Knowledge of leprosy is limited, and *erroneous beliefs and negative attitudes* exist (Romero-Salazar et al. 1995). Typically, the cognitive dimension of the representation of leprosy centers on the role of fortune and fate, sexual promiscuity, or heritage [heredity?] in the transmission of leprosy." Again we see an example of ethnomedical beliefs depicted as either dangerous to health or, at best, as an impediment to biomedical treatment.

A study of an Expanded Vaccination Program in Cameroon concluded that, "the immunization campaign was further *hindered by resilient cultural beliefs about disease causation.* Seventy-two percent of respondents stated that child mortality is a result of witchcraft or God's will. Impure water, germs, poor sanitation, and other known causes of disease were rarely cited" (Azevedo et al. 1991:1341). As a result of these "resilient cultural beliefs," "visits to a health center occur only when all other approaches have failed, or not at all, given the fatalism prevalent in the society" (p. 1341). The recommendation was for "education on the natural causation of disease and greater collaboration with and training of traditional healers" (Azevedo et al. 1991).

Whatever their research objectives, KAP surveys often measure what local people *don't* know, or what they know relative to a presumably infallible yardstick of correct health knowledge. There is often little or no attempt to measure what people *do* know. This seems a perversion of the term "ethnomedical beliefs," which is sometimes used in the titles of such studies. Usually the problem reported is that the natives are ridden with superstition; Western health education is needed to lead them out of darkness. But not always. A study of folk beliefs about diarrhea in

Thailand found that, "Most diarrhea in children under age one is considered to be . . . a normal developmental stage that requires no treatment. Thus, health messages concerning diarrhea are not considered by caregivers, which results in a delay in help-seeking and a risk factor of dehydration" (Shawyer et al. 1996). We see that whether natives view diarrhea as supernatural or natural, it is bad news to many health educators because, at best, ethnomedical belief delays seeking the type of help we want to provide. This deserves to be called a bulldozer approach: The Western public health way is the only way; adopt it or be crushed.

The Thai study went on to note that those surveyed "knew very little about the role of infection in diarrhea, the role of hygiene in prevention of diarrhea, and the place and function of oral rehydration solution, indicating important areas where education is still necessary." I wonder if mothers in the area surveyed did, in fact, use coconut water, rice water, or other commonly used, effective rehydrating liquids for their children who had diarrhea or were suffering from a locally recognized sunken fontanel syndrome, yet gave the wrong answer to a true/false question about something called ORS or ORT or "replacement fluid management."

Sound, health-promotive ethnomedical beliefs may be judged backward or dangerous if they differ at all from a narrow checklist of what is considered biomedically acceptable at the moment. A study in Nigeria found that "leading traditional remedies for diarrhea and/or dehydration" included native herbs and coconut water, leading the authors to conclude, "These results indicated the need to promote oral rehydration therapy (ORT)" (Ikpatt and Young 1992:222). It is doubtful whether the authors knew if local herbs for diarrhea are effective, but they should have known that coconut water *is* recognized as ORT. It is as effective as oral rehydration salts for dehydration.

A geographer, apparently from Africa, reviewed "pertinent literature" to examine four requirements of good health service often attributed to ethnomedicine (availability, accessibility, acceptability, and adaptability), only to conclude that African ethnomedicine fails on these (Anyinam 1987). The abstract notes:

A review of pertinent literature suggests that: (1) Accessibility of native healers may be less than generally assumed; (2) The availability of indigenous medical facilities varies between countries; (3) Many government officials appear indifferent toward ethnomedicine; and (4) It is uncertain whether ethnomedicine can adapt to changing conditions within Africa. (p. 803)

This is not the place to refute each point of this conclusion, but the author does not seem to understand what some of these four terms mean. For example, "acceptability" was misinterpreted as something to do with government attitudes of the day, rather than with the masses whose health the government wants to improve.

Anthropologists may also have this bias. As applied anthropologists work increasingly with health educators and others on multidisciplinary teams, they may come to adopt the public health mind set of "We know what's best for the medically unenlightened." This is especially so if the anthropologists' research is limited to quick-and-dirty sample surveys. Indeed, I have found myself thinking like this under such circumstances. I suppose if some of my conclusions had been challenged at critical times, I might have said something like: "Yes, well, the details of ethno-medical exotica are fascinating if you have the time to research them, but people around here are dying from preventable diseases. Yes, we applied medical anthropologists engage in social engineering based on quick and dirty research, but we are *saving lives!*"

For example, an article in an anthropological journal (by nonanthro-pologists) about childhood diarrhea perceptions in south India recognizes the importance of local pollution beliefs. Dehydration is seen as a state of pollution that results from a mother or her child having contact with a menstruating woman, a woman who has not bathed after intercourse, or a woman who has miscarried (Lozoff et al. 1975: 356). But pollution beliefs are depicted as misperceptions that lead to medically ineffective treatments such as chanting, burning incense, and other "ritual purifica-tion." Once again, ethnomedicine is shown in a negative light.

But what about other health promotive functions of pollution belief and practices (e.g., habits of cleanliness and hygiene that result from such beliefs, or quarantine of people when they may be infectious to others)? If a mother reported, "I kept my child with cholera and dehydration separate from other children until he was treated with recommended antibiotics," it would have meant a perfect score on the KAP survey. Instead, she might have said something like, "My child was unclean and so I kept him from other children until he was purified." This phraseology might earn a score of between 0% and 20%, depending on the disciplinary background of the scorer. Anthropologists might see something redeeming or suggestive of good health in the latter comment if they probed more deeply into pollution beliefs and behavior.

I am not proposing that the two answers are equivalent in their objective health consequences. Nor am I saying that "native genius," with health-promotive consequences, can be found in all ethnomedical belief and practices (see Chapter Eight for several counterexamples). But I am saying that we need a balanced view of ethnomedicine. A belief complex like pollution has positive as well as sometimes negative aspects even when measured with the Western, public health yardstick. We should take the trouble to investigate it in sufficient depth so that both aspects emerge. Let us go beyond the ethnocentric assumption that any health beliefs and practices that differ in substance and in idiom from ours is ipso facto deficient and something that stands in the way of progress.

Here is a comment I made a few years ago, in which I paraphrase an unpublished report of Harriet Ngubane:

> Western development planners and other professionals (including some Africans) tend to think of traditional systems—whether relating to health care, land tenure, communal ownership, kinship obligations, or ancestor veneration—as archaic and dysfunctional, as a way of life to be overcome if there is to be progress and development. What such a view fails to recognize is that traditional systems may be well-suited to the social, psychological, and other needs of participants in these systems; that traditional systems may be a great source of comfort to Africans under-going rapid culture change, providing security and continuity in an unpredictable, changing world; and that traditional systems tend to be genuine functioning systems whereas the same cannot as yet be said of the modern-urban alternative. (Green 1994a:31–32)

The same general comment applies to ethnomedicine, except that beliefs and practices of this sort may also be effective and beneficial to health, objectively or by public health standards.

GLOBAL EVIDENCE FOR ICT

We turn now to the second question: How widespread is indigenous contagion theory in other parts of the world? How generalizable beyond

Africa are the ICT findings presented here? As we will see, there is evidence that many communicable illnesses are conceived in ICT-like interpretative frameworks outside of Africa. Following is a survey of the anthropological and related literature for evidence of indigenous etiologies associated with contagious or infectious diseases.

First, two caveats. Surveys of indigenous etiologic belief are admittedly reductionistic. They ignore or at least oversimplify the multifactorial, multilevel, context-specific thinking usually found in explanations about illness causation—especially in medically pluralistic settings (Ngokwey 1988). However, I don't believe that these considerations should make us abandon efforts to take a broad, global look at illness causation theories and seek links between these *basic* theories and important behavioral consequences such as choice of treatment.

Second, there is the methodological problem that informants may be willing to speak more openly to outsiders about natural causes than about witchcraft. This is why I and my colleagues were so skeptical during our STD and diarrhea research in central Mozambique in 1991–92 when we found so much pollution and naturalistic infection theories and so little personalistic thinking. Yet, after trying in every way to find evidence of the latter (and we did find some), we reached a point where we felt we soon would be forcing informants to agree to propositions from Evans-Pritchard's fieldwork in the Sudan of the 1930s.

Now to the findings about ICT from the global search of literature on the etiology of contagious illnesses, much but not all of it based on anthropological or at least qualitative research.

Tuberculosis

In a Tzeltal community in southern Mexico, the majority of people were found to interpret a tuberculosis-like illness naturalistically rather than supernaturally. The Tzeltal term for tuberculosis translates as "white cough," which was contrasted with normal cough and a bronchitis-like illness considered self-limiting and respondent to treatment (Menegoni 1996:391).

According to Tzeltal informants, the cause of white cough was variously attributed to getting wet, bathing, getting cold in the river, not taking good care of oneself in general, hard work, poor food associated with poverty, or exposure to ashes from a volcano that are spread through the air. An indigenous germ concept known as *schanul* emerged; this was described as a tiny organism or living creature that carries illness. Some informants seemed to invoke *schanul* in white cough causation, but it is not clear to what extent (Menegoni 1996:388). There was some difference of opinion as to whether tuberculosis is contagious. Those who thought it was, believed it could be transmitted through eating utensils contaminated with *schanul* (p. 392). Menegoni felt that there has been a shift toward the former due to religion and the rise of modern medicine. Naturalistic beliefs are based on traditional notions of harmony and balance, and negative health effects are attributed to alterations in hot-cold equilibrium, lack of moderation, and extreme emotions such as *susto* (fright).

While some of the specific causes of white cough can be seen as related to harmony and balance, what about exposure to volcanic ashes that are spread through the air and the local germ concept? An interpretative framework such as indigenous contagion theory might be useful if there are sufficient indigenous Tzeltal beliefs related to contagion, illness-from-contact, illness-in-the-air, etc., that don't quite fit the humoral pathology paradigm that characterizes Latin America.

Acute Respiratory Infections (ARI)

Pneumonia and related upper respiratory infections (ARIs) are believed to be caused by "coldness" or "exposure to cold" in India and Pakistan, requiring "heat-producing" remedies to restore balance (Kundi et al. 1993; Mull and Mull 1994; Stewart et al. 1994). In West Java, "The most commonly perceived cause for ARI in children was air entering the body through some type of chill, exposure to draft or breeze, or change of weather" (Kresno et al. 1994). ARI is recognized by fever and rapid or "difficult" breathing.

A study of ARI based on interviewing child caretakers in the Philippines found that "very few informants indicated belief in supernatural causes of cough . . . ," the outstanding locally recognized symptom of ARI. Instead, attributed causes included change in temperature, "wind," having colds, and sprain from trauma, such as a child being handled incorrectly by mothers or elder siblings (McNee et al. 1995:1282–1283). A qualitative study of Quechua and Aymara Indians in Bolivia likewise found attributed causes of ARI to be cold and contagion, along with neglect of a lesser cold syndrome. These authors make the point often made by researchers that a "natural" ARI illness may be suspected as being of supernatural origin if standard treatments do not work and/or the conditions worsen, or if illness onset is unusually usually rapid and severe (Hudelson et al. 1995:1679). Standard treatments consist of herbal teas and baths, chest plasters, and body rubs.

Since I have not covered ARI in Africa, I will cite a largely qualitative study of ARI in Oyo State, Nigeria, that focused on mothers of small children (Iyun and Tomson 1996). Informants in this study seemed to associate ordinary "cough and cold" symptoms with the syndromes of interest to the researchers. These symptoms were believed "mostly caused by exposure to cold." "Coldness of the body" was believed to be a causal agent. The authors seemed a bit surprised that "none of them mention viruses, bacteria or germs as causal agents for ARI" (p. 440). Treatment consisted of mothers using a "remedy with warming and soothing properties" or "irritants to get rid of the cause of the disease (coldness) through vomiting, by forcing the child to swallow bitter remedies such as cow urine" (p. 440). Of course, treatment can be a clue to unclear etiology. It would appear that use of warming remedies to counteract coldness tells us that etiology is naturalistic. Use of irritants to cause vomiting, especially in Africa, may point to pollution beliefs. In either case, causes of ARI seem to be nonpersonalistic.

Dengue Fever

A comparative study in Mexico and Honduras by Kendall et al. (1991) showed that theories of dengue causation were similar in both countries, and they centered around winds, hot/cold balance, or sudden air temperature changes. Dengue was believed to be like other respiratory illnesses such as influenza, perhaps "seen as the expression of an endogenous imbalance precipitated by a mosquito bite, the wind, or other exogenous agent" (p. 263). Some key informants seemed to associate the illness with dirt, saying that dengue came from garbage.

Diarrhea

A global survey of diarrhea explanatory models (Weiss, quoted in Kaltenthaler and Drasar 1996:79), found that causal theories tend to fit the following categories:

1. foods that are fatty, not cooked adequately or heavy;
2. imbalance of heat and cold that may be associated with foods, exposure to draughts, or seasonal changes;
3. normal or poor-quality breast milk;
4. physical factors, such as a fall or poor care-taking;
5. supernatural causes, including possession, sorcery, or evil eye;
6. pollution from exposure to or inauspicious contact with ritually impure persons or things;
7. moral misbehaviour, including deeds of the sick person or a sick child's parents, especially promiscuous sex and sexual intercourse or pregnancy while breastfeeding;
8. natural consequence of developmental milestones, especially teething, crawling, and walking; and
9. infection that may be associated with hygiene and sanitation (but that may be difficult to distinguish from ideas about pollution).

Virtually all of these categories except evil eye are familiar from the African societies reviewed here. The questions for us are: How important are "supernatural causes" in Africa and globally? Is diarrhea perceived using indigenous constructs such as the contagion theory we find in Africa?

Let us look at some individual studies. Qualitative research of child diarrhea in Thailand showed that "Childhood diarrhoea was classified into two groups depending upon perceived causes: contagious and preventable, and not contagious and unpreventable" (Rauyajin et al. 1994:25). To prevent diarrhea in children, mothers reported that they avoid taboo food, avoid breastfeeding with "hot" milk, and visit local healers. The authors of this study conclude that health education programs should utilize local terminology. We see in the local etiology the familiar African notion that contagious illness is considered preventable. We also recognize familiar etiologic notions (hot milk and taboo foods).

A study of childhood diarrhea in Samoa showed the main locally perceived causes to be a child drinking bad or spoiled breast milk, the milk spoiling as a result of a nursing mother violating a local postpartum taboo by resuming sexual intercourse too soon. Other causes are eating bad foods or bad child care in general (Epling and Siliga 1967:141).

A study of diarrhea in Vellore, India, found that while diarrhea was considered natural and treatable by international medicine, "dehydration was believed to indicate a state of pollution that required ritual purification" (Lozoff et al. 1975:353). This provides a clue of why pollution beliefs are viewed and classified as supernatural by health researchers. The beliefs are seen as something arcane, requiring exotic native rites to resolve. It is one step from this to an assumption that spirits or spells are somehow involved, especially if pollution concepts arise in Africa. Lozoff et al., writing in an anthropology journal, make the reasonable recommendation that those involved in public health should somehow devise "therapeutic combinations" that satisfy biomedicine's requirement for getting rehydrating fluids into a child, with "the families' insistence on purification."

In Bangladesh, childhood diarrhea is often thought of as resulting from eating certain foods, and less often by the will of God, evil eye, or spirits (Ashraf 1984; Bhuiya 1992). A study by Farruque (1984) in northeast Bangladesh found that 71% of respondents attributed the cause of diarrhea to dirty water, while smaller groups cited food, worms, and dirty environment. In a nationally representative KAP survey of child diarrhea I directed in Bangladesh in 1985, we found that the most frequently attributed cause of diarrhea was bad, spoiled, or indigestible food (60%), followed by dirty or contaminated water (23%); heat or hot weather (7%); flies or exposed food (7%); worms (6%); evil spirits, evil eye, bad air, or God's will (4%) (this should have been two response categories); bad or spoiled breast milk (3%); and dirty hands or body (2%) (Green 1986:359).

Another Bangladesh study, this one of mother's beliefs and attitudes, found that a child's diarrhea during and after measles was considered beneficial. Mothers believed that it helped to flush out impurities from the body. They also believed that patients with measles should be kept in a clean environment (Shahid et al. 1983).

Studies of childhood diarrhea in Latin America tend to emphasize humoral pathology and hot/cold balance. For example, Escobar et al. (1983) observe that childhood diarrhea in Peru is "believed to be caused by invasion of the body by cold or by ingestion of foods designated as being 'cold.'" Such humoral beliefs are depicted as incompatible with Western infection theory and as leading to undesirable practices such as suspending breastfeeding. Another study of *mestiza* ethnomedicine in highland Ecuador revealed that there were two broad types of childhood diarrhea: those caused by "humoral imbalances," which were considered "not for the doctor," and those caused by "infection," which were "for the doctor" (McKee 1987:1148–1149). Diarrheas of the latter type are recognized by foul-smelling, watery stools and fever, suggesting that they are indeed infectious and serious. Their cause "is attributed to consuming dirt or contaminated food, putting dirty hands in the mouth, or eating 'heavy foods'" (p. 1148). McKee seems to interpret local "infection" theory as a folk interpretation of modern germ theory—as I would have several years ago—but informants' references to dirt and contamination would make me investigate indigenous pollution ideas to see whether these might be at least part of the mix, especially since "ritual cleaning" therapy is involved in one type of air illness (p. 1151).

A third class of so-called supernatural diarrheas is also described in the same study. One of these is from "evil air." This turns out to closely resemble the childhood diarrhea cause encountered in Africa. To quote a paraphrased explanation from an Ecuadoran informant: "If either of a married pair engages in an illicit love affair, the evil that sticks to them will cause their nursing infant to sicken . . ." (McKee 1987:1149). These words could have come from an informant in Mozambique or dozens of other African societies where this belief has been documented. Yet the cause seems to be impersonal rather than personalistic; the illness results from taboo violation where the immediate cause of illness is physical contact.

But perhaps I am looking too hard for ICT beliefs and giving inadequate attention to humoral pathology, which has been the focus of attention by Latin Americanist anthropologists. Therefore, before leaving Latin America, it may be instructive to look at two fairly recent studies that give overall descriptions of ethnomedical beliefs along with indications of where illnesses considered natural and contagious fit into the system.

A study of "pluralistic etiological systems in their social context" was carried out among the urban poor (local Indians and people of African and European descent) in Bahia, Brazil. The researcher found that "far from being dominated by supernatural considerations, non-Western etiological systems are instead ecologically oriented . . ." (Ngokwey 1988:793). Many locally recognized illnesses lie in "the natural domain" and rest on the premise that "exposure to environmental elements can be pathogenic," including excessive cold or heat, rain and humidity, sudden temperature change, and winds (believed to carry dust, cold, humidity, and "germs"). He found an indigenous concept of weak disposition or resistance (*fraqueza*), which was related to heredity, life style, and aging.

Contagion was often cited as a cause of illnesses biomedically regarded as such (e.g., gonorrhea), or not normally regarded as such (e.g., epilepsy, as in Africa, or asthma).

A study of religion, magic, and health beliefs among Huave Indians of Mexico (Cheney 1979) shows that although humoral pathology beliefs are important, hot/cold balance is not the whole etiologic story. Huaves classify illness into four categories based on attributed cause. The first, accounting for the greatest number and diversity of illness, is *ata mandar*, or "God-sent." This category "embraces afflictions that can be explained by natural phenomena and illnesses that can affect many people simultaneously" (Cheney 1979:66 and personal communication), in other words, contagious illnesses. Mentioned here are malaria, smallpox, common colds, and familiar childhood diseases. Other illness categories include those "resulting from strong emotional experiences"; sudden sickness or that caused by evil eye; and sickness caused by witchcraft or demon possession.

From these examples, and others cited in this chapter, it appears that humoral pathology does not account for all indigenous health beliefs in Latin America, perhaps most often those associated with contagious illnesses. For these, we at least sometimes encounter ICT constructs familiar from Africa and elsewhere.

Filariasis

Rauyajin et al.'s (1995) study of filariasis in Thai villages showed that "most villagers could correctly identify filariasis symptomatology and prognosis," meaning that the locally recognized illness and the disease were at least outwardly very similar. The illness was thought variously to be an inherited condition, an illness of "poor blood and air circulation," one of excessive physical labor, or something resulting from personal contact when a person has a fever (p. 1708). We see various naturalistic ideas in this etiology, including ICT (i.e., airborne illness and physical contact illness). Fewer informants spoke of offended deities or malicious ghosts as capable of bringing on the symptoms of the illness.

STIs in Cambodia and Suriname

It is useful to look at ethnomedical models of STIs outside Africa, since I have devoted considerable discussion to this type of contagious disease. In an ethnomedical study of STIs and AIDS in Cambodia, Eisenbruch (1998a, 1998b) provides considerable detail about Khmer STI causation theory. An illness that approximates syphilis and that translates as "crouching mango" is believed to result in a general way from men having sex with a woman, such as a prostitute, who has had many sexual partners. Traditional healer informants stressed that men only "acquire" crouching mango; women "create" it. Etiology is believed to work thus: If a woman has many sexual partners, the semen of different men is commingled in the womb of a single woman. Semen is believed to have different qualities (e.g., sweet, sour, or salty), and it is all derived from blood. Semen from different men do not mix. Such an ill-mixture "builds up a mouldy residue in (a woman's) uterus and, when this reacts with her sexual secretions . . . literally cooks up 'mango illness' or 'AIDS'" (p. 6). This process also leads to "black, terrible blood," which, when mixed with sperm, "reacts to create a new poison, called 'rice water' . . . or gonorrhea." This poison is believed to rise up a woman's spine and then spread to other parts of her body (Eisenbruch 1998a:6, 1998b).

Note the close similarity between the details of STI etiology of both the Khmer of today and the Kgatla (Tswana) of Botswana in the 1930s (Schapera 1940:196), as well as other Bantu speakers. For both, the proximate cause of STIs was the mixing of sperm or blood from different men in a single womb, and the general cause was a woman having many sexual partners. Note also the general compatibility of both with the biomedical view: (1) Sex with many partners leads to something that develops in the genital region and is then carried in the blood, making women and their new sexual partners sick; (2) AIDS is related in some way to syphilis and gonorrhea; (3) These illnesses spread to other parts of the body.

Another way to contract crouching mango, which is believed to lead to AIDS and leprosy, is from the steam of urine: Men catch this illness up their urethra when urinating on the spot where another person has urinated. Women likewise are vulnerable when they squat close to the ground to urinate. This parallels the belief described earlier among the Shona that the STI *kassinyonyo* can be transmitted by urinating at a crossroads where a dog has urinated. And it parallels the belief among the Macua that the STI germ-like organism can climb up the "bridge" formed by a stream of urine when someone urinates onto a puddle of urine left by a dog carrying this STI-carrying organism.

Crouching mango can "devour the bones, liver and heart, lungs, stomach, and brain" of a sufferer for months or years without outward skin symptoms. Khmer healers report that this STI used to take years to kill someone. Now, with patients dying with symptoms of chronic diarrhea and wasting, healers reckon that crouching mango has become "more savage" since 1992, becoming, in fact, the disease the world calls AIDS (Eisenbruch 1998a:9).

There is also belief among the Khmer of a mother-to-child transmission similar to transmission of genito-urinary *nyoka* illness among the Shona: "If, during intercourse (a) wife had a residue of black menstrual blood in her uterus, her blood, not (her partner's) contaminates the conceptus with the germ of 'jackfruit boils'" (these boils refer to a STI symptom manifest in children) (Eisenbruch 1998a:8).

The Khmer appear to recognize factors that account for vulnerability to AIDS: "Most healers felt that Cambodians, impoverished and malnourished, were particularly vulnerable to AIDS. Westerners, however, were fortified by their high-meat diet and, besides, could afford 'strong medicine' to combat AIDS" (Eisenbruch 1998a:8).

Note that these STI, including AIDS theories, closely parallel those found in Africa and elsewhere. They are nonpersonalistic and are expressed in the idiom of pollution, naturalistic infection, and environmental dangers (e.g., contact with a place where a sick person has urinated). We also find indigenous concepts that parallel those of biomedicine (e.g., perinatal transmission, the ability of the illness to become latent, the cofactor link between syphilis and AIDS—even the notion of weakened general immune system health leading to vulnerability to AIDS) (Duh 1991; Root-Bernstein 1993).

Khmer healers' treatment for crouching mango is highly symbolic and emphasizes restoration of moral equilibrium for the "lustful patient" who has "violated Buddhist precepts." Healers "recounted to patients proverbs such as 'Don't devour food according to your hunger, according to your whim; don't have appetite for rice at the market, eat rice at home'" (Eisenbruch 1998a:11). The researcher interpreted this as admonishing that safe sex, like healthy home cooking, is bland and predictable, but at least it is a safe meal. Thus, Khmer healers, like their counterparts in the societies of Africa we have reviewed, seem to have an approach and an ethnomedical foundation that could be built on to develop culturally meaningful AIDS and STI prevention messages, particularly those that aim at promoting fidelity, monogamy, or partner reduction. Such messages might be more of a stimulus to realistic and sustainable behavior change than the current dominant message, which is to always use a condom.

It might be useful to contrast this Khmer account of syphilis and AIDS with one from a Maroon society of Suriname. Maroons are descendants of slaves from West Africa who escaped the coastal plantations of former Dutch Guiana in the seventeenth and eighteenth centuries and established free societies in the interior Amazon rain forest. These societies were established on the basis of social organizational principles found in West Africa at the time, such as matrilineal descent (Green 1978; Price 1984). Therefore, there is a historical, cultural link between the Maroons of Suriname and sub-Saharan Africa that might account for parallels in ethnomedical beliefs, even if AIDS appxxeared centuries after this link was effectively severed. The findings that follow may also demonstrate the persistence of core ethnomedical beliefs, whatever the type and intensity of contact with other health systems.

I conducted long-term ethnographic research among the Matawai Maroons between 1971 and 1973, supplemented by three return trips between 1974 and 1980. In June 1997, I conducted some brief evaluation research with the neighboring Saramaka Maroons, who speak a dialect variant of the Matawai language. I conducted an in-depth interview in the Saramaka language with a septuagenarian traditional healer who claimed expertise in both STIs and AIDS. The following is taken directly from my field notes.

> A gonorrhea-like syndrome is locally known as *pandasi pasi*, literally the path to the agricultural plot, perhaps a reference to where recreational or unsanctioned sex takes place. A syphilis-like syndrome is referred to as *kandu*. Among the neighboring Matawais, this term refers to a type of protective sorcery that people (not just traditional healers) use to protect property. Perhaps *kandu* in the present context refers to protecting wives and lovers against seduction by other men. If so, such an interpretation of STIs (violation of norms regarding proper sexual behavior, especially rules of fidelity) links Maroon beliefs with those found in several parts of Africa.
>
> A third illness that comes from sexual intercourse is *pausei* (lit., beside the tree, again perhaps a reference to where recreational sex takes place). Its main symptom is pain in urination. *Pausei* was described as coming

from having sex in French Guiana (in Africa, several STDs are said to come from sex with outsiders, and syndromes might be named after a distant city). He had heard of the English word AIDS and said that Saramakas call it *jooka kandu* ("ghost *kandu*" or ghost syphilis. Syphilis that turns a sufferer into a ghost?).

This healer informant commented that more women than men seem to get the syphilis-like illness. He says he can cure all four of these illnesses, including the one called *jooka kandu* or AIDS. He says that patients have had their blood examined by a doctor's microscope and have been told they have AIDS, yet he has cured them. The cause of AIDS, according to this healer, is violation of the rules regarding when a widow can have sex after her husband has died. If the full mourning period has not elapsed, and the widow has not been ritually purified (*puu baaka*), a man who has sex with her will get *jooka kundu*.

In the language of ICT, this Saramaka interpretation may be classified as death pollution, a common interpretation of the cause of AIDS in central and southern Africa (e.g., *kaliondeonde* among the Bemba of Zambia). I will leave to the final chapter the intriguing question of why we find such parallels in ethnomedical beliefs about gonorrhea and other STIs, especially in societies as widely separated and as historically unconnected as Khmer and Tswana.

THE MISSING ANALYTIC CONSTRUCT

The analytic construct I have proposed, ICT, seems useful in analyzing and interpreting findings from diverse parts of the world. Researchers in the studies just reviewed seem at times not to know quite how to interpret disparate, arcane-appearing findings about winds, dirt, tiny animals, volcanic ashes in the air, and hot or bad breast milk. Broad ethnomedical constructs such as humoral theory have long helped unify and explain a great many ethnomedical findings in Latin America and the Indian subcontinent. But some findings related to communicable diseases do not quite fit such constructs, even in those areas. At the same time, we find germ-like ideas as well as those associated with pollution and environmental dangers in health belief systems in many diverse parts of the world. These ideas tend to be nonsupernatural in character and are associated with diseases biomedically classifiable as communicable. I wouldn't be surprised to find that they were mutually related as well, as are ideas about insects, dirt, and contaminants in the atmosphere in parts of Africa.

Tedlock (1987) observed that "The hot-cold categorization of humoral medicine has been referred to as the 'basic cognitive principle' of traditional medicine in Latin America" (p. 1069). Based on fieldwork with traditional healers in the Guatemala highlands, Tedlock commented that this framework has become a kind of "native etic" to which "native emic" explanations are supposed to conform, to the point that humoral explanations are found mostly "when anthropologists ask questions couched in humoral terms" (p. 1069). This is what I have been arguing about the personalistic native etic framework of Africa: Anthropologists and others interview African informants or make field observations expecting to find explanations that refer to magic, witchcraft, sorcery, or spirits. Not surprisingly, they find them. Anomalous, residual, none-of-the-above findings are classified and interpreted personalistically, as I suspect happened with the pollution and traces findings of Booyens, cited above.

An anthropologist colleague of mine provoked criticism in the 1970s for reporting a great deal of naturalism in African ethnomedicine, although his findings were based on painstaking, long-term ethnographic fieldwork (Warren 1974). Colleagues told him that he wasn't "looking deep enough," otherwise he would find the "real" personalistic explanations that motivated behavior. A study of leprosy among the Limba of Sierra Leone might provide an example of researchers not settling for anything less than witchcraft explanations. Opala and Boillot (1996) report that Limba explanations of leprosy include God's will; the role of maggots, gnats, flies, or leaches (said to merely reflect germ theory as explained by health assistants); stepping in excrement; sexual intercourse; bad water; poor working conditions; or breezes. Yet the authors wrote that "Limbas attribute serious illness to witchcraft" (p. 13). Limbas hide witchcraft explanations from outsiders, though, therefore "one must know the code they use to discuss this sensitive topic" (p. 13). The authors provide an example of using this interpretive code: "When one patient responded that his leprosy was caused by 'dreaming about palm oil,' Opala, realizing that both dreams and the red color of the oil are associated with witchcraft, asked if witchcraft is what he meant. He grudgingly agreed" (Opala and Boillot 1996:13).

These authors criticize other ethnomedical studies of leprosy for not being "as in-depth as they might be" (Opala and Boillot 1996:3). They argue that to understand how an illness is viewed in a particular culture, one must examine beliefs "within the wider context of the culture's world view" (p. 3)—in other words, witchcraft. But perhaps God's will (code for naturalistic explanation) or the many examples of the African ICT model found in the explanations Limbas actually gave should be taken seriously?[1]

A second ethnomedical study of leprosy, this one in northwestern Botswana, illustrates some of the same issues. Although research methods were described as qualitative, involving "ethnographic approaches such as in-depth interviews with key informants" including traditional healers, researchers had difficulty eliciting statements and explanations about perceived causes of leprosy, or the closest locally perceived syndrome (*ngara, lepero*). Many informants claimed they didn't know the cause, but those who ventured a cultural translation spoke of "bad blood," along with a few mentions of infection, heredity, and witchcraft (Kumaresan and Maganu 1994:538–539). The authors seem unsure about the meaning of the probable pollution code term bad blood, but, revealingly, they note that it is associated with sexually transmitted diseases and consuming foods that may be taboo, as well as with psychiatric illness. Kumaresan and Maganu opine that "the community had limited knowledge about the disease" (p. 537). Perhaps this is so, but the rest of us have limited knowledge about the *illness*, and therein lies the problem of communicating effectively with participants of "folk" medical systems and of designing culturally meaningful public health programs.

I realize that I am entering dangerous territory when I question the interpretation of findings from a society with which I have no experience. Yet little insects or contact with excrement or with bodily fluids (as happens in sexual intercourse), as well as bad blood and taboo violation, are common explanations for a variety of contagious illnesses in Africa and beyond. Why not in Sierra Leone and Botswana? If we begin with Pool's premise that, in the final instance, everything boils down to witchcraft, then we risk turning ethnography into an exercise in tautology or deductivism. We risk finding in fieldwork only those notions that we bring to it. I myself misinterpreted pollution and airborne illness as personalistic when I worked in Swaziland in the early 1980s, due, I now believe, to an expectation that most health beliefs were personalistic or due to fear that I might not be looking "deep enough."

If there has been undue attention on naturalistic beliefs in this book, it has been because there has been too much emphasis on personalistic beliefs in most other studies to date, and a corresponding neglect of naturalism. However, it should be emphasized here that witchcraft, sorcery, and other personalistic beliefs are part of the same conceptual universe as pollution, indigenous germ theory, and environmental dangers. Pragmatism and socially beneficial "functions" can be found in personalistic thought, including witchcraft beliefs, so disdained and dreaded by all but some anthropologists. Janzen has concluded from his extensive fieldwork in the Congo that witchcraft is such a loaded term, it should be dropped from the anthropologist's vocabulary. Local terms for "the W word," as he calls it, translate as "the power of words or oaths," or "words and thought in anger." It seems to him that for a society or cultural tradition to hold as a premise that words, thoughts, or anger can make people sick, this ought to be a mark of sophistication, not savagery (Janzen, personal communication).

I agree with this observation and see the "power of words and thoughts in anger" belief complex as a sophisticated symbolic construct closely related to the psychological and sociological domains, reflecting recognition of, and rules for, people to keep anger and words in check if there is to be any social harmony. If we accept this, indigenous contagion theory may be a sophisticated symbolic construct closely related to the domain of communicable disease, reflecting recognition of observable relationships in the environment, and, at some level, the value of biologically (epidemiologically) and socially useful rules, such as isolating individuals who have contagious diseases. There is further discussion of these ideas in Chapter Eight.

HISTORICAL CONTAGION THEORIES IN WESTERN MEDICINE

I have argued that there is a widespread belief complex that explains contagious illnesses in Africa and other parts of the developing world. Like witchcraft and sorcery explanatory frameworks, the ideas are used by outside interpreters of ethnomedical systems, but they arose from generalization and synthesis of indigenous, autochthonous models of illness. Thus, versions of these etic and emic models—which presumably resemble one another to a greater or lesser extent—exist in the minds of both outside analysts and natives. On the other hand, a general explanatory framework for contagious illness appears to exist in the minds of participants of indigenous medical systems in Africa and diverse other parts of the world, but it is not generally found in the minds of anthropologists and health researchers.

Beliefs and practices strongly resembling ICT are found historically in Western medicine. For example, pollution-like beliefs as well as those related to environmental dangers have been long associated with the more naturalistic, empirical side of health systems, sometimes in association with contagious disease. The ancient Egyptians were known to practice medicine based on the "empiric," as distinct from the magico-religious, school. Enemas and emetics were common practices for prevention and treatment, and daily lives were governed by hygienic laws concerning diet, sexual intercourse, burial of the dead, and bodily cleanliness (Marti-Ibanez 1962:50).

The Book of Leviticus in the Old Testament gave instructions for preventing the spread of leprosy (which might have included syphilis and gonorrhea), namely isolating "unclean" sufferers, requiring them to cleanse themselves and their clothes, and keeping them isolated from others until inspection determined that they had again become "clean" (Douglas 1966; Wilkenson 1993:1263).

Philosophers and healers of the Greco-Roman classical period are thought to have failed to observe, or observe adequately, the contagiousness of disease, according to most medical historians. But, as one notes:

> The classical contribution to concepts of contagion and infection relate less to the individual than to the environment. The term "infection" has root meaning "to put or dip into something," leading to *inficere* and *infectio*, staining or dyeing. This is a reminder that "an infection is basically a pollution." The same is true not only of "contagion," but also of the noun "miasma," which derives from the Greek verb *miaino*, a counterpart to the Latin *inficere*. Impurity is therefore a basic element in all three concepts. These derivations hark back to empirical observation, but also evoke the broad spectrum of religious and moral ideas clustering around notions of pollution and taboo. (Pelling 1993:327)

We see here both pollution and environmental dangers, including early evidence of miasma, the belief that odors or essences in the atmosphere or emanating from certain environments can poison or sicken. I might differ with this historian only about his apparent view of pollution being primarily a religious or moral idea. This medical historian finds further evidence of environmental dangers and naturalistic infection in the classical period:

> Finding or creating safe environments for human activity was an important preoccupation in classical literature. The Hippocratic emphasis on "airs, waters, and places" is well known, but observations on health are made in other contexts, especially by agricultural writers, who mentioned dangers arising from swarms of insects, the poisonous emissions of marshes, and vapours from the earth. In such contexts, the term "pestilential" is used to signify a concentrated degree of infectiousness. The air itself became infected. Of these writers, Varro (127–116 BC) is credited with a Lucretian explanation of natural phenomena and an idea of disease caused in particular localities by invisible animalcules taken in with the air, an idea both animalculist and miasmatist. (Pelling 1993:317)

Empirical-naturalistic medicine was also practiced in Medieval Europe in spite of the influence of the Christian church: "Apart from the curative power of the saints or holy relics, the foundation of medieval therapy was the expulsion of corrupt humors by purges, emetics, cupping, bleeding, enemas" (Marti-Ibanez 1962: 154). During the Black Death in fourteenth-century Europe, the sick were purged with aloes, blood was let, and attempts were made to purify the air with fire—pointing to belief in environmental dangers of the airborne variety—in addition to attempts to "soothe the humors" with medicines (Marti-Ibanez 1962:155). Historians have called the Black Death the Great Teacher, since it impressed on both medical and laypersons the lessons and nature of contagion and the value of isolation and quarantine (Wilkenson 1993:1264). Renaissance Europe also saw the first and sudden outbreak of syphilis. This new scourge was thought to be spread by sexual intercourse but also by other means, such as contaminated utensils, breath, or wet-nursing (Pelling 1993:318), beliefs we encountered in Africa.

Naturalistic infection theories developed in Europe long before the rise of modern germ theory, credited to Louis Pasteur. For example, Hieronymus Fracastorius from Verona, Italy, recognized in his *Opera Omnia* (1584) that some illnesses are caused by physical contact, involving minuscule, probably inanimate, particles not perceived by our senses (*insensibilibus particulis*). He recognized the contagiousness of tuberculosis, rabies, syphilis and measles. By the seventeenth century, van Leeuwenhook (1632–1723) spoke of the "little animals" of contagious disease—a term used today by Zulu, Swazi, and other African healers —and Athanasius Kircher (1602–1680), aided by new microscopes, propounded the doctrine of *contagium animatum* in infectious disease (Marti-Ibanez 1962:195; Pelling 1993:320).

Italian pathologists Francisco Acerbi in 1822 and Agostino Bassi in 1846 both spoke with certainty about tiny living organisms as the cause of contagious diseases (Marti-Ibanez 1962:245). For these post-Renaissance anticipators of modern germ theory, the minute entities causing illness were conceived as analogous to "insects or other lower organisms which have independent powers of movement" (Pelling 1993:313)—again, a widespread African idea.

Attribution of disease to conditions or dangers in the environment extend back to at least fifth century BC Greece. The Hippocratic texts *Airs, Waters, Places, Epidemics I* and *III*, and *On the Nature of Man* associate human health and disease with winds, bad air, and climatic changes as well as the type of water people are exposed to and the location of towns and the character of their sites. This period also gave rise (at least in recorded Western history) to the concept of miasma:

> The exact nature or character of these miasmas remained undefined, but general sources of the putrefaction of the air included stagnant marshes and pools, vapours from a variety of sources including corpses of humans and animals, sick persons, excreta, spoiled foodstuffs, decaying vegetable matter and exhalations that came from the ground through ruptures or clefts. The list contains sources of corruption that remained standard over the centuries and, as one or more of its elements could always be identified in a disease situation, they could form part of any attempt at explanation of disease causation. (Hannaway 1993:295)

We see again elements of pollution (vapors from corpses) beside other familiar themes from the ethnomedical literature of Africa and elsewhere concerning contagious illness. Hannaway (1993:292) has observed that attention to environmental factors in disease causation is well documented by historians of Western medicine, from classical Greece to at least the nineteenth century, and that this can be seen as an endeavor to find natural rather than supernatural explanations for disease. In Europe, belief in the air or atmosphere as the source or carrier of epidemic disease was prominent by the eighteenth century. Priestly and other leading scientists had developed "eudimeters," instruments designed to measure the healthy or unhealthy quality of air in places such as prisons, hospitals, and theaters (Hannaway 1993:305). These instruments failed to detect unhealthy air, so the search reverted to older methods, notably the presence of bad odors such as those found in graveyards, refuse dumps, cesspools, and tanneries (Hannaway 1993:305). Identification of such sites may also have been influenced by pollution beliefs. In any case, European beliefs about airborne illness led to campaigns to clean up such sites. These measures improved public health, even if the theories behind them can today be judged as deficient.

In sum, there is ample evidence of the three components of ICT in the history of Western medicine. We see empirical, naturalistic explanations developing alongside the magico-religious paradigms of the day, the former often associated with epidemics or with other contagious or infectious disease. Theories related to environmental dangers and pollution have the longest history.

WHY HAS ICT BEEN NEGLECTED?

If ICT in these familiar forms is so widespread in space and time, why has it been overlooked by most researchers of contemporary, non-Western societies? It may have been overlooked because of the assumption shared by Murdock and others that any germ-like ideas are simply a folk rendering of biomedical theory. Therefore, they are not of much anthropological interest because they are not truly part of the culture under study—they are merely recent imports from the dreary scientific world we already feel we know too well. Yet, even if germ theory has been borrowed from Western science—and it may not have been—medical anthropologists and other researchers ought to be interested in how it has been interpreted and adapted by different people in their health knowledge systems in order to better understand these systems as they influence behavior, perceptions, and attitudes today.

At the end of Chapter Two, I proposed a number of reasons why pollution beliefs may have been overlooked by ethnomedical interpreters, at least in Africa. Health beliefs linked to local environments may be somewhat more widely recognized, but still these have not often been shown to relate to broader indigenous theories of contagion, involving naturalistic infection and pollution theories, and perhaps some types of taboo violation. Ngokwey (1988), whose own research has emphasized the importance of ecological or environmental etiologies, has also wondered why anthropologists have overemphasized supernatural causation and underexplored natural, impersonal causation. One reason he mentions is a "pervasive evolutionism" in anthropology that assumes progression from supernaturalism in "simple societies," to naturalistic theories in "complex and more advanced" societies (Ngokwey 1988:794–795). This, along with overconfidence in science and a corresponding devaluation of ethnomedicine, is encountered in the attitude of a number of African doctors (e.g., the South African doctor who explained why he rejects indigenous medicine: "I believe in science . . . the law of cause and effect. If I swallow typhoid bacteria then I will get typhoid fever. But traditional medicine is often about evil spirits" (Motlana, in Paton 1997).

Another reason why ICT may not have arisen as an analytic construct among anthropologists has been discussed in this chapter. Odd-seeming ethnomedical findings about unseen insects, dangerous winds, volcanic dust, traces and tracks, bad blood, impure bodily fluids, hot breast milk, etc., may not fit the prevailing etic (or native etic) paradigm (e.g., witchcraft-sorcery-spirits for Africa, and humoral pathology for Latin America). Such findings often become ignored, marginalized, or remolded to fit the dominant paradigms.

NOTE

1. Neither Opala nor Boillot appear to be from Sierra Leone, but even if either were, I would still argue that an educated person native to the country in question could miss the significance of indigenous contagion theory.

CHAPTER EIGHT

THEORETICAL IMPLICATIONS

The widespread existence of the construct that I have called ICT begs for some sort of explanation. We may begin with the simple premise that uniform or similar patterns found in the same society, or in societies within a common region, or among societies that have had significant communication or historical links most likely owe their similarity due to diffusion of ideas from a common source. For example, parallel STI etiologies found among the Suriname Maroons and sub-Saharan African societies might well be due to cultural links. If, on the other hand, uniform or similar ideas are found in widely separated societies with no evident links, such as the Khmer and Tswana, these are most likely to have arisen independently.

Eisenbruch (1998a:14, 1998b) has advanced the notion of a fundamental "template of contagion" in his analysis of Khmer theories of STIs, AIDS, and leprosy. He notes that "most societies have long-held beliefs about the origins of horrible afflictions," such as leprosy and other serious, contagious diseases (1998a:14). He suggests that etiologic models that developed to explain "old diseases" like gonorrhea and leprosy became a template, or a basic overall model. Thus, when syphilis was introduced by Portuguese sailors in the sixteenth century and AIDS was introduced in the early 1990s, these new diseases were interpreted in ways that were compatible with the older models of contagion. In fact, all four illnesses (syphilis, gonorrhea, AIDS, and leprosy) are thought by Khmer healers to be related directly or indirectly to one another, just as we saw leprosy and STIs probably related in the Book of Leviticus.

The existence of archaic templates of contagion seems a reasonable way to explain why models of STIs, tuberculosis, gastroenteritis, and other contagious illness are similar among Bantu speakers. It also helps explain why syphilis, tuberculosis, schistosomiasis, and the newest illness, AIDS, are all thought to be related by some of the African healers and lay informants we have surveyed. In fact, given the historical links between the Bantu-speaking peoples of the Congo basin and southeast Africa and the major ethnic groups of West Africa, from which area Bantus migrated, it is reasonable to posit that archaic models of contagious illness developed before this southern migration—a few centuries BC—and have not changed in core assumptions.

But how can we explain similarities, especially close ones, in etiologic models found in widely separated peoples who lack historical and cultural connections? We have already seen how Schapera's Tswana informants of the 1930s and Khmer healers of the late 1990s interpreted certain prevalent STIs as a result of a woman having sex with many partners, with the immediate cause in both cases being the "mixing (of) strange sperms" or bloods of male partners in a woman's womb. Here we see the same metaphors as well as the same underlying process. Why?

For another example, we can compare the indigenous model of tuberculosis found in another two widely separated societies, the Tzeltal of Mexico and the Bemba of Zambia. The essential features of both models are summarized in Table 3.

Clearly, there are many parallels in ethnomedical constructs between these two widely separated societies. Even though both may have been influenced by Western biomedicine, new, foreign ideas were likely adapted to fit what Janzen (1981:189) has referred to as the symbolic center or inner core of an ethnomedical system. Janzen has suggested that although new health ideas and practices may be adopted, resulting in changes in the periphery of the system, there is a high degree of stability in the symbolic centers of at least African systems. And why not in Mesoamerican or Khmer systems? In other words, there may be reason to believe that present ethnomedical constructs of tuberculosis, and, for that matter, syphilis grew out of an archaic ICT template rather than, say, a witchcraft-sorcery template. In fact, the author of the Tzeltal study wrote that whereas present tuberculosis beliefs have been influenced by biomedicine, they grew out of earlier naturalistic beliefs such as hot-cold equilibrium (Menegoni 1996:388).

Table 3
Essential Features of Tuberculosis Models in Two Societies

	Tzeltal, Mexico	Bemba and Nyanja, Zambia
symptoms	cough	cough, blood-producing cough
locus of illness	chest, breathing	chest, breathing
cause	cold, ashes in the air, germ-like organism, overwork	breathing dust; exposure to cold, wind, or bad air; germ-like organism; contact with blankets, bed, etc.; sex with person w/this illness; pollution
predisposing factors	weakness, poor diet, poverty, not taking care of oneself	drinking alcohol, smoking, uncleanliness

But, again, why the parallels in the examples just provided? And, more broadly, why do we find the basic ideas that comprise indigenous contagion theory associated with contagious illness in societies widely separated by space and time? First, when dealing with illness and its interpretation, we are dealing with phenomena essentially the same in their manifestations. The symptoms, epidemiology, and other appearances and processes of cholera, leprosy, tuberculosis, and syphilis are rooted in biology and ecology and manifest themselves in roughly the same way wherever they are found. As Rubel and Hass (1996:122) note, "When cultural processes are anchored to physiological mechanisms, which are the same species wide, responses to those referents by different cultural groups can more readily be compared." When considering STIs, we can add the observation that the biology of the sexual drive is much the same interculturally, so it is not surprising that some basic behavioral patterns, such as the tendency to have sex outside of socially sanctioned marital bonds, is a virtual cultural universal.

Perhaps there is a limited range of logical deductions, given the same "problem" to explain, as when people anywhere are faced with understanding essentially the same biological factors (symptoms, course of illness) and the same cause-and-effect clues to etiology (e.g., a person develops genital sores after having sex with someone with similar symptoms). How many different logical deductions are there to explain illness where the cause-and-effect relationship between exposure and symptoms is quite apparent? In this case, a logical deduction is that something associated with the person who already has the illness must pass something to the other person. In societies (or subgroups) that lack the science and technology of biomedicine, this is likely to be conceived as dirt or pollution in its varied symbolic expressions, or as tiny, unseen creatures.

Here, the ICT agnostic might point out that evil spirits could just as well explain epidemic type illness. Spirits can be everywhere, and they are unseen; whole populations could presumably be cursed by, or exposed to, evil spirits. But consider the imputed nature of spirits, witches, and sorcerers. They bring illness (or allow it by withdrawing protection, in the case of African ancestral spirits) as punishment for some reason. Perhaps it is evident that too many children and innocent people are affected by contagious—especially epidemic—illness, therefore punishment theory is less reasonable than naturalistic contagion theories in explaining why certain illnesses usually (although not necessarily always) follow exposure. The former would have to postulate ill will and deliberate harm directed at a great number of people under a great variety of circumstances.

As noted earlier, any illness, including one recognized as contagious, can become interpreted as spirit- or sorcerer-caused if it does not develop in the normal way, and/or if it persists despite treatment that is thought to usually work (I use this language because many acute contagious/infectious diseases are self-limiting). But for contagious illness with an ordinary life cycle, explanations of the ICT sort seem to have more logical explanatory potential. They are more parsimonious; they do not require what would have to be complicated, convoluted theories of why a wide range of individuals engaged in the same activity (e.g., sexual intercourse with many partners or with a partner exhibiting characteristic symptoms) happen to be targeted by spirits or sorcerers for harm of the same sort (e.g., pain in urination, genital pus discharge). The range of explanations would seem to be most logically restricted in association with illnesses whose cause-and-effect relationship between exposure or contact and illness is most apparent (e.g., syphilis, measles, leprosy, and cholera).

When such a cause-and-effect relationship is less clear, as with malaria, schistosomiasis, or tuberculosis, we might expect that the etiologic models that develop in folk and tribal societies would appear more random or elaborate (Weller, personal communication). Here the problem or natural occurrence to explain is why many (but not all) people in a given area become sick with similar illness manifestations at roughly the same time (e.g., during the rainy season in the case of malaria). In these types, we often (but not always) seem to find ICT explanations of the environmental dangers sort, explanations that propose mass exposure to wind, air, cold, heat, dust, insects, or dangerous physical environments.

African informants have given anthropologists clues as to the logic of such interpretations. As mentioned in Chapter One, Bambara informants told Imperato (1974:15) that only wind has sufficiently widespread contact with people to cause smallpox. My Swazi traditional healer informants have expressed the same logic to explain why illnesses such as tuberculosis, certain types of colds (such as those we might classify as ARI), or severe (malarial?) headaches, tend to be interpreted as *tifo temoya*, or illnesses of the air or wind. If we consider the respiratory symptoms of the first two, the logic of involving wind or air in etiology becomes even stronger. In fact, the actual person-to-person contagiousness of illnesses such as those just mentioned may not be locally recognized. For example, Iyun and Tomson (1996) report this for ARI in southwest Nigeria, Hussain et al. (1997) report this for pneumonia among urban squatters in Karachi, and Menegoni (1996:388) reports it among some Tzeltal informants for tuberculosis in Mexico. Nevertheless, we usually find naturalistic including ICT rather than personalistic explanatory models associated with these diseases.

ADAPTATION

Health beliefs may arise and persist because they serve a useful function, because they are adaptive to a particular environment, or, in the context of our discussion, because they are adaptive to conditions in an environment that threaten health. Anthropologists interested in cultural adaptations (so-called biocultural or ecological anthropologists) have reported a number of behaviors that limit death from malaria. For example, some Vietnamese hill tribes build cooking and sleeping platforms on stilts, to just above the 10-foot flight ceiling of *Anopheles minimus* mosquitoes.

Another example is the widespread adoption of the fava bean, which appears to have antimalarial qualities, as a staple in the circum-Mediterranean (Brown et al. 1996: 196). And the hot/cold equilibrium model has been explained as "an important aspect of biocultural adaptation among the Maya of Yucatan, especially in the prevention of heatstroke and heat cramps, because it includes physiologically realistic rules for behavior during work in a hot climate" (McCullough 1973:32). Neumann (1977) has explained the existence of salt taboos among some native North American societies as a useful adaptation for people living under certain environmental and life-cycle conditions for whom there is a need for regulating sodium intake.

Finally, postpartum taboos against resuming sexual intercourse in Africa (and elsewhere) have been described as serving the latent function of improving chances for maternal and child health and survival, even though the expressed purpose for such taboos may be described as avoiding pollution of mothers' milk (van de Walle and van de Walle 1989). In fact, it has been suggested that much of social organization and behavior may serve such latent functions of preventing the spread of disease, even though their conscious purpose may be unrelated to health. In contrast, health behaviors related to *curing* the sick are usually conscious and deliberate (Brown et al. 1996:196).

To understand the parallels between the Khmer and Tswana models for syphilis/gonorrhea, we might draw on the adaptation paradigm and propose that a belief complex that teaches the dangers of having multiple sex partners serves to limit such behavior and hence, sexually transmitted diseases, a significant side effect of which can be infertility or subfecundity. True, infertility is more likely to result from gonorrhea or chlamydia than syphilis, but syphilis often results in premature or stillborn babies, that is, in fetal death due to bacterial transmission from infected mothers to fetus (Jones and Wasserheit 1991:19). With fertility and the survival of chromosomes at stake, we can say that natural selection itself selects for the Khmer-Tswana model of STI, over, say, a witchcraft model.

Biocultural or ecological anthropologists tend to restrict the concept of adaptation to those processes of change and adjustment that increase the chances of a particular population in a given environment to survive (McElroy and Townsend 1989:73, 76; Durham 1991). Alland (1990:342) notes that, "in order to avoid the problem of tautology inherent in the notion of adaptation ('What's adapted is there and what's there is adapted'), evolutionary biologists, particularly population geneticists, have developed an independent measure of adaptation—i.e., fitness based on relative fertility." Biocultural explanations have been defined as those that relate biological with sociocultural and environmental variables (McElroy 1990).

A competing paradigm in anthropology, cultural materialism, argues for the causal primacy of the infrastructural over the symbolic-ideational components of human social life. The former differs from the biological/ ecological and refers instead to the techno-economic, demographic, and environmental "activities and conditions directly linked to sustaining health and well-being through the social control of production and reproduction" (Harris 1979, 1992). Harris (1992) suggests that innovations in the symbolic-ideational component (where he would place ethnomedical beliefs) are likely to be selected if they are compatible with infrastructure, that is, if they "enhance productive and reproductive efficiency under specific environmental conditions" (p. 297). The importance of reproductive efficiency represents a point of agreement with biocultural anthropologists and evolutionary biologists.

Cultural responses to environmental challenges are also recognized by biocultural anthropologists, but perhaps not those that do not relate directly or indirectly to biology. Yet adaptive value is not only biological or related to reproductive success, as evolutionary biologists, ecologists, sociobiologists, and others have argued (Harris 1999). I suggest that an ethnomedical model also tends to be selected for if it can be shown to confer social value such as social harmony, preservation of marriage, and the unity of the kin group. Social harmony is an adaptation itself, even if we might also relate marriage and resulting kin groups to challenges in the environment, and/or to reproductive success.

Thinking again of the Khmer-Tswana STI model, or for that matter to the belief discussed in Chapter Four that unfaithful parental behavior leads to child diarrhea, we may account for the existence and persistence of either *in part* by proposing that a belief in the dangers inherent in having many sexual partners serves to reinforce the sanctity of marriage and the stability of resulting kin groups. Perhaps more importantly, it serves to limit strife and bloodshed to the extent that it regulates sexual intercourse, that is, socially nonsanctioned intercourse. We can say this because strife and bloodshed over adultery and other socially proscribed sexual relations are very nearly universal. We might argue whether natural selection favors societies with greater or lesser amounts of strife and bloodshed, but I contend that a trait that tends to mitigate against bloodshed also has adaptive value at a superorganic level (i.e., society and culture [recognizing that biology, society, and culture are interconnected in complex ways]). Such explanations may seem teleological: Society exists or at least develops in order to serve some useful end, to operate smoothly. But if culture is necessary for human survival, why should traits that result in society's smoother operation not tend to persist, not be selected for in some way?

Another way to look at the Khmer-Tswana STI model is to ask if everyone in the society benefits, or benefits equally, from its presumed functions (Edgerton 1992; Harris 1999). It appears that this model would function to enforce female chastity more directly than it would limit males who wish to have many sexual partners, since the danger lies in the mixing of different sperms in a single female rather than the mixing of different female essences in a single male. Of course, male sexual behavior would also be inhibited to some extent because men become ill if they chose as partners women who are sexually involved with other men at the same time. Still, this ethnomedical model could be interpreted as a mechanism for suppression of female sexuality while supporting a double standard. Added to this is the apparent blame factor, at least among the Khmer who believe that women "cook up" or create mango illness, while men do not create this but instead are on the receiving end from women (Eisenbruch 1998a:6).

Such interpretations are favored by critical and feminist anthropologists, and they certainly contribute a useful dimension to analysis of adaptation that is often missing from analyses of earlier generations of anthropologists. But adaptation analysis should not end with the question of who within a society may benefit and who may be oppressed. The net biological effect on the whole society of the STI model in our example would be to inhibit what in the AIDS era is called multipartnerism, and therefore limit STDs and their sequelae such as pelvic inflammatory disease, infertility, fetal loss, etc. Although the society as a whole benefits, many of these effects are of special value to women. One could add to these the apparent positive sociocultural effects (strife reduction, reinforcement of marriage, strengthening of kin group) and argue that on balance, the Khmer-Tswana STI model confers more benefits than oppression in its respective societies, even if some types of benefits may be unequally distributed by gender, social class, age or occupational group.

Of course, we find variation in ethnomedical and other adaptations. As Harris (1992:298) has said, "There is more than one way to shape an effective projectile, fashion a serviceable pot, design a computer program, or, in the vernacular, skin a cat." And there is more than one way to respond to challenges in the environment such as malaria or syphilis. We sometimes find models of pollution, sometimes of naturalistic infection, sometimes of environmental dangers, and indeed sometimes but less often of witchcraft or sorcery. For Harris, cultural responses might be "adaptively neutral" or "functionally equivalent," partly accounting for the variation found, "and capable of persisting tenaciously across the most fundamental sorts of infrastructural transformations and of influencing each other without feedback to infrastructure" (1992:297–298).

But what about ethnomedical and other beliefs and practices that even by the greatest stretch of the imagination are not found to function, or be adaptive, in any positive way? A number of contemporary anthropologists (e.g., Trotter, Edgerton, Landy, McElroy, and Townsend) hold that nutritional and ethnomedical practices and associated beliefs, among others, can be dysfunctional as well as functional. Trotter et al. (1989) offer the example of etiologic beliefs regarding *caída de mollera* (fallen fontanel syndrome) among Mexican Americans in the southwestern United States. This syndrome is believed to result from rough handling of a baby, such as its being dropped. Treatment accordingly has nothing to do with the biomedically known cause of this dehydration symptom, persistent diarrhea, but rather pushing up the baby's palate, holding the baby upside down, shaking it up and down, and other ineffective and potentially dangerous manipulations.

Robert Edgerton has written a provocative book on the subject of dysfunctional or maladaptive traits, beginning with the observation:

> There are some customs and social institutions in all societies that compromise human well-being. Even populations that appear to be well-adapted to their environments maintain some beliefs or practices that unnecessarily imperil their well-being or, in some instances, their survival.

253

> Populations the world over have not been well served by some of their beliefs such as, for example, those concerning witchcraft, the need for revenge, or male supremacy, and many of their traditional practices involving nutrition, health care, and the treatment of children have been harmful as well. (Edgerton 1992:1)

For Edgerton, people are rational, but not always. While some or many cultural traits are positively adaptive, others may be neutral, inefficient, or downright harmful by any objective measure; this includes science and science-based medicine.

Anthropologists have tended to overlook maladaptive traits for a number of reasons that Edgerton explores, including cultural relativism in its stronger forms, a romantic notion of primitive societies, a legacy of functionalism and cultural evolutionary theories in various forms, and an inclination to highlight the positive and overlook the negative when writing ethnographies (preferring the views of Redfield and Mead rather than of Oscar Lewis and Derek Freeman). McElroy and Townsend (1996:101) have added the observation that the anthropological quest to discover adaptive functions in every ethnomedical custom reflects a Western cultural bias that health is a high priority and that disease is ultimately preventable and controllable.

Whatever the reasons, in anthropology it is widely assumed that virtually all beliefs and resulting customs and practices are positively adaptive to the local environment. Anthropologists often go to great lengths to find positive adaptive value in all sorts of unsafe or unhealthy practices and their supporting beliefs, from infanticide to infibulation.[1] This seems as true in cultural materialism as in ecological, biological, or most other branches of anthropology; it is also found in psychology, evolutionary biology, sociobiology, and other related disciplines (Edgerton 1992: 30–32). Defending cultural materialism against Edgerton's charge of exaggerated cultural relativism, Harris cautions that anthropologists

> distinguish between cost-benefits that accrue equally to all segments, genders, classes, etc. and cost-benefits that accrue unequally, leaving some groups in the position of being dominated and exploited by others as in the case of slavery or colonialism. . . .
>
> Truly maladaptive or dysfunctional traits are beliefs and activities from which no one gains and everyone loses. (1999:146)

Edgerton, too, recognizes that maladaptive traits can develop some positive social functions at least for some group members, but he argues that they may still remain on balance maladaptive—in some cases, no one can be shown to gain and everyone loses. He speculates on how these might arise and persist. For example, a trait may be maladaptive from the start simply because people may make the wrong choices. Some maladaptive traits may arise as a result of predispositions rooted in human nature, such as selfishness, competition for mates, sexual jealousy, even ethnocentrism. Or a once-adaptive trait may cease to be so as the environment, technology, or other conditions change (Edgerton 1992).

It may be that adaptation is rarely an ideal or one-sided adjustment that is only positive or negative. At the biological level, human genetic adaptation can represent both a positive and a negative adaptation. For example, a genetic adaptation to malaria benefits some in a population but puts some at risk for sickle cell anemia. At the level of culture, an adaptation in the form of an ethnomedical model that results in holding a dehydrated baby upside down and sometimes shaking it up and down instead of providing rehydrating fluids is, as noted above, ineffective and potentially dangerous. However, *caída de mollera* is believed to result from rough handling of a baby, therefore a positive side of this belief is that babies without depressed fontanels (i.e., most babies) are probably handled carefully and gently, a health benefit.

A trait may have one effect biologically and quite another at the societal level. It has been argued that female circumcision, while harmful to individual health, maintains traditional role relationships and deeply held values (McElroy and Townsend 1996:114–115, quoting Greenbaum and Boddy). A trait may also have one effect on one group within a society yet quite another on a different group (e.g., female circumcision may be harmful for women but serve the interests of men wishing to control the sexuality of women). Or a trait may be beneficial in the short term but harmful in the longer term.

Highly committed cultural relativists might contend that even if something is demonstrably bad for individual health and survival, it might be beneficial for the group as a whole. Discarding colostrum might be bad, even fatal, for a baby but good for a group with poor resources living in a harsh environment and needing to keep its population numbers low to survive (Halperin, personal communication). If we argue this way, any manner of practices leading to death may be construed as good for a broader group. But if we use the main or sole criterion of bioculturalists, evolutionary biologists, cultural materialists, etc., namely reproductive success, then discarding colostrum must be seen as maladaptive for babies, mothers, and society. No one wins.

Culture by nature is conservative, Edgerton argues, so in the absence of selective pressures to change (usually requiring contact and interaction with other groups), maladaptive traits tend to persist, in part because of a tendency to do things as they have always been done. Neither the antiquity nor ubiquity of beliefs and practices is a guarantee of positive adaptiveness (e.g., the belief that semen resides in the brain, which led to headhunting in a number of societies).

In a chapter on maladaptive health beliefs and practices, Edgerton cites several examples to make the case that some are maladaptive. These include mothers discarding the colostrum or otherwise withholding it from newborns; taboos against pregnant or lactating mothers eating chickens or eggs; and *empacho* beliefs among Mexican Americans in the Southwest that lead to treatments that involve ingesting lead compounds, mercury, or toxic laundry bluing (Edgerton 1992:117). Edgerton also provides an example, which I already cited (Lozoff et al. 1975), of pollution interpretations for dehydration in children in south India. The imputed cause is transgression of the mother and the cure is that religious specialists chant rather than treat the child with, for example, rice water or coconut milk, practices that are found in a number of traditional societies and that do rehydrate a child.

The question also arises whether there is any conscious awareness on the part of members of a human group of the problems to be solved, or the adaptations that need to be made, by beliefs, customs, and the like. Common sense, not to mention long-term participant-observation research, suggests that there is often conscious awareness of problems facing groups. However, native informants seldom provide the kind of functionalist explanations that would make the work of anthropologists easy. ("We promote this cause of syphilis because we know we need to prevent sterility from untreated STDs, while at the same time we can reinforce the marital bond and avoid interpersonal conflict that always accompanies extramarital sex.")[2]

Edgerton offers several possible answers to this question. First, a response to some environmental or other challenge might originally have been chosen consciously, then, over the years it functioned so well that people eventually forgot why the response was developed. Or a response might have simply arisen fortuitously and unconsciously, and therefore its practical raison d'être was never understood by anyone in the group. This latter is acknowledged by biocultural anthropologists: "As a functionalist concept, adaptive strategy does not necessarily imply that human behavior and customs are the result of conscious planning or trial and error to reduce disease or increase well-being" (McElroy 1990:250). In fact, "positive biological feedback" may contribute to retention of those traits that have beneficial health or impact, whether or not they arose consciously or there is conscious awareness of what the benefits are (McElroy and Townsend 1996:102).

These last authors offer the example, already cited, of widespread postpartum taboos against intercourse, sometimes expressed in the idiom of pollution. The result is spacing of births, which has been proven to enhance maternal and child health and increase survival, even if a quite different explanation is provided for the practice. I suspect that *some* informants in such societies understand the value of postpartum beliefs and the like. I have interviewed many African healers who, apart from anything they might have learned from Western medicine, seem to clearly understand the health and survival benefits of spacing births by at least two or three years (Green and Altman 1997). And an Appalachian folk healer once surprised me by confessing that he deliberately manipulated myth and symbols in order to get his clients to drink goldenseal tea, which he believed was good for them.

David Landy recognizes that adaptation may be conscious and deliberate:

People bring to the solution of problems of health and disease not only customary behaviors and beliefs, but minds and bodies, or perhaps more accurately, minds in bodies. People are not only creatures and carriers, but creators of culture. Cultures are constantly being conserved, attenuated, and transformed at a much more rapid rate than biological changes in the human organism. (1990:359)

In a comment to Neumann's (1977) article on salt taboos, Baker (1977:296) notes that "People in general, or someone at least, perceived that they were less healthy or more likely to die if [Native Americans] ate salt during these life periods. . . ." Edgerton also sheds light on this issue:

> It would appear that people in folk societies sometimes do act very much like applied scientists. . . . Some folk populations have decision makers, such as prophets, war leaders, chiefs, big men, councils of elders, and the like, who deliberate about problems their societies face and try to make calculated decisions intended to enhance their well-being. (1992:196)

I submit that in the case of the development or reconsideration of illness explanatory models, the decision makers are likely to be indigenous healers, traditional birth attendants, and lay caretakers of children's health. They would be most likely to make cause-and-effect observations about predisposing factors and conditions and apparently resulting illness, as well as about treatment of some sort and apparent recovery. They would be in the best position to explain this to the rest of society. To the extent that the role of traditional healer is "professional" and esteemed, as it tends to be in much or most of Africa, the healers' model would likely be accepted because: (1) It would come from a respected, authoritative source; (2) It would not contradict common observations or experience; and (3) In less medically pluralistic times, there would be few competing theories. From the biocultural and perhaps cultural materialist perspectives, we would predict that the fundamental features of an ethnomedical model (the symbolic center, in Janzen's terms) would survive only if it interacted with ecological or infrastructural variables in ways that enhanced health and well-being.

TOWARD AN EXPLANATION FOR THE RELATIVE ADAPTIVENESS OF INDIGENOUS CONTAGION MODELS

We are left with the problem of explaining why some cultural traits, including ethnomedical models and associated behavior, are adaptive positively and some are not. I have suggested reasons in earlier chapters (e.g., that pollution beliefs might develop—or be selected for—because they often lead to the quarantine of sick people until they are no longer contagious). With death from epidemics at stake, we can say that the selection of pollution beliefs (at least those leading to withdrawing people considered contaminated or unclean from other people for some time) has biological survival value. And I have already suggested the objective measures of human survival and reproductive success for STIs, using the Khmer-Tswana STI model as an example. Konner (1991) observes,

It seems inconceivable that human marriage rules and sexual mores could have evolved without being in some degree a response to the burden of sexually transmitted diseases. . . . Infertility resulting from pelvic inflammatory disease caused by gonorrhea and chlamydia is as devastating from the viewpoint of reproductive success (and, consequently, natural selection) as death. (pp. 78–89)

STDs are not the only disease group that have provoked rational, positively adapted responses on the part of indigenous health systems. Other contagious and infectious diseases have also had that effect. It seems no coincidence that diseases such as malaria, tuberculosis, and filariasis also have a strong impact on fertility. In fact, some argue that it is even greater than that of STDs (McFalls and McFalls, quoted in Brown and Worthman 1991:86). This may get to the essence of the rationality and adaptiveness of indigenous contagion theory: Societies can ill afford to entertain witchcraft-sorcery-evil spirit theories of malaria, tuberculosis, STDS, filariasis, and the like because, with these, fecundity and hence group perpetuation and survival is at stake. And personalistic theories would more likely lead to ineffective treatment and prevention behaviors.

Recognizing this, we would expect to find just what we do find: a cluster of similar ethnomedical beliefs related to infectious and contagious diseases that are naturalistic and that tend to lead to behaviors that are often adaptive in some positive way. If they are not always positively adapted, they at least appear to be more so than the behaviors and practices that result from, say, witchcraft or sorcery beliefs. Edgerton (1992) has argued that witchcraft beliefs are often maladaptive. It is probably safe to say that such beliefs are more often maladaptive than naturalistic beliefs, using the bioculturalists' criteria of adaptation (i.e., survival and reproductive success).

We saw from ethnomedical studies cited above (e.g., Kimani 1981; Reid 1982) that mental illness tends often to be associated with personalistic etiologies, at least in Africa. I found this in my Swaziland research, and others have made the same observation (e.g., Akighir 1982; Edwards 1986; Azevedo et al. 1991). Perhaps an explanation for this lies in the nature of mental disorders and in differences between contagious and mental illnesses. Compared to mental illness, contagious diseases are more directly and immediately life threatening and more related to fertility and hence reproductive success. Serious mental illness may also have an effect on fertility and human survival, but to the extent that there is a strong, underlying organic component to schizophrenia and the psychoses—which there is now known to be—such illnesses are not easily prevented or cured in the way that contagious illnesses can be.

Contagious illnesses also offer empirically observable cause-and-effect relationships that provide etiologic and epidemiologic clues. Such clues are far less clear in the case of mental illness. Thus, with mental illness there is a greater range—perhaps we could say an unbounded range—of possible interpretations. With measles, tuberculosis, leprosy, or syphilis— illnesses where contact with, or exposure to, a sufferer can be seen without much difficulty to precede appearance of symptoms—a reasoned interpretation must account for the apparent cause-and-effect relationship between contact or exposure and symptoms. A similar logic is found in illnesses such as malaria or pneumonia, which seem to follow exposure to a place, or to wind, air, or cold.

Mental illnesses tend to afflict few individuals in any society. For example, the WHO estimates the worldwide prevalence of schizophrenia at 5.5 per 1,000 population. Examples of mass hysterical behavior aside (which would not be sustained over time), schizophrenia and the various psychoses do not have an epidemic nature, nor is there an observable cause-and-effect relationship between the symptoms of these and either contact with a sufferer or exposure to something in a common environment. Given such lack of objective clues from the environment, there would be nothing objective to refute a personalistic theory that explains why a particular individual has been singled out for misfortune or punishment in the form of mental illness. In fact, there would be selection for personalistic models since these excel in explaining why a particular person gets sick and others in the vicinity do not.

Additionally, there is a superficial resemblance between spirit possession and symptoms of some mental illnesses—suggesting or favoring theories that posit a spiritual cause of them. Thus, there could be at least two reasons that explain why contagious illnesses tend to be associated with naturalistic infection, pollution, and environmental dangers (i.e., ICT), while mental illnesses tend to be associated with witchcraft, sorcery, or spirits (i.e., personalistic explanations). First, the latter are more likely than the former to lead to positively adapted behavior, that is, behavior that better sustains life and reproductive success and that may provide benefits at the level of society and culture as well. Considering the nature of contagious illnesses (serious, sometimes fatal, and often linked with fertility and hence reproductive success), the payoff for the adapted behavior, or positive biological feedback, seems to serve as a powerful reinforcer. Such feedback is probably not associated with indigenous mental illness models and related behavior.

Second, there are observable cause-and-effect relationships with contagious illnesses (admittedly, with some more than others) that point to their contagiousness, discernable clues that are not found with mental illness. These observations probably restrict logically the range of explanations for the former, while leaving it open for the latter. That is, indigenous models about contagion have to account for certain etiologic and epidemiologic phenomena that do not vary much from place to place. This may account for fundamental resemblances between indigenous contagion models in traditional societies in diverse parts of the world, and between these and notions of contagion found historically in various parts of the world, and between these and the contemporary Western, biomedical model.

Consider also that most morbidity and mortality among children in poor countries is due to contagious and infectious disease, notably diarrhea, respiratory infections, and malaria. Children are highly valued in Africa and everywhere. Apart from instincts and emotions associated with parenting, people know that family, lineage, and broader group survival depend on healthy children, on children surviving the hazards of childhood. The high value placed on children's survival may be another factor selecting for adaptive ethnomedical models of contagious illness, models that usually result in relatively effective preventive and treatment behaviors. Relative, that is, to other illness in the same societies.

This is not to argue that indigenous ICT models always lead to positively adapted behaviors, nor that mental illness models never do. An example of maladaptive behavior not found in Edgerton's book but useful for our discussion because it concerns a highly contagious, fatal disease is in the description by Imperato and Traoré (1979) of Bambara beliefs about smallpox in Mali. According to these authors, the Bambara hold the ultimate cause of smallpox to be supernatural (spirit- or witch-sent), even though the proximate cause is the wind. Recall that "wind illness" is a characteristic expression of naturalistic ICT beliefs of the environmental dangers sort. Yet Bambara curative and preventive behaviors are said to result from the ultimate, supernatural etiologic theory. These behaviors take the form of talismans, charms, incantations, and other rituals. There are some herbal treatments for smallpox, but for the most part these are regarded as ancillary, "their real effectiveness depending on the outcome of the spiritual measures" (Imperato and Traoré 1979:16).

Disregard the fact that the researchers reporting this indigenous model were a physician and a schoolteacher rather than anthropologists and accept, for the sake of the argument, that this may be a good example of a maladaptive ethnomedical model of contagion. I suggest that such a model, leading to ineffective health-related behaviors, is unstable and a good candidate for replacement by a naturalistic model that recognizes clues from ecology and biology and that leads to behaviors that better sustain life. Given enough time, there is a tendency for indigenous models of contagion to do just that. For the reasons mentioned previously, there is less of a tendency for mental illness models to do so, and there may be less of a tendency for any illnesses that are noncontagious to do so. Think of serious, chronic, degenerative, noncontagious, nonmental illnesses such as cardiovascular disease, cancer, or multiple sclerosis, and compare these with contagious illnesses such as those I have discussed. The etiologic and epidemiologic clues for the former would not be so discernable, there would be less positive biological feedback in preventative/curative behavior associated with indigenous etiology, and there may even be a selective tendency to adopt a personalistic explanation that explains why some people are singled out for illness, while others in the same area are not.

The foregoing propositions—each of which can be stated as a hypothesis—can be encapsulated in a major testable hypothesis: Indigenous models of contagion are more likely to be naturalistic than models of other illnesses in a given society, and they are more likely to represent positive adaptations to prevailing conditions and to lead to life-sustaining health behaviors.

ICT AND POLITICAL ECONOMIC CONSIDERATIONS

Some anthropologists have criticized the adaptivist perspective of ecological anthropology for inadequately considering political and economic factors that affect the disease process (see, e.g., Alland et al. 1990; Baer 1990, 1995, 1997; Singer 1996). Singer (1996:506, 511) and others have used the term "unnatural selection" to suggest that nature (biology, environment) does not select for traits in human populations free from the interventions of political-economic factors. So-called critical medical anthropologists would doubtless consider my attempt to account for parallels in ethnomedical theories of contagion inadequate because it fails to deal with health systems as mechanisms for "maintaining and repro-ducing the working class," or for "imperialist expansion and bourgeois cultural hegemony" (Baer 1997:1568; and see Singer 1990).

I feel that these issues of political economy are very germane to med-ical anthropology—especially to analyses of Western biomedicine wher-ever it is found— but that they do not contribute substantially to solving the fundamental puzzle of why or how ICT developed the way it did in diverse parts of the world. For the purpose of this analysis, considerations such as the degree to which ethnomedical models may have arisen in the context of political or economic oppression or exploitation do not help us understand why naturalistic explanations tend to be chosen over per-sonalistic ones or why behaviors associated with either explanation can be seen to be positively adapted or not. Few people anywhere or at any time in history have been as oppressed as the Khmer in recent times (losing a third of their national population in a single generation to government-perpetrated genocide), yet their indigenous model of STI survived this and closely resembles that of the Tswana, who suffered no such genocide.

Likewise, a cultural materialist explanation would prefer to find causal primacy in a society's mode of production or reproduction. Harris explicitly rejects explanations about the health dangers of undercooked pork in his attempt to explain Muslim and Jewish taboos against eating pork. He argues instead that pig farming at the time appears to have been "a threat to the integrity of the basic cultural and natural ecosystems of the Middle East" (1974:40). Harris may be right in his interpretation of pork dietary taboos, but there seems to be too much infrastructural varia-tion in the societies considered in our survey of highly patterned ICT models— including those considered in our historical survey—to attribute these models to variations in infrastructure.

Therefore, explanation has been sought in biology, ecology, and the human mind-in-body. Political and economic factors have been held con-stant in this preliminary description and analysis of ICT. I have not detoured from the main analysis to consider who might suffer unfairly when, for example, people are judged contaminated or unclean as a result of local pollution theories. I acknowledge that such factors and considerations can be crucial, and that such considerations are useful and can shed light on important social justice issues.

Despite their anticipated disagreement with the broad, cross-cultural focus and adaptation paradigm favored in this book, I hope that critical medical anthropologists and cultural materialists will support the plea that all who work in international and public health take ethnomedical systems of non-Western peoples seriously and that we find value in indigenous knowledge systems and some role in public health programs for indigenous practitioners. This should put some brakes on the "imperialist expansion and bourgeois cultural hegemony" (Baer 1997:1568) of Western biomedicine, help maintain greater independence of indigenous health systems from the transformations and subordinations of the capitalist world-system, and lead to greater consumer choice and self-determination on the part of the poor in developing countries. This is the sort of social action normally advocated by critical medical anthropologists.

Medical anthropology has developed two somewhat distinct approaches to the study of health and illness. One is cultural-ethnomedical and focuses on definition of illness and social responses to illness. The other is biological-ecological and focuses on disease, environment, and population. Although there has been limited success to date in integrating these perspectives (Armelagos et al. 1992), the analysis offered here to explain the ubiquity and characteristic forms of ICT attempts to draw on both.

Health-related human beliefs and behavior are extremely complex. McElroy (1996) has suggested that this justifies the need for anthropologists to develop multiple models of health. McElroy (1990) has also noted, "Although criticized in recent years as being circular, teleological, too broad, or too functionalist . . . the adaptation paradigm continues to serve as a heuristic and conceptual tool for organizing data on human responses to environmental stressors, disease, disability, loss, and life transition" (p. 249).

I am not arguing that this paradigm is the only, or best, one for all or most research and analysis in medical anthropology. Just as ecological or biocultural anthropologists may have overlooked the importance of political or economic factors in pursuit of explaining certain phenomena, critical medical anthropologists have given inadequate attention to ecological factors, as Baer admits. Quoting Howard Parsons, he notes that economy and ecology are in fact inseparable since both deal with "bread-and-butter" matters that relate to the production and distribution of goods and services in the context of society and nature (Baer 1990:346).

FINAL COMMENTS ON PUBLIC HEALTH IMPLICATIONS

Apart from any light shed on comparative ethnography and competing anthropological paradigms, I hope I have underscored the public health significance of recognizing indigenous contagion theory in Africa and other parts of the developing world where official health interventions have often met with little success. Indigenous contagion and other naturalistic beliefs are an area of potential intersectoral interface between indigenous and cosmopolitan medicine.

Both agree that tiny or unseen agents of illness can be spread impersonally to anyone exposed to them, regardless of intent on the part of human or superhuman intelligence. Both are concerned with avoiding contact with persons or places considered impure or contagious. Both are also concerned with cleanliness and environmental sanitation, the danger of dirt, the value of clean, pure food and sometimes water, the isolation of those believed to be able to contaminate or infect others, the danger of multiple sexual partners, and the like. Both agree that the cause of contagious illness is impersonal and relates to conditions that may be avoidable or modifiable. To prevent contagion, some relatively mundane steps can be taken (e.g., avoiding a contagious [dirty, unclean, etc.] person or a dangerous place, refraining from sexual intercourse with unknown or multiple partners, or drinking a medicinal decoction rather than resorting to "supplication or manipulation" [i.e., religious or magical measures]). The evidence reviewed here suggests that magico-religious responses to illness are less likely to sustain life and promote reproductive success than responses characteristic of naturalistic models of illness.

There seems to be potential interface between ideas and practices related to prevention of contagion, although this needs to be much more fully explored in the context of specific illness/disease within individual cultural contexts. In any case, if public health messages can be framed in terms appropriate to indigenous contagion beliefs, they would take advantage of common ground that already exists. They would make more sense than messages that rely on medical jargon such as "electrolyte imbalance" or "oral rehydration," currently found in health education messages in Africa and elsewhere. As I have noted, use of medical concepts and jargon is often justified in the belief that local ethnomedical beliefs are so associated with witchcraft and spirits as to be unfit for adaptation in any form, therefore health promoters should start with a clean slate and teach undiluted, uncompromised medical science. My argument is that such an approach has proven largely ineffective; that ethnomedical beliefs pertaining to contagious illness/disease are *not* supernatural in Africa and many other parts of the world; that a widespread ethnomedical construct that we might call indigenous contagion theory has many parallels with Western biomedicine—especially in the form of public health—and that those of us who would promote public health in developing countries would do well to modify our approaches to accommodate and take advantage of these parallels.

The first workshop I attended for traditional healers and government health personnel—in Swaziland, in 1981—happened to concern a contagious disease, leprosy. The workshop was billed as a forum for exploring modern medical and Swazi beliefs and practices related to leprosy, with a view toward improving both approaches. A foreign physician expert on leprosy presided. Before long, it was clear that the invited traditional healers were to have no opportunity to speak. The organizer had previously decided that healers were there to listen and be shown the error of their ways. Toward the end of the day-long workshop, the healers stood up and complained that they felt insulted and so they were leaving. I later interviewed many of these healers, some of whom were among the most prominent, influential, and well educated of Swazi healers. They did not quickly forget their insult and were understandably wary about attending another "collaborative" workshop.

Considering that it is estimated that traditional healers provide at least 80% of all health services in Africa, and for that matter in many other poor, Third World countries, and considering their influence as opinion leaders in health (and often spiritual) matters, what good does it do to alienate them from formal health programs? I would say this even if we assumed, for the sake of argument, that all ethnomedical beliefs and practices were always damaging to health, which is highly unlikely. In view of the extremely high and growing iatrogenic morbidity and mortality found in the United States (Moore et al. 1998) and, indeed, virtually everywhere, no one can claim that Western biomedicine even approaches being completely beneficial. In any case, it is now widely acknowledged that significant gains in health and longevity are due to broad public health measures, such as improved water and sanitation, not to the availability of biomedical treatment. These broad measures are precisely where indigenous healers ought to fit in.

As this review of a number of studies including my own has shown, some beliefs and practices even when measured *only* by a Western, biomedical standard, promote health, others compromise it, and a sizable proportion does neither but may have a salutary social or psychological effect. The public health approach my colleagues and I have taken in several African countries has been, in its simplest form, to reinforce and promote useful ethnomedical beliefs and practices, discourage the harmful, and leave alone but respect that which has no direct health consequence. In addition, we introduce new health ideas and sometimes "technology" (e.g., oral rehydration salts, condoms) and try to enlist healers in public health efforts. We also use ethnomedical knowledge and beliefs gained from research with healers and their clients to develop and implement improved programs of what nowadays may be called "behavior change and communication" geared to the general population. Our approach is accommodative rather than confrontational whenever possible. Contagious and infectious diseases account for the greatest morbidity and mortality of children and adults in poor, developing countries. Ethnomedical models of such illnesses tend to be naturalistic and therefore often offer more of a basis of potential indigenous-biomedical collaboration than other types of disease.

The resulting collaboration can take the form of an intervention that is supported and can be implemented by both biomedical and traditional healers or lay caretakers. Examples include promoting fidelity and partner reduction for AIDS and STD prevention; discouraging use of unclean (unsterilized) razors for any type of treatment; promoting coconut or rice water for rehydration; dietary prescriptions and avoidances; and referrals to hospitals and clinics when biomedical treatment is proven superior to indigenous therapy. Such efforts have the best chance of developing and being sustained if a health communications strategy is developed and implemented in collaboration with indigenous healers and with the public at large. The strategy ought to be based on sufficient biomedical under-standing of ethnomedical beliefs and practices and ought to build on areas of interface and agreement, rather than confront the existing system.

267

Of course, to do this right, adequate research is needed. But how much and of what kind of research? Superficial observation including KAP surveys may be misleading. I have studied African ethnomedicine for nearly 20 years, but I have fallen into the trap of reaching conclusions based on what I thought was an adequate research foundation. For example, I have always discouraged use of purgative or emetic traditional medicines for children with dehydration, and, by extension, for children with diarrhea. Yet, recent phytochemical research has shown that the roots of *Mirabilis jalapa*, used in South Africa as a purgative, exhibit antibacterial activity against an impressive range of diarrhea-causing pathogens: *Staphylococcus aureus*, *Streptococcus pyogenes*, *Escherichia coli*, *Enterobacter sp.*, *Vibrio cholerae*, *Shigella flexneri*, and *Salmonella typhi* (Chifundera et al. 1991). This underscores that we must be cautious about categorical discouragement of any aspects of indigenous medicine and healing until we know what we are interfering with. This may require doing ethnopharmocological as well as ethnomedical research.

As it is, many who work in and define the approach of public health in developing countries already have opinions about ethnomedicine and traditional healers, based on no research, inadequate research, or clinical experience with a highly skewed sample of hospital patients who may have suffered negative effects of indigenous medicine. One such clinician who had worked for 33 years in a district hospital in Africa, wrote to *Tropical Doctor*:

> The assumption that traditional healers should be included in counselling and encouraged to treat AIDS sufferers is where many of us involved in the war against AIDS would part company with Dr. Staugaard [who had suggested this]. We should not assume that we could work as a team with those among traditional healers whose world view is that there are no pathogens in the universe, and that AIDS is caused by a broken taboo perhaps having no direct relationship with promiscuity. The view of our traditional health workers is that everything is curable if the offended spirits are placated and the proper corrective applied. (Foulkes 1992)

This writer apparently overlooked or did not believe Staugaard, who had reported, "Many indigenous concepts on the cause and transmission of HIV/AIDS are compatible with modern scientific concepts, although expressed in different terms and conceptual frameworks. AIDS is often considered an indigenous disease, caused by contact of blood and semen"

(Staugaard 1991:22). Still, this is relatively restrained language on the part of the clinician. The writer does not condemn all African healers; presumably those who believe in biomedically defined pathogens (rather than insects, darkness, or dirt) would, to some degree, be acceptable. And this author might recognize that taboos relevant to AIDS beliefs could serve to discourage promiscuity.

It is the last sentence in the quote that touches on the core argument in this book: "Everything is curable if the offended spirits are placated." I have argued that this may be the view for some African illnesses, but not for AIDS and most others biomedically defined as contagious. But such stereotypes of supernaturalism prevail in the absence of sufficient objective ethnomedical research in the domain of infectious, contagious disease. It is true that anthropologists are increasingly engaged in researching contagious disease—many on contract with powerful international health organizations and donors—and an increasing number of these are providing evidence supporting naturalistic ICT. But public health power brokers can still quote prominent anthropologists who have gone on record observing that African ethnomedicine is essentially supernatural and incompatible with germ theory and the rest of scientific medicine.

The approach I recommend—and already found in some more ethnomedically attuned health programs—would be unlikely to: (1) perpetuate witchcraft beliefs or the scapegoating of others; (2) impede acceptance of scientific thinking and perpetuate magical thinking; or (3) retard a patient's self-awareness or psychological maturation. Fear of such outcomes has been expressed by biomedical health promoters, in fact used as reasons not to accommodate indigenous health beliefs at all (Velimirovic and Velimirovic 1978:182–183; Asuni 1979; Velimirovic 1984; Paton 1997). Undue focus of anthropologists and others on witchcraft beliefs and practices, probably the area of *least* compatibility between indigenous medicine and Western public health, has not contributed to the incorporation of ethnomedical findings in public health programs—something many anthropologists bemoan as a serious oversight. We are more likely to see health programs informed by ethnomedical research if we place more emphasis where it deserves to be: on naturalistic understandings of contagious illnesses.

Undue focus on witchcraft beliefs and practices by anthropologists and others has not contributed to the incorporation of ethnomedical findings in public health programs—something many anthropologists bemoan as a serious oversight. However, we are more likely to see health programs informed by ethnomedical research if we place more emphasis where it deserves to be: not on witchcraft beliefs—which is probably the area of least compatibility between indigenous medicine and Western public health—but instead on naturalistic understandings of contagious illnesses.

NOTES

1. See Greunbaum (1996) for a recent relativist defense of female circumcision.

2. Occasionally they do. During my fieldwork in Suriname among the Matawai Maroons, a chief who lacked any formal education once explained to me how and why Maroon societies required unilineal descent systems as long as they practice swidden agriculture in a rain forest environment. His explanation combined the basic insights of cultural materialism with British structural-functionalism.

REFERENCES

Agyepong I. A. 1992. Malaria: Ethnomedical Perceptions and Practice in an Adangbe Farming Community and Implications for Control. *Social Science and Medicine* 35(2):131–137.

Airhihenbuwa, C. O. 1991. A Conceptual Model for Culturally Appropriate Health Education Programs in Developing Countries. *International Quarterly of Community Health Education* 11(1):53–62.

Ajai, O. 1990. The Integration of Traditional Medicine into the Nigerian Health Care Delivery System: Legal Implications and Complications. *Medicine and Law* 9(1):685–699.

Alland, A. 1990. Commentaries. *Medical Anthropology Quarterly* 4(3):342–344.

Alland, A., H. Baer, P. Kunstadter, C. Laderman, D. Landy, L. Romanucci-Ross, J. Trostle, S. J. Ulijaszek, and A. McElroy. 1990. Commentaries. *Medical Anthropology Quarterly* 4(3):342–344.

Akighir, A. 1982. Traditional and Modern Psychiatry: A Survey of Opinions and Beliefs Amongst People in Plateau State, Nigeria. *International Journal of Social Psychiatry* 28(3):203–209.

Anokbonggo, W. W., R. Odoi-Adome, and P. M. Oluju. 1990. Traditional Methods in Management of Diarrhoeal Diseases in Uganda. *Bulletin of the World Health Organization* 68(3):359–363.

271

Anyinam, C. 1987. Availability, Accessibility, Acceptability and Adaptability: Four Attributes of African Ethno-Medicine. *Social Science and Medicine* 25(7):803–811.

Armelagos, G. J., T. Leatherman, M. Ryan, and L. Sibley. 1992. Biocultural Synthesis in Medical Anthropology. *Medical Anthropology 14*(1):35, 52.

Ashraf, A. 1984. *Home Remedies and Rural Health Care*. Dakka: Christian Commission for Development in Bangladesh.

Asiimwe-Okiror, G. 1995. Brief Report on Population Based Survey in Jinja District. Kampala: STD/AIDS Control Programme, November.

Asuni, T. 1979. The Dilemma of Traditional Healing with Special Reference to Nigeria. *Social Science and Medicine 13*:33–39.

Avode, D. G., O. B. Capo-Chichi, P. Gandaho, B. Bouteille, and M. Dumas. 1996. Epilepsy Caused by Cysticercosis. Apropos of a Sociological and Cultural Investigation Conducted at Savalou in Benin. *Bulletin de la Societé de Pathologie Exotique 89*(1):45–47.

Awaritefe, A. 1989. Epilepsy: The Myth of a Contagious Disease. *Culture, Medicine, and Psychiatry 13*(4):449–456.

Azevedo M. J., G. S. Prater, and D. N. Lantum. 1991. Biomedicine and Child Mortality in Cameroon. *Social Science and Medicine 32*(12): 1341–1349.

Baer, H. A. 1990. Commentaries. *Medical Anthropology Quarterly 4*(3):344–347.

Baer, H. A. 1995. Medical Pluralism in the United States: A Review. *Medical Anthropology 9*(4):493–502.

Baer, H. A. 1997. The Misconstruction of Critical Medical Anthropology: A Response to a Cultural Constructivist Critique. *Social Science and Medicine 44*(10):1565–1573.

Baker, P. T. 1977. Commentary Re Neumann, T. W., A Biocultural Approach to Salt Taboos: The Case of the Southeastern United States. *Current Anthropology 18*(2):296.

Baptista, A. dos Santos. 1951. *Monographia etnografica sobre os Macuas*. Lisbon: Agencia Geral Do Ultramar.

Barnhoorn, F., and H. Adriaanse. 1992. In Search of Factors Responsible for Noncompliance among Tuberculosis Patients in Wardha District, India. *Social Science and Medicine 34*(3):291–306.

Beck, A. 1981. *Medicine, Tradition, and Development in Kenya and Tanzania, 1920–1970*. Waltham, MA: Crossroads Press.

Bentley, M., G. H. Pelto, and W. L. Strauss. 1988. Rapid Ethnographic Assessment: Applications in a Diarrhea Management Program. *Social Science and Medicine* 27(1):107–116.

Bhuiya, A. 1992. Village Health Care Providers in Matlab, Bangladesh: A Study of Their Knowledge in the Management of Childhood Diarrhoea. *Journal of Diarrhoeal Disease Research* 10(1):10–15.

Bibeau, G., E. Corin, M. H. Buganza, M. Mandela, M. Mahoya, M. K. Mukana, N. M. Makengo, R. Ahluwalia, and B. Mechin. 1980. *Traditional Medicine in Zaire*. Ottowa: International Development Research Centre.

Bichmann, W. 1979. Primary Health Care and Traditional Medicine. *Social Science and Medicine* 13B:175–182.

Bishaw, M. 1989. The Implications of Indigenous Medical Beliefs to Biomedical Practice. *Ethiopian Journal of Health Development* 3:75–88.

Bongaarts, J., P. Reining, P. Way, and F. Conant 1989. The Relationship Between Male Circumcision and HIV Infection in African Populations. *AIDS* 3(6):373–377.

Booyens, J. H. 1989. Aspekte van Populere Opvattinge oor Diareesiektes onder Tswanasprekende Stedelinge (Aspects of the Popular Attitude about Diarrhea among Tswana-Speaking Urbanites). *Curationis* 12(3–4):11–16.

Boster, J. S., and J. C. Johnson. 1989. Form or Function: A Comparison of Expert and Novice Judgements of Similarity Among Fish. *American Anthropologist* 91(4):866–889.

Boyd, M. R., Y. F. Hallock, J. H. Cardellina ll, K. P. Manfredi, J. W. Blunt, J. B. McMahon, R. W. Buckheit, Jr., G. Bringmann, M. Schaffer, G. M. Cragg, D. W. Thomas, and J. G. Jato. 1994. Anti-HIV Michellamines from *Ancistrocladus korupensis, Journal of Medicine and Chemistry* 37:1740–1745.

Brown, J., O. Ayowa, and R. Brown. 1993. Dry and Tight: Sexual Practices and Potential AIDS Risk in Zaire. *Social Science and Medicine* 37(8):989–994.

Brown, P. J., and C. M. Worthman. 1991. Review of J. A. McFalls and M. H. McFalls, *Disease and Fertility*. *Medical Anthropology Quarterly* 5(1):85–88.

Brown, P. J., M. C. Inhorn, and D. J. Smith. 1996. Disease, Ecology, and Human Behavior. In *Medical Anthropology: A Handbook of Theory and Methods*, 2d ed. C. F. Sargent and T. J. Johnson, eds. Pp. 183–218. Westport, CT: Praeger.

Brown, P. J., M. C. Inhorn, and D. J. Smith. 1998. Disease, Ecology, and Human Behavior. In *The Anthropology of Infectious Disease: International Health Perspectives*. M. C. Inhorn and P. J. Brown, eds. Pp. 241–266. Amsterdam: Gordon and Breach.

273

Bryant, A. T. 1966 [1909]. *Annals of the Natal Museum 2*, No. 1.

Buxton, J. 1973. *Religion and Healing in Mandari.* Oxford: Clarendon Press.

Bwayo, J., F. Plummer, M. Omari, A. Mutere, S. Moses, J. Ndinya-Achola, P. Velentgas, and J. Kreiss. 1994. Human Immunodeficiency Virus Infection in Long-Distance Truck Drivers in East Africa. *Archives of Internal Medicine 154*(12):1391–1396.

Caldwell, J. C., and P. Caldwell. 1994. The Nature and Limits of the Sub-Saharan African AIDS Epidemic: Evidence from Geographic and Other Patterns. In *Sexual Networking and AIDS in Sub-Saharan Africa: Behavioural Research and the Social Context.* I. O. Orubuloye, J. C. Caldwell, Pat Caldwell, and G. Santow, eds. Pp. 195–216. Canberra: Health Transition Centre, The Australian National University.

Caldwell, J. C., and P. Caldwell. 1996. The African AIDS Epidemic. *Scientific American 274*(3):62–68.

Cernea, M. 1990. Re-Tooling in Applied Social Investigation for Development Planning: Some Methodological Issues. Address to the Opening Plenary Session, International Conference on Rapid Assessment Methodologies for Planning and Evaluation of Health Related Programs, Pan American Health Organization, Washington, DC, November 12–15.

Cheney, C. C. 1979. Religion, Magic, and Medicine in Huave Society. In *From Tzintzuntzan to the "Image of Limited Good:" Essays in Honor of George M. Foster.* M. Clark, R. V. Kemper, and C. Nelson, eds. Pp. 59–73. Berkeley: Kroeber Anthropological Society.

Chhabra, S. C., R.L.A. Mahunnah, and E. N. Mshiu. 1990. Plants Used in Traditional Medicine in Eastern Tanzania. IV. Angiosperms (Mimosaceae to Papilionaceae). *Journal of Ethnopharmacology 29*(3):295–323.

Chifundera, K., B. Kizungu, and W. Mbuyi. 1991. Antibacterial Activity of Mirabilis Jalapa Seed Powder. *Journal of Ethnopharmacology 35*(2): 197–199.

Corish, J. L., ed. 1925. *Health Knowledge.* New York: Medical Book Distributors.

Cosminsky, S., and S. Scrimshaw. 1980. Medical Pluralism on a Guatemalan Plantation. *Social Science and Medicine 14B*:267–278.

Cunningham, A. B. 1993. Imithi-isiZulu: Trade in Traditional Medicines in Natal/KwaZulu. M. Soc. Sci. thesis, University of Natal, Durban.

Davies, D. 1972. *A Dictionary of Anthropology.* New York: Crane, Russak and Co.

de Sousa, J. F. 1991. Traditional Beliefs and Practices Related to Childhood Diarrhoeal Disease in a High-Density Suburb of Maputo. B.A. thesis (Sociology), University of Zimbabwe, Harare.

de Zoysa I., D. Carson, R. Feachem, B. Kirkwood, E. Lindsay-Smith, and R. Loewenson. 1984. Perceptions of Childhood Diarrhoea and Its Treatment in Rural Zimbabwe. *Social Science and Medicine 19*(7): 727–734.

Douglas, M. 1963. *The Lele of the Kasai.* London: Oxford University Press.

Douglas, M. 1975. *Implicit Meanings.* London: Routledge and Kegan Paul.

Douglas, M. 1992 [1966]. *Purity and Danger: An Analysis of Concepts of Pollution and Taboo.* London: Routledge and Kegan Paul.

Duh, S. V. 1991. *Blacks and AIDS: Causes and Origins.* Thousand Oaks, CA: Sage Publications.

Durham, W. H. 1991. *Coevolution: Genes, Culture and Human Diversity.* Stanford: Stanford University Press.

Durkheim, E. 1961 [1912, 1947 ed.]. *The Elementary Forms of the Religious Life.* Translated by J. Swain. New York: Collier Books.

Earthy, E. D. 1968 [1933]. *Valenge Women: The Social and Economic Life of the Valenge Women of Portuguese East Africa.* London: Frank Cass & Co., Ltd.

Edgerton, R. E. 1992. *Sick Societies: Challenging the Myth of Primitive Harmony.* New York: Free Press.

Edwards, S. D. 1986. Traditional and Modern Medicine in South Africa: A Research Study. *Social Science and Medicine 22*(11):1273–1276.

Eisenbruch, M. 1998a. Dr. Hansen and the Crouching Mango: The Anthropology of STI and HIV/AIDS in Cambodia. Paper presented at Association for Asian Studies 50th Annual Meeting, March 26–29, Washington, DC.

Eisenbruch, M. 1998b. Internet posting/letter, May 19.

Ekanem, E. E., and C. O. Akitoye. 1990. Child Feeding by Nigerian Mothers during Acute Diarrhoeal Illness. *Journal of the Royal Society of Health 110*(5):164–165.

Epling, P. J., and N. Siliga. 1967. Notes on Infantile Diarrhoea in American Samoa. *Journal of Tropical Pediatrics*, Sept.:139–149.

Escobar, G. J., E. Salazar, and M. Chuy. 1983. Beliefs Regarding the Etiology and Treatment of Infantile Diarrhea in Lima, Peru. *Social Science and Medicine 17*(17):1257–1269.

Evans-Pritchard, E. E. 1937. *Witchcraft, Oracles and Magic among the Azande*. Oxford: Clarendon Press.

Ezeabasili, N. 1982. Traditional Ibo Ideas about Disease and Its Treatment. Nigerian Prespectives on Medical Sociology. *Studies in Third World Societies*. O. A. Erinosho, guest ed. March:17–28.

Farruque, A.S.G. 1984. Home Remedies and Rural Health Care. Dhaka: Christian Commission for Development in Bangladesh, November, report.

Fassin, D., and E. Fassin. 1988. Traditional Medicine and the Stakes of Legitimation in Senegal. *Social Science and Medicine 27*(4):353–357.

Feinstein, A. R. 1967. *Clinical Judgment*. Huntington, NY: Robert E. Krieger.

Fernandez, E. L., and G. M. Guthrie. 1984. Belief Systems and Breast Feeding among Filipino Urban Poor. *Social Science and Medicine 19*(9):991–995.

Fierman, S. 1981. Therapy as a System-in-Action in Northeastern Tanzania. *Social Science and Medicine 15B*(3):353–360.

Fortes, M. 1976. Foreword. In *Social Anthropology and Medicine*. J. Loudon, ed. Pp. ix–xx. London: Academic Press.

Foster, G. 1976. Disease Etiologies in Non-Western Medical Systems. *American Anthropologist 78*(4):773–782.

Foster, G. 1983. Introduction to Ethnomedicine. In *Traditional Medicine and Health Care Coverage*. R. Bannerman, J. Burton, and Ch'en Wen-Chieh, eds. Pp. 17–24. Geneva: WHO.

Foster, L. M., S. A. Osunwole, and B. W. Wahab. 1996. Imototo: Indigenous Yoruba Sanitation Knowledge Systems and Their Implication for Nigerian Health Policy. In *Alaafia: Studies of Yoruba Concepts of Health and Well-Being in Nigeria*. F. Fairfax, B. W. Wahab, L. Egunjobi, and D. M. Warren, eds. Pp. 26–38. Studies in Technology and Social Change, No. 25. Ames, IA: Center for Indigenous Knowledge for Agriculture and Rural Development.

Foulkes, J. R. 1992. Traditional Health Workers (Letter). *Tropical Doctor 22*(3):121–122.

Freeman, M., and M. Motsei. 1992. Planning Health Care in South Africa: Is There a Role for Traditional Healers? *Social Science and Medicine 34*(11): 1183–1190.

Freund, P. J. 1989. Traditional Healers and Diarrhoea: Results of a Recent Survey in Zambia. Paper presented at the 117th Annual Meeting of the American Public Health Association (APHA), Chicago, October 22–26.

Gelfand, M. 1980. African Customs in Relation to Preventive Medicine. *The Central African Journal of Medicine* 27(1)1–7.

Gelfand, M., S. Mavi, R. B. Drummond, and B. Ndemera. 1985. *The Traditional Medical Practitioner in Zimbabwe*. Harare: Mambo Press.

Gessler, M. C., D. E. Msuya, M. H. Nkunya, A. Schar, M. Heinrich, and M. Tanner. 1995. Traditional Healers in Tanzania: Sociocultural Profile and Three Short Portraits. *Journal of Ethnopharmacology* 48(3):145–160.

Gibbs, S. 1992. Mozambique: From Dependency to Sustainability. What Role for Traditional Healers in the Move Towards a More Sustainable Health Service? B.A. thesis (Geography), University of Liverpool.

Glick, L. B. 1967. Medicine As an Ethnographic Category: The Gimi of the New Guinea Highlands. *Ethnology* 6:31–56.

Gluckman, M. 1945. How the Bemba Make Their Living: An Appreciation of Richards' "Land Labour and Diet in Northern Rhodesia." *The Rhodes-Livingstone Institute Journal* (June):55–75.

Good, C. M. 1987. *Ethnomedical Systems in Africa. Patterns of Traditional Medicine in Rural and Urban Kenya*. New York: Guilford Press.

Gottlieb, A. 1992. *Under the Kapok Tree*. Bloomington: Indiana University Press.

Green, E. C. 1978. Winti and Christianity: A Study of Religious Change. *Ethnohistory* 25(3):251–276.

Green, E. C. 1985. Traditional Healers, Mothers and Childhood Diarrheal Disease in Swaziland: The Interface of Anthropology and Health Education. *Social Science and Medicine* 20(3):277–285.

Green, E. C. 1986. Diarrhea and the Social Marketing of Oral Rehydration Salts in Bangladesh. *Social Science and Medicine* 21(4):357–366.

Green, E. C. 1987. Anthropology and the Integration of Modern and Traditional Health Sectors in Swaziland. In *Anthropological Praxis: Translating Knowledge into Action*. B.Wulff and S. Fiske, eds. Pp. 81–97. Boulder: Westview Press.

Green, E. C. 1989. *A Survey of Health, Fertility and Human Reproductive Knowledge and Attitudes among Nigerian Traditional Healers*. Washington, DC: The Futures Group.

Green, E. C. (with T. Tomas and A. Jurg). 1991. *A Program in Public Health and Traditional Health Manpower in Mozambique*. Maputo: Mozambique Ministry of Health and European Community.

Green, E. C. 1992. Unpublished Swaziland field notes (1981–92).

Green, E. C. 1994a. *AIDS and Sexually Transmitted Disease in Africa: Bridging the Gap between Traditional Healers and Modern Medicine.* Boulder and Oxford: Westview Press.

Green, E. C. 1994b. Unpublished Mozambique field notes (1990–94).

Green, E. C. 1995. Impacting on AIDS and STDS in Zambia: Report on the Traditional Healer Component of the Morehouse School of Medicine/Zambia AIDS Prevention Project. Lusaka, Zambia: USAID, Morehouse Medical School and Tulane University.

Green, E. C. 1997. Purity, Pollution and the Invisible Snake in Southern Africa. *Medical Anthropology 17*(2):83–100.

Green, E. C., and D. Altman. 1997. *Improving Child Spacing Awareness, Knowledge, and Services in Western Nampula Province, Mozambique.* Atlanta and Maputo, Mozambique: CARE International.

Green, E. C., A. Jurg, and A. Dgedge. 1993. Sexually Transmitted Diseases, AIDS and Traditional Healers in Mozambique. *Medical Anthropology 15*(3): 261–281.

Green, E. C., A. Jurg, and A. Dgedge. 1994. The Snake in the Stomach: Child Diarrhea in Central Mozambique. *Medical Anthropology Quarterly 8*(1): 4–24.

Green, E. C., A. Jurg, T. Tomas, and A. Dgedge. 1991. *Traditional Health Beliefs and Practices Related to Child Diarrheal and Sexually Transmitted Diseases.* Washington, DC: USAID and the Academy for Educational Development.

Green, E. C., and L. Makhubu. 1984. Traditional Healers in Swaziland: Toward Improved Cooperation between the Traditional and Modern Health Sectors. *Social Science and Medicine 18*(12):1071–1074.

Green, E. C., J. Marrato, and M. Wilsonne. 1995a. Ethnomedical Study of Diarrheal Disease, AIDS/STDs, and Mental Health in Nampula, Mozambique. Maputo: Mozambique Ministry of Health and Swiss Development Cooperation, Berne, August.

Green, E. C., and M. Nzima. 1995. The Traditional Healer Targeted Intervention Research Study in Zambia. Lusaka: Morehouse/Tulane AIDS Prevention Project, September, report.

Green, E.C., and B. Zokwe. 1993. Evaluation of the "Second Generation" of South African Traditional Healers Trained in HIV/AIDS Prevention and Management. Arlington: Family Health International, August, report.

Green, E. C., B. Zokwe, and J. D. Dupree. 1992. The Role of South African Traditional Healers in HIV/AIDS Prevention and Management. Arlington, VA: Family Health International, AIDSCAP Project.

278

Green, E. C., B. Zokwe, and J. D. Dupree. 1995b. The Experience of an AIDS Prevention Program Focused on South African Traditional Healers. *Social Science and Medicine 40*(4):503–515.

Gruenbaum, E. 1996. The Cultural Debate over Female Circumcision: The Sudanese Are Arguing This One Out for Themselves. *Medical Anthropology Quarterly 10*(4):455–475.

Grosskurth, H., F. Mosha, J. Todd, E. Mwijarubi, A. Klokke, K. Senkoro, P. Mayaud, J. Changalucha, A. Nicoll, and G. Gina. 1995. Impact of Improved Treatment of Sexually Transmitted Diseases on HIV Infection in Rural Tanzania: Randomised Controlled Trial. *The Lancet 346*:530–536.

Guillaume, A., and S. Rey. 1988. Morbidite par diarrhee: Quels recours therapeutiques? *Annales de l'Iford 12*(1):89–101.

Gumede, M. V. 1990. *Traditional Healers: A Medical Doctor's Perspective.* Johannesburg: Skotaville Publishers.

Hahn, R. A. 1984. Rethinking "Illness" and "Disease." *Contributions to Asian Studies 18*:513–522.

Hahn, R. A. 1995. *Sickness and Healing: An Anthropological Perspective.* New Haven: Yale University Press.

Hammond-Tooke, W. D. 1962. *Bhaca Society: A People of the Transkeian Uplands, South Africa.* London: Oxford University Press.

Hammond-Tooke, W. D. 1970. Urbanization and the Interpretation of Misfortune: A Quantitative Analysis. *Africa 2*(1):25–39.

Hammond-Tooke, W. D. 1981a. *Boundaries and Belief: The Structure of a Sotho Worldview.* Johannesburg: Witwatersrand University Press.

Hammond-Tooke, W. D. 1981b. Patrolling the Herms: Social Structure, Cosmology and Pollution Concepts in Southern Africa. Raymond Dart Lectures, No. 18. Johannesburg: Witwatersrand University.

Hammond-Tooke, W. D. 1989. *Rituals and Medicines.* Johannesburg: A. D. Donker, Ltd.

Handwerker, W. P., and D. F. Wozniak. 1997. Sampling Strategies for the Collection of Cultural Data: An Extension of Boas's Answer to Galton's Problem. *Current Anthropology 38*(5):869–875.

Hannaway, C. 1993. Environment and Miasmata. In *Companion Encyclopedia of the History of Medicine*, Vol. 1. W. F. Bynum and R. Porter, eds. Pp. 292–308. London and New York: Routledge.

Hanlon, J. 1990. *Mozambique: Who Calls the Shots?* Bloomington: Indiana University Press.

Haram, L. 1991. Tswana Medicine in Interaction with Biomedicine. *Social Science and Medicine 33*(2):167–175.

Harris, M. 1974. *Cows, Pigs, Wars and Witches.* New York: Vintage.

Harris, M. 1979. *Cultural Materialism.* New York: Random House.

Harris, M. 1992. Distinguised Lecture: Anthropology and the Theoretical Paradigmatic Significance of the Collapse of Soviet and East European Communism. *American Anthropologist 94*(2):295–305.

Harris, M. 1999. *Theories of Culture in Postmodern Times.* Walnut Creek, CA: AltaMira Press.

Helitzer-Allen, D., and H. Allen. 1992. *Focused Ethnographic Study of Sexually Transmitted Diseases in Thyolo, Malawi: Results.* Arlington, VA: FHI/AIDSCAP.

Helitzer-Allen, D., H. Allen, M. Field, and G. Dallabetta. 1996. Targeted Intervention Research on Sexually Transmitted Illnesses. *Practicing Anthropology 18*(3):20–23.

Hoernlé, W. 1946 [1937]. Magic and Medicine. In *The Bantu-Speaking Tribes of South Africa.* I. Schapera, ed. Pp. 221–245. Cape Town: Maskew Miller, Ltd.

Hoff, W., and N. Maseko. 1986. Nurses and Traditional Healers Join Hands. *World Health Forum 7*(2):412–416.

Hogle, J., and A. Prins. 1991a. *Prospects for Collaborating with Traditional Healers in Africa.* Arlington, VA: Management Sciences for Health (PRITECH Project).

Hogle, J., and A. Prins. 1991b. *Indigenous Knowledge and Management of Childhood Diarrhoeal Diseases.* Arlington, VA: Management Sciences for Health (PRITECH Project).

Honwana, A. 1994. *Nyamusoro*: Spirit Possession, Ritual and Social Change Among the Tsonga of Southern Mozambique. Ph.D. diss. (draft summary), University of London.

Hudelson, P., T. Huanca, D. Charaly, and V. Cirpa. 1995. Ethnographic Studies of ARI in Bolivia and Their Use by the National ARI Programme. *Social Science and Medicine 41*(12):1677–1683.

Hughes, J. 1991. Impurity and Danger: The Need for New Barriers and Bridges in the Prevention of Sexually Transmitted Disease in the Tari Basin, Papua New Guinea. *Health Transition Review 1*(2):131–141.

Hunter, D., and P. Whitten. 1976. *Encyclopedia of Anthropology.* New York: Harper & Row.

Hussain, R., M. A. Lobo, B. Inam, A. Khan, A. F. Qureshi, and D. Marsh. 1997. Pneumonia Perceptions and Management: An Ethnographic Study in Urban Squatter Settlements of Karachi, Pakistan. *Social Science and Medicine* 45(7):991–1004.

Ikpatt, N. W., and M. U. Young. 1992. Preliminary Study on the Attitude of People in Two States of Nigeria on Diarrhoeal Disease and Its Management. *East African Medical Journal* 69(4):219–222.

Imperato, P. J. 1974. Traditional Medical Practitioners among the Bambara of Mali and Their Role in the Modern Health-Care Delivery System. *Rural Africana* 26:41–54.

Imperato, P. J., and D. A. Traoré. 1979. Traditionl Bciefs about Smallpox and Its Treatment in the Republic of Mali. In *African Therapeutic Systems*. D. M. Warren, Z. Ademuwagun, J. Ayoade, and I. Harrison, eds. Pp. 15–18. Los Angeles: Crossroads Press for the African Studies Association.

Ingstad, B. 1990. The Cultural Construction of AIDS and Its Consequences for Prevention in Botswana. *Medical Anthropology Quarterly* 4(1):28–40.

Inhorn, M. C., and P. J. Brown. 1990. The Anthropology of Infectious Disease. In *Annual Review of Anthropology*, Vol. 19. B. J. Siegel, A. R. Beals, and S. A. Tyler, eds. Pp. 89–117. Palo Alto: Annual Reviews, Inc.

Inhorn, M. C., and P. J. Brown, eds. 1998. *The Anthropology of Infectious Disease: International Health Perspectives.* Amsterdam: Gordon and Breach.

Iyun B. F., and G. Tomson. 1996. Acute Respiratory Infections—Mothers' Perceptions of Etiology and Treatment in South-Western Nigeria. *Social Science and Medicine* 42(3):437–445.

Janzen, J. 1978. *The Quest for Therapy in Lower Zaire.* Berkeley: University of California Press.

Janzen, J. 1981. The Need for a Taxonomy of Health in the Study of African Therapeutics. *Social Science and Medicine* 15B(3):185–194.

Janzen, J. 1982. *Lemba 1650–1930: A Drum of Affliction in Africa and the New World.* New York: Garland Publishing.

Janzen, J. 1986. The Meeting of Allopathic and Indigenous Medicine in the African Context. Ms. published as Hippocrate de le Desserto, Galen de la Savanna, *Kos: Revista di Cultura e Storia Della Scienze Mediche*, III (Feb./Mar.) 20:39–61.

Janzen, J. 1989. Health, Religion, and Medicine in Central and Southern African Traditions. In *Caring and Curing: Health and Medicine in World Religious Traditions*. L. Sullivan, ed. Pp. 225–254. New York: MacMillan.

Janzen, J., and G. Prins. 1981. Causality and Classification in African Medicine and Health. *Social Science and Medicine 15B*(3):169–172.

Jones, R., and J. Wasserheit. 1991. Introduction to the Biology and Natural History of Sexually Transmitted Diseases. In *Research Issues in Human Behavior and Sexually Transmitted Diseases in the AIDS Era.* J. N. Wasserheit, S. Aral, and K. Holmes, eds. P. 25. Washington, DC: American Society for Microbiology.

Junod, H. 1962a [1926]. *The Life of a South African Tribe.* Vol. 1, *Social Life.* New Hyde Park, NY: University Books.

Junod, H. 1962b [1926]. *The Life of a South African Tribe.* Vol. 2, *Mental Life.* New Hyde Park, NY: University Books.

Jurg, A., T. Tomas, and J. de Jong. 1991. *Fornecedores e utentes de cuidados modernos ou tradicionais de saúde em Maputo, Mocambique: Opiniões e preferencias mutuas em Mocambique.* Maputo: National Institute of Health, GEMT.

Kaltenthaler, E. C., and B. S. Drasar. 1996a. Understanding of Hygiene Behaviour and Diarrhoea in Two Villages in Botswana. *Journal of Diarrhoeal Disease Research 14*(2):75–80.

Kaltenthaler, E. C., and B. S. Drasar. 1996b. The Study of Hygiene Behaviour in Botswana: A Combination of Qualitative and Quantitative Methods. *Tropical Medicine and International Health 1*(5):690–698.

Kay, M. A. 1993. Fallen Fontanelle: Culture-Bound or Cross-Cultural? *Medical Anthropology 15*(2):137–156.

Kendall, C., D. Foote, and R. Martorell. 1984. Ethnomedicine and Oral Rehydration Therapy: A Case Study of Ethnomedical Investigation and Program Planning. *Social Science and Medicine 19*:253–260.

Kendall, C., P. Hudelson, E. Leontsini, P. Winch, L. Lloyd, and F. Cruz. 1991. Urbanization, Dengue, and the Health Transition: Anthropological Contributions to International Health. *Medical Anthropology Quarterly 5*(3): 257–268.

Kimani, V. 1981. Attempts to Coordinate the Work of Traditional and Modern Doctors in Nairobi in 1980. *Social Science and Medicine 15B*(3):421–422.

Kluckhohn, C., and H. A. Murray. 1949. Personality Formation: The Determinants. In *Personality in Nature, Society, and Culture.* C. Kluckhohn and H. A. Murray, eds. Pp. 35–52. New York: Alfred A. Knopf.

Konner, M. 1991. The Promise of Medical Anthropology: An Invited Commentary. *Medical Anthropology Quarterly 5*(1):78–82.

Koumare, M. 1983. Traditional Medicine and Psychiatry in Africa. In *Traditional Medicine and Health Care Coverage*. R. H. Bannerman, J. Burton, and Ch'en Wen-Chieh, eds. Pp. 25–32. Geneva: WHO.

Kresno, S., G. G. Harrison, B. Sutrisna, and A. Reingold. 1994. Acute Respiratory Illnesses in Children under Five Years in Indramayu, West Java, Indonesia: A Rapid Ethnographic Assessment. *Medical Anthropology 15*(4): 25–434.

Krige, E. J. 1946. Individual Development. In *The Bantu-Speaking Tribes of South Africa*. I. Schapera, ed. Pp. 95–111. Cape Town: Maskew Miller, Ltd.

Krige, E. J. 1950 [1936]. *The Social System of the Zulus*. Pietermaritzburg: Shuter and Shuter.

Krige, E. J., and J. D. Krige. 1943. *The Realm of a Rain Queen*. London: Oxford University Press.

Kumaresan, J. A., and E. T. Maganu. 1994. Socio-Cultural Dimensions of Leprosy in North-Western Botswana. *Social Science and Medicine 39*(4):537–541

Kundi, M. Z., M. Anjum, D. S. Mull, and J. D. Mull. 1993. Maternal Perceptions of Pneumonia and Pneumonia Signs in Pakistani Children. *Social Science and Medicine 37*(5):649–660.

Kuper, A. 1973. *Anthropologists and Anthropology: The British School 1922–1972*. New York: Penguin.

Landy, D. 1990. Commentaries. *Medical Anthropology Quarterly 4*(3):358–368.

le Grand, A., and P. Wondergem. 1990. *Herbal Medicine and Health Promotion*. Amsterdam: Royal Tropical Institute.

Lieban, R. 1977. The Field of Medical Anthropology. In *Culture, Disease, and Healing*. D. Landy, ed. Pp. 13–31. New York: Macmillan.

Lozoff, B., K. R. Kamath, and R. A. Feldman. 1975. Infection and Disease in South Indian Families: Beliefs about Childhood Diarrhea. *Human Organization 34*(4):353–358.

Maina-Ahlberg, B. 1979. Beliefs and Practices Concerning Treatment of Measles and Acute Diarrhea Among the Akamba. *Tropical and Geographical Medicine 31*:139–148.

Marrato, J. 1991. Condições de enquadramento familiar da criança deficiente mental. B.A. thesis (Psychology), Maputo: Instituto Superior Pedagógico.

Marti-Ibanez, F. 1962. *The Epic of Medicine*. New York: Clarkson Potter.

Martinez, F. L. 1989. *O povo Macua e a sua cultura*. Lisbon: Ministry of Education, Institute of Tropical Scientific Studies.

Marwick, M. G., ed. 1970. *Witchcraft and Sorcery.* Harmondsworth: Penguin Books, Ltd.

McCorkle, C. M., and E. Mathias-Mundy. 1992. Ethnoveterinary Medicine in Africa. *Africa 62*(1):59–93.

McCullough, J. M. 1973. Human Ecology, Heat Adaptation, and Belief Systems: The Hot-Cold Syndrome of Yucatan. *Journal of Anthropological Research 29*(1):32–36.

McElroy, A. 1990. Biocultural Models in Studies of Human Health and Adaptation. *Medical Anthropology Quarterly 4*(3)243–265.

McElroy. A. 1996. Should Medical Ecology Be Political? *Medical Anthropology Quarterly 10*(4):519–522.

McElroy, A., and P. Townsend, eds. 1989. *Medical Anthropology in Ecological Perspective,* 2d ed. Boulder: Westview Press.

McElroy, A., and P. Townsend. 1996. *Medical Anthropology in Ecological Perspective,* 3d ed. Boulder: Westview Press.

McKee, L. 1987. Ethnomedical Treatment of Children's Diarrheal Illnesses in the Highlands of Ecuador. *Social Science and Medicine 25*(10):1147–1155.

McNee, A., N. Khan, S. Dawson, J. Gunsalam, V. L. Tallo, L. Manderson, and I. Riley. 1995. Responding to Cough: Boholano Illness Classification and Resort to Care in Response to Childhood ARI. *Social Science and Medicine 40*(9):1279–1289.

Menegoni, L. 1996. Conceptions of Tuberculosis and Therapeutic Choices in Highland Chiapas, Mexico. *Medical Anthropology Quarterly 10*(3):381–401.

Mitchell, J. C. 1965. The Meaning of Misfortune for Urban Africans. In *African Systems of Thought.* M. Fortes and G. Dieterlen, eds. Pp. 192–203. London: Oxford University Press.

Mitchell, R. C. 1973. Respondent Cooperation among Urban Yoruba. In *Survey Research in Africa. Its Applications and Limits.* W. M. O'Barr, D. H. Spain, and M. A. Tessler, eds. Pp. 252–260. Evanston: Northwestern University Press.

Moore, T. J., B. M. Psaty, and C. D. Furberg. 1998. Commentary: Time to Act on Drug Safety. *Journal of the American Medical Association 279*(19): 1571–1573.

Morely, P. 1978. Culture and the Cognitive World of Traditional Medical Beliefs: Some Preliminary Considerations. In *Culture and Curing.* P. Morely and R. Wallis, eds. Pp. 1–18. Pittsburgh: University of Pittsburgh Press.

Moses, Steven, F. Plummer, J. Bradley, J. Ndinya-Achola, N. Nagelkerke, and A. Ronald. 1994. The Association Between Lack of Male Circumcision and Risk for HIV Infection: A Review of the Epidemiological Data. *Sexually Transmitted Diseases* 21(4):201–210.

Mull, D. S., and J. D. Mull. 1994. Insights from Community-Based Research on Child Pneumonia in Pakistan. *Medical Anthropology* 15(4):335–352.

Mull, J. D., C. S. Wood, L. P. Gans, and D. S. Mull. 1989. Culture and "Compliance" among Leprosy Patients in Pakistan. *Social Science and Medicine* 29(7):799–811.

Murdock, G. P. 1959. *Africa: Its People and Their Cultural History*. New York: McGraw-Hill.

Murdock, G. P. 1980. *Theories of Illness*. Pittsburgh: University of Pittsburgh Press.

Murdock, G. P., C. S. Ford, A. E. Hudson, R. Kennedy, L. W. Simmons, and J.W.M. Whiting. 1961. *Outline of Cultural Materials, Behavior Science Outlines*, Vol. I, 4th rev. ed. New Haven: Human Relations Area Files, Inc.

Murphy, E. 1972. *History of African Civilization*. New York: Dell Publishing.

Nat, J. M. van der, W. G. van der Sluis, K.T.D. de Silva, and R. P. Labadie. 1991. Ethnopharmacognostical Survey of Azadirachta Indica A. Juss (Meliaceae). *Journal of Ethnopharmacology* 35(1):1–24.

Ndamba, J., N. Nyazema, N. Makaza, C. Anderson, and K. Kaondera. 1994. Traditional Herbal Remedies Used for the Treatment of Urinary Schistosomiasis in Zimbabwe. *Ethnopharmacology* 42(2):125–132.

Neumann, T. W. 1977. A Biocultural Approach to Salt Taboos: The Case of the Southeastern United States. *Current Anthropology* 18(2):289–308.

Ngokwey, N. 1988. Pluralistic Etiological Systems in Their Social Context: A Brazilian Case Study. *Social Science and Medicine* 26(8):793–802.

Ngubane, H. 1977. *Body and Mind in Zulu Medicine*. London: Academic Press.

Nichter, M. 1991. Use of Social Science Research to Improve Epidemiologic Studies of and Interventions for Diarrhea and Dysentery. *Review of Infectious Disease* 13(Suppl. 4):S265–271.

Noronha, C. V., M. L. Barreto, T. M. Silva, and I. M. Souza. 1995. A Popular Concept of Schistosomiasis Mansoni: Modes of Transmission and Prevention from the Perspective of Gender Differences. *Cadernos de Saude Publica* 11(1):106–117.

Nymongo, I. K. 1998. Lay People's Responses to Illness: An Ethnographic Study of Anti-Malaria Behavior among the Abagusii of Southwestern Kenya. Ph.D. diss. (Anthropology), University of Florida, Gainesville (Draft).

Nzima, M. M. 1995. Preliminary Programmatic Considerations: Questions and Related Analysis of the Targeted Intervention Research (TIR) Conducted in Collaborative Programs Involving Healers, Chimwemwe, Kitwe (June 13–24, 1994). Lusaka: Morehouse/Tulane AIDS Prevention Project.

Oaks, S., V. Mitchell, G. Pearson, and C. Carpenter, eds. 1991. *Malaria: Obstacles and Opportunities.* Washington, DC: National Academy Press.

Opala, J., and F. Boillot. 1996. Leprosy among the Limba: Illness and Healing in the Context of World View. *Social Science and Medicine 42*(1)3–19.

Oyebolo, D.D.O. 1980. Professional Associations, Ethics and Discipline among Yoruba Traditional Healers of Nigeria. *Social Science and Medicine 15B*:87.

Panizzo, E. 1994. Pesquisa sobre Convulsões na Criança. 1a Parte: Maputo. Unpublished study. Maputo: Ministry of Health.

Paton, C. 1997. Healers Are Bad Muti-Motlana. *Sunday Times* (South Africa), June 8.

Pelling, M. 1993. Contagion/Germ Theory/Specificity. In *Companion Encyclopedia of the History of Medicine*, Vol. 1. W. F. Bynum and R. Porter, eds. Pp. 309–334. London and New York: Routledge.

Pielemeier, J., S. de George, H. Fluty, W. O'Loughlin, D. Odhiambo, and K. Wagner. 1996. Process Evaluation of the AIDS Technical Support Project (ATSP). Unpublished report. Washington, DC: USAID, Division of HIV/AIDS.

Pierce, R. V. 1889. *The People's Common Sense Medical Adviser.* Buffalo: World's Dispensary Printing Office.

Pillsbury, B. 1978. *Traditional Health Care in the Near East.* Washington, DC: USAID.

Pitt, M, J. McMaster, T. Hartmann, and D. Mausezahl. 1996. Lay Beliefs about Diarrhoeal Diseases: Their Role in Health Education in a Developing Country. *Social Science and Medicine 43*(8):1223–1228.

Plummer, F. A., S. Moses, and J. O. Ndinya-Achola. 1991. Factors Affecting Female to Male Transmission of HIV-1: Implications of Transmission and Dynamics for Prevention. *Network Newsletter 2*(2):6–9.

Pool, R. 1994a. On the Creation and Dissolution of Ethnomedical Systems in the Medical Ethnography of Africa. *Africa 64*(1):1–20, 1994.

Pool, R. 1994b. *Dialogue and the Interpretation of Illness: Conversations in a Cameroon Village*. Oxford and Providence, RI: Berg Publishers.

Pool, R., M. Maswe, J. T. Boerma, and S. Nnko. 1996. The Price of Promiscuity: Why Urban Males in Tanzania Are Changing Their Sexual Behavior. *Health Transition Review 6*:203–221.

Price, S. 1984. *Co-Wives and Calabashes*. Ann Arbor: University of Michigan Press.

Radcliffe-Brown, A. R. 1952. *Structure and Function in Primitive Society*. London: Cohen & West, Ltd.

Rauyajin O., B. Kamthornwachara, and P. Yablo. 1995. Socio-Cultural and Behavioural Aspects of Mosquito-Borne Lymphatic Filariasis in Thailand: A Qualitative Analysis. *Social Science and Medicine 41*(12):1705–1713.

Rauyajin, O., V. Pasandhanatorn, V. Rauyajin, S. Na-nakorn, J. Ngarmyithayapong, and C. Varothai. 1994. Mothers' Hygiene Behaviours and Their Determinants in Suphanburi, Thailand. *Journal of Diarrhoeal Disease Research 12*(1):25–34.

Reid, M. B. 1982. Patient/Healer Interactions in Sukuma Medicine. In *African Health and Healing Systems: Proceedings of a Symposium*. P. S. Yoder, ed. Pp. 121–158. Los Angeles: Crossroads Press.

Reis, R. 1993. Evil in the Body, Disorder of the Brain. Paper presented at Epilepsy Workshop Heernstede, The Netherlands. June 25 (revised, draft).

Reis, R. 1994. Evil in the Body, Disorder of the Brain. *Tropical and Geographical Medicine, 46*(3, suppl.):S40–43.

Richards, A. 1956. *Chisungu: A Girl's Initiation Ceremony among the Bemba of Zambia*. London: Tavistock.

Richards, A. 1970 (1935). A Modern Movement of Witch-Finders. In *Witchcraft and Sorcery*. M. Marwick, ed. Pp. 164–177. Baltimore: Penguin Books.

Rivers, W.H.R. 1924. *Medicine, Magi and Religion*. London: Kegan Paul.

Romero-Salazar, A., M. C. Parra, C. Moya-Hernandez, R. Rujano, and J. Salas. 1995. The Stigma in the Social Representation of Leprosy. *Cadernos de Saude Publica 11*(4):535–542.

Root-Bernstein, R. 1993. *Rethinking AIDS: The Tragic Cost of Premature Consensus*. New York: Free Press.

Rosen, L. N. 1973. Contagion and Cataclysm: A Theoretical Approach to the Study of Ritual Pollution Beliefs. *African Studies 32*(4):229–246.

Rubel, A. J., and M. R. Hass. 1996. Ethnomedicine. In *Handbook of Medical Anthropology*. C. F. Sargent and T. M. Johnson, eds. Pp. 113–130 .Westport, CT: Greenwood Press.

Rwiza, H. T., W. B. Matuja, G. P. Kilonzo, J. Haule, P. Mbena, R. Mwang'ombola, and Jilek-Aall. 1993. Knowledge, Attitude, and Practice toward Epilepsy among Rural Tanzanian Residents. *Epilepsia 34*(6): 1017–1023.

Ryan, G. W. 1998. What Do Sequential Behavioral Patterns Suggest about the Medical Decision-Making Process?: Modeling Home Case Management of Acute Illnesses in a Rural Cameroonian Village. *Social Science and Medicine 46*(2):209–225.

Ryan, G. W., and H. Martínez. 1996. Can We Predict What Mothers Do? Modeling Childhood Diarrhea in Rural Mexico. *Human Organization 55*(1):47–57.

Schapera, I. 1940. *Married Life in an African Tribe*. London: Faber & Faber.

Schapera, I., ed. 1946 [1937]. *The Bantu-Speaking Tribes of South Africa*. Cape Town: Maskew Miller, Ltd.

Schapera, I. 1978. Some Kgatla Theories of Procreation. In *Social System and Tradition in Southern Africa*. J. Argyle and E. Preston-Whyte, eds. Pp. 165–182. Cape Town: Oxford University Press.

Scheinman, D., R. Nesje, E. Ulrich, and E. Malangalia. 1992. Treating HIV with Traditional Medicine. *AIDS and Society 3*(3):5.

Schneider, H. K. 1981. *The Africans: An Ethnological Account*. Englewood Cliffs, NJ: Prentice-Hall.

Scrimshaw, S.C.M., and E. Hurtato. 1987. *Rapid Assessment Procedures for Nutrition and Primary Health Care*. Tokyo: UCLA Latin American Center and United Nations University.

Seed, J., S. Allen, T. Mertens, E. Hudes, A. Serufilira, M. Carael, E. Karita, P. Van de Perre, and F. Nsengumuremyi. 1995. Male Circumcision, Sexually Transmitted Disease, and Risk of HIV. *Journal of Acquired Immune Deficiency Syndromes and Human Retrovirology 8*:83–90.

Seymour-Smith, C. 1986. *Dictionary of Anthropology*. Boston: G. K. Hall and Co.

Shahid, N. A. S. Rahman, K. M. Aziz, A. S. Faruque, and M. A. Bari. 1983. Beliefs and Treatment Related to Diarrheal Episodes Reported in Association with Measles. *Tropical Geographical Medicine 35*:151–156.

Shawyer, R., A. Sani bin Gani, A. N. Punufimana, and N.K.F. Seuseu. 1996. The Role of Clinical Vignettes in Rapid Ethnographic Research: A Folk Taxonomy of Diarrhoea in Thailand. *Social Science and Medicine 42*(1)111–123.

Simon, G., T. Zhuwau, R. M. Anderson, and S. K. Chandiwana. 1998. Is There Evidence for Behaviour Change in Response to AIDS in Rural Zimbabwe? *Social Science and Medicine 46*(3):321–330.

Singer, M. 1990. Reinventing Medical Anthropology: Toward A Critical Realignment. *Social Science and Medicine 30*(2):179–187.

Singer, M. 1996. Farewell to Adaptationism: Unnatural Selection and the Politics of Biology. *Medical Anthropology Quarterly 10*(4):496–515.

Singer, P. 1986. A Medical Anthropologist's View of American Shamans. *Free Inquiry 6*(2):20–23.

Sircar, B. K., and M. B. Dagnow. 1988. Beliefs and Practices Related to Diarrhoeal Diseases among Mothers in Gondar Region, Ethiopia. *Tropical Geography and Medicine 40*(3):259–263

Smith, E. W., and A. M. Dale. 1968 [1920]. *The Ila-Speaking Peoples of Northern Rhodesia.* Hyde Park, NY: University Books.

Sofowora, A. 1993. Recent Trends in Research into African Medicinal Plants. Second International Congress on Ethnopharmacology, Uppsala, Sweden, 2–4 July 1992. *Journal of Ethnopharmacology 38*(2–3):209–214

Soto-Ramírez, L. E., B. Renjifo, M. F. McLane, R. Marlink, C. Hara, R. Sutthent, C. Wasi, P. Vithayasai, V. Vithayasai, C. Apichartpiyakul, P. Auewarakul, V. Peña Cruz, D. S. Chui, R. Osathanondh, K. Mayer, T. H. Lee, and M. Essex. 1996. HIV-1 Langerhans' Cell Tropism Associated with Heterosexual Transmission of HIV. *Science l*(271):1291–1293.

Staugaard, F. 1991. Role of Traditional Health Workers in Prevention and Control of AIDS in Africa. *Tropical Doctor 21*(1):22–24.

Stayt, H. A. 1968. *The Bavenda.* London: Frank Cass & Co., Ltd.

Stewart, M. K., B. Parker, J. Chakraborty, and H. Begum. 1994. Acute Respiratory Infections (ARI) in Rural Bangladesh: Perceptions and Practices. *Medical Anthropology 15*(4):377–394.

Swantz, L. 1990. *The Medicine Man among the Zaramo of Dar es Salaam.* Uddevalla (Sweden): Scandanavian Institute of African Studies.

Tahzib, F. 1988. Sokoto Traditional Medical Practitioners Project. Second Progress Report. Unpublished paper, University of Sokoto, Nigeria.

Tedlock, B. 1987. An Interpretive Solution to the Problem of Humoral Medicine in Latin America. *Social Science and Medicine 24*(12):1069–1083.

Trotter, R. T., II, B. Ortiz de Montellano, and M. H. Logan. 1989. Fallen Fontanelle in the American Southwest: Its Origin, Epidemiology, and Possible Organic Causes. *Medical Anthropology 10*:211–221.

Turner, V. 1967. *The Forest of Symbols*. Ithaca: Cornell University Press.

Turner, V. 1987. Betwixt and Between: The Liminal Period in Rites of Passage. In *Betwixt and Between: Patterns of Masculine and Feminine Initiation*. L. C. Mahdi, S. Foster, and M. Little, eds. Pp. 3–22. La Salle, Illinois: Open Court.

van de Walle, E., and F. van de Walle. 1989. Postpartum Sexual Abstinence in Tropical Africa. Philadelphia: University of Pennsylvania, Population Studies Center, African Demography Working Paper No. 17. Paper presented at the IUSSP Seminar on Biomedical and Demographic Determinants of Human Reproduction, Baltimore, January 4–8, 1988.

Vecchiato, N. L. 1990. Ethnomedical Beliefs, Health Education, and Malaria Eradication in Ethiopia. *IQCEDN 11*(4):385–397.

Vecchiato, N. L. 1998. "Digestive Worms": Ethnomedical Approaches to Intestinal Parasitism in Southern Ethiopia. In *The Anthropology of Infectious Disease: International Health Perspectives*. M. C. Inhorn and P. J. Brown, eds. Pp. 241–266. Amsterdam: Gordon and Breach.

Velimirovic, B. 1984. Traditional Medicine Is Not Primary Health Care: A Polemic. *Curare 7*(1):61–79.

Velimirovic, B., and H. Velimirovic. 1978. The Utilization of Traditional Medicine and Its Practitioners in Health. In *Modern Medicine and Medical Anthropology in the United States–Mexico Border Population*. B. Velimirovic, ed. Pp. 172–185. Washington, DC: Pan American Health Organization.

Venter, C. P., and P. H. Joubert. 1988. Aspects of Poisoning with Traditional Medicines in Southern Africa. *Biomedical Environmental Science 1*(4): 388–391.

Ventevogel, P. 1992. *Aborofodee* (Whiteman's Things): Effects of Training Programme for Indigenous Healers in the Techiman District, Ghana. M.A. thesis, Free University of Amsterdam, The Netherlands.

Warren, D. M. 1974. Disease, Medicine, and Religion among the Bono of Ghana: A Study in Culture Change. Ph.D. diss. (Anthropology), Indiana University.

Warren, D. M. 1979. The Role of Emic Analysis in Medical Anthropology: The Case of the Bono of Ghana. In *African Therapeutic Systems*. D. M. Warren, Z. Ademuwagun, J. Ayoade, and I. Harrison, eds. Pp. 36–42. Los Angeles: Crossroads Press for the African Studies Association.

Warren, D. M. 1982. The Techiman-Bono Ethnomedical System. In *African Health and Healing Systems*. P. Stanley Yoder, ed. Pp. 85–105. Los Angeles: Crossroads Press for the African Studies Association.

Warren. D. M. 1986. The Expanding Role of Indigenous Healers in Ghana's National Health Delivery Systems: The Ghanain Experiment. In *African Medicine in the Modern World*. C. Fyfe and U. Maclean, eds. Pp. 73–86. Edinburgh: University of Edinburgh Press.

Warren, D. M. 1989. Utilizing Indigenous Healers in National Health Delivery Systems: The Ghanaian Experiment. In *Making our Research Useful: Case Studies in the Utilization of Anthropological Knowledge*. J. van Willigen, B. Rylko-Bauer, and A. McElroy, eds. Pp. 159–178. Boulder, CO: Westview Press.

Warren, D. M. 1995. Review of *Dialogue and the Interpretation of Illness: Conversations in a Cameroon Village*. *Man: The Journal of the Royal Anthropological Institute 1*(4):872–873.

Wasserheit, J. N. 1992. Epidemiological Synergy: Interrelationships Between HIV Infection and Other STDs. In *AIDS and Women's Health: Science for Policy and Action*. L. Chen, J. Sepulveda, and S. Segal, eds. Pp. 61–77. New York: Plenum Press.

Weiss, M. G. 1988. Cultural Models of Diarrheal Illness: Conceptual Framework and Review. *Social Science and Medicine 27*(1):5–16.

Weller, S. 1984. Cross-Cultural Concepts of Illness: Variation and Validation. *American Anthropologist 86*:341–348.

WHO. 1976. *Health Manpower Development*. Paper EB 57/21, Add. 2, p. 3, WHO 57th Session. Geneva: WHO.

Wilkenson, L. 1993. Epidemiology. In *Companion Encyclopedia of the History of Medicine*, Vol. 2. W. F. Bynum and R. Porter, eds. Pp. 1262–1282. London and New York: Routledge.

Wilson, K. B. 1992. Cults of Violence and Counter-Violence in Mozambique. Oxford: Oxford University, Refugee Studies Centre.

Winick, C. 1956. *Dictionary of Anthropology*. New York: Philosophical Library.

Wondergem P., K. A. Senah, and E. K. Glover. 1989. Ghana: An Assessment of the Relevance of Herbal Drugs in PHC and Some Suggestions for Strengthening PHC. Unpublished report. Legon: Department of Sociology, University of Ghana.

Worboys, M. 1993. Tropical Diseases. In *Companion Encyclopedia of the History of Medicine*, Vol. 2. W. F. Bynum and R. Porter, eds. Pp. 512–536. London and New York: Routledge.

World Bank. 1997. *Confronting AIDS: Public Priorities in a Global Epidemic.* New York: Oxford University Press.

Wu, C. 1995. Yin and Yang: Western Science Makes Room for Chinese Herbal Medicine. *Science News 148*:9.

Yoder, P. S. 1981. Knowledge of Illness and Medicine Among Cokwe of Zaire. *Social Science and Medicine 15B*:237–245.

Yoder, P. S. 1982. Introduction. In *African Health and Healing Systems: Proceedings of a Symposium.* P. S. Yoder, ed. P. 249. Los Angeles: Crossroads Press.

Yoder, P. S. 1991. Cultural Conceptions of Illness in the Measurement of Changes in Morbidity. In *The Health Transition: Methods and Measures.* J. Cleland and A. Hill, eds. Pp. 43–60. Canberra: Australian National University.

Yoder, P. S. 1995. Examining Ethnomedical Diagnoses and Treatment Choices for Diarrheal Disorders in Lubumbashi Swahili. *Medical Anthropology 16*:211–247.

Yoder, P. S., R. Drew, and Z. Zhong. Nd. Knowledge and Practices Related to Diarrhea Disorders, Oral Rehydration Therapy, and Vaccinations in Lubumbashi, Zaire. Pp. 12–14. Unpublished report. Philadelphia: University of Pennsylvania HEALTHCOM Project.

Young, J. 1998. SfAA President's Letter. *Society for Applied Anthropology Newsletter 8*(2):1–2.

AUTHOR INDEX

n identifies a note

Adriaanse, H., 220
Agyepong, I. A., 182
Ahluwalia, R., 53
Airhihenbuwa, C. O., 218
Ajai, O., 37
Akighir, A., 259
Akitoye, C. O., 117
Alland, A., 251, 262
Allen, H., 168, 178n2, 206, 207, 208, 214–215
Allen, S., 23
Altman, D., 257
Anderson, C., 197, 200
Anderson, R. M., 177
Anjum, M., 226
Anokbonggo, W. W., 110
Anyinam, C., 222–223
Apichartpiyakul, C., 181
Armelagos, G. J., 264
Ashraf, A., 229
Asiimwe-Okiror, G., 177
Asuni, T., 11, 37, 39, 74, 269
Auewarakul, P., 181
Avode, D. G., 205
Awaritefe, A., 205
Azevedo, M. J., 36, 221, 259
Aziz, K. M., 229

Baer, H. A., 262–263, 264, 265
Baker, P. T., 257
Baptista, A., 106n2
Bari, M. A., 229
Barnhoorn, F., 220

Barreto, M. L., 220
Beck, A., 182
Begum, H., 226
Bentley, M., 111
Bhuiya, A., 229
Bibeau, G., 53
Bichmann, W., 109
Bishaw, M., 31
Boerma, J. T., 174, 177
Boillot, F., 12, 236–237
Bongaarts, J., 23
Booyens, J. H., 92, 131–132
Boster, J. S., 30–31
Bouteille, B., 205
Bradley, J., 23
Brown, P. J., 12, 77, 250, 259
Bryant, A. T., 87n1, 101–102
Buckheit, Jr., R. W.
Buganza, M. H., 53
Buxton, J., 86

Caldwell, J. C., 23, 36, 77, 154
Caldwell, P., 23, 36, 77, 154
Capo-Chichi, O. B., 205
Carael, M., 23
Carpenter, C., 63
Carson, D., 17, 32
Cernea, M., 111
Chakraborty, J., 226
Chandiwana, S. K., 177
Changalucha, J., 137
Charaly, D., 227
Chavunduka, 110

Cheney, C. C., 231
Chhabra, S. C., 192
Chifundera, K., 268
Chui, D. S., 181
Chuy, M., 229
Cirpa, V., 227
Conant, F., 23
Corin, E., 53
Corish, J. L., 195–196
Cosminsky, S., 33
Cruz, F., 227
Cunningham, A. B., 102

Dagnow, M. B., 131
Dale, A. M., 58, 76, 182
Dallabetta, G., 206
Davies, D., 85
Dawson, S., 226
de George, S., 177
de Jong, J., 110, 192
de Silva, K.T.D., 192
de Sousa, J. F., 31, 94, 117–118
de Zoysa, I., 17, 32, 131.
Dgedge, A., 93, 103, 104, 110, 133n1,
    139, 142, 178, 214
Douglas, M., 50, 51–52, 59, 70, 80,
    81–82, 142, 144, 182, 208, 239
Draser, B. S., 130–131, 227
Drummond, R. B., 69, 104, 110
Duh, S. V., 233
Dumas, M., 205
Dupree, J. D., 174
Durham, W. H., 251
Durkheim, E., 59

Earthy, E. D., 57, 91, 100
Edgerton, R. E., 118, 252, 254–255,
    256, 257–258, 259
Edwards, S. D., 259
Eisenbruch, M., 144, 232, 233, 245–
    246, 252
Ekanem, E. E., 117
Epling, P. J., 228
Escobar, G. J., 229

Essex, M., 181
Evans-Pritchard, E. E., 18, 35, 72, 74
Ezeabasili, N., 43–44

Farruque, A.S.G., 229
Fassin, D., 53, 110
Fassin, E., 53, 110
Feachem, R., 17, 32
Feinstein, A. R., 12
Feldman, R. A., 223, 228
Fernandez, E. L., 221
Field, M., 206
Fierman, S., 32, 42–43, 48
Fluty, H., 177
Ford, C. S., 52
Fortes, M., 17
Foster, G., 12, 19, 31, 32, 34, 160,
    165–166, 172
Foster, L. M., 20n2, 39, 44
Foulkes, J. R., 11, 268
Freeman, M., 11, 36–37, 218
Freund, P. J., 39, 129
Furberg, C. D., 266

Gandaho, P., 205
Gans, L. P., 220
Gelfand, M., 69, 104, 110
Gessler, M. C., 183
Gibbs, S., 94–95
Gina, G., 137
Glick, L. B., 32
Glover, E. K., 291
Gluckman, M., 23
Good, C. M., 136
Gottlieb, A., 105
Green, E. C., 26, 31, 65, 78, 84, 93,
    95, 103, 104, 106n1, 110, 116, 125,
    133n1, 136, 139, 142, 148, 171,
    174, 178, 178n3, 189, 192, 203,
    214, 224, 229, 234, 257
Greunbaum, E., 270n1
Grosskurth, H., 137
Guillaume, A., 131
Gumede, M. V., 83–84

Gunsalam, J., 226
Guthrie, G. M., 221

Hahn, R. A., 12, 135
Hammond-Tooke, W. D., 63, 68, 69, 77, 78, 79–80, 82, 92, 101, 181–182, 214
Handwerker, W. P., 26
Hanlon, J., 108
Hannaway, C., 241–242
Hara, C., 181
Haram, L., 183
Harris, M., 33, 251, 252, 253, 263
Harrison, G. G., 226
Hartmann, T., 220
Hass, M. R., 32, 247
Haule, J., 205
Heinrich, M., 183
Helitzer-Allen, D., 168, 178n2, 206, 207, 208, 214–215
Hoernlé, W., 60, 102
Hoff, W., 110
Hogle, J., 103, 110, 116, 131
Honwana, A., 65, 78–79
Huanca, T., 227
Hudelson, P., 227
Hudes, E., 23
Hudson, A. E., 52
Hughes, J., 63
Hunter, D., 85
Hurtato, E., 111
Hussain, R., 249

Ikpatt, N. W., 222
Imperato, P. J., 14, 189, 249, 261–262
Inam, B., 249
Ingstad, B., 141, 215
Inhorn, M. C., 12, 77, 250
Iyun, B. F., 227, 249

Janzen, J., 14, 32, 33, 35, 48, 49, 67, 72, 86–87, 100, 246
Jilek-Aall, 205
Johnson, J. C., 30–31
Jones, R., 138, 139, 250

Junod, H., 55–57, 78, 91, 106n3
Jurg, A., 93, 103, 104, 110, 133n1, 139, 142, 178, 192, 214

Kaltenthaler, E. C., 130–131, 227
Kamath, K. R., 223, 228
Kamthornwachara, B., 220
Kaondera, K., 197, 200
Karita, E., 23
Kay, M. A., 118
Kendall, C., 227
Kennedy, R., 52
Khan, A., 226, 249
Kilonzo, G. P., 205
Kimani, V., 46, 48, 259
Kirkwood, B., 17, 32
Kizungu, B., 268
Klokke, A., 137
Kluckhohn, C., 25
Konner, M., 258–259
Koumare, M., 172
Kresno, S., 226
Krige, E. J., 61–62, 92
Krige, J. D., 87n2, 92
Kumaresan, J. A., 237
Kundi, M. Z., 226
Kunstadter, P., 262
Kuper, A., 62–63

Labadie, R. P., 192
Laderman, C., 262
Landy, D., 257
Landy, L., 262
Lantum, D. N., 36, 221, 259
le Grand, A., 54
Leatherman, T., 264
Lee, T. H., 181
Leontsini, E., 227
Lieban, R., 32
Lindsay-Smith, E., 17, 32
Lloyd, L., 227
Lobo, M. A., 249
Loewenson, R., 17, 32
Logan, M. H., 253.

Lozoff, B., 223, 229, 256

Maganu, E. T., 237
Mahoya, M., 53
Mahunnah, R.L.A., 192
Maina-Ahlberg, B., 93
Makaza, N., 197, 200
Makengo, N. M., 53
Makhubu, L., 110
Mandela, M., 53
Manderson, L., 226
Marlink, R., 181
Marrato, J., 94, 125, 206
Marsh, D., 249
Marti-Ibanez, F., 239, 240, 241
Martinez, F. L., 106n2
Martinez, H., 32, 33
Marwick, M. G., 53
Maseko, N., 110
Maswe, M., 174, 177
Mathias-Mundy, E., 48
Matuja, W. B., 205
Mausezahl, D., 220
Mavi, S., 69, 104, 110
Mayaud, P., 137
Mayer, K., 181
Mbena, P., 205
Mbuyi, W., 268
McCorkle, C. M., 47–48
McCullough, J. M., 250
McElroy, A., 218, 251, 254, 255, 257,
     262, 264
McKee, L., 230
McLane, M. F., 181
McMaster, J., 220
McNee, A., 226
Mechin, B., 53
Menegoni, L., 225–226, 247, 249
Mertens, T., 23
Mitchell, J. C., 53
Mitchell, R. C., 30
Mitchell, V., 63
Moore, T. J., 266
Morely, P., 51

Moses, S., 23
Mosha, F., 137
Motsei, M., 11, 36–37, 218
Moya-Hernandez, C., 221
Mshiu, E. N., 192
Msuya, D. E., 183
Mukana, M. K., 53
Mull, D. S., 220, 226
Mull, J. D., 220, 226
Murdock, G. P., 12, 13, 22, 23, 24, 35,
     37–38, 39–41, 46, 52, 55, 57,
     106n2, 111, 123, 127, 143, 206, 208
Murphy, E., 25
Murray, H. A., 25
Mwang'ombola, R., 205
Mwijarubi, E., 137

Na-nakorn, S., 228, 231
Nagelkerke, N., 23
Nat, J. M., 192
Ndamba, J., 197, 200
Ndemera, B., 69, 104, 110
Ndinya-Achola, J., 23
Neumann, T. W., 250, 257
Ngarmyithayapong, J., 228, 231
Ngokwey, N., 42, 225, 230, 243
Ngubane, H., 16, 63, 64–65, 66–67, 76,
     78, 80, 82, 101, 102, 164, 216n1,
     224
Nichter, M., 114
Nicoll, A., 137
Nkunya, M. H., 183
Nnko, S., 176, 177
Noronha, C. V., 220
Nsengumuremyi, F., 23
Nyamongo, I. K., 186
Nyazema, N., 197, 200
Nzima, M. M., 31, 136, 142

O'Loughlin, W., 177
Odhiambo, D., 188
Odoi-Adome, R., 110
Oluju, P. M., 110
Opala, J., 12, 236

Ortiz de Montellano, B., 253
Osathanondh, R., 181
Osunwole, S. A., 20n2, 39, 44
Oyebolo, D.D.O., 39, 109

Panizzo, E., 95
Parker, B., 226
Parra, M. C., 221
Pasandhanatorn, V., 228, 231
Paton, C., 243, 269
Pearson, G., 63
Pelling, M., 20n1, 42, 70, 239–241
Pelto, G. H., 111
Peña Cruz, V., 181
Pielemeier, J., 177
Pierce, R. V., 139
Pillsbury, B., 119, 121, 214
Pitts, M., 220
Plummer, F., 23
Pool, R., 12, 17, 72–74, 75, 149, 174, 177
Prater, G. S., 36, 221, 259
Price, S., 234
Prins, A., 103, 110, 116, 131
Prins, G., 14, 48, 49
Psaty, B. M., 266
Punufimana, A. N., 222

Qureshi, A. F., 249

Radcliffe-Brown, A. R., 59
Rahman, S., 229, 231
Rauyajin, O., 220, 228, 231
Rauyajin, V., 228
Reid, M. B., 43, 95, 259
Reingold, A., 226
Reining, P., 23
Reis, R., 31, 95, 101, 205
Renjifo, B., 181
Rey, S., 131
Richards, A., 60–61, 76, 78, 79
Riley, I., 226
Rivers, W.H.R., 32
Romanucci-Ross, J., 262
Romero-Salazar, A., 221

Ronald, A., 23
Root-Bernstein, R., 136, 179–180, 233
Rosen, L. N., 64
Rubel, A. J., 32, 247
Rujano, R., 221
Rwiza, H. T., 205
Ryan, G. W., 32, 33, 71–72
Ryan, M., 264

Salas, J., 221
Salazar, E., 229
Sani bin Gani, A., 222
Schapera, I., 60, 61, 78, 79, 87n2, 142, 169, 232
Schar, A., 183
Scheinman, D., 141
Schneider, H. K., 36, 59
Scrimshaw, S., 33
Scrimshaw, S.C.M., 111
Seed, J., 23
Senah, K. A., 291
Senkoro, K., 137
Serufilira, A., 23
Seuseu, N.K.F., 222
Seymour-Smith, C., 85
Shahid, N. A., 229
Shawyer, R., 222
Sibley, L., 264
Siliga, N., 228
Silva, T. M., 220
Simmons, L. W., 52
Simon, G., 177
Singer, P., 29, 262–263
Sircar, B. K., 131
Smith, D. J., 250
Smith, E. W., 58, 76, 182
Sofowora, A., 192
Soto-Ramírez, L. E., 181
Souza, I. M., 220
Staugaard, F., 141, 269
Stayt, H. A., 68–69, 182
Stewart, M. K., 226
Strauss, W. L., 273
Sutrisna, B., 226

Sutthent, R., 181
Swantz, L., 53, 110

Tahzib, F., 110
Tallo, V. L., 226
Tanner, M., 183
Tedlock, B., 236
Todd, J., 137
Tomas, T., 93, 110, 192
Tomson, G., 227, 249
Townsend, P., 218, 251, 254, 255, 257
Traoré, D. A., 261–262
Trostle, J., 262
Trotter, R. T., 253
Turner, V., 35, 105

Ulijaszek, S. J., 262

Van de Perre, P., 23
van de Walle, E., 250
van de Walle, F., 250
van der Sluis, W. G., 192
Varothai, C., 228, 230
Vecchiato, N. L., 46–47, 99–100
Velimirovic, B., 74, 269
Velimirovic, H., 269
Ventevogel, P., 71
Vithayasai, C., 181
Vithayasai, V., 181

Wagner, K., 177
Wahab, B. W., 20n2, 39, 44
Warren, D. M., 17, 31, 40, 70–71, 75,
    110, 236
Wasi, C., 181
Wasserheit, J. N., 136, 138, 139, 250
Way, P., 23
Weiss, M. G., 108
Weller, S., 72
Whiting, J.W.M., 52
Whitten, P., 85
WHO, 109
Wilkenson, L., 239, 240
Wilson, K. B., 109

Wilsonne, M., 125
Winch, P., 227
Winick, C., 85
Wondergem, P., 54, 110
Wood, C. S., 220
Worboys, M., 187
World Bank, 110, 174, 176
Worthman, C. M., 259
Wozniak, D. F., 26
Wu, C., 54n2

Yablo, P., 220
Yoder, P. S., 17, 32, 44–45, 48, 93,
    100, 107, 111, 131
Young, J., 75
Young, M. U., 222

Zhuwau, T., 177
Zokwe, B., 95, 174

SUBJECT INDEX

The following typographical conventions used in this index are: *f* and *t* identify figures and tables, respectively; *n* identifies a note.

Abagusii (Kenya), 186
ABC approach to AIDS prevention, 176
abortion, 62, 146
abstinence, sexual, 175–177
    see also AIDS, prevention
Academy for Educational Development, 27
acquired immunodeficiency syndrome, *see* AIDS
acute respiratory infection, 226–227
adaptation, cultural, to illnesses, 249–256
adultery, as cause for disease, 80, 81, 103, 124
Africa, general health beliefs in, 31–34
agriculture, 22, 23, 24
AIDS
    causes for, 160–162, 171–172, 232–233
    as incurable, 162, 166
    prevention, 162, 171, 175–177, 233–234 (*see also* condoms, public health)
    symptoms of, 160
    traditional healers and, 136, 141, 150, 161–162, 170–171
    transmission, 136, 161, 180–181
    tuberculosis and, 150, 160, 180, 193
    see also behavior, sexual; circumcision; GEMT, AIDS prevention program; HIV; knowledge, attitudes, and practices survey; individual peoples

AIDSCAP, *see* AIDS Control and Prevention project
AIDS Control and Prevention project, 27–29
akamukolwe (genital warts), 158
akankulila, 150
akasele (STI), 150, 151–152, 154, 162, 167, 170
akashishi, 147–148, 160
akaswende (STI), 150, 151, 155, 156–157, 162, 167
amabolo ukufimba (testicular disease), 150
animal husbandry, 22, 23, 24
Anopheline mosquitoes, 47, 250
anthropologists, 29–30, 75
anthropology, medical, 17, 31–32, 264
antibiotics, attitude toward use of, 167–168
ARI, *see* acute respiratory infection
atchi-koko, 124, 147–148
Aymara Indians, 226–227
Azande, 35, 72

Bahia (Brazil), 230–231
balance, as metaphor for health, 46–47
Bangladesh, childhood diarrhea study in, 229
Bantu, 24–25, 68–70
barrenness, 50, 92
BaVenda, *see* Venda
behavior, sexual, 174
behavior, therapy-seeking, 32–33

299

beliefs, naturalistic, 50–51
    see also infection theory, naturalistic, pollution
beliefs, personalistic, 12, 35–36
    see also sorcery, witchcraft
beliefs and practices, maladaptive, 253–256
Bemba, 60–61, 76
    AIDS and, 160–161
    childhood diarrhea and, 129–130
    tuberculosis and, 193–194
Beng (Ivory Coast), 105
Bhaca (South Africa), 181
bias, Western medical ethnocentric, 73, 217–224
bichinho (tiny worm), 147
bilharzia, 196–204
biomedicine, Western, 20n1
    as cause for infertility, 167
    collaboration with traditional healers, 26–31, 86–87, 154
    contagion theories, historical, 42, 238–242
    traditional medicine and, 171–172, 214
    see also public health
blood
    bad/dirty, 169–172, 183
    as cause for AIDS, 161, 162, 170–172
    menstrual, 41, 62
    as pollution, 58
    siki illnesses and, 142
    strong/weak, concept of, 169
    traditional concepts of, 168–172
blood-in-urine, *see* bilharzia
blood transfusion, 160, 161, 180
bolabola (STI), 151, 154–156, 170
    see also utushishi
Bolivia, 226–227
Bono (Ghana), causal theories of illness, 70–71
Botswana, 61
Brazil, 220, 230

breastfeeding, 103, 124, 165, 229
breast milk, 66, 113, 115, 124, 228
    see also colostrum
bride-price, 22, 23
bride-service, 23, 54n1
bridewealth, 24, 54n1

Caida de mollera, 255
Cambodia, *see* Khmer
Cameroon, 36, 71–72, 221
Cental Bantu, 22–23
chancroid, 138, 173
    see also bolabola
Chawama
    AIDS and, 161–162
    gonorrhea-like illness and, 152–153
    malaria and, 184–191
chicasameti (STI), 103
chicazamentu (STI), 139, 143, 144
chichuna (child disease), 103, 104
chikahara (sunken fontanel), 114, 116, 118
chikamba (diarrhea), 114, 116, 118, 122
chikeke (STI), 139
childbearing, as polluting, 62
childbirth, as polluting, 79
chimanga (STI), 135, 139, 141, 143–144
chinhamukaka (diarrhea), 113–114, 116, 119, 122
chinzonono (gonorrhea), 152, 153
chipande, 118
chipata, 145
chlamydia, 138, 151
cholera, 115
cifuba, see icifuba
Cimwemwe
    and AIDS, 162–163
    and gonorrhea-like illness, 151–152
    and malaria, 184–191
circumcision, 23, 62, 255
cleanliness, 44, 99, 191–192
    see also diarrhea, childhood, causes of

CMV, 180
code words, 77, 78, 78t2, 131, 143–144, 163
Cokwe (Zaire), 44–45
colostrum, 118, 255, 256
condoms
  beliefs and attitudes about, 153, 173–174
  education on, 148
  promotion of usage, 127, 170–171, 176
  STD incidence and, 174, 175
  use of, for disease prevention, 162, 173
Condylomata, flat, 138
Condylomata acuminata, 138–139
congenital illnesses, 165
Congo, Democratic Republic of, 67, 80
consumption, 57, 182
  see also tuberculosis
contagion, 55
  bodily fluids and, 142
  Botswana healers ideas about, 183
  see also Murdock, George, typology of illness
contagion, mystical, 55
  see also Murdock, George, typology of illness, pollution
contagion theory of illness, 13–16, 38*f*1, 39–41
contamination, as codeword for pollution, 143–144
contraceptive social marketing (CSM), 176
"coolness," 67
Copperbelt (Zambia), study in, 150–152
cough, indigenous syndrome, 195
crouching mango, 232–233
  see also syphilis
CSM, *see* contraceptive social marketing

Death, contact with
  as cause for diarrhea, 115

as polluting, 41, 61, 62, 66, 79
  see also Macua, *mahithé*, pollution beliefs
dehydration, *see* sunken fontanel
dengue fever, 227
Department of Traditional Medicine (Mozambique), *see* GEMT
depressed fontanel, *see* sunken fontanel
diarrhea, 129–132
  see also diarrhea, childhood
diarrhea, childhood, 98
  African causal theories of, 128–129, 131–132
  causes of, 111–116, 120–122, 123–125
  dietary advice for, 117–118
  enemas used to cure, 103
  environmental causes of, 65
  global causal theories of, 228
  indigenous treatment for, 116–118
  prevention, 127, 130
  symptoms of, 118–119
  treatment of, 116–118
  see also GEMT, individual peoples, *nyoka*
diet, as cause for disease, 186
dirt, as a term, 128
dirt/dirty, as codewords for pollution, 163
disease
  airborne, 204
  causation theories, historical, 186–187
  contagious, 20*n*1, 260–261
  inborn, *see* illness, inherited
  infectious, 20*n*1, 248–249
    as a term, 12
  see also individual diseases
diviner-mediums, 46–47, 66
divining bones, 56
"drop," 152, 178*n*3
Durkheim, E., 59

EBV, 180

Ecuador, childhood diarrhea in, 229–230

Edgerton, R., 253–257

Egyptians, ancient, 239

ekkissinomo, 145

empacho, 32, 256

enemas and emetics, 69, 85–86, 101–105

environment, as cause for disease, 14, 41, 63–65, 78*t*2, 239–242

epilepsy, 95, 205–206

equilibrium model of health, 34, 166

equissonyonyo, 145

eruku (shadow of death), 127–128

erungu, see eruku

esulo, see sunken fontanel

esuloy eronela, see sunken fontanel

Ethiopia, 46–47

    causal theories of diarrhea in, 131

    worm/snake belief in, 99–100

ethnoveterinary medicine, 47–48

ethogo, 146

etiologic models, global similarities of, 12, 245–249

etiology

    African, 35–37, 41–47

    and predicting heath treatment, 31–32

evil eye, *see* personalistic disease causation

exogamy, 22

Family Health International, 27

fatalistic, Africans as, 16, 35–36, 221

fava bean, 250

FES, *see* focused ethnographic study

FGD, *see* focus group discussion

fisa (heat), 82

flies, as disease vector, 198–199

fluids, bodily, and contagion, 142–144

FMD, *see* foot and mouth disease

focused ethnographic study (FES), 206–208

focus group discussion (FGD), 27

fontanel, sunken, *see* sunken fontanel

foot and mouth disease (FMD), 48

Foster, G., 34–35, 160

Frazer, Sir James, 59

Frelimo party, 108–109

Gaza Province (Mozambique), 57

gcunsula, 102

GEMT

    AIDS prevention program, 135–136, 137

    background of, 108–111

    childhood diarrhea programs, 111–128

genital lice, 156

genital ulcer disease (GUD), 145

genital ulcers, *see mula*

genital warts, 158, 173

    see also ibele

genito-urinary illnesses, *see* bilharzia

germ theory, 37, 77, 240–241

gobela (STI), 139

go fisa (heat), 79–80

gonorrhea

    clinical symptoms of, 138

    see also akasele (STI), gonorrhea-like illnesses

gonorrhea-like illnesses, 152–154

Greeks, ancient, 239–240, 241

Guardian of Bodily Purity, 93, 104

Guatemala, 33

GUD, *see* genital ulcer disease

Hamosho (worm/snake), 99–100

hanga, 82

HAV, 180

HBV, 180

healers

    indigenous, *see* traditional healers

    Islamic, 127

    traditional, *see* traditional healers

    Zionist Christian faith, 103

helminthic infections, 180

hepatitis B, 180

herbalists, 111
herbs, medicinal, 102, 116, 167, 200
HIV
    subtypes, 181
    transmission of, 136–137, 165
    see also AIDS; blood; knowledge,
        attitudes, and practices survey
HIV/AIDS programs and condom pro-
    motion, 176
HIV-1 viral subtypes, 181
homicide, as polluting, 66
Honduras, dengue fever in, 227
"hotness," 61, 67
HSV1, 180
HSV2, 180
HTLV, 180
human immunodeficiency virus, *see*
    HIV
hydrocele, 145, 159
hygiene, personal, and illness, 143, 155,
    156–157, 162

Ibele (genital warts), 46, 150, 151, 158,
    165
Ibo (Nigeria), 43–44
icambu, 150
(i)chifuba, see icifuba
icifuba, 192–196
icipelo, 150
iciwane, 148
ICT, *see* indigenous contagion theory
idrop, 102
ikando (prolonged menstrual period),
    150, 159
Ila, 58
illness
    airborne, 48, 66, 189–190, 249
    inherited, 45*t*, 46, 114, 158, 165,
        195
    naturally caused, 43, 44, 172
    public health implications of, 16–17
    as a term, 12
    see also individual illnesses, *nyoka*,
        tuberculosis

illness, cause(s) for
    ancestors as, 43, 62, 66–67, 68, 69
    historical, 42
    natural, 44, 47
    pollution as, 16, 66–67
    sorcery as, 35, 43
    see also individual illnesses,
        witchcraft
illnesses, African, typologies of, 37–41
illnesses of God, 42–43, 44
illnesses, *siki*, 104, 142
    causes of, 139
    derivation of term, 139
    treatment, 140
imbune, 102
immune system, 136, 179–180
imótótó (cleanliness), 44
(i)mpepo, 185
incest, 80, 81
indangali, 156
India, 15, 220, 226, 228–229
indigenous contagion models
    adaptiveness of, 258–262
    global similarity of, 245–249, 250–
        253, 263
indigenous contagion theory (ICT), 13,
    77
    elements of, basic, 78*t*2
    global evidence for, 224–235
    ignored by researchers, 242–243
    political economic considerations of,
        262–265
    public health implications of, 265–
        270
    as similar to modern germ theory,
        18
    and STIs, 141–142
    see also illness, airborne
indigenous germ theory, 77, 78, 183
indigenous medicine, African, stereo-
    type of, 11
infections, helminthic, 180
infection theory, naturalistic, 37–39,
    38*f*1, 171–173

infertility, 153, 154, 161, 167, 250, 259
Inhambane Province (Mozambique), 27
   internal snake and, 97–98
   traditional healers, 104
insokanda, 99, 130
insula (testicular disease), 150, 159
intercourse, *see* sexual intercourse
internal snake
   as cause for disease, 57
   differences in beliefs among
      societies, 100
   diseases caused by, 90
   historical beliefs about, 91–92
   pollution beliefs and, 93–94, 105
   as positive concept, 89, 91, 93, 97,
      101
   as symbol for pollution beliefs, 105
   see also kokwana, nyoka, individual
      peoples
inthoci, see sunken fontanel
invisible snake, *see* internal snake
inyoka (internal snake), 89, 97
inyoni, see umphezulu
Ivory Coast, causal theories of diarrhea
   in, 131

Jooka kundu (AIDS), 235
"jumping the hair," 128

Kaliondeonde, 147, 160
Kalombo Mwane (AIDS), 160
kandu, 234
KAP, *see* knowledge, attitudes, and
   practices survey
kasele, 152
kassinono, 145
kassinyonyo, 145, 147, 232
kaswende, 156
Kenya, 45–46
Kgatla, 61, 80, 160
Khmer
   AIDS and, 144, 232–234
   disease theories, 245–246
   STIs, and, 232–234

Khmer-Tswana STI model, 250–253
khoma (dirt), 104, 139, 148, 163
Kikuyu (Kenya) diviners, causal categories of illnesses, 45–46, 45*t*
knowledge, attitudes, and practices survey (KAP), 26, 56, 229
   results as skewed, 219–222
kokwana (internal snake), 92, 132
Kom (Cameroon), causal theories of
   illness, 71–72
Kongo, 86–87
kraals, 24
kuamwissira (diarrhea), 115
kuhabula (diarrhea), 65, 103
kusuma amenshi, 158
kutulula, 129

"Leaking," *see* gonorrhea-like illnesses
Lele pollution theory, 50, 80, 182
Lenge, 57, 91
lepero, 237
leprosy, 220, 221, 232, 236–237, 239
liciwane, 148
Life of a South African Tribe, The,
   55–56
likhubalo, 203–204, 215
likodzo, 215
linkin'gi, 151, 152
lobola, see bride-price
Lovedu, internal snake and, 92
lufhila (consumption), 182
lugola, 102
lukhuba, 203
lukozo (blood-in-urine), 197, 198, 199

Macua
   childhood diarrhea and, 123–127
   pollution beliefs, 127–128
   STIs among, 147–148
mahithé, 146–147
makhumo, 56
malaria, 184–192
   biomedical causes for, 188
   environmental causes for, 187

migration and, 63
prevention, 191–192
symptoms of, 185
traditional causes for, 185–187
transmission of, 182–183, 185–187, 188–190
treatment, indigenous vs. hospital, 192
see also Anopheline mosquitoes, fava bean
Malawi, 24
adult illnesses, causes for, 209–213
focused ethnographic survey in, 206–215
Manica healers, 111–122, 139–141
Manica Province (Mozambique), 104
as research site, 110–111
STIs in, 137–141
manyoka (diarrhea), 112–113, 117, 121
manyoka ekufambissa, 112
manyoka kuhambisa asinadriru, 112–113
marginalization, social, 66, 77
Maroons, 234–235
matrilineal descent, 22
mavuca, 123, 127
measles, 124, 229
medical materialism, 52
medical professionals, African, 36–37
medicine, African, stereotype of, 11–12, 17–18
see also beliefs, personalistic
menstrual blood
as agent of contagion, 142–143
as pollution, 60–61, 62, 124
as taboo, 56, 58
menstruation
as polluting, 79, 93–94
prolonged, 150
taboos associated with, 58
see also chicazamentu, women
mental illness, 259–260
Mexican Americans and fallen fontanel syndrome, 253

Mexico, 32, 227
see also Huave Indians, Tzeltal
migration, 63, 79
mihaco (illness-associated worm), 95
Ministry of Health (Mozambique), 27
miscarriage, as polluting, 62, 79, 146
monogamy, 175–177
Morehouse School of Medicine/Zambia AIDS Prevention Project, see Morehouse/Tulane AIDS project
Morehouse/Tulane AIDS project, 28, 148–149, 173
mosquitoes, as disease vector, 186, 191, 198
see also Anopheline mosquitoes
Mozambique
cultural diversity within, 90
incidence of hepatitis B in, 180
independence, 108–109
internal snake belief in, 92–99
National AIDS Program, 136
National Health Service, 110
pollution beliefs in, 57
research project in, 27
STI etiologic belief in, 170–171
see also GEMT, Manica healers, Manica Province, Maputo Province, Nampula Province
mpepo (cold), 185
mpepo mutupi, 185
muacharia, 123, 125
muanan'hama, 123
muanan'luku, 123
mubulale muwamuwala (airborne illness), 189
mukolwe, 150, 164–165
mukunko (prolonged menstrual period), 150, 164–165
mula (genital ulcers), 139, 143, 145, 146
Murdock, G., 13, 14, 22, 35
typology of illness, 37–41, 38f1, 52, 55
mussekeneke, 145, 146

mussequeneque, see mussekeneke
mwana, 123
mystical retribution, 38*f*1, 40

Nampula Province (Mozambique), 27, 95
childhood diarrhea in, 123–127
namuili, 146
National AIDS Program (Mozambique), 136
National Health Service (Mozambique), 110
natural, as a term, 48–49
naturalism, African, 72–75
naturalistic infection, 13
 see also indigenous germ theory
naturalistic medical system, defined, 34
naturalistic theories of causation, 209–214
ndjaka, 56–57
ndjoka, see nyoka
ndzoka, see nyoka
ngara, 237
Nguni, 23–24, 78
Nigeria, 43–44, 227
njoka (noxious worm), 130
nkombola (genital warts), 158
nsoka (noxious worm), 99, 130
ntsanganiko (diarrhea), 114–115
nursing, *see* breastfeeding
Nyakwadi (internal snake), 58, 89, 91
Nyanja
 AIDS and, 161–162
 bilharzia and, 197–200
 childhood diarrhea and, 129–130
 tuberculosis and, 194–195
nyoga, see nyoka
nyoka, 98–99
 "calming" the, 96, 100, 116, 122
 as inborn, 96, 98
 pollution beliefs and, 93–94
 sunken fontanel caused by, 96, 114, 118–119

 see also diarrhea, childhood, epilepsy, internal snake
nyoka dzo kusorora, 112, 120
nyoka dzoni (STI), 140, 143
nyoka kundu (STI), 94, 140
nyoka kusorora (simple diarrhea), 112
nyokana, see tinyokana
nyokane, 95
nyokani, 98
nyongo, 115
nyowa, see nyoka
nzoka (snake), 96–97

Ohara, 123
okala ovenya, 146
omtupha, 123
omuaculela muana, 127 .
oporar, 123, 124
oral rehydration solution, 108, 119–120, 126, 222
oral rehydration therapy, 222
ORS, *see* oral rehydration solution
ORT, *see* oral rehydration therapy
Outline of Cultural Methods (1961), 52
ovialua, 123
Oyo State (Nigeria), 227

Pakistan, 220, 226
pandasi pasi, 234
papillomaviruses, clinical symptoms of, 138–139
Papua (New Guinea), 63–64
patrilineal descent, 23, 24
pausei, 234
personalistic disease causation, 72–75, 160, 166, 202
 and childhood diarrhea, 228–229
personalistic medical system, defined, 34
Peru, childhood diarrhea in, 229
Philippines, 221, 226
phiringaniso (diarrhea), 113, 114, 116, 119, 121

phthisis (consumption), 195–196
pollution, 13–14
  as cause for childhood diarrhea, 121–122, 124
  code words, 77, 78*t*2, 131
  compared to indigenous germ theory, 77
  as impersonal process of contagion, 66, 76–77
  sources of, 41, 50, 57, 78–80
  treatments, characteristic, 78*t*2
  see also "hotness," individual peoples
pollution beliefs, 13–14, 40, 76, 78–87, 171–173
  historical, 55–67, 76
  as means of social control, 80–81
  as naturalistic, 50–53
pollution studies, African, as under-researched, 52, 54*n*3, 70, 83–87
polygyny, 22, 24
Portugal, 108
possession, *see* personalistic disease causation
pregnancy, 57, 65
prevention, disease, *see* individual diseases
prohibitions, sexual, 146
promiscuity
  as cause for barrenness, 50
  and condom usage as promoting, 173–174
  role as cause of illness, 162, 194
prostitutes, 153, 154
prostitution, 154, 161
public health
  indigenous contagion beliefs and, 17–18, 218–219
  intervention studies, 26–31
  see also GEMT
purification, 60, 61, 65, 79, 128, 235

Quechua Indians, 226–227

Renamo party, 109–110
Rhodesia, 58, 60–61
rikaho, 204
Ronga, 94–95
rukawe, 204
Rural Water-Borne Disease Control Project, 26

Salt, prohibition against for babies, 117–118
Samoa, childhood diarrhea in, 228
schanul, 226
schistosomiasis, *see* bilharzia
schistosomiasis haematobium, *see* bilharzia
seizures, *see* epilepsy
sex, extramarital, 113
sexual intercourse
  as polluting, 60, 79, 80–82, 124, 142–143
  restrictions on, 61
  as taboo, 62, 214
  transmission of AIDS and, 136
sexually transmitted disease
  defined, 135
  HIV transmission and, 136–137
  prevalence of, 136
  symptoms, clinical, 138–139
  see also individual diseases, sexually transmitted illness
sexually transmitted illness
  causation theories, 162–164
  defined, 135
  as naturalistic, 147
  nyoka-related, 140
  pollution belief and, 142, 144
  prevention, 171–173
  treatment, 165–167
  see also individual illnesses, sexually transmitted disease
Shadow of Death, 127–128, 146–147
Shambaa (Tanzania) causal theories of illness, 42–43

Shona/Thonga linguistic groups, 23
Shona (Zimbabwe), 69, 104
SIDA, 141
Sidama (Ethiopia), 46–47, 99–100
sifuba (tuberculosis), 189
slim disease, see AIDS
Smith, R., 59
snails, as disease vector, 198–199, 202
sombra do morto (shadow of death), see
    mahithé
songeia (STI), 139, 141, 143
sorcery, 35, 43, 203–204, 215
    see also witchcraft
South Africa, 27–28, 68–69
STD, see sexually transmitted disease
stereotype, of African indigenous med-
    icine, 11, 17–18
STI, see sexually transmitted illness
Sukuma (Tanzania), 43, 97
sunken fontanel, 125–127
    caused by nyoka, 96, 114, 118–119
    causes for, 125–126
    treatment of, 126–127
    see also chikahara, chinhamukaka,
        phiringaniso
supernatural causes of disease, see per-
    sonalistic disease causation
Suriname, see Maroon
Swazi
    airborne illness and, 189–190
    internal snake concept and, 84, 97
    use of enemas and emetics, 102
Swaziland, 24
    bilharzia in, 200–201
    Rural Water-Borne Disease Control
        Project in, 26
symptoms, of disease, see individual
    diseases
syphilis, 135, 165
    symptoms, clinical, 138
    see also crouching mango
syphilis-like illnesses, 156–157
syringes and AIDS, 160, 161

Taboo, 62, 214
    associated with menstruation, 58
    postpartum, 80, 250, 257
    violation of, 157
taboo beliefs, as superstition, 59
Tanzania, 24, 42–43
    internal snake belief in, 97
    malaria in, 182–183
tapeworms, 91
Targeted Intervention Research (TIR),
    129, 148–149
"tattooing," see vaccination
tattoos, as site for medication, 167
testicular disease, 150, 159
Thailand, 220, 221–222, 231
    childhood diarrhea in, 228
theories of causation
    natural, 37–39, 38f1
    STI, 162–165
    supernatural, 37, 38f1, 39–40
    see also individual peoples
therapy choice, 214–215
thomela, see sunken fontanel
Thonga, 23, 40–41, 55, 56, 57
tibamo, 183
tifo temanti, 204
tifo temoya, 189–190
tilonza, 102
timvilapo, 102
tinyokana, 91
TIR, see Targeted Intervention Research
Togo, causal theories of diarrhea in,
    131
"tracks," 64, 132
traditional healers, 199
    adult illnesses, names for, 150–151
    AIDS and, 136, 141, 150, 161, 162,
        170–171
    bilharzia treatment by, 199–200
    on causes of childhood diarrhea,
        111–112, 120–122
    on causes of malaria, 182–183
    on causes of STIs, 140, 147–148,
        162–163

on causes of sunken fontanel, 126–127

childhood diarrhea treatment by, 116–118

collaboration with biomedicine, 26–31, 86–87, 110–111, 154

condoms and, 173–174

gonorrhea-like illnesses treatment by, 153–154

internal snake concept and, 94–96, 100–101

knowledge sharing by, 112, 118–119

versus laypersons as knowledge source, 30–31

malaria treatment by, 192

modernization, effect upon numbers of, 53

ORS and, 119–120

preference of, over Western medicine, 167–168

ratio of, to population, 110

STI treatment by, 104, 139–140, 146, 166–167

as sympathetic, 168, 215

treatment of sunken fontanel by, 126–127

witchcraft and, 164

worldwide use of, 7

see also GEMT, individual diseases, individual peoples, Manica healers, traditional medicine

traditional medicine

as impediment to science, 74

as treatment for tuberculosis, 196

and Western biomedicine, 75

see also traditional healers

transmission of disease

congenital, 140, 162

through breastfeeding, 103, 124, 165

see also individual diseases

Tsonga (Thonga) ethnolinguistic group

and internal snake concept, 94

sources of pollution for, 65–66, 78–79

Tswana

causal theory of diarrhea, 131–132

STI etiology, 232

tuberculosis beliefs, 183

see also Kgatla, Khmer-Tswana STI model

tuberculosis, 225–226

AIDS and, 150, 160, 180, 193

causes of, 45t1, 46, 193–194, 225–226

historical beliefs about, 195–196

as naturalistic, 183, 195

prevention, 196

symptomless, 193

symptoms of, 193

transmission, 193–195

see also sifuba

tumukolwe (vaginal warts), 150, 151, 162

see also utushishi

twins, birth of, as polluting, 79

Tzeltal, 225–226, 247t3

Ubulwele bwa mpopo, 183

ubusako (prolonged menstrual period), 150

ubwamba ukukanaima, 150, 165

Uganda, 175

ukondoloka (slim disease), 160

Ukupolomya, 129

ukusunda umulopa (blood-in-urine), 197, 198, 199

ulcers, genital, see mula

ulushinga, 150, 165

ulusula (prolonged menstrual period), 150

umfundzan-ngati (blood-in-urine), 196

umkhondo, see "tracks"

umkhuhlane, 84

umnyama (blackness), 66, 102

umphezulu (diarrhea), causes of, 65, 103, 130

umthundungati (blood-in-urine), 196, 203, 204

umukunko, 150
UNAIDS, 27, 176, 177, 179, 206
  Rural Water-Borne Disease Control
    Project, 26
UNICEF, 179
urbanization, pollution illness and,
  85–86
USAID, 176, 177, 179
utulonda (STI), 151
utumani twabulwele (egg of illness),
  164
utushishi (disease-causing insect), 162–
  164

Vaccination, 69–70, 153
Valenge, and internal snake concept,
  100
Vellore (India), diarrhea in, 228–229
Venda, 68–69
viruses common to Africans, 180

Wacia, 123
water, dirty/stagnant, *see* bilharzia
West Africa, causal theories of illness
  in, 70–72
WHO, 179, 260
will of God, as cause for illness, 36
Wimbum, 73, 75
witchcraft, 17–18, 43
  as cause for diarrhea, 104, 120, 124
  as cause for epilepsy, 205, 206
  as cause for illnesses, 35, 36, 62, 68,
    69, 172, 195
  as cause for leprosy, 236–237
  as cause for STIs, 164
  internal snake concept and, 92, 101
  modernization and, 53–54
  relationship to naturalistic belief,
    238
  see also personalistic disease causa-
    tion sorcery
women
  circumcision and, 255
  as diviners, 66

as impure, 56, 57, *see also nyoka
  dzoni*
newly delivered, as pollution, 57, 65
pregnant, behavior of, as cause for
  childhood diarrhea, 65
see also breastfeeding, breast milk,
  "hotness," *ikando* (prolonged
  menstrual period), *kusuma amenshi, umnyama*

World Bank, 179
worm, as cause for disease, 99–100,
  130

Xenophilia, 29–30, 83
Xhosa, and internal snake concept,
  95–96

Yoruba (Nigeria), 44
Yucatan, *see* Maya

Zaire, 44–45
Zambia
  childhood diarrhea, 129
  condom use, rate of, 155
  gonorrhea-like illnesses in, 151–154
  infectious disease in, 184–206
  malaria in, 184–192
  model of tuberculosis in, 247*t*3
  research project in, 28
  sexually transmitted illness in, 148–
    150, 171–173
Zimbabwe, 24, 69
  childhood diarrhea in, 131
  traditional healers, 200
Zimbabwe National Traditional Healers'
  Association, 200
Zionist church, 87
zombo (child disease), 103, 104
Zulu, 24, 61–62, 63
  body-cleansing practices of, 69,
    101–102
  pollution beliefs of, 40, 62, 63,
    64–65, 66, 76, 78, 79, 80, 86

ABOUT THE AUTHOR

Edward C. Green, Ph.D., is a Washington, D.C.–based applied medical anthropologist. He consults for a number of international development organizations and is a board member of several nonprofit organizations. His work in developing countries has spanned Africa, Latin America, the Caribbean, and Asia, and he has worked as an adviser to the ministries of health in both Swaziland (1981–83) and Mozambique (1994–95). A specialist in AIDS and other sexually transmitted diseases, he has also been involved in projects or research in family planning, child survival, maternal and child health, water and sanitation, and children affected by war. He is an internationally recognized authority on African indigenous healers, and has worked to develop programs in which indigenous healers work collaboratively with conventional medical personnel to achieve public health goals. Green is the author or editor of four previous books, including *Indigenous Healers and the African State* (1996, Pact Publications), *AIDS and STDs in Africa* (1994, Westview Press), and *Practicing Development Anthropology* (1986, Westview Press), as well as more than 200 journal articles, book chapters, presented papers, and commissioned reports.